Democracy and Political Culture in Eastern Europe

What is the relation between democracy and political culture in countries undergoing major systemic change? Have subjective political orientations of citizens been important in shaping the development of democracy in central and eastern Europe after the fall of communism?

These key questions are addressed by an international group of political scientists, the majority of whom have their home-base in the 13 central and eastern European countries covered in the book. The analysis draws on a unique set of data collected and processed by the contributors to this volume within the framework of the World Values Survey project. This empirical data enables the assembled authors to establish similarities and differences in support of democracy between a large number of countries with different cultural and structural conditions as well as historical legacies.

This new book will be a valuable reference tool for students and researchers of the relationship between democracy and culture; eastern European politics; transitions from autocracy to democracy; and the EU's eastward enlargement.

Hans-Dieter Klingemann is Professor of Political Science (emeritus) at the Freie Universität, Berlin, and Director (emeritus), Social Science Research Center Berlin, Germany. **Dieter Fuchs** is Professor of Political Science at the University of Stuttgart, Germany. **Jan Zielonka** is Ralf Dahrendorf Fellow in European Politics at St Antony's College, University of Oxford, UK.

Routledge research in comparative politics

1 **Democracy and Post-Communism**
Political change in the post-communist world
Graeme Gill

2 **Sub-State Nationalism**
A comparative analysis of institutional design
Edited by Helena Catt and Michael Murphy

3 **Reward for High Public Office**
Asian and Pacific Rim states
Edited by Christopher Hood and B. Guy Peters

4 **Social Democracy and Labour Market Policy**
Developments in Britain and Germany
Knut Roder

5 **Democratic Revolutions**
Asia and Eastern Europe
Mark R. Thompson

6 **Europeanisation and the Transformation of States**
Edited by Bengt Jacobsson, Per Lagreid and Ove K. Pedersen

7 **Democratization**
A comparative analysis of 170 countries
Tatu Vanhanen

8 **Determinants of the Death Penalty**
A comparative study of the world
Carsten Anckar

9 **How Political Parties Respond to Voters**
Interest aggregation revisited
Edited by Kay Lawson and Thomas Poguntke

10 **Women, Quotas and Politics**
   Edited by Drude Dahlerup

11 **Citizenship and Ethnic Conflict**
   Challenging the nation-state
   Haldun Gülalp

12 **The Politics of Women's Interests**
   New comparative and international perspectives
   Edited by Louise Chappell and Lisa Hill

13 **Political Disaffection in Contemporary Democracies**
   Social capital, institutions and politics
   Edited by Mariano Torcal and José Ramón Montero

14 **Representing Women in Parliament**
   A comparative study
   Edited by Marian Sawer, Manon Tremblay and Linda Trimble

15 **Democracy and Political Culture in Eastern Europe**
   Edited by Hans-Dieter Klingemann, Dieter Fuchs and Jan Zielonka

Democracy and Political Culture in Eastern Europe

Edited by Hans-Dieter Klingemann, Dieter Fuchs and Jan Zielonka

Routledge
Taylor & Francis Group

LONDON AND NEW YORK

First published 2006
by Routledge
2 Park Square, Milton Park, Abingdon, Oxon OX14 4RN

Simultaneously published in the USA and Canada
by Routledge
270 Madison Ave, New York, NY 10016

Routledge is an imprint of the Taylor & Francis Group, an informa business

© 2006 Hans-Dieter Klingemann, Dieter Fuchs and Jan Zielonka for
selection and editorial matter; individual contributors, their
contributions.

Typeset in Baskerville by Wearset Ltd, Boldon, Tyne and Wear
Printed and bound in Great Britain by TJI Digital, Padstow, Cornwall

British Library Cataloguing in Publication Data
A catalogue record for this book is available from the British Library

Library of Congress Cataloging in Publication Data
A catalog record for this book has been requested

ISBN10: 0-415-38602-0 (hbk)
ISBN10: 0-203-08597-3 (ebk)

ISBN13: 978-0-415-38602-9 (hbk)
ISBN13: 978-0-203-08597-4 (ebk)

Contents

List of contributors   ix

Preface   xi

**Introduction: support for democracy and autocracy in
eastern Europe**   1
HANS-DIETER KLINGEMANN, DIETER FUCHS,
SUSANNE FUCHS AND JAN ZIELONKA

**PART I
Comparative perspectives**   23

1 **Democratic communities in Europe: a comparison between
East and West**   25
DIETER FUCHS AND HANS-DIETER KLINGEMANN

2 **East European value systems in global perspective**   67
RONALD INGLEHART

3 **Historical and cultural borderlines in eastern Europe**   85
GABRIEL BĂDESCU

**PART II
National perspectives**   99

4 **The Czech Republic: critical democrats and the persistence
of democratic values**   101
ZDENKA MANSFELDOVÁ

5 Slovenia in central Europe: merely meteorological or a
   value kinship?   119
   VLADO MIHELJAK

6 Hungary: structure and dynamics of democratic
   consolidation   148
   CHRISTIAN W. HAERPFER

7 Slovakia: pathways to a democratic community   172
   SILVIA MIHALIKOVA

8 Poland: citizens and democratic politics   203
   RENATA SIEMIENSKA

9 Latvia: democracy as an abstract value   235
   ILZE KOROLEVA AND RITMA RUNGULE

10 Lithuania: civic society and democratic orientation   256
    RASA ALISAUSKIENE

11 Estonia: changing value patterns in a divided society   277
    MIKK TITMA AND ANDU RÄMMER

12 Romania: fatalistic political cultures revisited   308
    ALINA MUNGIU-PIPPIDI

13 Bulgaria: democratic orientations in support of civil society 336
    ANDREY RAICHEV AND ANTONY TODOROV

14 Russia, Belarus and Ukraine: construction of democratic
    communities   355
    ELENA BASHKIROVA

    Bibliography   379
    Index   389

Contributors

Rasa Alisauskiene is Associate Professor at the Vilnius University and Director of the General "Baltic Surveys" (The Gallup Organization), Vilnius, Lithuania.

Gabriel Badescu is Associate Professor at the Political Science Department, Babes-Bolyai University, in Cluj-Napoca, Romania.

Elena Bashkirova is President of the Romir Monitoring Group, Romir Monitoring, Moscow, Russia.

Dieter Fuchs is Professor for Political Theory and Comparative Analysis of Democracies at the Institute for Social Sciences, University of Stuttgart, Stuttgart, Germany.

Susanne Fuchs is Senior Researcher at the Social Science Research Centre in Berlin, Germany.

Christian W. Haerpfer is Professor of Political Science in the Department of Politics at the University of Vienna, Director of the Center of Strategic Development at the Institute for Advanced Studies, Vienna, Austria and Visiting Professor in the School of Slavonic, Central and Eastern European Studies at the University of Glasgow, United Kingdom.

Ronald Inglehart is Professor of Political Science, University of Michigan, Ann Arbor, Michigan, USA, and President of the World Values Survey Association, Stockholm, Sweden.

Hans-Dieter Klingemann is Professor of Political Science at the Free University and Director at the Social Science Research Centre in Berlin, Germany. He is also a Research Fellow at the Center for the Study of Democracy, University of California, Irvine and Directeur de Recherche Associé, Institut d'Études Politiques de Paris.

Ilze Koroleva is Researcher at the Institute of Philosophy and Sociology, University of Latvia, Riga, Latvia.

Zdenka Mansfeldová, PhD, is Senior Research Fellow at the Institute of Sociology, Academy of Sciences of the Czech Republic, Prague, Czech Republic.

Silvia Mihalikova is Associate Professor and Jean Monnet Chair in European Integration at the Comenius University, Bratislava, Slovak Republic.

Vlado Miheljak is Associate Professor of Social and Political Psychology and Researcher at the Center for Public Opinion Research and at the Faculty of Social Sciences, University of Ljubljana, Slovenia.

Alina Mungiu-Pippidi is Director of the think-tank, Romanian Academic Society, and Professor of Political Science at the Romanian National School of Government and Administration, Bucharest, Romania.

Andu Rämmer is a Researcher at the Department of Sociology, University of Tartu, Estonia.

Andrey Raichev is a Senior Researcher and Director of BBSS Gallup – TNS, Sofia, Bulgaria.

Ritma Rungule is a Researcher at the Institute of Philosophy and Sociology, University of Latvia, Riga, Latvia.

Renata Siemienska is Professor of Sociology and Director of the Institute for Social Studies, Warsaw University, Warsaw, Poland.

Mikk Titma is Professor of Sociology, University of Tartu, Tartu, Estonia.

Antony Todorov is Dean and Associate Professor at the New Bulgarian University, Sofia, Bulgaria.

Jan Zielonka is Ralf Dahrendorf Fellow in European Politics at St Antony's College, University of Oxford, UK.

Preface

What is the relation between democracy and political culture in countries undergoing major systemic change? Have subjective political orientations of citizens been important in shaping the development of democracy in central and eastern Europe after the fall of communism? These questions have been a core concern of an international group of 20 political scientists, of which 16 are based in the 13 central and eastern European countries covered in this book. The analysis draws from a unique set of data collected and processed by the contributors to this volume within the framework of the World Values Survey project. These data enabled authors to establish similarities and differences in support of democracy between a large number of countries with different cultural and structural conditions as well as historical legacies.

The macro-level findings of the book tend to support the proposition that support for democracy declines the further east one goes. In contrast, it has been found that micro-level relationships are astonishingly similar. For example, support for democracy is always positively related to higher levels of education – no matter where an individual citizen happens to live. The question thus becomes: what makes the proportion of democrats grow? Throughout the book, we try to avoid normative judgments. However, the volume makes it evident that, for some countries to consolidate their democracy, a major shift in political culture is required. Democracy cannot be built without democrats. It is hoped that the book will contribute to a better understanding of what makes democracies strong and resistant to autocratic temptation.

The project was part of the program of the research unit, "Institutions and Social Change," of the Wissenschaftszentrum Berlin für Sozialforschung. We are grateful for its continuing and gracious support. Our thanks also go to the European University Institute in Florence which hosted the initial planning conference in June 1999, and also provided the resources necessary for bringing the group together in Brussels in December 2002. The authors owe a great deal to Nora Fisher and Susanne Fuchs who helped with the editorial work and did all the technical work necessary to deliver the volume to the publisher.

Without their support the book would have never seen the light of day. Finally, we are grateful to Heidi Bagtazo, Editor – Politics and International Studies at Routledge, and to Hannah Dolan for their crucial help in getting this book published.

Hans-Dieter Klingemann
Dieter Fuchs
Jan Zielonka

Introduction

Support for democracy and autocracy in central and eastern Europe

Hans-Dieter Klingemann, Dieter Fuchs, Susanne Fuchs and Jan Zielonka

This book shows how subjective orientations to politics – value orientations in particular – have shaped democracy in central and eastern Europe after the fall of communism. It does so by examining the evolving map of democratic and autocratic attitudes among citizens of 13 countries in the region. The analysis draws from a unique set of data collected and processed by the contributors to this book within the World Values Survey and European Values Study projects.

The book tells an interesting story of how different central and eastern European publics perceived ongoing democratic consolidation, but it would be wrong to assume that the book is written for students of a single region only. First of all, central and eastern Europe are scrutinized in a broader European and global context. Moreover, the book develops a set of general theoretical propositions concerning the congruence of political culture and democratic political institutions. Students of transitions from autocracy to democracy may also find this book useful, because it shows how cultural factors behind democratic consolidation interact with other domestic and international factors identified within this field. The volume starts with a presentation of conceptual and comparative frameworks, followed by in-depth analyses of the individual countries undergoing democratic consolidation.

This introductory chapter will first try to conceptualize the relationship between democracy and political culture, especially in countries undergoing major systemic change. It will then present the answer to the most important question raised in this volume: how much support can we find in central and eastern Europe for democracy and autocracy? We will point to macro-differences in distributions of political orientations and structural similarities of their micro-relationships within and beyond the region. We will then present the structure and contents of the volume and highlight important findings from the comparative and national analyses.

Political culture and democracy

After the breakdown of the communist system in central and eastern Europe, all countries in the region embarked on the road of democracy building. Huntington (1991) has classified this transformation as part of a "third wave" of democratization, and the study of democratic transitions and consolidations has become extremely popular among social scientists. However, from the very beginning it was clear that the successful democratic experiment cannot be taken for granted (Dawisha and Parrot 1997; Holmes 1997; Pridham and Ágh 2001). In countries such as Belarus or Ukraine, democratic reforms were more a matter of rhetoric than practice. All too often, institutions were being crafted to suit the power-holders' partisan aims with little room for genuine public participation and fair political competition. In countries such as Russia or Romania, violence has been used as a means of democracy-building, and this was obviously quite controversial. For instance: Was it justified that presidential tanks pounded the site of parliament in the name of democracy, as was the case in Moscow in 1993? In other cases, democracy was confronted with ethnic violence, especially in the Balkans, but also in other countries in the region.

In many cases, democracy-building went hand-in-hand with state-building. The Baltic countries in particular raised the question: can a newly liberated nation-state afford to grant full democratic rights to a sizable national minority made up of its previous occupiers? Historians and political anthropologists have pointed to the persistent Soviet legacy in the region (Jowitt 1996; Ekiert and Hanson 2003). Sociologists have pointed to the initially weak civil society and underdeveloped middle class (Schöpflin 1993). There was also the difficult question about the economic prerequisites of democracy. Can poor countries such as Albania or Bulgaria ever manage to consolidate their democratic systems? Can democratic reforms proceed simultaneously with market liberalization and privatization? Will market-building prove incompatible with democracy-building as Offe and Przeworski have argued (Offe and Przeworski 1991; Diamond and Plattner 1996; Greskovits 1997)? Even Huntington (1991) himself has acknowledged that, in the past, various waves of democratization have been followed by a "reverse wave." Democratic Italy, Germany, Spain and Portugal fell victim to autocratic or totalitarian rule despite their mature middle classes and relatively high levels of economic development.

Thus, persistence of democratic regimes cannot be taken for granted. For democracy to persist and become consolidated, it is usually not enough to enjoy favorable internal and external structural conditions. Nor is it enough to skillfully engineer institutions. With the passage of years and an increasing body of empirical insight, it has become evident that it is difficult to understand the trajectories of democracy-building without considering political culture.

This hardly comes as a surprise because modern political science has been aware of a close interaction between democratic institutions and democratic culture for several decades already. As Almond and Verba have argued since the 1960s, democracies are only able to persist if they enjoy a political culture which is congruent to and supportive of its democratic structures (Almond and Verba 1963; Almond 1980). This congruence between democracy and culture has increasingly been acknowledged by students of democratic transitions (Linz and Stepan 1996; Diamond 1999; Merkel 1999). However, the nature of this congruence is still a matter of discussion. Concepts such as culture and democracy or democratic consolidation are multi-dimensional and thus not prone to simple generalization. Almond and Verba understood political culture in terms of attitudes and behavior of citizens. But obviously a political culture is linked to a multitude of political attitudes and behavior. The relevance of particular sets of attitudes and behavior for the issue of democratic consolidation is much disputed.

In this volume, Fuchs and Klingemann make a theoretical effort to specify such sets of political attitudes and behaviors that are characteristic of democratic communities and congruent to various democratic regimes. The following empirical analysis in this chapter, however, is restricted to attitudes of democracy and autocracy as ideal forms of government. These attitudes are – without any doubt – important for consolidation and persistence of democracy. If a majority of citizens object to the general principles of democratic rule, then we would expect the democratic regime of any country to be in deep trouble. On the other hand, it is assumed that the higher the degree of support of democracy as an ideal form of government is, the higher the potential for consolidation of democracy will be.

This basic hypothesis governs our empirical study of central and eastern Europe's new democracies. First, we define support of democracy and measure the degree of support in all countries under investigation. Second, we examine socio-demographic, attitudinal and behavioral correlates of support for democracy in these countries. Results are compared to similar analyses conducted in three countries representing democratic benchmarks: the USA, Norway and West Germany.

As mentioned earlier, data for this analysis are generated in the context of the World Values Survey and the European Values Study. Fieldwork extends from May 1995 (USA) to February 1999 (second Polish survey). Modal time of fieldwork is in the years of 1996/7 when ten of the 16 surveys were conducted. Thus, results describe the situation in the new democracies of central and eastern Europe in the second half of the 1990s. These were quite crucial years for these countries with new democratic constitutions and institutions already in place in most of the cases (Zielonka 2001).

Scale construction, index formation as well as all single items used in the analysis are described in the Appendix and will not be detailed here.

Relationships are assessed by Pearson's correlation coefficient. A two-tailed significance test applies. In order to be accepted as significant, relations have to reach the 0.001 level.

Support for democracy as an ideal in 13 countries

Democratic values are basic to the legitimation of democratic regimes. It is obvious that "democracy" is a core value of any set of democratic values. Thus, one of the most important preconditions of a successful legitimation of democracy in a particular country has to be the degree to which this value or the principle of democracy is accepted by its citizens. The outcome of this analysis will demonstrate empirically the degree to which this is the case in the central and eastern European countries and in the three democratic "reference countries" mentioned above.

We assume that the concept of democracy is of relevance to citizens and that the meaning of democracy which citizens accord to the concept taps the concept of democracy as theoretically defined. This assumption has been supported by various empirical studies (Fuchs *et al.* 1995; Thomassen 1995). The results of these analyses lend credence to the assumption that support of the principle of democracy can be measured by questions directly proposing "democracy" to ordinary citizens as an attitude object. The survey questions and items used to measure attitudes towards democracy as an ideal form of government – which were part of a larger battery of items – read as follows:

> (1) I am going to describe various types of political systems and ask what you think about each as a way of governing this country. For each one would you say it is a very good, fairly good, fairly bad or very bad way of governing this country?
>
> "Having a democratic political system."
>
> (2) I am going to read off some things that people sometimes say about a democratic political system. Could you please tell me if you agree strongly, agree, disagree, or disagree strongly?
>
> "Democracy may have its problems but it's better than any other form of government."

The following two items were meant to measure preferences for autocratic rule and to control the proper understanding of the democracy items:

> (3) I am going to describe various types of political systems and ask what you think about each as a way of governing this country. For each one would you say it is a very good, fairly good, fairly bad or very bad way of governing this country?
>
> "Having a strong leader who does not have to bother with parliament and elections."

(4) "Having the army rule."

Responses to these four items have been combined to form a democracy–autocracy scale. Scale values presented in Table I.1 are collapsed. The resulting index distinguishes "strong democrats," "weak democrats," "undecided citizens," and "autocrats" (details of scale and index construction are described in Appendix I.1).

As a core element of our concept of a democratic community, we have proposed in this volume the following operational definition: "the stronger support is for democracy and the more strongly autocracy is rejected, the more closely the societal community will correspond to a democratic community."

Empirical results, shown in Table I.1, demonstrate that the proportion of citizens supporting democracy as an ideal varies a great deal in the countries under study. The proportion of "strong democrats," which is citizens who strongly prefer democracy over autocracy, unequivocally is – as expected – significantly higher in the three reference countries (USA,

Table I.1 Democracy–autocracy index: proportion of democrats and autocrats

	Strong democrats (%)	Weak democrats (%)	Undecided citizens (%)	Autocrats (%)	N
Reference countries					
USA	44	49	4	3	1,360 (88)
Norway	60	36	2	2	1,097 (97)
West Germany	56	41	2	1	969 (95)
Central Europe					
East Germany	32	64	3	1	939 (93)
Poland*	20	64	8	8	823 (75)
Czech Republic	33	62	3	2	1,017 (89)
Slovakia	34	60	3	3	959 (88)
Hungary	42	51	3	4	540 (83)
Romania	28	58	6	8	917 (74)
Bulgaria	11	68	9	12	644 (60)
Europe					
Estonia	27	63	6	4	855 (84)
Latvia	10	76	8	6	970 (81)
Lithuania	7	75	11	7	685 (68)
Belarus	10	67	11	12	1,364 (65)
Ukraine	7	67	13	13	1,351 (48)
Russia	4	54	16	26	1,210 (59)

Notes
* 1999 EVS Survey.
Figure in parenthesis: percentage of total sample.

Norway, and Germany) than in all eastern European countries. In the reference countries, the percentage of "strong democrats" varies between 60 percent in Norway and 44 percent in the USA. In comparison, among the central and eastern European countries, Hungary can count on the highest (42 percent) and Russia on the relatively lowest (4 percent) proportion of "strong democrats." In general there is a gap between the "reference countries" on the one hand and the central and eastern European countries on the other. However, the differences within the group of the central and eastern European countries are rather significant, too. In general there seems to be an East–West axis which is connected with a diminishing degree of support for democracy as an ideal. Of course, as always there are exceptions to this rule. This is particularly true for Poland and Estonia with both countries showing a higher than expected proportion of non-democrats.

Table I.1 also shows that non-response to any one of the four items is rather high in Ukraine (52 percent), Russia (41 percent), Bulgaria (40 percent), Belarus (35 percent), and Lithuania (32 percent). This is an indication that a firm opinion about democracy or autocracy as the ideal form of government is still lacking in wide sections of the populace.

All told, there is no doubt that aggregated attitudinal differences between countries are substantial. However, in this analysis we shall demonstrate that these aggregate between-country differences diminish substantively when it comes to the correlates of attitudes toward democracy and autocracy on the individual level.

Correlates of support for democracy and autocracy

Table I.2 presents relations of classic socio-demographic characteristics – gender, age, education – and the democracy–autocracy scale. Systematic relations can be expected with respect to age and education. Socialization theory would predict that older citizens who have lived through communist times should express less support for democracy, while the reverse should be true for younger citizens who have already experienced liberal democracy. Social cognition theory would expect that the higher-educated would not only command a higher level of information but would also be better equipped cognitively to gauge the pros and cons of democratic and autocratic regimes. Thus, the probability of support for democracy is expected to be higher in the group of the higher-educated. There is no readily available theory to propose an equally plausible a priori assumption of a systematic relationship between gender and a preference for democracy over autocracy. Nor do empirical results offer room for inductive speculation as far as gender is concerned. Not a single significant correlation could be observed. The expectation based on socialization theory is supported in five out of 13 central and eastern European countries. In these five countries, age correlates negatively with

Table I.2 Socio-demographic correlates of the democracy–autocracy scale

	Gender		Age		Education	
	r	*N*	*r*	*N*	*r*	*N*
Reference countries						
USA	0.01	1,360	0.15*	1,340	0.20*	1,357
Norway	0.04	1,097	0.11*	1,097	0.24*	1,094
West Germany	0.06	969	−0.12*	968	0.31*	964
Central Europe						
East Germany	0.06	939	−0.00	933	0.23*	922
Poland**	0.00	900	0.05	823	0.25*	821
Czech Republic	0.03	1,017	0.09	1,017	0.24*	986
Slovakia	0.02	959	−0.06	959	0.19*	930
Hungary	0.02	540	−0.05	539	0.18*	532
Romania	0.06	917	−0.10*	917	0.14*	910
Bulgaria	−0.04	644	−0.12*	626	0.19*	644
Eastern Europe						
Estonia	−0.02	855	−0.01	855	0.14*	855
Latvia	−0.01	970	−0.07	970	0.21*	970
Lithuania	−0.01	685	0.01	685	0.15*	685
Belarus	−0.02	1,364	−0.16*	1,364	0.23*	1,363
Ukraine	0.04	1,351	−0.11*	1,351	0.13*	1,346
Russia	0.03	1,210	−0.08*	1,209	0.21*	1,210

Notes
* significant at 0.001 level.
** 1999 EVS Survey.

support for democracy which means that – as expected – the young are more supportive of democracy than the elderly. In the majority of cases, however, there are no systematic relationships of age and support for democracy. At least two ex post explanations are possible. First, the socialization effort of the old regime may – in part – have failed. Second, the experiences with the new regime may have been both positive and negative, with the latter prevailing. The USA and Norway – two of the three reference countries – show a significant and positive correlation. This is what was expected of the citizens of these two old liberal democracies. The negative signs of the correlation coefficients observed in West Germany may have to do with this country's somewhat checkered and shorter democratic tradition.

The expected positive relation of education and preference for democracy over autocracy has been found to be empirically significant in all countries included in the analysis. This is an impressive result. Thus, it is safe to say that support for democracy varies positively with level of education.

Support for democracy as a form of government is not a sufficient condition for democracy to be "the only game in town" to use Linz and

Stepan's expression (1996). Rather, it is important that acceptance of democracy as the principle of a good polity is embedded in a broader set of attitudes which – taken together – constitute a democratic belief system. Even more important: political elites as well as ordinary citizens are expected to share the key characteristics of this democratic belief system for democracy to function and persist.

Principles governing the interrelationships of citizens are of importance in this context. For example, citizens should trust each other at least to a certain degree as a precondition for the possibility of a political division of labor. Such cooperation will also be easier if citizens can count on a certain degree of acceptance of deviant behavior (tolerance). In addition, citizens should agree that violence is not regarded as a legitimate mode of political participation and competition. Table I.3 presents correlates of three related indicators – trust in others, acceptance of deviant behavior, rejection of violence (for details of measurement, compare Appendix I.2) – and the democracy–autocracy scale.

Table I.3 Attitudinal correlates of the democracy–autocracy scale: trust, acceptance of deviant behavior and rejection of violence

	Trust in others		Acceptance of deviant behavior		Rejection of violence	
	r	*N*	*r*	*N*	*r*	*N*
Reference countries						
USA	0.15*	1,360	0.18*	1,233	0.25*	1,330
Norway	0.21*	1,097	0.22*	1,065	0.16*	1,095
West Germany	0.20*	969	0.26*	941	0.25*	963
Central Europe						
East Germany	0.17*	939	0.21*	918	0.17*	934
Poland**	0.04	823	0.12*	759	–	–
Czech Republic	0.06	1,017	0.02	932	0.18*	985
Slovakia	0.09	959	0.11*	885	0.15*	934
Hungary	0.08	540	0.18*	495	0.22*	532
Romania	−0.01	917	0.13*	857	−0.01	873
Bulgaria	0.10	644	0.09	538	0.13*	624
Eastern Europe						
Estonia	0.06	855	0.20*	775	0.22*	850
Latvia	0.09	970	0.09	891	0.07	956
Lithuania	−0.00	968	0.02	599	0.09	625
Belarus	−0.01	1,364	0.21*	1,165	0.20*	1,323
Ukraine	0.08*	1,364	0.11*	1,086	0.17*	1,302
Russia	0.01	1,210	0.21*	1,057	0.13*	1,170

Notes
* significant at 0.001 level.
** 1999 EVS Survey.
Cell entries are Pearson's *r*. In Poland the scale "acceptance of deviant behavior" has been constructed without the item "prostitution."

As expected, one can observe a significant relationship between rejection of violence as a means of political competition and support for democracy in the reference countries as well as in almost all (nine out of 12) countries of central and eastern Europe. A systematic and positive relation of acceptance of deviant behavior and support of democracy as measured by the democracy–autocracy scale has been found in all countries under consideration. In a majority of countries (12 out of 16), this relationship is statistically significant at the 0.001 level. As far as trust in others is concerned, results confirm expectations only in the three reference countries, as well as East Germany and the Ukraine. In these countries, associations are significant although the correlation coefficient is rather low in the Ukraine. East Germany should be regarded as a special case due to the fact that it became part of the Federal Republic in 1990. These results suggest that the emergence of trust toward other citizens seems to depend on long-term experience of positive political cooperation in a democratic setting.

In contrast to autocracy, democracy relies on citizen participation in politics. Political motivation as well as involvement in protest behavior can be regarded as indicators of their readiness to participate politically. Table I.4 summarizes the relation of these two indicators (for details, compare Appendix I.2) and the democracy–autocracy scale.

Significant correlations of political motivation and support for democracy are present in the three reference countries and in practically all the more central (as opposed to more eastern) countries in the region – with the exception of Bulgaria. This relationship, however, does not exist in the countries which had been republics of the former Soviet Union, except for Estonia. In general, however, the division line runs between the established democracies of the West and the central European countries on the one hand, and the east European countries on the other. The inclination to engage in protest behavior shows a positive and significant relationship in 12 of the 16 countries under consideration. Thus, with some small exceptions, elite-challenging political participation can also be regarded as a general correlate of support of democracy in the more eastern European countries.

To sum up, the empirical analysis of the relative preference for democracy over autocracy and its correlates has generated quite different results in the countries under consideration. First, large differences could be observed in the various countries and regions as far as the proportion of democrats and autocrats is concerned. These differences can easily be located on an East–West axis. As Fuchs and Klingemann (in this volume) demonstrate, the distribution of democrats shows two thresholds. The first threshold separates the established democracies of the West and all of the newly established democracies under investigation. The second threshold separates the central from the eastern European countries.

Second, correlates of the democracy–autocracy scale are surprisingly similar across all countries and regions; a result which is also confirmed by country-level dimensional analyses (not documented; available upon

Table I.4 Attitudinal and behavioral correlates of the democracy–autocracy scale: political motivation and protest behavior

	Political motivation		Protest behavior	
	r	N	r	N
Reference countries				
USA	0.22*	1,322	0.25*	1,295
Norway	0.29*	1,097	0.25*	1,092
West Germany	0.27*	961	0.32*	946
Central Europe				
East Germany	0.24*	920	0.27*	900
Poland**	0.22*	812	0.14*	814
Czech Republic	0.16*	1,003	0.09	893
Slovakia	0.14*	947	0.17*	832
Hungary	0.15*	534	0.21*	520
Romania	0.13*	893	0.10	735
Bulgaria	0.08	617	0.13*	469
Eastern Europe				
Estonia	0.10*	846	0.10	811
Latvia	0.08	943	0.14*	893
Lithuania	0.09	668	0.20*	568
Belarus	0.08	1,325	0.24*	1,283
Ukraine	0.05	1,223	0.07	1,175
Russia	0.07	1,195	0.11*	1,144

Notes
* significant at 0.001 level.
** 1999 EVS Survey.
Cell entries are Pearson's r.

request). This means that mechanisms of assessment of political information and the generation of political attitudes follow similar rules and regularities. If this assumption proves to be true, political attitudes and behavior of citizens in eastern Europe are – in the end – bound to converge with those of central Europe and the established liberal democracies in the West. An important precondition of this assumption, however, is that over a longer period of time, citizens in the new democracies have positive experiences with the workings of their democratic institutions. In all likelihood, this precondition will turn out to be different for various regions of central and eastern Europe. Thus, an uneven development of support for democracy in the new democracies of central and eastern Europe is the most likely scenario.

Comparative patterns within and beyond the region

This introductory chapter discusses the basic concept of a democratic community on a cultural, structural and procedural level. It distinguishes between a libertarian, liberal, republican, and socialist type of democratic community and suggests variables to indicate the modal distribution of these types of democratic communities in the region. Special attention is also paid to cultural legacies, such as dominant religion and type of imperial legacy, duration of socialist rule and socio-economic features of modernity. The chapter tests empirically and subsequently qualifies the notion of a cultural border along religious lines, as outlined by Huntington (1996). Taking into account the imperial legacy, duration of socialist rule, and the level of socio-economic modernity allows us to paint a more differentiated picture than the one emerging from Huntington's analysis in particular as it applies to a more subtle geographic classification of types of democracy. The arguments presented by Klingemann and Fuchs are later mirrored in parts of the case studies presented in the book. Of particular interest are the analyses of those countries such as Estonia and Bulgaria which deviate from general expectations as formulated by Klingemann and Fuchs. (We did not try to enforce a strict analytical framework for examination of the case studies. However, the authors had access to various drafts of the chapter by Hans-Dieter Klingemann and Dieter Fuchs and were encouraged to consider the analytical propositions outlined therein).

Ronald Inglehart's chapter deals with eastern European countries in a global comparative context. He uses data from the World Values Survey/European Values Study to map the location of different countries on a two-dimensional Cartesian system of co-ordinates. Although the Industrial Revolution, and with it the main incentive for socio-economic modernization, began 200 years ago, the distinction between a traditional versus secular–rational orientation and a survival versus self-expression orientation persists, and it proves crucial for the relative position of most of the countries on Inglehart's cultural map. He shows that, although economic development seems to push countries from different cultural backgrounds toward a common developmental path, the influence of cultural heritage is still very strong indeed. Inglehart's findings are in line with the results of the case studies presented in this book. For instance, several case studies explicitly endorse his conclusion that some central and eastern European countries often still lack a structure of value-orientations which would back-up their democratic institutions.

The last of the three more general theoretical chapters combines theoretical expectations and empirical findings in Transylvania. The case is interesting because Transylvania shows that significant cultural borders also exist within individual states. More importantly, the evidence provided by this case openly challenges theoretical propositions about the strong link between culture, religion, and democracy, as proposed by Huntington and Braudel (Braudel 1987; Huntington 1997). In his chapter, Gabriel Badescu adopts the theoretical frameworks outlined in this volume by Dieter Fuchs, Hans-Dieter Klingemann, and Ronald Inglehart. He also takes into account the different indicators proposed in the preceding two chapters, as there are: levels of socio-economic modernity, type of imperial legacy, time spent under a Leninist regime and post-materialist versus materialist value-orientation. Transylvania shares some, but not all, characteristics with the rest of Romania. Most notably, Transylvania is Catholic while the rest of Romania is Orthodox. Before 1918, Transylvania was part of the Habsburg Empire, while the other parts of Romania were part of the Ottoman Empire until 1877 and became independent thereafter. Badescu asks: does the institutional design of autocratic regimes suppress the power of cultural heritage? Do different cultural traditions impact on the current political attitudes of the population? His answers, based on the existing evidence, are quite surprising: although the two regions differ in many respects, they do not differ in the direction predicted by theory. The more "modern" region, Transylvania, does not host the more democratically oriented population, while the more-traditional part of the country does (excepting Bucharest). The only significant difference between the two regions predicted by the cultural border theory concerns the overall level of membership in voluntary associations. However, this difference might well be the result of infrastructural differences that are at least partly caused by non-cultural reasons.

Badescu's chapter is followed by country case studies providing insights in the specific features of the individual democratic communities. Nevertheless, the case studies also offer some more general hypotheses. First of all, democracy seems to be accepted as the only game in town in the majority of the countries under study (with the notable exception of Russia).

However, although there is a general tendency that core elements of democratic beliefs are consistently related, there seem to be exceptions. A strong leader, who is not controlled by parliament and elections, seems to be compatible with the idea of democracy in countries such as Lithuania and Latvia. In addition, in some countries it seems as if democracy as an ideal and how the democratic process unfolds in one's own country cannot always be properly distinguished. This, too, is an exception from the rule (Klingemann 1999) but, as such, all the more interesting. Thus, in these instances one has to be cautious when it comes to the delineation of the group of the "dissatisfied democrats" (Klingemann 1999).

Similar observations apply to the findings related to the collective or pluralist dimensions of democracy. Tolerance as an abstract quality is cherished by a majority of citizens. However, when it comes to toleration of different lifestyles, intolerance and rejection often prevails.

Another feature seems to be common to many of the 13 countries: at the beginning of the twenty-first century, grandparents and grandchildren tend to be closer to each other in terms of political values and beliefs than parents and children (e.g. Bulgaria, Lithuania). However, this observation is probably caused less by socialization experiences in early adulthood –

we may safely assume that the circumstances have changed between the 1930s and 1990s – than by the *failure* or *absence* of such socialization efforts or experiences when being raised under a socialist regime. What "failure" or "absence" actually means remains an open question. It may well be that core values such as individual or "negative" freedom are hard to change by any socialization effort.

Political-participation levels are quite low in all the countries under consideration in the period studied. In many countries, frustration about the possibility and willingness to be involved in politics individually is explicitly voiced. As Hirschman indicates in his essay on "Shifting Involvements" (Hirschman 1982), this may not by necessity signify a complete withdrawal from politics on the part of citizens in these countries, but rather the beginning of a cycle of participation waves which are also common in the "old" democracies.

As mentioned earlier, the share of strong democrats and autocrats in the countries under study changes in relation to geographic location. In the countries situated more to the East, the share of autocrats is higher, while the share of democrats is lower. It is probably not a coincidence that the countries with the largest shares of autocrats tend to be former Soviet republics. However, there are notable exceptions to this trend. Bulgaria resembles Ukraine more than other non-Soviet states do. Estonia, on the other hand, does not reveal the typical post-Soviet pattern. Poland, according to our data, has a surprisingly low share of strong democrats and a high share of autocrats. All this suggests that broad comparisons have limitations and that case studies are necessary to refine our analysis. It is worth mentioning that 15 of the 20 authors of this book come from the regions under consideration. All country chapters – with the exception of Hungary (which has been written by an Austrian) – are contributed by colleagues from the central and eastern European countries under investigation. Most of them have been involved in the data-gathering operation. They stand for authenticity and their critical objections went far toward preventing the editors from engaging in quick but premature generalizations.

Peculiarities of individual countries

In the first case study, Zdenka Mansfeldová analyzes the prevalence of democratic values in the Czech Republic. According to her data, the Czech Republic has a more democratically oriented population than is the case in many other countries of the region. However, the author points out that her country lacks the civil, more informal structures that are the pillars of a smoothly functioning democracy.

Vlado Miheljak analyzes the case of Slovenia. Slovenia has many advantages, such as a relatively developed urban structure and a small-scale industry, factors contributing to a predisposition for democratic consolidation. The country also has a homogeneous ethnic composition which places it in an even better position than most of the other post-communist countries. However, Slovenia's democratic transformation has been more troublesome than originally expected. Miheljak points out, for instance, that Slovenia lacks a tradition of democratic statehood. Thus, the undeniable advantages that enabled Slovenia's rather smooth economic transformation did not lead to an equally fast and stable inscription of democratic values onto the public's cognitive map.

The Hungarian case is presented by Christian Haerpfer. He argues that the specifics and the success of the Hungarian transformation lay in their slow and gradual nature. Proto-forms of pluralism and a free-market economy under the regime of "Goulash Communism" – a very much admired communist regime type – preceded the non-violent political change and allowed for a comparatively "soft" transition from autocracy to democracy. Thus, "nostalgia" for the Kadar regime co-exists with rather strong democratic attitudes and a high level of support for a tolerant and pluralist society.

Silvia Mihalikova considers the Slovak case. She starts her contribution with a description of the historical roots of Slovak national identity. This identity was reinforced by a short period of independent statehood under autocratic rule. Starting in 1993, independent Slovakia has followed a democratic path. However, while Meciar's "defective democracy" enjoyed support, Slovak citizens hold rather pro-democratic views which are roughly on the same level as in the Czech Republic. Thus, Slovak citizens still appear to be torn between seemingly contradictory appeals of a social-ist ethos on the one hand and the longing for a democratic community on the other.

Renata Siemienska's chapter deals with the Polish case. She describes a civil society that preceded and nowadays sometimes undermines its polit-ical establishment. Surprisingly, the share of strong democrats is rather low in a country that was at the forefront of democratization in central and eastern Europe. It is quite possible that the principles and the civil norms that guided the Polish population in its struggle for democracy were the first to clash with the realities of democratic transition.

Ilze Koroleva and Ritma Rungule analyze the Latvian case. According to their analysis, the concept of democracy seems to be blurred in the minds of the Latvian respondents. The authors describe precisely how various attitudinal patterns are formed. As mentioned above, "tolerance" as an abstract concept enjoys high support among Latvian respondents. However, "real" tolerance as defined by acceptance of different lifestyles does not seem to enjoy high currency.

Rasa Alisauskiene presents the Lithuanian case and draws similar conclusions. She paints a picture of a rather successful structural transformation which, however, is not always perceived as such by Lithuan-ian citizens. She highlights the difficulties arising from supporting democracy as an ideal and the evaluation of the functioning of the democratic process in one's own country. In particular, the values of a libertarian type of democracy which emphasizes self-responsibility and competition do not seem to go together with democracy as an ideal in times of personal economic hardship, increasing inequality, and social stratification.

The Estonian case is quite unusual when compared to other post-Soviet republics. The distribution of democrats and autocrats is closer to non-Soviet rather than post-Soviet countries – including the two other Baltic States. Mikk Titma and Andu Rämmer argue that this could be explained by the historic influence of German culture in Estonia. Moreover, Estonia, unlike some other Soviet republics, experienced sovereign statehood and parliamentary democracy before World War II. Titma and Rämmer put special emphasis on the analysis of two ethnic communities in Estonia and their fundamentally changed relations after 1991. The Russian minority makes up 29 percent of the overall population in Estonia, and it experienced a dramatic decrease in its status following Estonian independence. A large proportion of Russians living in Estonia do not even have (or want to have) an Estonian passport. The differences in perceptions especially of Estonian institutions seem to mirror the different statuses of the two communities. The authors also point to a modernization gap between ethnic Russians and ethnic Estonians, which might be related to their different cultural heritage. Nevertheless, in concluding, the authors suggest that the Russians and Estonians seem to be coming nearer to each other under the new democratic regime. They show, for instance, that the "modernization gap" becomes smaller when looking at young Russians born and raised in Estonia.

In her analysis of Romania, Alina Mungiu-Pippidi focuses on the dichotomy of institutions and culture. Her approach is different from the one taken by Badescu, but it arrives at a rather similar conclusion: "Governance matters and no nation is doomed to perpetual poor governance." According to Mungiu-Pippidi, the similarities between pre-war and post-communist Romania result from similar institutional failures and deficiencies of the political process – not from political culture.

Andrey Raichev and Antony Todorov discuss the Bulgarian case. They outline the development of a country which never was a Soviet republic but which embraced socialist (and Soviet) rule to a greater extent than even some ex-Soviet republics. Not surprisingly, therefore, the pattern of distribution of democrats and autocrats resembles that of many of the former Soviet republics. Apparently the close Bulgarian–Russian relationship and the specific nature of the Zhivkov regime – commonly regarded as one of the most Soviet-friendly regimes in eastern Europe – resulted in political beliefs similar to those found in the former Soviet republics. The authors correctly argue that, in Bulgaria, "Sovietization" was first and foremost understood as "modernization." In addition, the Soviets were never seen as an occupation force by the Bulgarian population. Thus the dichotomy between ex- and anti-communists had much less ideological meaning for Bulgarian citizens. Raichev and Todorov also point to a peculiar pattern of political socialization in Bulgaria, which is also found in some other east European countries. This pattern can be described as follows: Bulgarian grandparents and grandchildren tend to share more political values than Bulgarian parents and their offspring. Raichev and Todorov's chapter develops a detailed typology of various cohorts and this typology explains to a large extent generational differences in political attitudes and values.

Elena Bashkirova examines three countries, Ukraine, Belarus, and Russia. She focuses especially on the Russian path to democracy. Her analysis shows that its weakness derives particularly from the weakness of an accepted legal framework ("Rechtsstaat") and from the lack of an executive able to enforce the existing rules, especially in the early stages of democracy-building in Russia. She also points to the remaining power of the *nomenclatura* of the old Soviet regime, and to a Russian society seemingly unable to play a constructive role in building and supporting a strong democratic community. The share of strong democrats in Russia is the lowest overall in the region. According to Table 1.1, only 4 percent of Russian respondents could be defined as strong democrats, while 26 percent must be counted as autocrats and 59 percent are uncertain what to believe. Bashkirova also offers a comparison of the Ukraine and Belarus with Russia. In addition, these three countries are contrasted to West Germany as a yardstick of Western democracies.

Conclusions

It was quite clear to all those involved in this book project that it would be difficult to write responsibly about the relation of democratic culture and democratic structure without a reliable set of empirical data. The data generated by the World Values Survey and European Values Study projects have offered the authors of this volume a unique opportunity, and all tables in this volume, if not otherwise attributed, are based on the data derived from these surveys. Not only did the projects generate comparable data on all 13 central and eastern European cases, but they allowed an analysis of central and eastern Europe in a broader European and global context. With the help of these data we were able to establish similarities and differences between a large number of countries with different cultural and structural conditions as well as historical legacies. We were able to quantify some of the assumptions of leading cultural theories which are currently based on a different, and often much more limited, type of comparable empirical evidence. In addition, we propose different types of democratic communities for theoretical reasons, test them empirically and show their modal distribution in the greater Europe. Results are important to answer the question of whether or not there is, or shall be, a potential for a democratic European demos in the future.

This book reflects the editors' strong support for comparative approaches, but it also bears witness to the utility of country-by-country analysis. While it was easy to identify some general patterns within the region and even beyond it, each country proved to have its own peculiarities. Individual case studies explain the historical and political context of democratic orientations expressed by the respondents. This shows that similar patterns are often generated by different factors, and they help us to explain the many unexpected results emerging from the statistical evidence.

Throughout the book we have tried to avoid normative judgments. However, it is evident that for some countries to consolidate their democracy a major shift in political culture is required. Democracy cannot be built without democrats, and in some of the countries studied, large segments of the respondents expressed ideas that are more conducive to autocracy than to democracy. We hope that this volume will contribute toward a better understanding of what makes democracies strong and resistant to autocratic temptation.

Appendix I.1 Fieldwork of surveys and number of cases (N)

Countries	Start of fieldwork	N
Reference countries		
USA	May 1995	1,542
Norway	October 1996	1,127
West Germany	March 1997	1,017
Central European countries		
East Germany	March 1997	1,009
Poland	February 1997	1,153
	February 1999	1,095
Czech Republic	November 1998	1,147
Slovakia	November 1998	1,095
Hungary	December 1998	650
Romania	June 1998	1,239
Bulgaria	December 1997	1,042
Eastern European countries		
Estonia	October 1996	1,021
Latvia	October 1996	1,200
Lithuania	July 1997	1,009
Belarus	December 1996	2,092
Ukraine	September 1996	2,811
Russia	November 1995	2,040

Appendix I.2 Scales and indices used in the analysis

Democracy–autocracy scale

Scores of two items measuring attitudes toward autocracy as a form of government are added and subtracted from the sum of scores of two items measuring democracy as an ideal.

The two "democratic" items are worded as follows:

> I am going to describe various types of political systems and ask what you think about each as a way of governing this country. For each one would you say it is a (4) very good, (3) fairly good, (2) fairly bad or (1) very bad way of governing this country?
>
> > "Having a democratic political system."
>
> I am going to read off some things that people sometimes say about a democratic political system. Could you please tell me if you (4) agree strongly, (3) agree, (2) disagree, or (1) disagree strongly?
>
> > "Democracy may have its problems but it's better than any other form of government."

The two "autocratic" items are worded as follows:

> I am going to describe various types of political systems and ask what you think about each as a way of governing this country. For each one would you say it is a (4) very good, (3) fairly good, (3) fairly bad or (1) very bad way of governing this country?
>
> > "Having a strong leader who does not have to bother with parliament and elections."
>
> (d) "Having the army rule."

Values of the democracy–autocracy scale are calculated as follows:

> Democracy–autocracy $= ((a + b) - (c + d))$

Scale values run from $+6$ (democracy) to -6 (autocracy). List-wise deletion of missing values applies.

Index "Democrats" – "Undecided citizens" – "Autocrats"

"Strong democrats" (scale values 5–6) assess democracy very positively and autocracy negatively. "Democrats" (scale values 1–4) differ from strong democrats in that their assessment of democracy is, on balance, less expressed. The group of "undecided citizens" (scale value 0) is composed of respondents who express an equal of preference for both democracy and autocracy. "Autocrats" (scale values $-1--6$) are those respondents who give a more favorable evaluation of autocracy as compared to democracy.

Trust in others

Trust in others is measured by the following question:

> "Generally speaking, would you say that most people can be trusted or that you can't be too careful in dealing with people? (1) Most people can be trusted; (0) Can't be too careful (including don't know and no answer)."

Acceptance of deviant behavior

Factor scores were calculated in each country using the following four items:

> "Please tell me for each of the following statements whether you think it can (10) always be justified, (1) never be justified or something in between, using this card."

- – Homosexuality.
- – Prostitution.
- – Abortion.
- – Divorce.

List-wise deletion of missing values applies.

Rejection of violence

Rejection of violence is measured by the following question:

> "Here's one more statement. How strongly do you agree or disagree with it? (4) strongly agree, (3) agree, (2) disagree, (1) strongly disagree.
>
> Using violence to pursue political goals is never justified.

Political motivation

Factor scores were calculated in each country using the following three items:

> "Please say, for each of the following, how important it is in your life. Would you say politics is (4) very important, (3) rather important, (2) not very important or (1) not at all important?"

"How interested are you in politics? (4) very, (3) somewhat, (2) not very or (1) not at all interested?"

"When you get together with your friends, would you say you discuss political matters (3) frequently, (2) occasionally, or (1) never?"

List-wise deletion of missing values applies.

Protest behavior

Factor scores were calculated in each country using the following three items:

"Now I'd like you to look at this card. I'm going to read out some different forms of political action that people can take, and I'd like you to tell me, for each one, whether you have actually (3) done any of these things, (2) whether you might do it, or (1) would never, under any circumstances, do it."

- signing a petition
- joining in boycotts
- attending lawful demonstrations

List-wise deletion of missing values applies.

References

Almond, G.A. (1980) "The Intellectual History of the Civic Culture Concept," in Almond, G.A. and Verba, S. (eds) *The Civic Culture Revisited*, Boston: Little, Brown and Company.

Almond, G.A. and Verba, S. (1963) *The Civic Culture*, Princeton: Princeton University Press.

Braudel, F. (1987) *Grammaire des Civilisations*, Paris: Arthaud – Flammarion.

Dawisha, K. and Parrott, B. (eds) (1997) *The Consolidation of Democracy in East-Central Europe*, vol. 1, Cambridge: Cambridge University Press.

Diamond, L. (1999) *Developing Democracy*, Baltimore: The Johns Hopkins University Press.

Diamond, L. and Plattner, M.F. (eds) (1996) *The Global Resurgence of Democracy*, Baltimore, London: Johns Hopkins University Press.

Ekiert, G. and Hanson, S.E. (eds) (2003) *Capitalism and Democracy in Central Eastern Europe: Assessing the Legacy of Communist Rule*, Cambridge: Cambridge University Press.

Fuchs, D., Guidorossi, G. and Pale, S. (1995) "Support for the Democratic System," in Klingemann, H. and Fuchs, D. (eds) *Citizens and the State*, Oxford: Oxford University Press.

Greskovits, B. (1997) *The Political Economy of Protest and Patience*, Budapest: Central European University.

Hirschman, A.O. (1982) *Shifting Involvements: Private Interest and Public Action*, Princeton: Princeton University Press.

Holmes, L. (1997) *Post Communism: an Introduction*, Oxford: Polity Press.

Huntington, S.P. (1991) *The Third Wave: Democratization in the Late Twentieth Century*, Norman: University of Oklahoma Press.

Huntington, S.P. (1996) *The Clash of Civilizations and the Remaking of World Order*, New York: Simon and Schuster.

Jowitt, K. (1996) "The New World Disorder," in Diamond, L. and Plattner, M. (eds) *The Global Resurgence of Democracy*, Baltimore: The Johns Hopkins Press.

Klingemann, H. (1999) "Political Support in the 1990s: a Global Analysis," in Norris, P. (ed.) *Critical Citizens*, Oxford: Oxford University Press.

Linz, J.J. and Stepan, A. (1996) *Problems of Democratic Transition and Consolidation*, Baltimore: The Johns Hopkins University Press.

Merkel, W. (1999) *Systemtransformation. Eine Einführung in die Theorie und Empirie der Transformationsforschung*, Opladen: Leske und Budrich.

Offe, C. (1991) "Capitalism by Democratic Design? Democratic Theory Facing the Triple Transition in East Central Europe," *Social Research* 58.

Pridham, G. and Ágh, A. (eds) (2001) *Prospects for Democratic Transformation in East-Central Europe*, Manchester: Manchester University Press.

Schöpflin, G. (1993) *Politics in Eastern Europe 1945–1992*, Oxford: Blackwell.

Thomassen, J. (1995) "Support for Democratic Values," in Klingemann, H. and Fuchs, D. (eds) *Citizens and the State*, Oxford: Oxford University Press.

Zielonka, J. (ed.) (2001) *Democratic Consolidation in Eastern Europe. Vol. 1: Institutional Engineering*, Oxford: Oxford University Press.

Part I
Comparative perspectives

1 Democratic communities in Europe

A comparison between East and West

Dieter Fuchs and Hans-Dieter Klingemann

The issue

Until the Maastricht Treaties (1991), the European Community was primarily an economic community legitimated by economic efficiency criteria (Lepsius 1999). Maastricht, however, initiated the transformation of the Community into a European Union, which continued with the Treaty of Amsterdam (1997). These treaties vest greater powers in EU institutions. The EU is thus increasingly a supranational regime, substantially restricting member states' scope for action, and whose decisions directly affect citizens' lives. These decisions also affect politically sensitive areas that have hitherto been dealt with at the nation-state level (including social and moral issues). These developments have been politicizing the EU and, consequently, engendering legitimation problems. The discussion on the democratic deficiencies of the EU, which has arisen only since this transformation of the European Community, is an expression of the legitimation issue. Many feel the EU can attain democratic legitimacy only if a European demos with a collective identity takes shape (Grimm 1995; Kielmansegg 1996; Scharpf 1999). This can be maintained even if the democratic deficiencies of the EU were to be eliminated institutionally by substantially expanding the rights of the European Parliament. A viable European democracy requires a European demos that conceives of itself as a collectivity, considers itself represented by the Parliament, and makes the latter the addressee of relevant demands. However, in view of the cultural plurality and heterogeneity of European nation-states, it is doubtful whether the constitution of a European demos with a tenable collective identity is possible at all (Lepsius 1999).

A further transformation of the EU must increase these doubts. At the 1992 Copenhagen summit, the then EU heads of government decided that the countries of central and eastern Europe could become members of the EU if they so desired and if they meet certain criteria for accession. Eight post-communist countries are already EU members and several others may join soon. For a number of reasons, eastward enlargement is likely to make it even more difficult to develop a European identity.

This is true, first, because the territorial limits of Europe are vague: where does it end in the East, or where should it end? A clearly defined territory is a useful, indeed necessary precondition for the cognitive constitution of an "us" that distinguishes itself from "others" and which is the vehicle of a collective identity (Fuchs *et al.* 1993). Second, including additional nation-states increases the cultural plurality of the EU still more. And, third, it cannot be excluded that, over and above this pluralization, there is a cultural gap between western Europe and central and eastern Europe. Such a gap can be caused by different traditions and historical events in the distant past, but also by socialization and experience in the opposing societal systems in which people in eastern and western Europe lived from the end of the Second World War until the collapse of the communist states.

A collective identity can develop only on the basis of commonality among the members of a definable community. It is an open question of how comprehensive this commonality must and can be in the case of a European demos. We assume that homogenizing the plurality of national cultures to form a European nation is a project that is neither practicable nor useful. For a European demos, before which the EU regime can be legitimated and which participates in the democratic processes in Europe, common political values and behaviors are presumably quite sufficient. With this premise in mind, our empirical goal is to establish the extent to which such commonality exists in individual countries, or whether there are serious and systematic differences.

This analysis is structured by two theoretical considerations. First, we assume that political value orientations and behaviors can be organized in meaningful patterns. In determining these patterns, we draw on the concepts of the democratic community and various types of democratic community. The most important criterion is support for democratic rule and rejection of autocratic rule. The greatest possible agreement on these preferences is a necessary condition for a European demos. However, fundamental support for democracy reveals nothing about the ideas held on how democracy should be specifically implemented and structured. To settle this question, further values and behaviors must be taken into account. They form specific patterns, and, with reference to the democratic theory debate, we distinguish different types of democratic community.

Second, our analysis of differences in political values and behaviors considers not only individual countries, but groups or families of countries. The country groups are distinguished on the basis of criteria proposed by Huntington (1996), Reisinger (1999) and Lipset (2000).

The planned analysis can contribute only to discovering the *potential* for the formation of a European demos with a collective identity. Empirically established, objective commonality can have an identity-forming effect only if it is perceived as such and finds its place in the self-description of the collectivity. However, this transformation of objective commonality into the subjective self-understanding of a collectivity presupposes a great deal. In the case of a European demos, one of the prerequisites is certainly a European public (Gerhards 1993) that can make latent commonality visible and allow it to become part of people's self-conception. However, this is not the subject of our study. We limit ourselves to the priority investigation of whether there is such commonality at all.

The study proceeds in three steps. First, the concepts of democratic community and types of democratic community are presented. The empirical analysis follows. It begins by explicating the classification of countries and by stating a number of theoretical expectations. In the empirical analysis itself, we first establish the extent to which the societal community in individual countries and groups of countries can be considered democratic at all. We then determine what type of democratic community predominates in these countries and groups of countries. In a third and final step, we summarize the empirical findings and draw a number of conclusions on the formation of a European demos with a collective identity.

The concept of the democratic community

The demos of a democracy is a certain form of societal community. And, like every societal community, it is constituted through two mechanisms (Fuchs 1999b, 2000). First, by *drawing a boundary* that defines who is included and who is excluded. In modern societies, nationality provides a formal boundary. But it can have a constitutive effect only if it is subjectively assimilated by members of the community. This requires cognitively identifiable criteria, and one important such criterion is a clear territorial boundary. Second, a societal community takes shape through the *ties* between members on the basis of things actually or presumed to be shared. Only through these two mechanisms does a mere aggregate of individuals become a community that presents and can describe itself as such, and with which members can also identify.

The form of societal community that interests us is the demos, which, as the subject of a democratic form of government, should be a democratic community (Berry 1989; Chapman and Shapiro 1993). If it is to be accepted as such, it has to exhibit certain minimal characteristics. The institutional order of a democracy (*kratos*) can function only if there is a corresponding community (*demos*). In determining the properties of a democratic community we draw on an analytical model that divides democracy into three hierarchically structured levels (Fuchs and Roller 1998; Fuchs 1999a, 2000). The topmost level is that of *political culture*, whose constitutive elements are the fundamental values of a democracy. The next level is that of *political structure*, which consists of the democratic system of government of a country, generally laid down by the constitution. This structure can be understood as a selective implementation of the cultural values of a community for the action context of politics, and this system of government is also legitimated by recourse to these values. The lowest level in the hierarchy is that of the *political process*. The political process is concerned with the realization of the collective goals of a community by the actors. Their action is controlled by the political structure, and this means, among other things, that normative expectations about the behavior of political actors is associated with the constituted system of government in a given country. The three levels thus form a control hierarchy that begins with culture and ends with the process or actual activity on the part of actors. What attributes must a community have at these three levels if it is to be deemed democratic?

At the *cultural level*, a democratic community is characterized above all by support for the fundamental values of democracy. They include the idea of self-government or sovereignty of the people. And this includes mutual recognition of citizens as free and equal. Since the birth of democracy in ancient Athens, the two values of freedom and equality have been essentially bound up with democracy (Sartori 1987; Hansen 1991).

A democratic community cannot be as clearly identified at the *structural level* as at the cultural level. On the one hand, it must be expected that the regime in the citizens' own country is supported in so far as it is a democracy and not an autocracy. Otherwise approval of the idea of democracy would be completely non-committal. On the other hand, the idea of a democracy can be institutionally embodied in different ways. For this reason many people may basically want a democracy, but not in the form that exists in their country. People may therefore support or criticize the democracy implemented in their country for a variety of reasons (Fuchs 2000). They may support it because it is a democracy and as such has institutionalized the idea of democracy. They may criticize it because they feel that the reality of democracy in their country fails to meet their own normative ideas of democracy, and because they also assume there are alternative forms of implementation that produce a better democratic reality. Such people can be described as "critical democrats" (Klingemann 1999). Both possibilities are compatible with the prerequisites for a democratic community.

The *process level* is concerned with the realization of political objectives by producing collectively binding decisions. In pluralistic societies, such goals are always controversial, and conflicts about them are the very essence of democratic processes. A democratic community is thus not characterized by consensus, however understood, about the political goals to be attained, but only by actual compliance with the procedural norms for taking action as laid down by the constitution, and which are intended to regulate everyday political conflicts.

Table 1.1 shows these attributes of a democratic community in the form of "the more/the more" statements. They constitute operational definitions that provide a point of reference for later empirical analysis. As we

Table 1.1 Operational definitions of a democratic community

System level	Basic elements	Operational definitions
Culture	Values	The stronger support is for a democracy, and the more strongly autocracy is rejected, the more closely the societal community will correspond to a democratic community. The more strongly other citizens are recognized as free and equal, the more closely the societal community will correspond to a democratic community.
Structure	Rules and institutions	The stronger support for or critique of democracy in one's own country is based on democratic norms, the more closely the societal community will correspond to a democratic community.
Process	Actions	The less citizens use force as a political means, the more closely the societal community will correspond to a democratic community. The more closely citizens conform to the democratically determined norms of action, the more closely the societal community will correspond to a democratic community.

have seen, a democratic community is characterized at the process level by compliance with the democratically established legal norms. The prohibition of violence or force as a political instrument has pre-eminent status among these legal norms, because it affects the essence of successful integration into a community. The table therefore contains an independent operational definition of force as a means of politics.

Having established the characteristics of a democratic community, we proceed to differentiate different types. For the purpose of our study, we combine a theoretical with a pragmatic approach. Theoretically, we follow the contemporary discussion in political philosophy (including Nozick 1974; Barber 1984; Taylor 1989; Etzioni 1993; Rawls 1993), and pragmatically we are guided by indicators available in the 1995–9 World Values Survey. We begin with a simplified description of the types. We bring in a dimension at the cultural level that has hitherto been neglected by empirical democracy research, namely the ethos of a community. It has two points of reference; first, the ethical values by which a person orders his or her life and, second, the ethical values governing relations with other members of the societal community.

This ethos of the community is the subject of one of the most important democracy theory debates to have been conducted in recent decades. We will not deal with it in detail at this point, but merely reiterate the aspects that are important for our analysis – the differentiation of the democratic community. The debate has been provoked by the tension between the freedom of individuals and the demands of the community. Differing normative positions are apparent primarily in the priority given to the one or the other. This general continuum, with the poles of individualism and community, can be divided into two dimensions, which have already been mentioned in discussing the ethos of the community. The one dimension addresses the fundamental question: who bears the principal responsibility for shaping and determining a person's life – the individual or the state (in as much as the state represents a specific form of community institutionalization)? The other dimension is concerned with the equally fundamental question of how relations between individuals should be. The one alternative is performance-driven competition between individuals in the various marketplaces, and the other is cooperation and solidarity in dealing with one another (Chapman and Shapiro 1993). Crossing these two dichotomous dimensions produces a typology with four normative models of democracy and the corresponding types of democratic community: libertarian, liberal, socialist, republican and communitarian (see Figure 1.1).

The contrasting and, as it were, pure models are the libertarian and socialist communities. On both dimensions they give clearest priority to one or other alternative. The liberal model differs from the libertarian primarily through equality of opportunity in competition between individuals in the economic and political markets as a criterion of justice. And justice is the most important standard by which to evaluate societal institutions. The most prominent advocate of this model is Rawls (1993). Given differences in ability and temperament, equality of opportunity can be ensured only through legal regulation and redistribution by government. Government thus plays an extremely important role in shaping the life of the individual. The liberal model differs from the socialist model in three ways. First, redistribution by government is concerned only with the most equal possible distribution of the primary goods that are absolutely necessary for the individual to organize his or her life autonomously. Second, the principles of competition and performance are constitutive for the relationship between individuals in everyday interaction in the marketplace, in politics and in other areas of society. And, third, in the event of

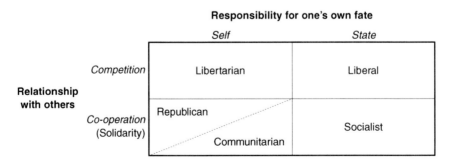

Figure 1.1 Types of a democratic community.

conflict, individual freedom always has unrestricted priority over the equal distribution of the other primary goods.

Among other things, this means that, in contrast to the socialist model, basic social rights ought not to be included in the constitution. Ensuring equality of opportunity can be only a political task, which, in practical terms, results in the establishment of a more or less comprehensive welfare state. Overall, the role of government in the liberal model is thus relatively less restricted than in the socialist model. This difference is not visible in the dichotomized typology. From an institutional point of view, the ethical values of the libertarian community mean as little government as possible and as comprehensive a market as possible; and those of the socialist community mean a comprehensive welfare state and a limited market. The liberal community occupies an intermediate position.

The republican community differs most strongly from the others. Moreover, it can be considered the normatively most demanding. In contrast to the liberal community, common values are of crucial importance, and, in case of doubt, are given priority over the unrestricted freedom of the individual. The lifestyle of a republican community is "essentially co-operative and solidaristic" (Post 1993). It differs from the liberal and especially from the socialist community by a fundamentally anti-etatist and anti-paternalist attitude. In this regard it resembles the libertarian community. According to republican ideas, community values should by implemented not by government, and thus on behalf of the citizens, but by the community of citizens themselves (Etzioni 1996). For this reason the self-organization of the citizenry in local units is an essential republican postulate. The republican community is thus a participatory community which emphasizes solidarity. The solidarity concept differs considerably from that upheld in the socialist community. It presents itself as voluntary support for people in need through no fault of their own, or as voluntary charitableness. Solidarity in a socialist community, by contrast, is exercised through collectively binding decisions by the state and, moreover, is characterized by a strong concept of equality.

The ideas about a republican community that were developed in the context of normative democracy theory have been taken up in an empirical research context, especially by Putnam (1993). Putnam himself uses the concept of *civic community*. The dimensions and attributes of the civic community are compatible with our analytical distinctions. Putnam assumes from the outset that the civic community is democratic, and accordingly exhibits corresponding attitudes toward the democratic system of government. He therefore concentrates on the ethos of the community and the behavior of its members that it engenders. At the level of political culture, Putnam sees several values as characteristic of the community. In the first place he emphasizes political equality, while stressing – fully in keeping with the republican tradition – that this includes equal rights *and* duties for all. This value is particularly important for the relationship between individual members of the community and its institutions. The other values are concerned with interactions among members of the community. They should be guided by solidarity, tolerance and trust. The citizens of a civic community are thus explicitly not egoistic–rational people, as is assumed, for example, in the libertarian model of democracy.

A decisive characteristic of a civic community is, according to Putnam, a strong commitment among citizens to political participation. Putnam makes two specifications in this regard. First, an orientation toward the public good: "Participation in a civic community is more public-spirited, more oriented to shared benefits" (Putnam 1993: 88). On the other hand, the decisive form of participation is in voluntary associations. According to Putnam, active membership in voluntary associations contributes to the generation of the values mentioned and the associated ability and willingness for cooperative behavior in realizing the public good. In the same cell in Table 1.1, a distinction is once again drawn between a republican and a communitarian community. The two exhibit largely the same attributes. But, unlike the republican community, a communitarian community is characterized by concepts of the good and proper life, which it considers binding on all. A well-known example of communitarian ideas is the ethical moralism of Protestant sects in the United States. It has strongly affected American culture, and, according to Lipset (1996), is a central attribute of "American exceptionalism." Although this ethical moralism is concerned mainly with private issues of the family, marriage, sexuality and the like, corresponding ethical ideas also carry over into the public sphere, as the many scandals involving politicians and the bitter conflicts on abortion show (Ferree *et al.* 2000). A further characteristic of communitarianism among Protestant sects that has had a major impact on American culture as a whole is, according to Lipset (1996), a pronounced work ethic that derives ultimately from the idea of "predestination."

Table 1.2 shows the five types of democratic community schematically in terms of the attributes described above. The two dimensions underlying the typology in Figure 1.1 have naturally been taken into account. A characteristic is used in describing a type of democratic community only if this is clearly justified on the basis of the democracy theory discussion.

Empirical analysis

Classification of countries and theoretical expectations

As the predecessor of the European Union, the European Community came into being during the period of the East–West conflict. It therefore included only western European states, with France and Germany as the core countries. They provided relative economic and cultural homogeneity, and the border question did not arise. To the West, north, and south,

Table 1.2 Types of a democratic community (schematic description)

	Libertarian	Liberal	Socialist	Republican	Communitarian
Cultural level					
Responsibility for one's own life	Self	Self + State competition +	State	Self	Self
Relationship with others	Competition	Equal opportunities	Solidarity (abstract)	Solidarity (specific)	Solidarity (specific)
Ethic idea of the good		Tolerance		Tolerance	Moralism
Work ethic					Well-developed
Trust in others				High	High
Structural level					
Ownership of means of production	Private ownership	Private ownership	Private ownership + State property		
Management of enterprises	Entrepreneur		Entrepreneur + Employee		
Process level					
Political motivation				High	High
Civic engagement (voluntary associations)				High	High

the border was defined by the coastline, and to the East by the Iron Curtain. After the collapse of communism, the eastward border dissolved, and the question of where the eastern bounds of Europe ought to be set and who should be considered potential members of the EU came on to the agenda (Huntington 1996).

Depending on what criteria are applied, this question finds a variety of answers. The criterion of our study is the similarity of political communities in the countries of central and eastern Europe to those of the western European countries that have hitherto constituted the European Union. The basic assumption is that the potential for the formation of the European demos with a collective identity is proportionate to the similarity of political values and behaviors. Before we tackle the empirical analysis, we classify the countries under study and attempt on this basis to formulate what we expect of the analysis.

Political values and behaviors are influenced by various factors; most importantly, perhaps, by durable cultural traditions (Putnam 1993; Huntington 1996; Inglehart 1998). A useful starting point for classifying countries is thus the distinction between civilizations drawn by Huntington (1996). He postulates an historical cultural borderline within Europe that divides the western Christian peoples from the Muslim and Orthodox peoples. This dividing line ultimately goes back to the division of the Roman Empire in the fourth century, consolidated in the sixteenth century. If one were to take account only of this cultural border, the frontier of Europe would be clearly definable. It would run where Western Christianity ends and Islam begins (Huntington 1996). This definition is based above all on religion, and this is dichotomized: Protestant and Catholic versus Orthodox and Muslim. For the purposes of our analysis, this is too great a simplification. We therefore draw on two further criteria to produce a more differentiated classification of countries, basing our procedure on democracy theory approaches and findings (Reisinger 1999; Lipset 2000).

These two additional criteria are the different empires in which the peoples concerned lived for centuries, namely the British, Habsburg, Russian and Ottoman empires. The links between these empires and specific religions (Protestant, Catholic, Orthodox and Muslim) are obvious, but it can be assumed that the respective system of government has an independent impact on fundamental values. They are, for example, to be associated with the extent of autocratic rule in the different empires or with the different degree of separation between State and Church.

The Soviet Empire can be regarded as a specific variant. To distinguish it from these old empires, we refer to it as an imperium. Russia formed the centre of this imperium, and its sphere of influence included first the other Soviet republics, and second the countries of central and eastern Europe within the Iron Curtain. Unlike the empires, the Soviet Union and its satellite states had definitely no religious basis. The impact on the political attitudes and behaviors of the citizenry is affected by the autocratic system of government and the egalitarian ideology (Fuchs 1999b; Rohrschneider 1999). Reisinger (1999) suggests that this impact varies depending on the length of time during which a country had a Leninist regime.

In addition to religion, empire and Leninist regime, we draw on a fourth characteristic, the level of socio-economic modernity. It is opera-tionalized by per capita GDP. The modernity and wealth of a country are among the most important preconditions for the formation and stability of a democracy and for the development of democratic and liberal values. This has been repeatedly established by Lipset (1959, 1994, 2000), and can be considered one of the best confirmed findings of empirical demo-cracy research.

Tables 1.3 and 1.4 classify countries in terms of the dimensions explained. Description in terms of "empire" and "modernity" (Table 1.3) is relatively unproblematic. It is a little more complicated with "religion," since most countries are mixed in this respect. Table 1.4 shows the shares of individual religions in each country as a percentage. In the last column (CL) the country is classified in terms of modal denomination. The columns PC (Protestant and Catholic) and OM (Orthodox and Muslim) demonstrate the dominant dividing line postulated by Huntington (1996).

Countries have been assigned to one of seven groups on the basis of the four dimensions (see Tables 1.3 and 1.4). Although our study is con-cerned with European countries, the United States, Australia and New Zealand have also been taken into account. According to Huntington (1996), these countries form an independent culture complex within western Christian civilization that differs systematically from Europe. This difference has also recently been empirically established at the level of political attitudes and behaviors (Fuchs and Klingemann 2000). Including this group of countries provides a contrastive backdrop to the particularity of European nations. Moreover, they most clearly represent one of the types of democratic community that we have identified (libertarian community).

We have chosen to label the groups of countries by geographical region. Such regions are relatively neutral concepts, while being, in a certain sense, effective factors in generating common characteristics. Spatial proximity between countries and peoples facilitates communica-tion and increases the probability of similar historical experience. All four dimensions relate systematically to the formation and stability of demo-cracies on the one hand, and to the development of democratic and liberal attitudes and behaviors on the other (Huntington 1996; Reisinger 1999; Lipset 2000).[1] Since we cannot make any precise assumptions about the relative weight of individual dimensions and relations between the various scale points, only limited a priori assumptions are possible on the

Table 1.3 Cultural heritage: a classification of countries by empires (imperia), duration of Leninist regimes and modernity

Countries	Empires (Imperia) (crude classification)	Modernity (GDP ppp in US $)
Anglo-American countries		
USA	British (–)	29.080
Australia	British (–)	19.510
New Zealand	British (–)	15.780
Western European countries		
Norway	None (Sweden) (–)	24.260
Sweden	None (–)	19.010
Finland	Russian (–)	19.660
West Germany	None (Prussia) (–)	24.345
Spain	None (Spain) (–)	15.690
Central European countries		
East Germany	None (Prussia)/Le 41	17.995
Czech Republic	Habsburg/Le 41	10.380
Slovakia	Habsburg/Le 41	7.860
Hungary	Habsburg/Le 43	6.970
Slovenia	Habsburg/Le 18	11.880
Croatia	Habsburg/Le 18	4.930
Baltic countries		
Estonia	Russia/Le 50	5.090
Latvia	Russia/Le 50	3.970
Lithuania	Russia/Le 50	4.140
South-eastern European countries (mainly Orthodox)		
Yugoslavia	Ottoman/Le 18	3.500
Romania	Ottoman/Le 43	4.270
Bulgaria	Ottoman/Le 43	3.870
South-eastern European countries (mixed-Muslim)		
Macedonia	Ottoman/Le 18	3.180
Bosnia-Herzegovina	Ottoman/Le 18	2.358
Albania	Ottoman/Le 45	2.170
Eastern European countries		
Russia	Russia/Le 74	4.280
Ukraine	Russia/Le 74	2.170
Belarus	Russia/Le 74	4.820
Moldova	Ottoman/Le 50	1.450

Notes
Le = years of Leninist rule (Reisinger 1999 and own calculations for Albania, East Germany, and the former Yugoslav states); Modernity: GDP purchasing parity power in US dollars 1997.

basis of this classification. We begin with the "democratic community," which is characterized by acceptance of the fundamental values of every democracy. In this regard, the situational factor of the collapse of the communist systems is likely to have an effect. We therefore expect a democracy to be supported by a majority in every country. The factors we have

Table 1.4 Cultural heritage: a classification of countries by denomination (%)

Countries	P	C	PC	O	M	OM	S	T	CL
Anglo-American countries									
USA	*36*	25	**61**	0	0	1	18	80	**P**
Australia	*48*	26	**74**	1	1	2	3	79	**P**
New Zealand	*60*	14	**74**	0	0	0	4	78	**P**
Western European countries									
Norway	*82*	1	**83**	1	1	2	4	89	**P**
Sweden	*81*	5	**86**	1	4	5	1	92	**P**
Finland	*80*	3	**83**	2	0	2	1	86	**P**
West Germany	*39*	33	**72**	0	1	1	1	74	**P**
Spain	1	*82*	**83**	0	0	0	1	84	**C**
Central European countries									
East Germany	*18*	5	**23**	0	0	0	1	**24**	**T**
Czech Republic	2	*39*	**40**	0	0	0	3	43	**C**
Slovakia	10	*73*	**83**	0	0	0	3	86	**C**
Hungary	17	*55*	**72**	2	0	2	1	75	**C**
Slovenia	2	*69*	**71**	2	1	3	1	75	**C**
Croatia	0	*82*	**82**	1	1	1	1	85	**C**
Baltic countries									
Estonia	10	0	**10**	*16*	0	**16**	2	**28**	**T**
Latvia	*19*	18	**37**	18	0	18	5	60	**P**
Lithuania	2	*77*	**79**	4	0	4	2	85	**C**
South-eastern European countries (mainly Orthodox)									
Yugoslavia	1	6	**7**	*64*	8	**72**	2	81	**O**
Romania	2	5	**6**	*87*	0	**87**	3	96	**O**
Bulgaria	1	1	**2**	*52*	12	**64**	1	67	**O**
South-eastern European countries (mixed-Muslim)									
Macedonia	0	1	**1**	*45*	24	**69**	0	70	**O**
Bosnia-Herzegovina	2	14	**16**	26	*27*	**53**	1	70	**M**
Albania	0	6	**6**	20	*67*	**87**	0	93	**M**
Eastern European countries									
Russia	0	0	**0**	*48*	5	**53**	1	54	**O**
Ukraine	0	6	**6**	*56*	0	**56**	1	63	**O**
Belarus	0	8	**8**	*54*	0	**54**	0	62	**O**
Moldova	0	0	**0**	*83*	0	**83**	1	84	**O**

Notes
P = Protestant; C = Catholic; PC = sum of Protestant + Catholic; O = Orthodox; M = Muslim; OM = sum of Orthodox + Muslim; S = Sects; T = proportion of respondents mentioning a denominational affiliation; CL = generalized denominational classification. Cell entries are data generated by the World Values Survey 1995–9.

used in classifying countries would therefore have to take effect in *relative differences* between countries and groups of countries. If the major historical dividing lines postulated by Huntingdon (1996), separating the western Christian peoples from the Muslim and Orthodox peoples, is indeed the decisive borderline, the Anglo-American, western European, central European and Baltic countries would be more democratic that the south-eastern and eastern European lands.

If all four dimensions – not only "religion" but also "empire," "Leninist regime" and "modernity" – are taken into account, expectations are somewhat more differentiated. On the basis of these dimensions, we can posit the following ordinal sequence in the extent to which a democratic community exists: (1) the Anglo-American and western European countries (perhaps Spain and Finland might be somewhat marginal); (2) the central European countries; (3) the Baltic countries; (4) the south-eastern European countries (with the exception of Albania); (5) the eastern European countries (including Albania). In all the following tables of empirical results, the groups of countries are listed in this presumed order. If one wishes to provide an empirically testable simplification, the extent to which a democratic community exists in individual countries can be assumed to vary along a geographical north-west–south-east axis.

Two central criteria were applied in differentiating between types of democratic community (see Figure 1.1). First, whom the citizens feel should bear primary responsibility for a person's fate (the individual or the state), and, second, how relations between fellow citizens ought to be (competitive or based on solidarity). The two criteria can also be understood as a specification of the more general individualism–collectivism dimension. In formulating our expectations, we drew on a study by Lipset (1996). He postulates a substantial difference between American and European cultures, an "American exceptionalism." In this context, he is concerned only with western Europe. The distinction Lipset makes resembles that proposed by Huntington (1996) between North American and the cultures of western Europe. However, Lipset focuses on different aspects. In his view, the exceptionality of American culture has been primarily determined by the ethos of the Protestant sects that immigrated from Britain. Central to the American ethos is a marked individualism with a strong ethic of self-responsibility and an anti-etatist attitude. This has produced a society with a weak central government and a strong market. Lipset contrasts this American ethos with the etatist and solidary attitudes among Europeans, which have led to the formation of welfare states. Of the factors given in Tables 1.3 and 1.4 that shape the political attitudes and behaviors of the citizenry, Lipset thus cites British origins and the tradition of the British Empire, and the religion of the Protestant sects. However, since the ethic of the Protestant sects and the structure of the political and economic systems grounded on it are considered the most important causes for the extraordinarily successful modernization process in the United States, the modernity factor also comes into play. On the basis of Lipset's study, we can formulate a number of expectations about the type of democratic community in the countries under study.

Lipset (1996) takes no account of central and eastern European countries. If we assume that autocratic regimes – like those of the Ottoman and

Russian Empires and the Soviet imperium – foster etatist orientations and weaken individualist attitudes, we can on this basis formulate expectations about the type of democratic community to include the countries of central and eastern Europe. We restrict ourselves to the two criteria underlying the typology in Figure 1.1, on the assumption that, at a more general level, both are based on the individualism–collectivism (or etatism) dimension. On this dimension, at least three types of democratic community can be placed. The libertarian community is closest to the individualist pole, the socialist community to the collectivist pole, with the liberal community between the two. If we apply these criteria, the Anglo-American countries can be assumed to exhibit a tendency toward the libertarian community, western European countries toward the liberal community and the countries of central and eastern Europe toward the socialist community. The latter is likely to apply most strongly for the Slav successor countries to the Soviet Union.

Democratic community

Two questions are to be settled in the first step of the empirical analysis. First, the extent to which the societal communities in the countries under study are democratic and, second, how marked the similarities or differences between these countries are. The analysis is guided by the expectations formulated in the previous section.

The criteria for a democratic community have been established as operational definitions (see Table 1.1). With the exception of "mutual recognition as free and equal citizens," indicators of all the attributes of a democratic community are contained in the World Values Survey 1995–9. The distributions of attitudes and behavioral dispositions measured by these indicators are shown in Table 1.5.

We will not interpret the empirical findings shown in Table 1.5 in any detail. as the indicators and indices are described in greater detail in Appendix 1.1. They serve primarily as background information for the following systematic comparison to which we can refer as needed. Before we tackle this comparison, a few remarks on our methods are appropriate.

We describe and localize the countries under study by aggregating individual characteristics of citizens. The advantages and disadvantages of this strategy are well known, and they have been comprehensively discussed. Our approach differs from most in that we make a priori assumptions that are theoretically justified. On the one hand, we define the democratic community in general and the types of democratic community on the basis of a number of specific characteristics. On the other hand, we determine which countries best represent the democratic community and its types. These are the benchmark countries of our analysis. We assume that all respondents can be described and related to the benchmark countries through a combination of the properties constitutive to the respective

Table 1.5 Empirical evidence of citizen support for a set of criteria for a democratic community (%)

Countries	Culture		Structure		Process	
	DEM	AUT	PSC	CGI	VIO	LAW
Anglo-American countries						
USA	88	5	35	27	83	98
Australia	83	6	30	23	85	97
New Zealand	88	3	14	11	87	95
Western European countries						
Norway	93	3	67	60	91	97
Sweden	93	5	27	39	88	93
Finland	75	10	34	23	91	94
West Germany	93	1	40	20	85	88
Spain	92	8	31	25	76	97
Central European countries						
East Germany	91	2	38	12	85	90
Czech Republic	88	4	33	18	80	86
Slovakia	88	4	36	30	73	82
Hungary	83	5	32	30	80	89
Slovenia	82	6	28	24	70	85
Croatia	95	13	45	38	87	74
Baltic countries						
Estonia	85	6	30	36	83	91
Latvia	79	8	24	19	83	83
Lithuania	87	15	29	23	76	90
South-eastern European countries (mainly Orthodox)						
Yugoslavia	88	10	24	29	74	92
Romania	89	22	11	16	77	94
Bulgaria	80	19	36	43	79	96
South-eastern European countries (mixed-Muslim)						
Macedonia	73	15	21	16	79	89
Bosnia-Herzegovina	87	26	32	57	72	97
Albania	98	65	43	35	93	92
Eastern European countries						
Russia	51	20	7	16	82	85
Ukraine	75	17	13	29	78	81
Belarus	75	17	12	26	83	80
Moldova	71	16	14	33	66	82

Notes
DEM: Support of democratic rule; AUT: Support of autocratic Rule; PSC: Support of political system of one's own country; CGI: Confidence in governmental institutions; VIO: Illegitimacy of violence; LAW: Law-abidingness. Cell entries are percentage of positive support.

community. By using discriminant analysis as a statistical technique we are able to answer two questions. First, how important the specific characteristics (indicators) are in predicting the membership of a respondent in the predefined group on the one hand, and in the undefined group on the other. Second, for every respondent from the undefined group, the probability of his or her belonging to the defined or known group can be determined.

The tables show several figures useful in assessing results. First, correlations of the variables with the discriminant function: the higher the correlation, the more important is the variable or the indicator for discriminating between the known group and the group of other countries. Second, eigenvalues and canonical correlations: both high eigenvalues and high canonical correlations mean that the two groups are well separated by the given set of variables. Third, group centroids are reported. These figures are simply average scores for respondents belonging to each of the predefined groups. Fourth, we show simplified classification results. Each respondent is allocated to a group according to his or her greatest probability – given the set of variables for the prediction. The share of correctly classified respondents is an indictor of the goodness of fit.

Discriminant analysis allows us to assign a probability of belonging to a group that is defined a priori to represent a certain theoretical category. We use this capability in our analysis. Although the initial score is allocated to the individual respondent, we use this variable in our analysis mainly to describe nation-states by averaging the respective information.

The standard against which we determine the extent to which the societal community in specific countries is democratic is a group of countries that undoubtedly represent such a community. The countries concerned are, first, the United States and Australia and, second, Sweden and West Germany. These are the benchmark democracies for the discriminant analysis. Table 1.6 shows how strongly the eight attributes of a democratic community distinguish between the benchmark democracies and the other countries. With one exception – "confidence in governmental institutions" – all correlations of the variables with the discriminant function are statistically highly significant. The highest correlations are in "support for autocracy (-0.799) at the cultural level and "law-abidingness" (0.583) at the process level. Some 60 percent of respondents were correctly classified on the basis of this weighted combination of characteristics.

However, our analysis is concerned with the categorization and comparison of countries and groups of countries. For this purpose we have aggregated the results at the individual level. Table 1.7 shows the mean of probability for respondents in a country to belong to the group of benchmark democracies as defined by the characteristics stated in Table 1.6. Countries are classified in terms of the geographical groups explained in the theoretical section. The name of each geographical group is given over the countries, and the mean and standard deviations for these groups

Table 1.6 Differentiation between benchmark democracies and other countries

	Democracies[a] r^b		
Cultural level			
Support of democracy	0.446		
Support of autocracy	−0.799		
Structural level			
Support for current political system	0.252		
Confidence in government institutions	0.048[c]		
Process level			
Illegitimacy of violence	0.264		
Law-abidingness	0.583		
Eigenvalue	0.059		
Canonical correlation	0.236		
Group centroids			
Groups to classify	−0.121		
Democracies	0.486		
Classification results		Group	
	1		2
1 Group to classify	0.58		0.42
2 Democracies	0.32		0.68
Correctly classified		60	

Notes

a Benchmark countries: USA, Australia, Sweden and West Germany.

b Pooled within-group correlations between discriminating variables and canonical discriminant function.

c Not significant at the 0.001 level.

are also stated. The expectation formulated in the theoretical section relative to the geographical country groups postulates the following ordinal sequence in degrees of democratic community: (1) the Anglo-American and western European countries; (2) the central European countries; (3) the Baltic countries; (4) the south-eastern European countries; (5) the eastern European countries.

This assumption is essentially confirmed by empirical findings. The deviant group is the Baltic nations, which rank after the Orthodox south-eastern European countries. However, the results for individual Baltic countries differ greatly. Whilst the mean for Estonia corresponds more or less to that for Slovenia and Croatia in central Europe, Latvia and Lithuania trail behind the south-eastern European Muslim countries. Estonia's distinctiveness can be attributed to the country's greater modernity in comparison with the other two Baltic nations (see Table 1.3) and to the high proportion of the population – in comparison with all the countries under study – with no religious ties (see Table 1.4).

By far the greatest misclassification of a country in a geographical group is Albania. Of all the countries, Albania shows the lowest mean and

Table 1.7 Closeness of countries to the benchmark democracies

Countries	Mean[a]	Sd[a]	N[a]
Anglo-American countries	*0.552*	*(0.118)*	*3,749*
USA[b]	0.562	(0.12)	1,235
Australia[b]	0.538	(0.12)	1,726
New Zealand	0.565	(0.11)	788
Western European countries	*0.536*	*(0.123)*	*4,494*
Norway	0.579	(0.11)	1,077
Sweden[b]	0.530	(0.12)	862
Finland	0.493	(0.13)	796
West Germany[b]	0.551	(0.11)	896
Spain	0.511	(0.12)	863
Central European countries	*0.497*	*(0.135)*	*4,980*
East Germany	0.539	(0.12)	888
Czech Republic	0.512	(0.13)	935
Slovakia	0.482	(0.13)	868
Hungary	0.512	(0.13)	494
Slovenia	0.486	(0.14)	807
Croatia	0.460	(0.14)	988
Baltic countries	*0.436*	*(0.131)*	*2,168*
Estonia	0.477	(0.13)	782
Latvia	0.418	(0.12)	894
Lithuania	0.403	(0.12)	492
South-eastern European countries (mainly Orthodox)	*0.468*	*(0.135)*	*2,382*
Yugoslavia	0.494	(0.13)	1,013
Romania	0.453	(0.14)	804
Bulgaria	0.444	(0.12)	565
South-eastern European countries (mixed-Muslim)	*0.405*	*(0.133)*	*2,091*
Macedonia	0.429	(0.12)	589
Bosnia-Herzegovina	0.436	(0.13)	966
Albania	0.322	(0.10)	536
Eastern European countries	*0.374*	*(0.127)*	*3,796*
Russia	0.362	(0.13)	1,011
Ukraine	0.380	(0.13)	1,008
Belarus	0.382	(0.12)	1,054
Moldova	0.373	(0.13)	723
Total	0.477	(0.12)	23,660
Eta[2]	0.228	–	–

Notes
a Mean = Mean membership probability of respondents belonging to the group of benchmark democracies, defined by the set of eight characteristics of democratic community; Sd = Standard deviation; N = Number of cases.
b Benchmark democracies.

thus the greatest distance to the benchmark democracies. The result cannot be explained with reference to the country classification criteria. Possibly the regime of Enver Hodscha plays a role, certainly the most total-itarian among comparable regimes in Europe.

As we expected, the Slav successor countries to the Soviet Union, here termed "eastern European countries," show by far the lowest mean score of all regional groups (see Table 1.7). They thus correspond least to the benchmark democracies. However, a majority in Moldova, Belarus and Ukraine also clearly favors democracy, while only a minority is in favor of autocracy (see Table 1.5). Relative distance from the benchmark demo-cracies thus does not necessarily mean that the citizens of the country con-cerned do *not* form a democratic community. The relatively least support for democracy (51 percent) and a relatively high support for autocracy (20 percent) among eastern European countries is to be found in Russia. Of all the countries under study, Russia, together with Albania, has the lowest mean score. These two countries are accordingly the least demo-cratic as far as the attitudes and behaviors of their citizens are concerned.

Among the Anglo-American and western European countries, two deviate relatively strongly from the others: Spain and, above all, Finland (see Table 1.7). In the case of Spain this is attributable above all to the below-average rejection of violence as a political instrument, and in the case of Finland to the below-average support for democracy (see Table 1.5). The explanation *ex post factum* may be the tradition of violent con-frontation in Spain and the geographical proximity of Finland to Russia and the Soviet Union. Finland is the only country in western Europe that belonged to an autocratic empire (Russia) for a longer period. These two deviant cases also explain the difference in the mean between the Anglo-American countries and the countries of western Europe.

For the further analysis of the democratic community we made two sim-plifications in comparison with the discriminant analysis. First, we restricted ourselves to the three characteristics: "support of democracy," "support of autocracy" and "law-abidingness." We thus renounce attitudes to the political system in the respondents' own country, the theoretical status of which is not fully clear. The three attributes taken into account, are, however, also those that most clearly distinguish the group of bench-mark democracies from the group of other countries (see Table 1.6). Second, we make no a priori assumption in the form of a reference group (benchmark democracies). We localize the countries in a two-dimensional space (see Figure 1.2). The one dimension is the proportion of respon-dents that clearly support democracy while rejecting autocracy. These respondents are termed "solid democrats" (Klingemann 1999). The second dimension is the proportion of respondents that exhibit differing degrees of law-abidingness.

The countries are relatively widely scattered in the two-dimensional space. Although there is a significant linear relationship between the two

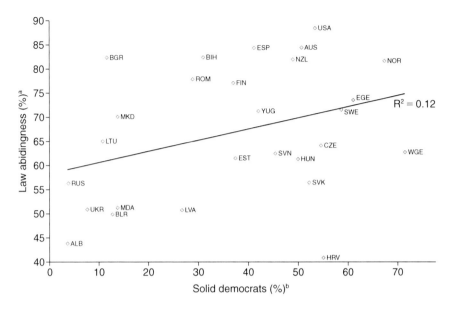

Figure 1.2 Location of countries in a two-dimensional space of democratic community.

dimensions, it is not very marked ($R^2 = 0.12$). Nevertheless, certain patterns can be identified that correspond to the results of the discriminant analysis. Countries with a pronounced democratic community are located in the top right-hand area of the space, the Anglo-American countries and some western European countries. Of the western European countries, Spain and West Germany deviate most. Finland and Spain exhibit above average law-abidingness and an only average proportion of solid democrats. With West Germany exactly the opposite applies.

The left-hand bottom part of the space is occupied by countries whose societal community can be described as least democratic. Here we find the same countries that scored lowest in the discriminant analysis: the eastern European countries and Albania. Combining clear support for democracy and rejection of democracy produces an even more marked result. In all five countries (Russia, Ukraine, Belarus, Moldova, Albania) solid democrats are a minority of less than 25 percent. At the same time, the level of law-abidingness is below average. The central European countries (Czech Republic, Slovakia and Hungary), although spatially somewhat apart from the North American and western European countries, are still much closer to them than to the eastern European countries and Albania. This finding, too, conforms to the discriminant analysis.

Types of democratic community

A democratic community is characterized by its members exhibiting attitudes and behaviors that meet the minimum demands of a democracy. However, a democracy can be differently realized and appointed in light of the different normative ideas which citizens' may possess. On the basis of the democratic theory discussion, we have distinguished five normative models of democracy and the corresponding five types of democratic community (see Figure 1.1). Having in the preceding section empirically analyzed the similarities and differences between countries with regard to the democratic community, we proceed in this section to do the same for the types of democratic community.

In Table 1.2 the five types of democratic community are described in terms of characteristics that are theoretically relevant and for which indicators are available in the World Values Survey 1995–9. The distributions of the specific attitudes and behaviors are shown in Tables 1.8 and 1.9. The detailed description of the indicators and indices is to be found in the Appendix 1.2. In this case, too, we will not deal with the distributions in detail but turn directly to the comparison between countries.

In this comparison we proceed as with the democratic community. The statistical method used is discriminant analysis, and we define benchmark countries as the point of reference for classifying individual countries. As explained above, our definition of benchmark democracies draws primarily on the study by Lipset (1996) and a follow-up empirical analysis (Fuchs and Klingemann 2000). According to these studies, the United States is to be considered a libertarian democracy with republican and communitarian elements. For the sake of simplicity, we take recourse in Table 1.10 and the following tables and figures only to the characterization as libertarian democracy. Australia has structural properties similar to those of the United States (see Tables 1.3 and 1.4) and exhibits similar political attitudes and behaviors. In our analysis, Australia – in addition to the United States – therefore represents the libertarian type of democracy, and the two countries form the corresponding benchmark group.

In contrast to the individualism of the United States, western European countries have a pronounced etatist tradition. This was realized in the development of welfare states, whose functions include ensuring the greatest possible equality of opportunity for individuals competing in the markets. These welfare states correspond to the liberal model of democracy, and a societal community with the relevant attitudes and behaviors is therefore to be termed a "liberal" community. The benchmark countries we have chosen to represent this liberal type of community are Sweden and West Germany. Both are indubitably welfare states, but they have developed different forms (Roller 2000). By taking these two countries into account, the relevant spectrum of western European welfare

Table 1.8 Citizen support of different types of democratic community at cultural level (%)

Countries	Culture				
	SRE	SOL	TRU	WET	ETO
Anglo-American countries					
USA	66	21	35	68	9
Australia	47	29	40	61	18
New Zealand	45	34	47	61	21
Western European countries					
Norway	37	19	65	42	22
Sweden	67	49	57	49	40
Finland	42	41	48	57	20
West Germany	41	75	40	25	45
Spain	24	67	29	55	23
Central European countries					
East Germany	19	86	24	33	35
Poland	36	61	17	32	5
Czech Republic	23	51	27	43	30
Slovak Republic	14	52	26	45	17
Hungary	12	82	22	43	13
Slovenia	24	53	15	58	20
Croatia	11	62	23	54	22
Baltic countries					
Estonia	16	56	21	57	5
Latvia	17	66	24	52	8
Lithuania	24	74	21	33	3
South-eastern European countries (mainly Orthodox)					
Yugoslavia	16	65	29	45	4
Romania	31	63	18	63	6
Bulgaria	22	71	24	52	14
South-eastern European countries (mixed-Muslim)					
Macedonia	16	74	7	35	2
Bosnia-Herzegovina	17	59	27	60	3
Albania	14	62	24	88	2
Eastern European countries					
Russia	16	79	23	48	3
Ukraine	14	76	29	43	3
Belarus	17	70	23	52	4
Moldova	14	75	22	54	3

Notes
SRE: Self-responsibility; SOL: Solidarity; TRU: Trust in others; WET: Work ethic; ETO: Ethic tolerance.
Cell entries are percentage positive support (for details compare Appendix 1.2).

Table 1.9 Citizen support for different types of democratic community at structural and process levels (%)

Countries	Structure		Process	
	PRO	MAN	PMO	CIV
Anglo-American countries				
USA	74	55	52	52
Australia	62	51	45	45
New Zealand	52	64	41	35
Western European countries				
Norway	46	34	43	25
Sweden	48	36	41	24
Finland	59	35	17	12
West Germany	61	30	55	25
Spain	34	37	17	13
Central European countries				
East Germany	37	29	47	16
Poland	31	15	27	0
Czech Republic	38	42	27	7
Slovak Republic	23	21	28	6
Hungary	40	24	24	9
Slovenia	49	22	14	8
Croatia	75	34	24	13
Baltic countries				
Estonia	33	40	26	3
Latvia	36	37	25	5
Lithuania	47	38	25	2
South-eastern European countries (mainly Orthodox)				
Yugoslavia	42	25	21	4
Romania	55	37	21	9
Bulgaria	40	27	23	2
South-eastern European countries (mixed-Muslim)				
Macedonia	58	37	21	8
Bosnia-Herzegovina	49	25	37	20
Albania	78	48	19	7
Eastern European countries				
Russia	14	16	23	3
Ukraine	32	23	25	1
Belarus	25	20	38	1
Moldova	20	23	23	5

Notes
PRO: Private ownership; MAN: Management of enterprise; PMO: Political motivation; CIV: Civic engagement.
Cell entries are percentage of positive support (for details compare Appendix 1.2).

Table 1.10 Differentiation between benchmark types of democracies and other countries

Type of democracy	Libertarian democracy[a] r^c	Liberal democracy[b] r^c
Cultural level		
Self-responsibility	0.464	0.513
Solidarity with the disadvantaged	−0.504	0.095
Trust in others	0.114	0.333
Work ethic	0.178	−0.226
Ethic tolerance	0.012	0.722
Structural level		
Private ownership	0.354	0.182
Management of enterprise (owners)	0.286	−0.035
Process level		
Political motivation	0.232	0.318
Civic engagement	0.786	0.291
Eigenvalue	0.294	0.096
Canonical correlation	0.476	0.296
Group centroids		
Group to classify	−0.193	−0.075
Liberal democracies	1.522	1.274

Classification results	Group		Group	
	1	2	1	2
1 Group to classify	84	16	76	24
2 Liberal democracies	30	70	23	77
Correctly classified	82		76	

Notes
Benchmark countries:
a United States and Australia.
b Sweden and West Germany.
c Pooled within-group correlations between discriminating variables and canonical discriminant functions.

states, and thus of western European liberal democracies, has been covered.

The correlations of the indicators of the discriminant function in Table 1.10 show how strongly the individual characteristics distinguish between the benchmark countries and the other countries. In the case of libertarian democracy, the highest correlations are for "self-responsibility" and "solidarity with the disadvantaged," as well as "civic engagement." The first two characteristics are also those with which a libertarian democracy can most strongly be identified in accordance with our theoretical assumption (see Figure 1.1 and Table 1.2), and "civic engagement" is typical of republican and communitarian democracies (see Figure 1.3). For liberal democracy, the highest correlations are for "self-responsibility" and "ethic tolerance."

These characteristics are also to be found in the description of the liberal community in Table 1.2. The proportion of correctly classified respondents is much higher for these two types of democratic community than for the democratic community in general. For "libertarian democracy" the figure is 82 percent, and for "liberal democracy" 76 percent.

This indicates that the difference between the reference group and the group of other countries is relatively large. We will be dealing with this in greater detail later in the chapter.

The socialist community has not been included in the comparative analysis. The reason is a simple one: there is no western country that can plausibly represent this type of community. There is also no western country that represents the republican and the communitarian communities in a "pure" form. However, the United States and Australia exhibit some republican and communitarian properties. Although the benchmark group composed by these two countries predominantly represents a libertarian community, it has additional attributes.

In contrast to the democratic community in general, there are considerable differences between countries with regard to the type of democratic community. We will deal first with the *libertarian community*. Three gaps are identifiable between groups of countries. The first is between the Anglo-American and the western European countries. For the first the mean is 0.656 and for the second 0.376. Since the western European countries still have the highest mean of the European groups, the difference between Anglo-America and Europe posited by Lipset (1996) is impressively confirmed. Within the European countries, however, there are still substantial differences. The next gap in mean ranking is between western European countries (0.376) and Muslim south-eastern European countries (0.282). Right at the end of the scale come the Baltic and eastern European countries. The mean for both groups of countries is lower than 0.200. The democratic communities in Europe can thus definitively not be considered libertarian but at least liberal (western European countries), if not even socialist.

There are some striking deviations within groups of countries. Among western European countries, Spain, and among central European countries, Hungary, have a markedly lower mean than the other countries in their groups. And among the Muslim south-eastern European countries, Bosnia-Herzegovina has by far the highest mean. This relatively greater proximity of Bosnia-Herzegovina to the benchmark democracies is, however, attributable less to the libertarian characteristics of the two countries that constitute the group than to the communitarian attribute of moral rigorism (see Table 1.8).

As the correlations of the *liberal community* characteristics with the discriminant function show (see Table 1.10), "self-responsibility" (0.513) and especially "ethic tolerance" (0.722) distinguish most clearly between the benchmark countries and the others. By the first (self-responsibility), a liberal community distinguishes itself above all from a socialist community, and by the second (ethic tolerance) from a communitarian community. Thus, the results of the discriminant analysis do not inevitably fit the libertarian–liberal–socialist continuum. In the liberal community, too, there are very clear differences between groups of countries. Also in keeping with theoretical expectations, western European countries most strongly represent the liberal community (mean: 0.524). The Anglo-American and central European countries follow after clear intervals, 0.449 and 0.380, respectively. The most striking difference is apparent between the central European countries and the other groups. Among these other groups of countries, the Orthodox south-eastern European countries have the relatively highest mean (0.289) and the eastern European countries the relatively lowest (0.247). As far as the liberal community is concerned, the major cultural dividing line suggested by Huntington (1996) does exist, separating the western Christian civilization (including central Europe) from the Orthodox–Muslim civilization in eastern Europe.

Since characteristics that can relate to other types have been included in the two discriminant analyses on libertarian and liberal democracy, we omit characteristics that are theoretically quite unambiguous from the following considerations. In Figure 1.3, countries are localized in a two-dimensional space mapping the proportion of citizens with a strong sense of self-responsibility and those with a strong sense of solidarity. The regression line shown in the figure represents the underlying libertarian–liberal–socialist continuum: strong self-responsibility and weak solidarity

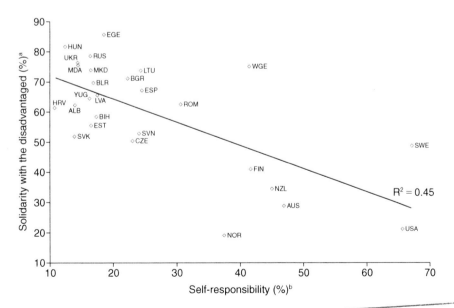

Figure 1.3 Location of countries on the libertarian–liberal–socialist dimension.

Table 1.11 Closeness of countries to liberal and libertarian types of democracy

Countries	Libertarian democracy[a]			Liberal democracy[b]		
	Mean[c]	Sd[e]	N[x]	Mean[c]	Sd[e]	N[x]
Anglo-American countries	*0.656*	*(0.30)*	*3,122*	*0.449*	*(0.26)*	*3,122*
USA	0.752	(0.27)	1,016	0.426	(0.26)	1,016
Australia	0.621	(0.31)	1,528	0.455	(0.27)	1,528
New Zealand	0.580	(0.29)	578	0.473	(0.25)	578
Western European countries	*0.376*	*(0.28)*	*3,652*	*0.524*	*(0.27)*	*3,652*
Norway	0.470	(0.28)	970	0.494	(0.24)	970
Sweden	0.431	(0.28)	662	0.682	(0.21)	662
Finland	0.334	(0.26)	708	0.424	(0.24)	708
West Germany	0.360	(0.29)	604	0.657	(0.26)	604
Spain	0.251	(0.25)	708	0.406	(0.27)	708
Central European countries	*0.240*	*(0.24)*	*4,317*	*0.380*	*(0.25)*	*4,317*
East Germany	0.224	(0.23)	687	0.505	(0.28)	687
Czech Republic	0.263	(0.24)	794	0.413	(0.23)	794
Slovakia	0.199	(0.20)	834	0.331	(0.22)	834
Hungary	0.184	(0.20)	467	0.340	(0.23)	467
Slovenia	0.277	(0.25)	731	0.330	(0.24)	731
Croatia	0.274	(0.25)	804	0.360	(0.24)	804

	Mean	(Sd)	N	Mean	(Sd)	N
Baltic countries	*0.191*	*(0.20)*	*2,227*	*0.268*	*(0.19)*	*2,227*
Estonia	0.200	(0.20)	761	0.247	(0.18)	761
Latvia	0.192	(0.20)	844	0.290	(0.19)	844
Lithuania	0.179	(0.18)	622	0.262	(0.19)	622
South-eastern European countries (mainly Orthodox)	*0.225*	*(0.22)*	*2,380*	*0.289*	*(0.22)*	*2,380*
Yugoslavia	0.180	(0.19)	1,073	0.252	(0.20)	1,073
Romania	0.305	(0.25)	819	0.296	(0.22)	819
Bulgaria	0.189	(0.19)	488	0.358	(0.23)	488
South-eastern European countries (mixed-Muslim)	*0.282*	*(0.26)*	*2,193*	*0.254*	*(0.19)*	*2,193*
Macedonia	0.223	(0.22)	627	0.240	(0.18)	627
Bosnia-Herzegovina	0.321	(0.29)	917	0.267	(0.19)	917
Albania	0.287	(0.29)	649	0.249	(0.17)	649
Eastern European countries	*0.143*	*(0.16)*	*4,719*	*0.247*	*(0.19)*	*4,719*
Russia	0.136	(0.16)	1,294	0.251	(0.25)	1,294
Ukraine	0.134	(0.14)	1,381	0.256	(0.20)	1,381
Belarus	0.146	(0.15)	1,255	0.264	(0.19)	1,255
Moldova	0.168	(0.20)	789	0.197	(0.17)	789
Total	0.297	(0.23)	22,610	0.352	(0.22)	22,610
Eta²	0.22	–	–	0.09	–	–

Notes

a Libertarian democracy: benchmark countries USA and Australia.

b Liberal democracy: benchmark countries Sweden and West Germany.

c Mean = Mean membership probability of respondents belonging to the group of benchmark democracies, defined by the set of nine characteristics; Sd = Standard deviation; N = Number of cases.

characterize a libertarian community and, vice versa, a socialist community is characterized by strong solidarity and weak self-responsibility, with the liberal community located between the two. The variance of no less than 45 percent explained by the regression shows that the assumption of this underlying continuum is justified. If we take the 50 percent threshold in each case to ensure better orientation in the spatial classification of countries, the only country that simultaneously scores high on self-responsibility and low on solidarity is the United States. Accordingly, the United States is by far the most libertarian community, and "American exceptionalism" (Lipset 1996) is clearly in evidence. Surprisingly, an above-average proportion of Swedes have a pronounced sense of self-responsibility, while evincing much greater solidarity than Americans. In the upper-left-hand part of the space, which is defined by strong solidarity and weak self-responsibility, thus delimiting a socialist community, we find all the countries from central and eastern Europe – plus Spain as the only western European country. Within this cluster of countries, no further differentiation by geographical region is possible. For example, two of the countries we have assigned to central Europe – Hungary and East Germany – together with the eastern European countries of Russia, Ukraine and Moldova, form the outermost fringe of the cluster, thus representing the relatively most socialist communities. In contrast, two central European countries – Slovenia and the Czech Republic – together with Romania are gathered at the opposite fringe of the cluster in the direction of the Western countries. The countries deviating most from the regression line are West Germany and Norway. They are average on self-responsibility, but solidarity is below-average in Norway and above-average in West Germany.

The two dimensions in Figure 1.5 relate to the constitutive characteristics of a republican or civic community. A fundamental normative concept in this type of democratic community is that the individual and not government should bear primary responsibility for the individual's affairs (see Figure 1.1). The same is demanded by libertarians; but, in contrast to libertarians, republicans do not assume that collective goals can be attained only indirectly through the mechanisms of the market. They stress active cooperation between citizens to realize common projects (Putnam 1993; Fukuyama 1999). The resource on which such cooperation can draw is termed *social capital*. Social capital consists primarily in shared values and norms of reciprocity and cooperation. A consequence of the mutual assumption that such values and norms apply, and of experience with relevant action, is *trust* or *confidence* in the other members of the community. Trust in others is therefore frequently used as an indicator of the social capital of a community. Cooperative values and norm orientations induce citizens to participate actively in voluntary associations, and this in its turn stabilizes the social capital. Putnam (1993) therefore refers to civil or voluntary associations as "social structures of co-operation." In

Figure 1.4, active participation by citizens in two or more voluntary associations is termed "civic engagement."

The link between "civic engagement" and "trust in others" that Putnam
posits is controversial. As the regression analysis shows ($R^2 = 0.344$), this
assumption is confirmed by our data at least at the aggregate level of the
countries under study. The classification of countries in the two-dimensional space of a republican community reveals a marked difference
between Anglo-American and western European countries on the one
hand, and the countries from central and eastern Europe on the other.
The latter show less trust in others as well as less civic engagement.
The only western European country in the group is Spain. Taking the
analysis results of this section for central and eastern Europe as a whole,
we find a positive and a negative aspect: they relatively clearly represent a
socialist community and just as clearly do *not* represent a republican
community.

Among the Anglo-American and western European countries, there is
none that exhibits both strong confidence in others and strong civic
engagement. Thus, we cannot identify a "pure" case of a republican
community. Two configurations among these countries are evident. First,
the two Nordic countries, Norway and Sweden, with an average level of
civic engagement and a high level of trust in others and, second, the two
Anglo-American countries, Australia and the United States, with an
average level of trust in others and a high level of civic engagement.

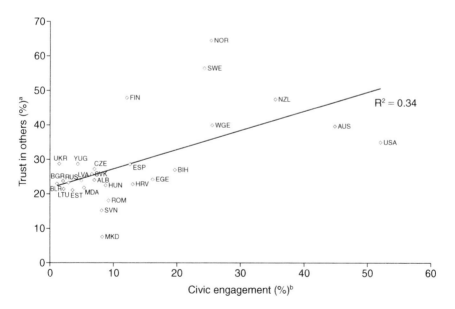

Figure 1.4 Location of countries in a two-dimensional space of republican
community.

Summary and conclusions

Development toward a politically integrated and geographically more comprehensive Europe appears to be irreversible. But the general dynamic of development offer fundamental options that have yet to be decided. One is the extent of political integration through European institutions. The central issue is how strongly the competence to make binding decisions is to be transferred from the nation-states to the supranational regime of the EU. Another is the matter of the eastern border, the question of which countries should belong to the EU. This is the point of reference for our study. Besides economic aspects, the question of the eastward enlargement of the EU is of strategic importance for the formation of a European demos. Every institutional arrangement of the EU needs to be legitimated, and the more strongly the decisions of these institutions directly impact the life world of the citizen, the greater is the need for legitimation. The addressee of this legitimation of a European regime and European politics is a European demos. For legitimation to be successful, a merely formal demos is presumably insufficient. Over and above legally defined membership, it should constitute a political community with a collective identity citizens can subjectively attribute to themselves and with which they can identify.

We proceed from two premises. First, that the collective identity of the European demos is grounded in subjectively perceived commonality in political values and behaviors; second, that objectively demonstrable commonality in both regards provides the potential for the formation of a collective identity. Against this background, we have attempted to answer two questions. First, the extent to which political values and behavior are shared by the citizens of European countries; second, the extent to which there are systematic differences between western, central and eastern Europe, and where possible cultural borders lie. The most important results of our analysis can be summed up as follows.

Regardless of what institutional form the regime of the EU will ultimately take, it will be a democratic form of government. Moreover, one of the key criteria for a country to join the EU is that it has a stable democracy. However, a democracy can function and survive only if the demos, as the ultimate sovereign, also exhibits appropriate values and behavior. In a first step, we have therefore empirically determined the extent to which societal community in the countries under study can be described as democratic, and what differences there are between countries and groups of countries.

Differences are apparent between groups of countries, but – with one exception – they are not very pronounced. They can be mapped on a geographical west–east axis. The relatively most democratic communities are to be found in the Anglo-American and western European countries. The countries in which the democratic community is least developed are the Muslim countries in south-eastern Europe and the eastern European countries. Leaving aside the Anglo-American countries and regressing the scores of individual countries for the democratic community on a geographical west–east axis, no less than 62 percent of variance can be explained. In certain measures, this result is in keeping with Huntington's (1996) theory. However, in contrast to Huntington's assumptions, no threshold can be identified between West and East, only a continuous decline in the extent of a democratic community.

The exception mentioned above is concerned with the countries of eastern Europe and, in our parlance, this means the Slav successor states to the Soviet Union (Russia, Ukraine, Belarus, Moldova). Albania also belongs to the group. In all of these countries, "law-abidingness" is clearly below average, and in every case there are fewer than 25 percent "solid democrats" among the citizenry (see Figure 1.2). According to our criteria, there is, therefore, at least currently, no democratic community in these countries. Besides the longer-term factors we have mentioned (religion, empire, Leninist regime and modernity), the party systems are presumably responsible for this result. In all these countries, the party system is shaped by parties that support at least the introduction of autocratic elements into the existing governmental system, if not the imposition of autocratic systems as a whole (Klingemann and Hofferbert 2000). The democratic transformation of the party system, in addition to economic development, is therefore a structural prerequisite that could strengthen the democratic community in these countries.

While there are relatively slight differences between the countries under study as regards the democratic community in general, this is far from being the case with the types of community. This is particularly clear if one considers the libertarian–liberal–socialist dimension. According to our analysis, the United States is indubitably a libertarian community. The vast majority of American citizens consider that not the state but the individual is responsible for his own life; at the same time solidarity with the disadvantaged is very weak (see Figure 1.3). *All* the countries of central and eastern Europe offer a contrast to the United States. In these countries, strong self-responsibility is evinced by less than a third of citizens, and in most countries by less than 20 percent. A majority, however, exhibit strong solidarity with the disadvantaged. Thus, on the basis of these two characteristics, the countries of central and eastern Europe can be considered socialist communities.

The two other Anglo-American countries (Australia and New Zealand), as well as the western European countries, score between the United States and the central and eastern European countries on self-responsibility. On solidarity the figures are at a similarly low level as that of the United States, the only exception being West Germany. Overall, these countries can therefore be classified as liberal communities, which are, however, closer to the libertarian United States than to the socialist central and eastern European communities.

Following on from the studies by Putnam (1993) and Fukuyama (1999), we have operationalized the republican community by the two dimensions "civic engagement" and "trust in others." The classification of countries in the space defined by these two dimensions again shows a clear West–East difference. Most republican are the Anglo-American countries United States, Australia and New Zealand. Decidedly not republican, in contrast, are the countries of central and eastern Europe – "civic engagement" is weak, "trust in others" is weak. The strong etatist orientation among citizens in central and eastern Europe is thus complemented and accordingly still further stabilized by a lack of civic society elements.

The question of the eastward enlargement of the EU can be discussed and answered from a variety of standpoints. For example, economic or geopolitical considerations can play a role. The perspective taken by our analysis is that of the implications of eastward enlargement for the development of a European demos. This, in turn, is the condition for a viable European democracy. The greater the differences are between countries, the lower is the potential for a European identity on which a European demos can be based.

Our study identifies three substantial dividing lines. The first runs between America and Europe, as already posited by Lipset (1996). For our purposes, however, this is of secondary importance. The second divides western Europe from central and eastern Europe. The countries in these two parts of Europe represent different types of democratic community. At this political cultural level, Huntington's (1996) thesis of a cultural dividing line within Europe is confirmed to a certain extent. According to the theoretical premises of our analysis, every eastward enlargement poses integration problems and increases the difficulty of constituting a European demos. The West–East difference we have described is concerned with differing types of democratic community. Between the countries of Europe there is little difference in the political values and behavior that are essential to a democracy. The potential for Europeans in western, central and eastern Europe to consider each other as democrats, and to integrate this understanding in their collective identity, is thus considerable.

The Slav successor nations to the Soviet Union (Russia, Ukraine, Belarus and Moldova), together with Albania, are the exception. They cannot, at least not yet, be considered democratic communities, and in all the analyses we have conducted, they offer a serious contrast to the western European countries and, to some extent, also to the countries in central and eastern Europe. This is the third dividing line we identify. Taking account only of political cultural points of view (while, of course, considering the question of timing), the eastern border of the EU would have to be drawn before these countries.

Appendix 1.1 Criteria for a democratic community

Cultural level

1 Support of democratic rule

Item 1 "I'm going to describe various types of political systems and ask what you think about each as a way of governing this country. For each one, would you say it is a very good, fairly good, fairly bad or very bad way of governing this country?"

"Having a democratic political system."

Item 2 "I'm going to read off some things that people sometimes say about a democratic political system. Could you please tell me if you agree strongly, agree, disagree or disagree strongly, after I read each one of them?"

"Democracy may have problems but it's better than any other form of government."

Scores of the two items are added to form the index, "Support of democratic rule." Scale values run from 2, "low support for democratic rule," to 8, "high support for democratic rule." Table 1.3 presents proportion of respondents with scale values 6–8.

2 Support of autocratic rule

Item 1 "I'm going to describe various types of political systems and ask what you think about each as a way of governing this country. For each one, would you say it is a very good, fairly good, fairly bad or very bad way of governing this country?"

"Having a strong leader who does not have to bother with parliament and elections."

Item 2 "I'm going to describe various types of political systems and ask what you think about each as a way of governing this country. For each one, would you say it is a very good, fairly good, fairly bad or very bad way of governing this country?"

"Having the army rule."

Scores of the two items are added to form the index, "Support of autocratic rule." Scale values run from 2, "low support of autocratic rule," to 8, "high support of autocratic rule." Table 1.3 presents proportion of respondents with scale values 6–8.

Structural level

3 Support for current political system of own country

Item 1 "People have different views about the system for governing this country. Here is a scale for rating how well things are going: 1 means very bad and 10 means very good."

"Where on this scale would you put the political system as it is today?"

Scale values run from 1, "very bad," to 10, "very good." Table 1.3 presents the proportion of respondents with scale values 6–10.

4 Confidence in governmental institutions

"I am going to name a number of organizations. For each one, could you tell me how much confidence you have in them: is it a great deal of confidence, quite a lot of confidence, not very much confidence or none at all?"

Item 1 "Political parties."
Item 2 "The government in..."
Item 3 "Parliament."

Scores of the three items are added to form the index, "Confidence in governmental institutions." Scale values run from 3, "low confidence," to 12, "high confidence." Table 1.3 presents proportion of respondents with scale values 8–12.

Process level

5 Illegitimacy of violence

Item 1 "Here's one more statement. How strongly do you agree or disagree with it? (agree strongly, agree, disagree, disagree strongly)."

"Using violence to pursue political goals is never justified."

Scale values run from 1, "disagree strongly," to 4, "agree strongly." Table 1.3 presents proportion of respondents with scale values 3–4.

6 Law-abidingness

"Please tell me for each of the following statements whether you think it can always be justified, never be justified, or something in between, using this card" (Interviewer: read out statements. Code one answer for each statement).

Item 1 "Claiming government benefits to which you are not entitled."
Item 2 "Avoiding a fare on public transport."
Item 3 "Cheating on taxes if you have a chance."

Scores of the three items are added to form the index, "Law-abidingness." Scale values run from 3, "low degree of law-abidingness," to 30, "high degree of law-abidingness." Table 1.3 presents proportion of respondents with scale values 24–30.

Appendix 1.2 Criteria of different types of democratic community

Cultural level

1 Self-responsibility

Item 1 "Now I'd like you to tell me your views on various issues. How would you place your views on this scale? 1 means you agree completely with the statement on the left; 10 means you agree completely with the statement on the right; and if your views fall somewhere in between, you can choose any number in between."

   1 "The government should take more responsibility to ensure that everyone is provided for."
   10 "People should take more responsibility to provide for themselves."

Scale values run from 1, "low self-responsibility," to 10, "high self-responsibility." Table 1.4 presents proportion of respondents with scale values 7–10.

2 Solidarity with the disadvantaged

Item 1 "Why in your opinion, are there people in this country who live in need? Here are two opinions: Which come closest to your view?"

   1 "They are poor because of laziness and lack of will power."
   2 "They are poor because society treats them unfairly."

Item 2 "In your opinion, do most poor people in this country have a chance of escaping from poverty, or is there very little chance of escaping?"

   1 "They have a chance."
   2 "There is very little chance."

Scores of the two items are added to form the index, "Solidarity with the disadvantaged." Scale values run from 2, "low solidarity," to 4, "high solidarity." Table 1.4 presents proportion of respondents with scale value 4.

3 Trust in others

Item 1 "Generally speaking, would you say that most people can be trusted or that you can't be too careful in dealing with people?"

    1   "Most people can be trusted."
    0   "Can't be too careful, don't know, no answer."

Table 1.4 presents proportion of respondents with scale value 1.

4 Work ethic

Item 1 "Now I'd like you to tell me your views on various issues. How would you place your views on this scale? 1 means you agree completely with the statement on the left; 10 means you agree completely with the statement on the right; and if your views fall somewhere in between, you can choose any number in between."

    1   "Hard work doesn't generally bring success – it's more a matter of luck and connections."
    10   "In the long run, hard work usually brings a better life."

Table 1.4 presents proportion of respondents with scale values 7–10.

5 Ethic tolerance

"Please tell me for each of the following statements whether you think it can always be justified, never be justified, or something in between, using this card."

Item 1 "Homosexuality."
Item 2 "Prostitution."
Item 3 "Abortion."
Item 4 "Divorce."

Scores of the four items are added to form the index, "Ethic tolerance." Scale values run from 4, "low ethic tolerance," to 40, "high ethic tolerance." Table 1.4 presents proportion of respondents with scale values 29–40.

Structural level

6 Private ownership

Item 1 "Now I'd like you to tell me your views on various issues. How would you place your views on this scale? 1 means you agree completely with the statement on the left; 10 means you agree completely with the statement on the right; and if your views fall somewhere in between, you can choose any number in between."

    1   "Government ownership of business and industry should be increased."

   10 "Private ownership of business and industry should be increased."

Table 1.4 presents proportion of respondents with scale values 7–10.

7 Management of enterprise

Item 1 "There is a lot of discussion about how business and industry can be managed. Which of these four statements comes closest to your opinion?"

    1   "The owners should run their business or appoint the managers."

    0   "The owners and the employees should participate in the selection of managers;

         The government should be the owner and appoint the managers;

         The employees should own the business and should elect the managers."

Table 1.4 presents proportion of respondents with scale value 1.

Process level

8 Political motivation

Item 1 "Please say, for each of the following, how important it is in your life. Would you say...

    "Politics"

is very important, rather important, not very important or not at all important?

   Item 2 "How interested would you say you are in politics?"

    very interested, somewhat interested, not very interested, not at all interested?

Scale values run from 2, "low motivation," to 8, "high motivation involvement." Table 1.4 presents proportion of respondents with scale values 6–8.

9 Civic engagement

"Now I am going to read off a list of voluntary organizations; for each one, could you tell me whether you are an active member, an inactive member or not a member of that type of organization?"

Item 1 "Church or religious organization."
Item 2 "Sport or recreation organization."
Item 3 "Art, music or educational organization."
Item 4 "Labor union."
Item 5 "Political party."
Item 6 "Environmental organization."
Item 7 "Professional organization."
Item 8 "Charitable organization."
Item 9 "Any other voluntary organization."

Scores of the nine items ("active membership") are added to form the index, "Civic engagement." Scale values run from 0, "no civic engagement," to 9, "high civic engagement." Table 1.4 presents proportion of respondents with scale values 2–9.

Acknowledgment

This chapter is a revised version of "Eastward Enlargement of the European Union and the Identity of Europe" which appeared in a special issue of *West European Politics*, vol. 25, 2 (April 2002). The authors gratefully acknowledge permission to build on this publication.

Note

1 Religion: 1 Muslim or Orthodox, 2 Catholic, 3 Protestant or secular; Empire: 1 Ottoman or Russian, 2 Hapsburg, 3 British or none; Leninist regime: 1 yes (duration in years), 2 no; modernity: continuous (the higher the score the more favorable to democracy and vice versa).

References

Barber, B.R. (1984) *Strong Democracy: Participatory Politics For a New Age*, Berkeley: University of California Press.
Berry, C.J. (1989) *The Idea of a Democratic Community*, New York: St. Martin's Press.
Chapman, J.W. and Shapiro, I. (eds) (1993) *Democratic Community. Nomos No. XXXV*, New York: New York University Press.
Etzioni, A. (1993) *The Spirit of Community: the Reinvention of American Society*, New York: Touchstone, Simon & Schuster.

Etzioni, A. (1996) *The New Golden Rule: Community and Morality in a Democratic Society*, New York: Basic Books.

Ferree, M.M., Gamson, W.A., Gerhards, G. and Rucht, D. (2000) *Collective Actors and the Public Sphere: Abortion Discourse in the U.S. and Germany*, Cambridge: Cambridge University Press.

Fuchs, D. (1999a) "Soziale Integration und politische Institutionen in modernen Gesellschaften," in Friedrichs, J. and Jagodzinski, W. (eds) *Soziale Integration. Sonderheft 39 der Kölner Zeitschrift für Soziologie und Sozialpsychologie*, Opladen: Westdeutscher Verlag.

Fuchs, D. (1999b) "The Democratic Culture of Germany," in Norris, Pippa (ed.) *Critical Citizens: Global Support for Democratic Government*, Oxford: Oxford University Press.

Fuchs, D. (2000) "Die demokratische Gemeinschaft in den USA und in Deutschland," in Gerhards, J. (ed.) *Die Vermessung kultureller Unterschiede: USA und Deutschland im Vergleich*, Opladen: Westdeutscher Verlag.

Fuchs, D., Gerhards, J. and Roller, E. (1993) "Wir und die anderen. Ethnozentrismus in den zwölf Ländern der europäischen Gemeinschaft," in *Kölner Zeitschrift für Soziologie und Sozialpsychologie* 45.

Fuchs, D. and Klingemann, H. (2000) "A Comparison of Democratic Communities: American Exceptionalism and European Etatism," paper presented at the conference, "Re-thinking Democracy in the New Millennium," University of Houston, 17–20 February.

Fuchs, D. and Roller, E. (1998) "Cultural Conditions of Transition to Liberal Democracies in Central and Eastern Europe," in Barnes, S.H. and Simon, J. (eds) *The Postcommunist Citizen*, Budapest: Erasmus Foundation and Hungarian Academy of Sciences.

Fukuyama, F. (1999) *The Great Disruption: Human Nature and the Reconstitution of Social Order*, New York: Free Press.

Gerhards, J. (1993) "Westeuropäische Integration und die Schwierigkeiten der Entstehung einer europäischen Öffentlichkeit," *Zeitschrift für Soziologie* 22.

Grimm, D. (1995) "Does Europe Need a Constitution?," *European Law Journal* 1.

Hansen, M.H. (1991) *The Athenian Democracy in the Age of Demosthenes: Structure, Principles and Ideology*, Oxford: Blackwell.

Huntington, S.P. (1996) *The Clash of Civilizations and the Remaking of World Order*, New York: Simon & Schuster.

Inglehart, R. (1998) "Clash of Civilizations of Global Cultural Modernization? Empirical Evidence from 61 Societies," paper presented at the 1998 meeting of the International Sociological Association, Montreal, 27–31 August.

Kielmansegg, P.G. (1996) "Integration und Demokratie," Jachtenfuchs, M. and Kohler-Koch, B. (eds) *Europäische Integration*, Opladen: Leske + Budrich.

Klingemann, H. (1999) "Mapping Political Support in the 1990s: a Global Analysis," in Norris, Pippa (ed.) *Critical Citizens: Global Support for Democratic Government*, Oxford: Oxford University Press.

Klingemann, H. and. Hofferbert, R.I. (2000) "The Capacity of New Party Systems to Channel Discontent," in Klingemann, H. and Neidhardt, F. (eds) *Zur Zukunft der Demokratie*, Berlin: edition sigma.

Lepsius, M.R. (1999) "Die Europäische Union. Ökonomisch-politische Integration und kulturelle Pluralitätn," in Viehoff, R. and Segers, R.T. (eds) *Kultur, Identität,*

Europa. Über die Schwierigkeiten und Möglichkeiten einer Konstruktion, Frankfurt a.M.: Suhrkamp.

Lipset, S.M. (1959) *Political Man: the Social Bases of Politics,* Garden City: Doubleday.

Lipset, S.M. (1994) "The Social Requisites of Democracy Revisited," *American Sociological Review,* 59.

Lipset, S.M. (1996) *American Exceptionalism: a Double-Edged Sword,* New York: W.W. Norton.

Lipset, S.M. (2000) "Conditions for Democracy," in Klingemann, H. and Neidhardt, F. (eds) *Zur Zukunft der Demokratie,* Berlin: edition sigma.

Nozick, R. (1974) *Anarchy, State, and Utopia,* New York: Basic Books.

Post, R.C. (1993) "Between Democracy and Community: the Legal Constitution of Social Form," in Chapman, J.W. and Shapiro, I. (eds) *Democratic Community. Nomos No. XXXV,* New York: New York University Press.

Putnam, R.D. (with Robert Leonardi and Raffaella Y. Nanetti) (1993) *Making Democracy Work: Civic Traditions in Modern Italy,* Princeton: Princeton University Press.

Rawls, J. (1993) *Political Liberalism,* New York: Columbia University Press.

Reisinger, W.M. (1999) "Reassessing Theories of Transition Away from Authoritarian Regimes: Regional Patterns among Postcommunist Countries," paper presented at the 1999 Annual Meeting of the Midwest Political Science Association, Chicago, 15–17 April.

Rohrschneider, R. (1999) *Learning Democracy: Democratic and Economic Values in Unified Germany,* Oxford: Oxford University Press.

Roller, E. (2000) "Ende des sozialstaatlichen Konsenses? Zum Aufbrechen traditioneller und zur Entstehung neuer Konfliktstrukturen in Deutschland," in Niedermayer, O. and Westle, B. (eds) *Demokratie und Partizipation,* Opladen: Westdeutscher Verlag.

Sartori, G. (1987) *The Theory of Democracy Revisited,* Chatham, NJ: Chatham House.

Scharpf, F.W. (1999) "Demokratieprobleme in der europäischen Mehrebenenpolitik," in Merkel, W. and Busch, A. (eds) *Demokratie in Ost und West. Für Klaus von Beyme,* Frankfurt a.M.: Suhrkamp.

Taylor, C. (1989) "Cross-purposes: The Liberal–Communitarian Debate," in Rosenblum, N. (ed.) *Liberalism and the Moral Life,* Cambridge, MA: Harvard University Press.

2 East European value systems in global perspective

Ronald Inglehart

Introduction

To what extent does a common culture exist among the countries of central and eastern Europe? Are their worldviews relatively similar? And to what extent are their basic value systems compatible with those of the publics of western Europe?

Modernization theorists, from Karl Marx to Max Weber to Daniel Bell, have argued that economic development brings pervasive cultural changes that tend to erase traditional cultural boundaries. Analyzing evidence from the four waves of the World Values Surveys, this study finds evidence of major cultural changes *and* the persistence of distinctive cultural traditions.

The publics of central and east European countries have relatively similar basic values, in broad global perspective. Their values differ from those prevailing in western Europe. While both eastern and western European societies are among the most secular–rational countries in the world, the European Union publics rank substantially higher than most central and east European publics on survival/self-expression values – a syndrome of tolerance, trust, well-being, and emphasis on self-expression that is closely linked with democracy. To some extent, these differences seem to reflect whether or not a given society has experienced communist rule and how long it was dominated by communism. The cultural heritage of a society also seems to play a significant role. Large differences exist between value systems of the historically Catholic or Protestant ex-communist societies of central and eastern Europe, and the historically Orthodox ex-communist societies. These values are changing over time, but the impact of a society's historical heritage remains clearly visible in the value systems of its public today.

Modernization and cultural change

In the nineteenth and early twentieth centuries, modernization theorists from Marx to Weber predicted the future of industrial society, emphasizing the rise of rationality and the decline of religion. In the twentieth century, non-Western societies were expected to abandon their traditional cultures and assimilate the technologically and morally superior ways of the West.

In the opening years of the twenty-first century, it has become clear that modernization is more complex than these early views anticipated. Hardly anyone today expects a proletarian revolution, and it is evident that religion has not vanished, as predicted. Moreover, it is increasingly apparent that modernization cannot be equated with westernization. Non-western societies in east Asia have surpassed their western role models in key aspects of modernization, such as rates of economic growth and high life expectancy. Few observers today attribute moral superiority to the West.

Although few people would accept the original Marxist version of modernization theory today, one of its core concepts still seems valid: the insight that, once industrialization begins, it produces pervasive social and cultural consequences, from rising educational levels to changing gender roles. Industrialization is the central element of a modernization process that impacts on most other elements of society. Marx's failures as a prophet are evident, but he correctly foresaw that industrialization would transform the world. When he was writing *Das Kapital*, only a handful of societies were industrialized. Today, almost every society on Earth is at some stage of the industrialization process.

This chapter explores this thesis with data from the World Values Surveys and European Values Studies, which have measured the beliefs and values of the people of 80 societies containing almost 85 percent of the world's population.[1] These surveys provide time-series data from the earliest wave of democratization in 1981 to the most recent wave, completed in 2002, offering an unprecedentedly rich source of insight into the relationships between economic development and social and political change. These surveys show that substantial changes have occurred in the values and beliefs of the publics of these societies, even during the relatively brief time span since 1981. These changes are closely linked with the economic changes experienced by a given society. However, we find evidence of both massive cultural change and the persistence of traditional values. As we will demonstrate, economic development is associated with predictable changes away from absolute norms and values, toward a syndrome of increasingly rational, tolerant, trusting, and post-industrial values.

Values of the rich and poor

The World Values Survey data demonstrate that the worldviews of the people of rich societies differ systematically from those of low-income societies across a wide range of political, social, and religious norms and beliefs. In order to focus our comparisons on a small number of important dimensions of cross-cultural variance, we carried out a factor analysis of each society's mean level on scores of variables, replicating the analysis in Inglehart and Baker (2000).[2] The two most significant dimensions that emerged reflected, first, a polarization between traditional and secular–rational orientations toward authority and, second, a polarization between privileging of survival or self-expression.

By "traditional" we refer to orientations that are relatively authoritarian, place strong emphasis on religion, and emphasize male dominance in economic and political life, respect for authority, and relatively low levels of tolerance for abortion and divorce, and have relatively high levels of national pride. Advanced or secular–rational societies have the opposite characteristics.

The second major dimension of cross-cultural variation is linked with the transition from industrial society to post-industrial societies – which brings a polarization between the weight accorded to survival and that given to self-expression. A central component of this dimension involves the polarization between materialist and post-materialist values, reflecting a cultural shift that is emerging among generations who have grown up taking survival for granted. Self-expression values give high priority to environmental protection, tolerance of diversity, and rising demands for participation in decision-making in economic and political life. These values reflect mass polarization over the response to statements such as: "When jobs are scarce, men have more right to a job than women"; "A university education is more important for a boy than a girl"; and, "Men make better political leaders than women." This emphasis on gender equality is part of a broader syndrome of tolerance of outgroups, including foreigners, gays, and lesbians. The shift from survival values to self-expression values also includes a shift in child-rearing values, from emphasis on hard work toward emphasis on imagination and tolerance as important values to teach a child. And it goes with a rising sense of subjective well-being that is conducive to an atmosphere of tolerance, trust, and political moderation. Finally, societies that rank high on self-expression values also tend to rank high on interpersonal trust. This produces a culture of trust and tolerance, in which people place a relatively high value on individual freedom and self-expression, and have activist political orientations. These are precisely the attributes that the political culture literature defines as crucial to democracy.

The unprecedented wealth that has accumulated in advanced societies during the past generation means that an increasing share of the population has grown up taking survival for granted. Thus, priorities have shifted from an overwhelming emphasis on economic and physical security toward an increasing emphasis on subjective well-being, self-expression, and quality of life. Inglehart and Baker (2000) demonstrate that orientations have shifted from traditional toward secular–rational values, and from survival values toward self-expression values in almost all advanced industrial societies that have experienced economic growth. But "modernization" is not linear – when a society has completed industrialization and starts becoming a knowledge society, it moves in a new direction.

Figure 2.1 shows a two-dimensional cultural map on which the value systems of 80 societies are depicted. The vertical dimension represents the traditional/secular–rational dimension, and the horizontal dimension reflects the survival/self-expression values dimension. Both dimensions are strongly linked with economic development: the value systems of rich countries differ systematically from those of poor countries. Germany, France, Britain, Italy, Japan, Sweden, the U.S.A., and all other societies with a 1995 annual per capita GNP over $15,000 rank relatively high on both dimensions – without exception, they fall in the upper right-hand corner.

On the other hand, every one of the societies with per capita GNP below $2,000 fall into a cluster at the lower left of the map; India, Bangladesh, Pakistan, Nigeria, Ghana, and Peru all fall into this economic

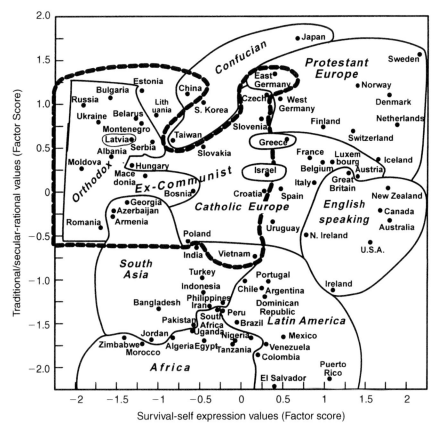

Figure 2.1 Central and eastern European values in global perspective.

zone that cuts across the African, south Asian, ex-communist, and Orthodox cultural zones. The remaining societies fall into two intermediate cultural–economic zones. Economic development seems to move societies in a common direction, regardless of their cultural heritage.

Economic development interacts with a society's cultural heritage

Nevertheless, distinctive cultural zones persist two centuries after the Industrial Revolution began. Different societies follow different trajectories even when they are subjected to the same forces of economic development, in part because situation-specific factors, such as a society's cultural heritage, also shape how a particular society develops. Huntington (1996) has emphasized the role of religion in shaping the world's eight major civilizations or "cultural zones": western Christianity, Orthodox Christianity, Islam, Confucianism, Japan (Shintoism), Hinduism, Africa, and Latin America. These zones were shaped by religious traditions that are still powerful today, despite the forces of modernization.

Economic development is strongly associated with both dimensions of cultural change. But a society's cultural heritage also plays a role: all four of the Confucian-influenced societies (China, Taiwan, South Korea, and Japan) have relatively secular values, constituting a Confucian cultural zone, despite substantial differences in wealth. The Orthodox societies constitute another distinct cultural zone, as Huntington argued. The 11 Latin-American societies show relatively similar values. And, despite their wide geographic dispersion, the English-speaking countries constitute a relatively compact cultural zone. Similarly, the historically Roman Catholic societies (e.g., Italy, Portugal, Spain, France, Belgium, and Austria) display relatively traditional values when compared with other societies with the same proportion of industrial workers such as Confucian or ex-communist societies. Finally, virtually all of the historically Protestant societies (e.g., West Germany, Denmark, Norway, Sweden, Finland and Iceland) rank higher on both the traditional–secular rational dimension and the survival/self-expression dimension than do the historically Roman Catholic societies.

Religious traditions appear to have had an enduring impact on the contemporary value systems of the 80 societies. But a society's culture reflects its entire historical heritage. A central historical event of the twentieth century was the rise and fall of a communist empire that once ruled one-third of the world's population. Communism left a clear imprint on the value systems of those who lived under it. East Germany remains culturally close to West Germany, despite four decades of communist rule, but its value system has been drawn toward the communist zone. Although China is a member of the Confucian zone, it also falls within a broad communist-influenced zone. Similarly, Azerbaijan, though part of the Islamic cluster, also falls within the communist superzone that dominated it for decades. Changes in GNP and occupational structure have important influences on prevailing worldviews, but traditional cultural influences persist.

Almost all EU member countries of western Europe fall into a broad cultural zone in the upper-right hand corner of Figure 2.1, although both Ireland and Portugal (the two poorest members shown here) are outliers. But this zone is widely dispersed, overlapping with the English-speaking zone (in the case of Ireland) and bordering on both the Latin-American zone and the ex-communist zone (in the case of Portugal). Interestingly, two western European countries that are not members of the European Union, Switzerland and Iceland, fall squarely inside the European Union zone. Their high levels of economic development and their Protestant historical traditions seem to have played much more important roles in shaping their basic values systems than any possible influence of membership in the European Union. Iceland and Switzerland fall readily into the Protestant sub-cluster of the European Union cultural zone: they are culturally closer to the historically Protestant members of the European Union than are the historically Catholic members.

The ex-communist societies of central and eastern Europe all fall into the upper left-hand quadrant of our cultural map, ranking high on the traditional/secular–rational dimension (toward the secular pole), but low on the survival/self-expression dimension (falling near the survival-oriented pole). A broken line encircles all of the societies that have experienced communist rule, and they form a reasonably coherent group. Although by no means the poorest countries in the world, the societies of central and eastern Europe's experience of the collapse of communism shattered their economic, political, and social systems, and brought a pervasive sense of insecurity. Thus, Russia, Ukraine, Bulgaria, Romania, and Moldova rank lowest of any countries on Earth on the survival/self-expression dimension – exhibiting lower levels of subjective well-being than much poorer countries such as India, Bangladesh, Zimbabwe, Uganda, and Pakistan. People who have experienced stable poverty throughout their lives tend to emphasize survival values; but those who have experienced the collapse of their social system (and may, as in Russia, currently have living standards and life expectancies far below where they were 15 years ago) experience a sense of unpredictability and insecurity that leads them to emphasize survival values even more heavily than those who are accustomed to a lower standard of living. Not surprisingly, communist rule seems conducive to the emergence of a relatively secular–rational culture. As Figure 2.2 demonstrates, the ex-communist countries in general, and those that were members of the Soviet Union in particular (and thus experienced communist rule for seven decades, rather then merely four decades), rank higher on secular–rational values than non-communist countries. To an equally striking extent, ex-communist countries in general, and former Soviet countries in particular, tend to

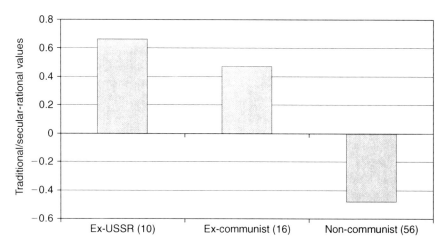

Figure 2.2 Traditional/secular–rational values and experience under communist rule.

emphasize survival values far more heavily than societies that have not experienced communist rule (Figure 2.3).

Yet there is wide diversity within the former communist zone. The basic values prevailing in the Czech Republic, Slovenia, Croatia, and East Germany are very close to those of west European societies on both major dimensions. Significantly, these societies have experienced relatively successful transitions from communism to market economies – and they were historically shaped by the Protestant or Roman Catholic religious traditions, rather than by the Orthodox tradition. This is part of a broader

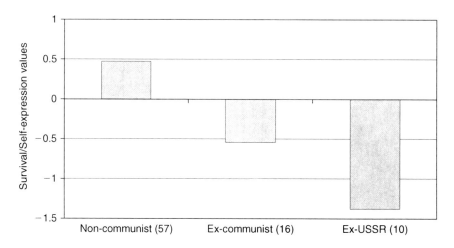

Figure 2.3 Survival/self-expression values and experience under communist rule.

pattern. The historically Protestant or Roman Catholic ex-communist societies show a marked tendency to rank higher on self-expression values than the historically Orthodox societies. (Table 2.1 shows the historically dominant religion of each society). A society's position on this dimension has important political implications. As we have shown elsewhere (Inglehart and Welzel, 2005: 155), there is a 0.90 correlation between self-expression values and the extent to which effective democracy is actually practiced in that society.

Figure 2.4 shows the relative position of each of the nine major cultural regions on the traditional/secular–rational dimension. When the broad "non-communist" category is broken down into these finer categories, it is clear that both Protestant Europe and the Confucian cultural region are even more secular than the Orthodox cultural region: experience under communist rule probably contributed to the relatively secular worldviews held by the publics of Orthodox societies, but the forces of modernization seem to have secularized Protestant Europe even more effectively than the conscious efforts that communist regimes made to stamp out religion. The Confucian cultural heritage, of course, has emphasized a relatively secular, this-world orientation for many centuries. The English-speaking publics remain significantly more traditional in their orientations than those of other rich countries – though they are markedly less so than the publics of developing societies in South Asia, the Islamic region, Latin America, and Africa, the most traditional cultural region of all.

Although they lag behind other rich societies in their degree of secularization, the English-speaking peoples place greater emphasis on self-expression values than the people of any other cultural region, as Figure 2.5 demonstrates. Protestant Europe comes next; on the two-dimensional map

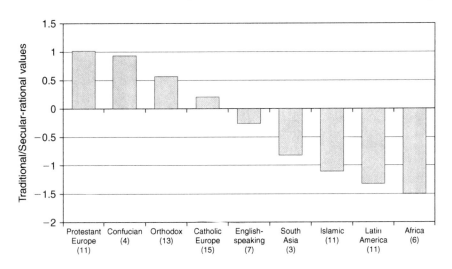

Figure 2.4 Traditional/secular–rational values in eight cultural regions.

Table 2.1 Cultural regions

Protestant Europe	English-speaking	Catholic Europe	Confucian	Orthodox	Latin America	South Asia	Islamic	Africa	Mixed	Unique
W. Germany	Britain	France	Japan	Belarus	Mexico	India	Pakistan	S. Africa	Bosnia	Israel
Netherlands	Ireland	Italy	S. Korea	Bulgaria	Argentina	Philippines	Turkey	Nigeria		
Denmark	N. Ireland	Belgium	China	Romania	Puerto Rico	Vietnam	Azerbaijan	Ghana		
Norway	USA	Spain	Taiwan	Greece	Brazil	Bangladesh	Zimbabwe			
Sweden	Canada	Hungary	Ukraine	Chile	Indonesia	Tanzania				
Iceland	Australia	Poland	Russia	Peru	Albania	Uganda				
Finland	New Zealand	Czech Rep.	Moldova	El Salvador	Egypt					
Switzerland	Slovenia	Georgia	Venezuela	Morocco						
E. Germany	Portugal	Armenia	Uruguay	Iran						
Latvia	Austria	Serbia	Dominican	Jordan						
Estonia	Lithuania	Montenegro	Republic	Algeria						
	Lithuania	Macedonia	Colombia							
	Croatia									
	Slovakia									
	Luxembourg									

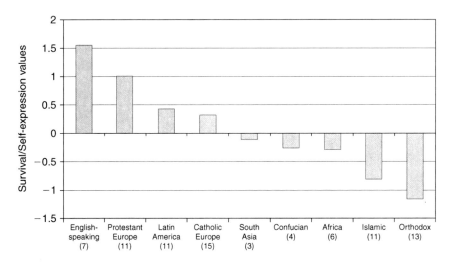

Figure 2.5 Survival/self-expression values in eight cultural regions.

as a whole, this region exhibits the most modern outlook of any cultural region. The Orthodox societies rank at the opposite extreme, placing less emphasis on self-expression values (and more on survival values) than the people of any other cultural zone. Catholic Europe as a whole places relatively strong emphasis on self-expression values, despite the fact that roughly half the members of this group have experienced communist rule (along with two societies of Protestant Europe). Decades of communist rule had a significant impact on the values and beliefs of those who experienced it, but a given cultural heritage can partially offset or reinforce its impact. Thus, as Inglehart and Baker (2000) demonstrate with multiple regression analysis, even when we control for level of economic development and other factors, a history of communist rule does account for a significant share of the cross-cultural variance in basic values (with seven decades of communist rule having more impact than four decades). An Orthodox tradition seems to reduce emphasis on self-expression values, by comparison with societies historically shaped by a Roman Catholic or Protestant cultural tradition. Central and east European countries have a shared experience of communist rule, but their respective religious traditions appear to have set them on distinct trajectories that were not erased by communism.

We have compared the belief systems of the people of central and east European societies with those of other regions on two major dimensions of cross-cultural variation. This provides a useful overview, but it is operating at a high level of generalization. Now let us examine how these societies differ on some of the specific variables linked with each of the two main dimensions.

Table 2.2 shows cross-cultural variation in five of the most important

Table 2.2 Regional differences in the components of traditional/secular–rational values – experience under communist rule

	% Saying "God is very important in my life"	% Very proud of nationality	% Favoring more respect for authority	% Low on Autonomy Index	% Saying abortion is never justifiable	Mean score on traditional/secular–rational values
Ex-USSR (10)	24	33	58	51	28	0.664
Ex-communist (16)	27	47	56	50	30	0.471
Non-communist (54)	53	62	62	64	49	−0.481
Overall mean (80)	44	56	60	60	42	−0.159

variables that are closely linked with the traditional/secular–rational dimension (dozens of other variables are also strongly correlated with this dimension, but these five illustrate the general pattern). This table shows the percentage emphasizing the traditional pole, so high scores indicate traditional values. On all five variables, the publics of the ex-communist countries are much less likely to have traditional values than the publics in societies that did not experience communist rule. For example, the publics of the Soviet successor states are less than half as likely to say that "God is very important in my life" than are the publics of non-communist societies; they also rank much lower on national pride, are less likely to say that "more respect for authority would be a good thing," are more likely to emphasize independence and determination as important things for a child to learn (autonomy versus obedience), and are less likely to believe that abortion is never justifiable. The largest gap is between communist and non-communist societies, but the publics of the Soviet successor states tend to be even more secular than the publics of the other ex-communist societies.

When we examine the results from each of the nine cultural regions, we find a more complex picture (Table 2.3). Overall, Protestant Europe has the most secular public, but the ranking varies on given variables. The Confucian publics actually show more secular orientations than the Protestants on four of the five variables, but rank slightly behind them on the index as a whole. The publics of the Orthodox countries consistently rank about third, ranging from as high as second to as low as fourth on these variables. The publics of Catholic Europe are slightly *less* likely to say that "God is very important in my life" than are the publics of the Ortho-dox societies, but they rank slightly behind them on the other four variables. Overall, the rankings of given cultural zones are remarkably consistent across all five variables: if you know the region's ranking on one of them, you can predict where it will fall on the other four with a great deal of accuracy. The Protestant and Confucian cultural zones *always* fall among the three lowest-ranking regions, and at the opposite extreme, sub-Saharan Africa and Latin America *always* fall among the three highest-ranking regions.

Table 2.4 provides details concerning variables closely linked with the survival/self-expression dimension. High scores indicate that a given region emphasizes self-expression values relatively strongly. Thus, the non-communist countries in general have a score on the materialist/post-materialist values index of −11, indicating that the materialists outweigh the post-materialists by 11 percentage points. The preponderance of mate-rialists is much stronger in societies that have experienced communist rule: materialists outnumber post-materialists by 43 percentage points in the Soviet successor states and by 31 percentage points in the other ex-communist societies. Similarly, happiness levels and tolerance of homo-sexuality are much lower in the Soviet successor states than in the societies

Table 2.3 Regional differences in the components of traditional/secular–rational values – by cultural region

	% Saying "God is very important in my life"	% Very proud of nationality	% Favoring more respect for authority	% Low on Autonomy Index	% Saying abortion is never justifiable	Mean score on traditional/secular–rational values
Protestant Europe (11)	12	38	43	37	18	1.018
Confucian (4)	9	23	28	36	31	0.937
Orthodox (13)	30	42	57	55	29	0.571
Catholic Europe (14)	27	47	59	55	31	0.210
English-speaking (7)	33	59	68	59	32	−0.259
South Asia (3)	64	79	64	66	55	−0.816
Islamic (11)	80	71	69	79	63	−1.105
Latin America (11)	78	79	79	75	69	−1.322
Africa (6)	74	75	65	78	72	−1.499
Overall mean	44	56	61	60	43	−0.164

Table 2.4 Regional differences in the components of survival/self-expression values – experience under communist rule

	Postmat minus materialist	% Very happy	Some tolerance, homosexuality	Have signed petition	Trust People	Disagree, men make better politicians	Mean score, survival/ self-expression values
Non-communist (54)	−11	33	50	37	29	55	0.472
Ex-communist (16)	−31	16	36	27	26	50	−0.542
Ex-USSR (10)	−43	7	29	17	25	28	−1.380
Overall mean (80)	−19	26	45	33	28	53	0.053

that have not experienced communist rule, with the other ex-communist societies falling in between these two extremes: in the never-communist zone, 33 percent of the public describes themselves as "very happy," as compared with only 7 percent in the ex-Soviet societies, and 16 percent in the other former communist societies. Attitudes toward homosexuality are negative throughout the world. Respondents were asked to rate the acceptability of homosexuality on a ten-point scale, ranging from 1 as never justifiable to 10 as always justifiable. Over half of the respondents in the world as a whole chose point 1, indicating total rejection; the remaining respondents were distributed over points 2 through 10. Thus, this table differentiates between those who indicated "some" tolerance of homosexuality (choosing points 2 through 10) versus those who indicated that it was completely unacceptable. In the non-communist world, 50 percent express "some" tolerance – but in the Soviet successor states, only 29 percent do so, and in the other ex-communist countries the figure is 36 percent. The percentage who report having signed a petition in the last five years also varies greatly, with 37 percent of the public in non-communist societies reporting that they have done so, as compared with only 17 percent in the ex-Soviet societies. This variable has shown a steady upward trend from 1974 to the present in established democracies; but in the new democracies, this and other forms of unconventional political participation were at a high point during the transition to democracy around 1990, but have subsequently declined in almost all new democracies, in a "post-honeymoon" phenomenon (Inglehart and Catterberg 2003). Differences in interpersonal trust are relatively small across communist and non-communist societies, but there are large differences in attitudes concerning gender equality. In the 54 non-communist societies as a whole, a clear majority – 55 percent – disagree with the statement that "men make better political leaders than women." But in the Soviet successor states, only 28 percent disagree – a heavy majority agree. These large differences in tolerance of outgroups such as gays and women have political implications – for tolerance of outgroups among the public is closely correlated with stable democracy at the institutional level. Although overwhelming majorities of the publics of former communist societies endorse democracy as a general goal, they show much lower levels on such underlying qualities as tolerance and the post-materialist valuation of freedom of speech and political participation as goods in themselves. These attributes seem to play a crucial role in the emergence and survival of liberal democracy.

Table 2.5 shows how each of these orientations breaks down across the nine cultural zones. Again, the rankings on one variable are generally very consistent with the rankings on the other variables. And the societies shaped by the Orthodox tradition rank lowest of all nine cultural zones on two of the six variables, and among the three lowest groups on all of the remaining variables. Overall, the Orthodox cultural zone ranks lowest of any region in emphasis on self-expression values – even lower than the

Table 2.5 Regional differences in the components of survival/self-expression values – by cultural region

	Postmat minus materialist	% Very happy	Some tolerance, homosexuality	Have signed petition	Trust People	Disagree, men make better politicians	Mean score, survival/self-expression values
English-speaking (7)	10	40	68	66	38	79	1.553
Protestant Europe (11)	−9	29	73	53	46	84	1.007
Latin America (11)	−5	40	46	23	16	64	0.428
Catholic Europe (14)	−14	21	57	42	24	57	0.323
South Asia (3)	−29	38	35	15	29	43	−0.113
Confucian (4)	−36	21	40	35	42	53	−0.268
Africa (6)	−25	39	19	15	14	42	−0.288
Islamic (11)	−36	19	8	18	26	33	−0.814
Orthodox (13)	−39	10	31	18	23	43	−1.161
Overall mean	−19	26	43	33	28	51	0.050

Islamic cultural zone. Given the remarkably strong linkage that has been found between self-expression values and stable democracy (Inglehart and Welzel 2005), this is a sobering finding.

A society's position on the survival/self-expression index is very strongly correlated with its level of democracy, as indicated by its scores on the Freedom House ratings of political rights and civil liberties. This relationship is remarkably powerful and it is clearly not a methodological artifact or an intra-cranial correlation, since the two variables are measured at different levels and come from different sources. Virtually all of the societies that rank high on survival/self-expression values are stable democracies. Virtually all of the societies that rank low on this dimension have authoritarian governments. The correlation of 0.90 between survival/self-expression values and democracy is significant at a very high level, and probably reflects a causal linkage. But what is causing what?

One interpretation would be that democratic institutions give rise to the self-expression values to which they are so closely linked. In other words, democracy makes people healthy, happy, non-sexist, tolerant, trusting, and instills post-materialist values. This interpretation is appealing and if it were true, it would provide a powerful argument for democracy, implying that we have a quick fix for most of the world's problems: adopt democratic institutions and live happily ever after.

Unfortunately, the experience of the Soviet Union's successor states does not support this interpretation. Since their dramatic move toward democracy in 1991, they have not become healthier, happier, more trusting, more tolerant, or more post-materialist – most have moved in exactly the opposite direction. The fact that their people are living in economic and physical insecurity seems to have more impact than the fact that their leaders are chosen by free elections.

Democratic institutions do not automatically produce a culture that emphasizes self-expression values. Instead, it seems that economic development gradually leads to social and cultural changes that make democratic institutions more likely to survive and flourish. That would help explain why mass democracy did not emerge until a relatively recent point in history, and why, even now, it is most likely to be found in economically more-developed countries – in particular, those that emphasize self-expression values over survival values.

This is cause for concern, but by no means a reason for resignation. During the past few decades, most industrialized societies have moved toward increasing emphasis on self-expression values, in an intergenerational cultural shift linked with economic development. We believe that the low levels of emphasis on self-expression values currently found in ex-communist countries – and above all in the Soviet successor states – is linked with the traumatic conditions many of these societies have experienced in the wake of the collapse of communist political, economic and social systems. This will not endure forever. In the long run, these societies will recover, continuing a process of economic development that has been temporarily disrupted. The seeds of an intergenerational shift toward rising emphasis on self-expression values and a political culture that supports democracy are already present. For, throughout central and eastern Europe, the younger generations place markedly greater emphasis on self-expression values than do the older generations. In the long run, the process of intergenerational population replacement is working to make these values more widespread. Their progress will be greatly enhanced insofar as economic recovery and political stability are attained.

Notes

1 For detailed information about these surveys, see the WVS websites at wvs.isr. umich.edu and www.worldvaluessurvey.org, and the EVS website evs.kub.nl.
2 For details of these analyses at both the individual and the national level, see Inglehart and Baker 2000.

References

Huntington, S.P. (1996) *The Clash of Civilizations and the Remaking of World Order*, New York: Simon and Schuster.

Inglehart, R. and Baker, W. (2000) "Modernization, Cultural Change and the Persistence of Traditional Values," *American Sociological Review* 65, 1.

Inglehart, R. and Catterberg, G. (2003) "Trends in Political Action: the Developmental Trend and the Post-Honeymoon Decline," *International Journal of Comparative Sociology* 44, 1.

Inglehart, R. and Welzel, G. (2005) *Modernization, Cultural Change and Democracy: The Human Development Sequence*, New York: Cambridge University Press.

3 Historical and cultural borderlines in eastern Europe

Gabriel Bădescu

Introduction

Political values and current political behavior are important indicators for the level and type of democracy a given society has achieved. A democratic institutional framework will work only if minimal standards are shared within the respective community (see Tóka 1995; Fuchs and Roller 1998).

The goal of this chapter is to examine the hypothetical relationship between the cultural conditions of a transition from communism to a liberal democracy and the political history of the respective territory. Therefore, I will examine the relationship between political orientations and behavior of the Romanian population and the pre-communist past of the territory of contemporary Romania.

Some authors assert that the characteristics of a democratic community are significantly influenced by durable "inherited" cultural traditions. In order to classify nations or sub-national political communities according to these traditions, we employ the following indicators: a) the dominant religion (Huntington 1996); b) the Empire in which ancestors of the present citizens lived for centuries (Reisinger 1999); c) the length of time spent under a Leninist regime (Fuchs 1999; Rohrschneider 1999); d) the level of socio-economic modernity (Lipset 1959, 1994); and e) characteristics of the respective civil society in the past (Putnam 1993).

The cited authors agree that different patterns of political behavior not only reflect current experiences and values but also the socialization experiences of the past, elements of which may have been passed down over many generations. However, the expectation that influences from the pre-communist era are still observable after a forty-year experience of authoritarianism seems rather tenuous. Nonetheless, the links between institutions and political values, orientations and norms which are somehow congruent in democratic political communities, may be rather incongruent in autocratic society. In a democratic political community, "cultures set limits to elites as well as mass behavior – shaping the political and economic systems, as well as being shaped by them" (Inglehart 1997: 15). Under an autocratic regime, and especially under communism, cultural factors might matter less, since people's voice's do not count much and can be very easily coerced. In addition, under communism, many political decisions were heavily influenced by the Soviet Union, a foreign power with very different political traditions. Thus, one might expect that the harsh and imposed political institutions would have made it difficult for indigenous political culture to persist over a long period of time. If some political values, orientations or behaviors did indeed preserve their distinct national or regional distribution – despite radical transformations in the social, political and economic spheres during the last 40 years, initiated mainly from the outside – then the cultural-historical perspective for explaining the democratic transition of a country like Romania would gain credence.

The following analysis is based on the assumption that cultural characteristics of a society influence the modalities of political change. More specifically, I assume that the concept of a democratic political community (Fuchs and Klingemann 2000) includes political values, norms and patterns of behavior that are relevant for the transition of the countries under consideration. My analysis will focus on some of these characteristics as dependent variables. Empirical data are taken from the World Values Survey.

Whereas most empirical studies explore the long-term effects of the historical context on democratic communities by a comparative analysis of different countries, my research strategy is to compare regions within a country that differ in terms of historical characteristics. The two approaches are complementary, and have their specific strengths and weaknesses. The cross-country comparison allows for the inclusion of a larger number of cases, reducing non-systematic measurement error. After all, there are 28 post-communist countries engaged in a process of transition from autocratic to democratic rule (Rose *et al.* 1998: 68). However, results of an analysis based on the comparison of regions within countries are less affected by factors that increase the error in cross-national studies because one does not have to control for divergent country characteristics such as, for example, legal framework or constitutional arrangements. In addition, the danger of introducing ambiguity due to translation is negligible in a country of linguistic homogeneity.

The main part of the analysis reported in this chapter is based on a comparison of political values and behavior in two large Romanian regions. Theories that hypothesize a causal relation between the cultural heritage of a political community and current political attitudes and behaviors of its members would predict that two regions within the same country, but with cultural heritages which typically differ in their support of democracy, are expected to display a different degree of democratization and, probably, a significant variation in terms of support for a democratic community. This expectation will be empirically tested with indicators developed on the basis of data taken from the 1995–9 World Values Survey.

It will be shown that the distribution of democratic attitudes in the two regions does not differ in the way predicted by cultural heritage theory. This implies that political culture is not immune to institutional change. Moreover, the division of European territory along historical–cultural borderlines such as Catholic, Protestant, Slavic-Orthodox or "modern" and "traditional" as described by Ferdinand Braudel's *longue durée* (Wagner 2001), is problematic and needs further testing with proper empirical research.

The Romanian democratic community in a comparative perspective

There are several cross-national surveys that include Romania. Their results provide largely consistent categorizations of the former communist countries based on the distribution of democratic attitudes and behavior in the respective societies.

Relying on the 1995–9 World Values Survey data, Dieter Fuchs and Hans-Dieter Klingemann (2000: 34) found a continuous but not very pronounced decline in the quality and the level of consolidation of democratic communities between west and east European countries. According to the authors' criteria, the political communities of some of the successor states of the former Soviet Union as well as Albania could not be classified as democratic communities.

Based on the New Democracy Barometer surveys, Richard Rose *et al.* (1998) estimated for every post-communist country the share of respondents who support the present regime, and the share of those who support autocratic alternatives. The Czech Republic scored highest with regard to the prevalence of democratic attitudes among its populace; Belarus and Ukraine scored lowest. Romania occupied a middle position, close to Bulgaria, Slovakia, Poland, Hungary and Slovenia. Another comparative study (based on national surveys conducted in 11 former communist countries between 1990 and 1992) evaluated the level of respondents' satisfaction with the way democracy works in their countries. The largest proportion of satisfied respondents was found in Romania, whereas Ukraine, Hungary, Krasnoyarsk (a Russian region) and Estonia displayed the smallest share of content citizens (Fuchs and Roller 1998: 297). A similar question was asked in a more recent series of cross-national surveys, the Comparative Study of Electoral Systems (CSES), which were conducted between 1996 and 2000. The level of satisfaction with the democratic process as measured by the CSES surveys conducted in different post-communist countries is summarized in Table 3.1.

The Czech Republic, East Germany and Poland display a very similar distribution of satisfaction and dissatisfaction with the democratic process. Romanian respondents are slightly more satisfied with their current political regime than Hungarians and Lithuanians, whereas Ukrainians show a

Table 3.1 Level of satisfaction with the democratic process, %, Romania (1998)

Country	Satisfied	Fairly satisfied	Not very satisfied	Not at all satisfied	Total
Czech Republic	3.7	54.0	33.0	6.0	100
East Germany	5.7	51.2	35.4	7.7	100
Hungary	1.4	40.8	41.6	16.2	100
Lithuania	12.9	21.6	53.3	12.1	100
Poland	5.8	57.3	29.2	7.7	100
Romania	20.4	23.5	38.6	17.5	100
Ukraine	2.2	7.0	37.5	53.3	100

very low level of satisfaction. Altogether, these results do not seem to support the *longue durée* perspective, because no clear threshold can be detected between the central European and the south-eastern European countries, including Romania.

Different premises for two Romanian regions: the type of democratic community

The two regions that will be compared in this chapter are Transylvania[1] (Region 1) and the rest of the country (Region 2), excluding the capital, Bucharest. As will be discussed below, this choice maximizes differences in terms of the type of cultural heritage prevalent in the two regions. Bucharest, which is not a part of Transylvania, is excluded from the analysis because of the specific socio-demographic characteristics of its inhabitants.

It is important to note that migration between these two regions has been modest. Therefore, there is not much support for the possibility of a homogenization of political values and attitudes through significant population exchange between the respective regions. According to the 1992 census, less than 5 percent of the population in Transylvania was born outside this region, whereas the share of native Transylvanians living in Region 2 was negligible. In 1966 and 1977, the corresponding figures were even lower, and after 1992 migration between regions decreased further (Rotariu and Mezei 1999). Historically the two regions belonged to different Empires and showed a distinct distribution of ethnic origin and religious denomination of its residents, as well as different levels of social and economic modernity before World War II.

Transylvania was part of the Habsburg Empire until 1918, whereas the rest of the country belonged to the Ottoman Empire until 1877, when it became independent. Transylvania was more heterogeneous in terms of ethnicity and religious denomination than Region 2. In 1930, 57.8 percent of Transylvanian inhabitants were Romanians, compared to 88.5 percent in the rest of the country (including Bucharest with 81.2 percent; Livezeanu 1995: 20, 226). In 1857, about half of the Romanians from

Transylvania were Greek Catholics and the other half were of Orthodox denomination. Most of the non-Romanian inhabitants of Transylvania were Catholics and Protestants, whereas more than 90 percent of the Romanians of the rest of the country were Orthodox (Rotariu *et al.* 1996). The Greek Catholic Church was established in Transylvania in 1700 when the Habsburg regime persuaded the local Orthodox clergy that their acceptance of the Catholic dogma and the authority of the Pope would earn them a status equal to the Catholic and Protestant clergy. The communists banned the Greek Catholic Church in late 1948, and forced it to merge with the Orthodox Church (Stan and Turcescu 2000).

Several characteristics of the Transylvanian socio-economic development point to the fact that Transylvania entered the twentieth century on a significantly higher level of socio-economic modernity than Region 2, that this difference began to emerge before 1900 and that it persists. For example, in Transylvania birth rates started to decrease around 1880, about 30 years earlier than in Region 2, and at the same time as in Italy, Hungary, Serbia and Poland. This difference between Transylvania and Region 2 still exists today (Ghețău 1997: 15; Mureșan 1999: 179–80) and this is also true when ethnic non-Romanians are excluded from the analysis (Rotariu 1993). Furthermore, the literacy rate was higher in Transylvania than in Region 2: 51.1 percent as compared to 39.3 percent in 1897–1912, and 67 percent as compared to 55.8 percent, in 1930 (Livezeanu 1998: 48).

If we accept that higher levels of socio-economic modernity are generally connected with a stronger tendency to support democratic values and behavior, we expect greater support of democracy among the Transylvanians.

Results of the 1990, 1992 and 1996 general elections seem to support the idea that significant differences exist between the two regions with respect to political values and behavior, and that these differences survived the leveling power of the communist regime. The most successful party in these elections, the Party of Social Democracy in Romania (PDSR),[2] won significantly different shares of the electorate in the two regions (Table 3.2).

The Romanian Democratic Convention (CDR), the largest party coalition in the period of 1992–2000, which in general favored rapid reform of political and economic institutions than the PDSR, enjoyed significantly

Table 3.2 The electoral support for PDSR in 1990, 1992 and 1996, %, Romania

| | *Year of the general elections* | | |
	1990	*1992*	*1996*
Region 1	43.58	8.88	11.76
Region 2	79.07	24.21	28.96

greater support in Region 1 than in Region 2. Even if we control for ethnic heterogeneity and size of locality, significant differences between the two regions can still be observed (Table 3.3).

Empirical analysis

Contrary to the theory of enduring cultural traditions and their impact on political attitudes and behavior, we might presume that institutional arrangements characteristic of the communist regime suppressed any lingering cultural differences between Regions 1 and 2. In democratic societies the respective institutional design is at least, to some degree, influenced by cultural factors. Under an autocratic regime, and especially in countries under a strong Soviet influence, the existing rules and laws were rather disconnected from popular political values and beliefs. Here, attitudes of the national political elites and their relations to the Soviet ruling class were probably more influential in shaping the system than values and beliefs popular among in the population of the pre-communist era.

The two Romanian regions constitute a perfect opportunity to test the hypothesis of the impact of enduring cultural traditions on political values and behavior since political development after 1990, and the failures and successes of subsequent government policies did not vary systematically across Romania. Differences between the two regions with regard to support of democracy may therefore be rooted in and accounted for by a more distant past.

Most of the dependent variables used describe citizens' attitudes toward democracy and serve as criteria for the distinction of different types of political communities (Fuchs and Klingemann 2000). The empirical data

Table 3.3 The effects of region and size of locality on the proportion of the Romanians who voted in the 1996 general elections for PDSR, and CDR respectively, multiple regression.[a]

	Effects on votes for PDSR[b]		Effects on votes for CDR[c]	
	Standardized coefficient	Standard error	Standardized coefficient	Standard error
Region[d]	−0.70	0.37	0.33	0.34
Size of locality[e]	−0.14	0.01	0.19	0.01

Notes
a The unit of analysis is locality of residence.
b The dependent variable in the first regression model is the proportion of votes for PDSR.
c The dependent variable in the second regression model is the proportion of votes for CDR.
d Region: people from the Region 1 are coded "1," those from the Region 2, "0."
e Size of locality: the number of Romanians 18 years and older.

are taken from the Romanian World Value Survey (1993, 1998), and from the Romanian Public Opinion Barometer Surveys. In my analysis, I will proceed as follows. First, I discuss the impact of socio-economic standard variables on democratic attitudes and behaviors for Region 1 and Region 2. Second, regional differences which have been observed will be discussed. Third, I will focus on generational influences. Thus, I will discuss variations of the relationship of region and various dependent variables across age cohorts. The distribution of the attitudes and behavioral dispositions in the two Romanian regions discussed are presented in Tables 3.4 to 3.6.

After a first broad comparison we can conclude that there are, indeed, differences between the two Romanian regions. However, the differences

Table 3.4 Empirical evidence of citizen support for a set of criteria for a democratic community, 1998, %, Romania

	DEM	AUT	PSC	CGI	VIO	LAW
Romania	88.6	22.0	11.0	15.8	77.0	77.8
Region 1	85.1	24.2	12.7	14.9	74.6	78.3
Region 2	90.3	19.2	10.0	16.3	78.7	77.7

Notes
DEM: Support of democratic rule; AUT: Support of autocratic rule; PSC: Support of political system of one's own country; CGI: Confidence in governmental institutions; VIO: Illegitimacy of violence; LAW: Law-abidingness. Cell entries are % positive support.

Table 3.5 Citizen support of different types of democratic community at the cultural level, 1998, %, Romania.

	SRE	SOL	TRU	WET	ETO
Romania	31.0	63.0	18.0	63.0	6.0
Region 1	29.8	52.7	19.6	60.5	6.7
Region 2	28.7	67.4	19.3	64.6	6.0

Notes
SRE: Self-responsibility; SOL: Solidarity; TRU: Trust in others; WET: Work ethic; ETO: Ethic tolerance. Cell entries are % positive support.

Table 3.6 Citizen support for different types of democratic community at the structural and process level, 1998, %, Romania

	PRO	MAN	PMO	CIV
Romania	55.0	37.0	21.0	9.0
Region 1	56.3	33.1	18.1	11.1
Region 2	55.2	37.9	20.3	3.8

Notes
PRO: Private ownership; MAN: Management of enterprise; PMO: Political motivation; CIV: Civic engagement. Cell entries are % positive support.

observed do not square with what the theory of the *longue durée* would have predicted. Democratic attitudes are not more prominent in Region 1 and citizens from this region do not show less support for etatist policies than people from Region 2. On the contrary, there are significant differences showing that citizens of Region 2 express a higher support for democracy (DEM), a lower support for autocratic rule (AUT), and they reject violence as a legitimate political mode of political competition (VIO). In addition, citizens from Region 1 display a lower level of solidarity with the poor (SOL), a less pronounced individualistic work ethic (WET) and a lower level of support for private ownership (MAN) than citizens from the Region 2. The only democratic values and behaviors on which citizens from Region 1 score higher than citizens from Region 2 are those referring to participation. Membership in voluntary organizations in Region 1 is significantly higher than in Region 2. The same is true for citizens who have signed petitions, participated in boycotts, or taken part in lawful demonstrations.

Ideally, we should be able to compare similarly structured populations for every independent variable. Data of the World Values Survey allow us to control for effects of the level of formal education, the size of the local community, age and ethnicity. Table 3.7 shows the effect of region on each dependent variable (estimated by a multiple regression model). Effects of region on dichotomous dependent variables, such as member-

Table 3.7 The effect of region on indicators of the quality of democratic community, multiple regression models,[a] Romania

Dependent variable	Standardized coefficient of region	t
DEM	−0.15	−4.20
AUT	0.11	3.28
PSC	0.04	1.10
CGI	−0.06	−1.83
VIO	0.00	0.04
LAW	0.02	0.60
SRE	−0.04	−1.34
SOL	−0.09	−2.61
WET	0.02	0.66
ETO	−0.11	−3.41
PRO	−0.06	−1.74
MAN	0.07	1.90
PMO	0.04	1.10

Notes
a Each row describes a multiple regression model; the dependent variable is specified in the first column; cell entries in the second and third columns describe the effect of region ("0" for Region 1, "1" for Region 2) on the respective dependent variable.
DEM: Support of democratic rule; AUT: Support of autocratic rule; PSC: Support of political system of one's own country; CGI: Confidence in governmental institutions; VIO: Illegitimacy of violence; LAW: Law-abidingness. SRE: Self-responsibility; SOL: Solidarity; TRU: Trust in others; WET: Work ethic; ETO: Ethic tolerance; PRO: Private ownership; MAN: Management of enterprise; PMO: Political motivation.

ship in associations, social trust, signing petitions, participating in boycotts and participating in demonstrations, are estimated by a logistic regression model (Table 3.8).

The multivariate analyses confirm the results of the bi-variate analyses: the hypothesis that the population of Region 1 is more democratically oriented than inhabitants of Region 2 is not just rejected – the inverse is true.

There are several possible explanations for this finding. It may be the case that the two regions were more similar in the distant past than we had reason to assume. However, it may also be the case that different political belief systems existed until the end of World War II and that they disappeared under the leveling effect of the autocratic regime. Its new political institutions may have been inspired (and sometimes implemented) by the Soviet Union as the hegemon and have "represented a much stronger call for uniformity than the Ottoman, Russian, Habsburg or German empires had ever dared – or, for that matter, wanted – to raise" (Berglund and Aarebrot 1997: 152).

Another empirical test would allow us to reduce the range of plausible explanations to some extent. The analysis of the relation between region and democratic attitudes and behaviors by age cohorts, that is by those born before the communist period and those born afterwards,[3] may help to decide whether there have ever been significant differences between the two regions, or whether the leveling effect of the postwar institutional settings has successfully extinguished these differences. If the elderly in Region 1 tend to be more supportive of democracy than the elderly in Region 2, we would have found at least some support for a historical differentiation that did not survive communist rule. In all other cases, we are left with two distinct possibilities: a) before Word War II the two regions did not vary with regard to modal political values, beliefs and behavior to the extent expected; or b) the leveling effect of communist institutions was so strong that it cancelled out all effects of an early socialization. The overall result of this analysis, however, is that people from Region 1 who were born before the communist period do not tend to display more democratic attitudes than the elderly in Region 2.[4]

Table 3.8 The effect of region on political values and behavior, logistic regression models,[a] Romania

Dependent variable	b coefficient of region	Standardized error	Exp. b
CIV	1.02	0.15	2.77
Trust	0.02	0.17	1.02

Notes
a Each row describes a logistic model; the dependent variable is specified in the first column, cell entries in the second, third, and fourth columns describe the effect of REGION ("0" for Region 1, "1" for Region 2) on the respective dependent variable.
TRU: Trust in others; CIV: Civic engagement.

There is one indicator that discriminates between the two regions. This indicator can also be used as a criterion to classify *types* of democratic community. According to the results of the 1998 Romanian WVS data, Region 1 hosts a significantly higher share of citizens who are members in voluntary organizations than Region 2. The percentage of active membership in at least two organizations amounts to 15.2 percent in Region 1 as compared to 3.8 percent in Region 2. Although the questions on membership are probably not very reliable in Romania,[5] all available survey data document a marked advantage for Region 1 in this respect (Bădescu 2003). Thus, is civil society more deeply rooted in Region 1 than in Region 2, or is this difference determined by other, non-cultural factors? If the analysis is extended to other forms of civil participation, a similar difference emerges between the two regions. People who signed a petition, took part in a boycott or participated in a lawful demonstration are found more often in Region 1 than in Region 2 (Table 3.9).

Which factors account for this difference? At least three conditions support political and societal participation: civic values and attitudes, social resources and the capability to mobilize (Verba *et al.* 1995). In our case, it is hard to determine whether values play a significant role in explaining the discrepancy between the two regions. The different levels of membership in voluntary organizations and participation between the two regions may be entirely the result of better developed recruitment and mediation networks in Region 1. There are some arguments in favor of this explanation. First, there are attitudes and values usually associated with the notion of a civic community, and these should be positively correlated with volunteering and participation (Putnam 1993). Yet the prevalence of these attitudes does not vary between the two regions in the expected direction (Table 3.5). Second, Region 1 is indeed characterized by better-developed social networks than Region 2 (Sandu 1999). Thus, the flow of information between citizens, which in turn influence their capacity to be mobilized for civic activities, is more intense in Region 1 than in Region 2. Third, a significant part of voluntary membership is tied to the existence of non-governmental organizations. A majority of these organizations were established with foreign aid from western Europe, and many still depend on external support (Dakova *et al.* 2000; Kuti 2001). Region 1 hosts a considerably larger number of NGOs than does Region 2, and this is probably a result of geographical proximity.[6]

Table 3.9 Types of political participation, 1998, %, Romania

	Petition	*Boycotts*	*Demonstrations*
Romania	17.0	3.0	20.0
Region 1	19.5	4.4	22.3
Region 2	12.3	2.1	17.8

To summarize, different levels of civic activism in the two regions do not necessarily imply a similarly distinguished distribution of democratic values, but may be rooted in different levels of the development of social and administrative infrastructures.

Conclusions

If democratic attitudes and patterns of behavior are among the most important determinants of the quality and speed of the process of democratization, then the question about their resistance to institutional change is clearly significant. The analysis of changing cultural orientations under the influence of a communist regime and its specific institutional settings might provide insights into the potentialities as well as limitations of a country's transition to a liberal democracy.

Historico-cultural legacy theories assert that political values, beliefs and behavior shaped by the societal and institutional designs of the pre-communist era are preserved and important determinants of current political culture. There are two propositions which, if true, would support the historical cultural legacy approach. One is that different distributions of values in two different populations is the result of differentiated experiences of historical socialization prior to the introduction of a radically new institutional context and re-allocation of societal resources.[7] A second and related possibility is that a particular historical cultural formation would predispose a community toward exhibiting certain types of political values even after a long interval. If these propositions are valid then, in the case of Romania, we would expect age cohorts who have been socialized under pre-communist rule to differ from those who grew up under communist rule.

This chapter has explored the long-term effects of historical context on political attitudes and behavior using Romania as an example. The design has allowed us to compare two regions of the country which are different in their historical and cultural heritage. Moreover, a comparison across countries showed that the degree of support for democracy in Romania is not systematically lower than in any other central and east European country formerly dominated by communism. This initial finding does not confirm what historical cultural legacy theories would predict.

The two Romanian regions I compare are, according to Huntington (1996), border areas of two different types of European civilizations. If we assume that this hypothesis of a cultural divide is true, we should find a lasting effect of this divide reflected in a different distribution of support for democratic values and patterns of political behaviors in these two regions. We expect a significant variation because these two regions. First, Region 1 and Region 2 belonged to different Empires – one was under the reign of the Habsburgs, the other under the Ottomans. Second, they are home to people of different religious denominations and ethnicities – one region is dominated by Roman and Greek Catholics, whereas belief in the Orthodox faith is characteristic of the other region. Third, their levels of social and economic modernity before World War II were significantly different. However, our results show that the distribution of democratic values and political behavior does not fit the expectations based on historical cultural legacy theories. What differences exist simply do not align in accordance with the predictions of such theories.

Thus, our findings indicate that the two lines of reasoning on which the historical cultural legacy approach is grounded cannot explain the Romanian case. The current distribution of political values and attitudes cannot be related to the pre-communist era and the earlier historical circumstances, such as the Empires the regions belonged to, the dominant religions or the levels of socio-economic modernity. This conclusion may be challenged because the two regions neighbor one another and therefore diffusion of attitudes and lifestyles cannot be excluded (even if migration seems to be of no importance during the last 25 years). However, even if diffusion had occurred, one would expect that differences should show in the older age cohorts' political values and beliefs in comparison to those who were born after World War II. It is an empirical fact that this is not the case. Therefore, we have to assume that either there were no differences of political values, beliefs and behavior in pre-communist times, or that communist institutions destroyed and changed the effects of early socialization experiences. There may be some other explanation for this phenomenon but the fact remains that values were not transmitted from the pre-communist period across the communist era into the present.

The more general implication of our findings is that different types of historical cultural legacies are not necessarily linked with current cultural conditions of a transition from communism to a liberal democracy. The Romanian case cannot be used to fully demonstrate that pre-communist period characteristics have no impact on or are unimportant to present political culture. However, at least it indicates that only when more refined historical attributes will be taken into account and when their variance across regions is large enough, a causal effect on today's democratic values, beliefs and behavior can be posited.

Notes

1 Currently, the name "Transylvania" does not have any administrative meaning and historically it does not refer to exactly the same territory as today. In this analysis, "Transylvania" includes the regions Banat, Crisana-Maramures and Transylvania, which are identified by the codes 5, 6 and 7 in the World Values Surveys data.
2 Until 1992, the PDSR was called the Democratic Front of National Salvation (FDSN).
3 At the time of survey, 60 years of age was used as a threshold between the two cohorts.

4 In each of the log linear models that included REGION, AGE and an indicator for democratic attitudes, the third order effects were not significant at the 0.05 level.
5 There are large differences between survey results on membership in at least one voluntary association due to the way questions are asked. In eight national surveys, the minimum is 3.7 percent and the maximum is 25.7 percent (Bădescu 2003).
6 Region 1 is closer to the west European countries, and also has more flight connections to the capital city and to foreign destinations.
7 Robert Putnam's study on regional differences in Italy (1993) is an example for this category.

References

Bădescu, G. (1999) "Miza politică a încrederii," *Sociologie româneasca*, New series 2.
Bădescu, G. (2003) "Încredere și democrație în țările foste comuniste," in Pop, L. (ed.) *Valori ale tranzitiei. O perspectiva empirică*, Iași: Polirom.
Berglund, S. and Aarebrot, F. (1997) *The Political History of Eastern Europe in the 20th Century: the Struggle Between Democracy and Dictatorship*, Cheltenham: Edward Elgar.
Dakova, V., Dreossi, B., Hyatt, J. and Socolovschi, A. (2000) *Review of the Romanian NGO Sector: Strengthening Donor Strategies*, report commissioned by Charles Stewart Mott Foundation and Charity Know How (CAF).
Fuchs, D. (1999) "The Democratic Culture of Germany," in Norris, P. (ed.) *Critical Citizens: Global Support for Democratic Government*, Oxford: Oxford University Press.
Fuchs, D. and Klingemann, H. (2000) *Eastward Enlargement of the European Union and the Identity of Europe*, Discussion Paper, WZB.
Fuchs, D. and Roller, E. (1998) "Cultural Conditions of the Transition to Liberal Democracy," in Barnes, S.H. and Simon, J. (eds) *The Postcommunist Citizen*. European Studies Series of the Hungarian Political Science Association and the Institute for Political Sciences of the Hungarian Academy of Sciences, Budapest: Erasmus Foundation and Hungarian Academy of Sciences.
Ghețău, V. (1997) "Evoluția fertilității în România. De la transversal la longitudinal," *Bibliotheca Demographica No. 5/1997*, Bucharest: Romanian Academy.
Huntington, S.P. (1996) *The Clash of Civilizations and the Remaking of the World Order*, New York: Simon & Schuster.
Inglehart, R. (1997) *Modernization and Postmodernization: Cultural, Economic, and Political Change in 43 Societies*, Princeton: Princeton University Press.
Kuti, É. (2001) *Nonprofit Organizations as Social Players in the Period of Transition: Roles and Challenges*, unpublished manuscript.
Lipset, S.M. (1959) "Some Social Requisites of Democracy," *American Political Science Review*, 53, 1.
Lipset, S.M. (1994) "The Social Requisites of Democracy Revisited," *American Sociological Review*, 59: 1.
Livezeanu, I. (1995) *Cultural Politics in Greater Romania: Regionalism, Nation Building and Ethnic Struggle, 1918–1930*, Ithaca: Cornell University Press.
Mureșan, C. (1999) *Evoluția demografică a României. Tendințe vechi, schimbări recente, perspective (1870–2030)*, Cluj-Napoca: Presa Universitară Clujeană.
Putnam, R.D. (with Robert, L. and Nanetti, R.Y.) (1993) *Making Democracy Work: Civic Traditions in Modern Italy*, Princeton: Princeton University Press.

Reisinger, W.M. (1999) "Reassessing Theories of Transition Away From Authoritarian Regimes: Regional Patterns among Postcommunist Countries," paper presented at the 1999 Annual Meeting of the Midwest Political Science Association, Chicago, 15–17 April.

Rohrschneider, R. (1999) *Learning Democracy: Democratic and Economic Values in Unified Germany*, Oxford: Oxford University Press.

Rose, R., Mishler, W. and Haerpfer, C. (1998) *Democracy and its Alternatives: Understanding Post-Communist Studies*, Baltimore: The Johns Hopkins University Press.

Rotariu, T. (1993) "Aspecte demografice in Transilvania, la începutul secolului al XX-lea," *Sociologie Românesca*, 4, 2.

Rotariu, T. and Mezei, E. (1999) "Asupra unor aspecte ale migraţiei interne," *Sociologie românesca*. Serie noua 3.

Rotariu, T., Semeniuc, M. and Pah, I. (1996) *Studia Censualia Transilvanica. Recensământul din 1857*, Bucuresti: Editura Staff.

Sandu, D. (1999) *Spaţiul social al tranziţiei*, Iaşi: Polirom.

Stan, L. and Turcescu, L. (2000) "The Romanian Orthodox Church and Post-Communist Democratization," *Europe-Asia Studies*, 52, 8.

Tóka, G. (1995) "Political Support in East-Central Europe," in Klingemann, H.D. and Fuchs, D. (eds) *Citizens and the State*, Oxford: Oxford University Press.

Verba, S., Schlozman, K.L. and Brady, H.E. (1995) *Voice and Equality: Civic Voluntarism in American Politics*, Cambridge, MA: Harvard University Press.

Wagner, P. (2001) "Transformation in Eastern Europe: Beyond 'East' and 'West'," unpublished manuscript.

Part II
National perspectives

4 The Czech Republic

Critical democrats and the persistence of democratic values

Zdenka Mansfeldová[1]

Introduction

The current democratic regime in the Czech Republic did not develop in the classic "bottom-up" way in which the pre-war democracy of the Czechoslovak Republic emerged. The latter was a product of anti-feudal protest and it institutionalized democratic impulses from within an already existing civil society. Although the current democratic regime resulted from a revolt against communist rule, its institutional "skeleton" was established from above. The institutions were structured and established *a priori* instead of expressing and codifying democratization a posteriori.

However, this institutional skeleton has been in place for years, and seems to have contributed to consolidation of Czech democracy (Merkel 1996a, b; Lauth and Merkel 1997). After the consolidation of the institutional setting, delayed by the split of Czechoslovakia in 1993, a party system developed comparatively fast and served as a structure of interest mediation and political representation. Democracy is increasingly accepted as a regime able to produce and channel dynamic change. The years of stability and "crystal changelessness" (Havel 1989) are over.

Democracy as a political regime has no serious contenders today. Still, the skeleton lacks more flesh, i.e. a functioning civil society. The existing civil society of the pre-war Czechoslovak Republic was a complex network of various voluntary associations which was destroyed first during Nazi occupation and then through communist totalitarianism. However, a democratic community cannot be established from above, and the existing associations and interest organizations do not yet constitute a fully functioning civil society (Brokl 1997). This may explain a number of problems encountered in Czech democracy.

Low levels of participation in both parties and voluntary associations may result in policies that lack responsiveness to the interests of people and concentrate on macro-problems instead. Additionally, absent civic participation may promote the development of a "sclerotic" bureaucracy. Since the structure of interests that should be represented via the party system is not yet fully developed, politicians tend to waste their energy in petty struggles that confuse both the public and commentators in the media. Altogether, democracy in the Czech Republic seems to function on the formal level, while it suffers from a deficient political culture. The big business of politics is hard to handle for a young democratic regime that is not firmly rooted in national and European values and still struggles to find its own identity.

In the following sections we describe support for democracy and autocracy, political involvement, confidence in institutions, as well as attitudes relevant to an assessment of the ethos of political and civil community. In addition, the analysis allows us to inspect two hypotheses. The first is that Czech society maintained democratic values in spite of the communist regime and embraces democracy as an ideal form of government. From this follows the second proposition that efforts of the communist regime to socialize the older generation into an autocratic mind set were not successful in the Czech Republic.

Support of democracy and autocracy

Support of democracy and autocracy is measured by an index that combines the respondents' attitudes toward democratic and autocratic rule. With this index we distinguish strong democrats, weak democrats, autocrats and undecided citizens. Almost 90 percent of Czech respondents belong to the category of democrats. A third of them represent "strong democrats" (31 percent) who hold strong positive views about democracy, while 58 percent of citizens belong to the group of "weak democrats," who accept the democratic political system, with some reservations. An altogether autocratic orientation is expressed by 4.3 percent of the respondents, and 6 percent remain undecided.

Though citizens cherish the idea and values of democracy, they are rather critical of the way the political system currently works. Only a minority of (strong as well as weak) democrats considers the performance of the current regime as very good. The group where an autocratic orientation prevails exhibits the most critical attitude toward the performance of the political system. The group of strong democrats is least critical, while weak democrats, as indicated in Table 4.1, are less satisfied with the current political system.

Citizens aged 40 years and older are more likely to be found among democrats than younger respondents. In the group of strong democrats, 18.9 percent are forty-to-fifty years of age, 21.8 percent are between 50 and 60 years old and 29.5 percent citizens are over sixty years of age. In the group of weak democrats, the situation is very similar (20.1 percent, 20.5 percent and 23.8 percent, respectively).

With regard to party-political orientation, strong democrats are located predominantly in the center and right part of the political landscape. Weak democrats occupy the center-left. The group of autocrats is mar-

Table 4.1 Satisfaction with the performance of the current political system, 1998, %, Czech Republic

	The political system works				
	Very poorly				Very well
Strong democrats	13.2	19.0	42.3	23.8	1.7
Weak democrats	19.3	34.6	32.6	12.3	1.7
Autocrats	36.5	34.6	21.2	5.8	1.9
Undecided	33.3	31.3	22.9	10.4	2.1

ginal (4.1 percent). They are mostly situated in the center and the left part of the political spectrum.

The stable prevalence of democratic orientations among the respondents, a comparatively even distribution in the political spectrum with centrist accents and a small representation in the extreme left and right, as well as the critical and informed attitude of citizens with regard to the performance of the current political system, gives an impression of a civil society in which democratic values are safely rooted.

Delving into views on democracy in greater detail, we see that Czech respondents clearly favored democracy (86.4 percent) over other possible regimes. Only 8.8 percent assessed democracy negatively (Table 4.2). Another 4.8 percent were not able to answer the question.

Similarly, a majority (84.8 percent) agreed with the statement, "Democracy may have problems but it's better than any other form of government," while only 8.5 percent disagreed. "A strong leader who does not have to bother with parliament and elections" was disapproved of by 78.4 percent of the respondents; only 14.8 percent supported this idea. Yet these 15 percent will be misunderstood if plainly classified as "autocrats." The survey was conducted shortly after the end of the Klaus government, which was heavily criticized for its ultra-liberal policies that relied on a kind of "invisible hand." In the media, the "rule of a strong hand" was debated as a way out of the crisis and as an alternative to the Klaus style of

Table 4.2 Attitudes toward democracy, 1998, %, Czech Republic

	Very good	Fairly good	Fairly poor	Very poor	Don't know
Having a democratic political system	37.0	48.7	7.1	1.7	4.8
	Strongly agree	Agree	Disagree	Strongly disagree	Don't know
Democracy may have problems but it's better than any other form of government	32.4	52.4	6.9	1.6	6.7

governance. However, this alternative was never meant to be beyond parliamentary control. It might well be the case that at least some of the respondents who supported a strong leader in the World Values questionnaire did not realize that they expressed a preference for autocratic rule.

The army ruled was rejected by a majority of 91.4 percent of the respondents, while only 4.9 percent consider the armed forces as appropriate rulers (see Table 4.3).

An interpretation of the respondents' assessments of the efficiency of a democratic regime must distinguish the current democratic regime in the Czech Republic with its various forms during the last eight years from the ideal, the theoretical concept of democracy. However, respondents do not necessarily do the same when they evaluate democracy. They judge the regime on the basis of their experience; therefore, skeptical assessments do not automatically indicate autocratic attitudes (see Table 4.4).

A majority of the respondents (54.4 percent) does not agree with the statement, "In democracy the economic system runs badly," while 37.2 percent agreed; 8.5 percent remained indecisive. Those belonging to the thirty-seventh percentile group may have been individuals who have endured economic hardships over the last eight years due to the democratic regime. That said, these hardships derive from an industrial structure which is a product of Austro-Hungarian times. No regime has ever solved this problem, so democracy is no exception here.

Table 4.3 Autocratic attitudes, 1998, %, Czech Republic

	Very good	Fairly good	Fairly poor	Very poor	Don't know
Having a strong leader who would not have to respect parliament and elections	3.8	11.0	29.7	48.7	6.7
Having the armed forces rule	1.0	3.9	16.6	74.8	3.7

Table 4.4 Effectiveness of democratic rule, 1998, %, Czech Republic

	Strongly agree	Agree	Disagree	Strongly disagree	Don't know
In democracy, the economic system runs poorly	10.1	27.1	45.2	9.2	8.5
Democracies are indecisive and there is too much squabbling	10.2	43.4	34.0	5.3	7.1
Democracies are no good at maintaining order	7.7	32.8	43.9	8.3	7.4

Democracy was assessed as an "indecisive system which has too much squabbling" by 53.6 percent of the respondents, while 39.3 percent disagreed with this statement. These respondents refer to the current political situation in the Czech Republic, rather than to a generally negative attitude toward democracy. This is also indicated by the large share of respondents who agree that "Democracy may have problems but it's better than other forms of government" (85 percent), and the disagreement of 52 percent with the statement that "Democracies aren't good at maintaining order."

Political involvement

Democratic politics rest on citizen participation. How involved is the Czech populace in politics? What about political interest, electoral and other types of political participation, as well as membership in voluntary organizations?

Interest in politics

Among such activities as with the family, friends, at leisure time and work, politics is least important for the majority of respondents. However, religion may be even less important than politics. Subjective importance of politics reached its peak in the period after the revolution of 1990. Since then it decreased from 37.4 percent to 25.8 percent. At the time of the first free elections in 1990, almost every citizen was interested in politics (very interested: 72.5 percent; interested: 27.5 percent). In 1998, political interest declined to a level of 55.9 percent (very interested: 14.6 percent; interested: 41.3 percent). There are at least two possible explanations for the downward trend. First, it could be interpreted as a process of normalization. The extraordinary events of the revolution attracted a high level of attention, while mastering the problems of day-to-day life thereafter directed the attention of citizens to other spheres of life. Second, decline of political interest may have been caused by what was perceived "dirty" or "bad" politics. In this case, it is plausible to assume that people turned their back on political matters.

Political participation

Two types of political participation are considered here: electoral participation and non-institutionalized modes of participation such as signing petitions, lawful demonstrations, boycotts and the like.

The most widespread type of political participation is voting in general elections. Since the first free elections in 1990, voting levels decreased continuously from 96.8 percent in the elections to the Czech Parliament in 1990 to 74 percent in the 1998 elections. Apparently voting behavior has also "normalized." The reported preferences of voters surveyed regularly in opinion polls roughly correspond with the current representation of parties in parliament. In future elections, the number of parties in parliament will probably increase with the participation of the Green Party and the so-called Movement of Independents. The Communist Party and the right-wing Republicans are the most extremist political factions and they are rejected by a large majority of citizens.

Apart from voting, there are many other ways to participate in politics and public matters. When it comes to non-institutionalized modes of participation, signing petitions, participating in lawful demonstrations or boycotts, political participation is quite popular. The same is not true for activities such as participating in wild-cat strikes or occupying buildings. In these cases, the Czech population remains rather passive. These findings may explain why there have been comparatively few demonstrations or strikes in the country, despite of the fact that opinion polls indicate public dissatisfaction with the current political and/or economic situation.[2]

The transformation of the Czech Republic also involved a revival of civic associations within a renewed legislative framework. Citizens' interests demanded new intermediating associations. Apart from organizations that existed before the regime change, many new organizations were established.[3] The number of organizations does not indicate the level of active involvement of citizens. However, the associational landscape became more pluralized after 1990, and thus, the chances to participate increased.

Yet membership in voluntary organizations seems to be rather low.[4] The most popular associations are sport and leisure-time related. Membership in labor unions remains important, although their membership decreased.[5] A comparatively large share of the active labor force is organized in labor unions (roughly 40 percent). After the initial loss of prestige in 1990, the public image of labor unions gradually improved. This may also be promoted by increased cooperation between labor unions and the government.

Table 4.5 Membership in voluntary organizations, 1998, %, Czech Republic

Organization		*Active member*	*Inactive member*	*Not a member*
Political organizations	Political party	2.5	4.2	92.9
	Labor union	3.2	12.4	81.4
	Professional organization	3.6	5.3	90.5
	Church or religious organizations	4.7	11.9	83.2
	Environmental organizations	1.5	3.4	94.6
Societal organizations	Charitable organizations	1.1	2.6	95.7
	Art, music and education organizations	3.4	5.5	95.7
	Sport and recreation organizations	11.2	12.4	76.1
	Any other voluntary organization	7.8	9.5	82.0

The churches and religious organizations occupy the third rank with regard to level of civic membership. Although the newly achieved religious freedom did not lead to a massive increase in formal church membership, the willingness to work for charities (which have resumed their activities after 40 years of suppression) went up.

Confidence in institutions

To properly function, a democratic government and an open, pluralistic society need institutions that give citizens confidence to play by the rules. In this section we will present data about subjective confidence in government institutions, in the legal system and administration, in societal organizations and the mass media. The interpretation takes into account that low levels of confidence may reflect the attitude of a critical citizen. In addition, it is well known that most respondents have a tendency not to react to a particular institution as an abstract, generalized concept. Rather, they also consider the people who visibly represent these institutions. Whenever data from the 1990 World Values Survey are available in addition to the 1998 survey they will be compared.

Confidence in institutions of government

Institutions of government such as political parties or the parliament are part of an ongoing process of political competition which is often evaluated negatively by the citizen. Harmony and compromise are preferred over struggle and debate.

This attitude shows most clearly with respect to political parties. Barely 14.3 percent of respondents report confidence in political parties (a great deal of confidence: 0.8 percent; quite a lot of confidence: 13.5 percent), 81.8 percent do not trust political parties (not very much confidence: 54.2 percent; no confidence at all: 27.6 percent). Most respondents have an opinion; the proportion of respondents who say "don't know" is rather low (3.8 percent). These results may also be influenced by former President Havel who openly expressed that he favored political and social movements over political parties. Since he enjoyed high esteem by the public, his assessment of the emerging political parties may well have been influential.

If we compare confidence in political parties and confidence in the ecology movement and the women's movement, this expectation seems to be supported. The ecology movement attracted public attention from 1995 when – with the help of foreign allies – it started to organize a number of protest activities. The protest was directed against environmental destruction and pollution by large industrial plants, as well as against the government, in the conflict over the completion of an atomic power plant in Temelín. Roughly half of the respondents (52.6 percent) trusted Czech ecological movements: 46.9 percent expressed quite a lot of confidence, while 39 percent of the respondents did not trust these movements and 31 percent expressed not very much confidence.

Until recently, the women's movement has not been very well established in the Czech Republic. This may be explained in part by the fact that, in most instances, gender equality was formally achieved early on. In the Czech Republic, female labor-market participation has been at relatively high levels since World War II. Female suffrage was achieved as early as 1920. The communist party featured women's emancipation among their most important ideological topoi and thus won a high share of the female electorate in the last semi-free elections in 1946. Additionally, the communist regime institutionalized equal representation of women in political and societal organizations. Thus, female interests were, and are at least rhetorically, addressed in Czech society, and equality between men and women has been legally guaranteed for decades. Czech women are constantly told that their social surrounding is not gendered at all. This particular feature of post-communist societies makes it difficult to address women's problems for what they are, since the ideological denial of gender inequalities in a (post)socialist society systematically erased the need to think of such inequalities' existence. In 1998, 32.5 percent of the respondents expressed confidence in the women's movement. Of this group, 30.2 percent expressed quite a lot of confidence. Approximately the same share, 35.1 percent expressed not very much confidence, and 14.1 percent reported having no confidence at all. The percentage of respondents who "don't know" how to evaluate "women's movements" (21 percent) is very high. This points to the fact that the attitude object is not very familiar and many respondents may express an attitude that is not firmly crystallized. It is also possible that they rather refer a movement they know to exist in other countries. Nevertheless, confidence levels for these social movements are very much higher than confidence levels for political parties.

The parliament is the core institution of representative democracy. In 1990, 44 percent of respondents said that they had confidence in parliament. This figure dropped to 19.8 percent in 1998. Data provided by the Czech Institute for Public Opinion Polls (IVVM) indicate similar trends. The proportion of respondents having confidence in the parliament remained at the same high level until January 1992, with a slight decrease shortly before the summer elections in 1992 (40 percent). After the elections this percentage started to decrease until it reached the low level of 1998.

Finally, confidence levels are measured for two supra-national institutions of government, the European Union (EU) and the United Nations (UN). Both institutions are not part of the day-to-day Czech political competition, and it is expected that confidence levels are relatively high.

In 1990, 64.5 percent respondents reported having confidence in the

European Union; 33.9 percent did not. In 1998, this proportion had dropped to 43.7 percent, while 46.1 percent had no confidence. Apparently, in 1990, the vision of a fast and unconditional accession of the Czech Republic was widely shared and the public image of the EU was very positive. In 1998, the situation had changed. Czech citizens had realized that EU interests were not always compatible with their own, and that most of the time it was up to the Czech Republic to adapt. As a consequence, the proportion of indecisive citizens increased. In 1990, 11.4 percent of the respondents reported having a great deal of confidence in the EU, 6.4 percent indicated that they have no confidence at all and only 1 percent answered "I don't know." In 1998, 13.6 percent of respondents reported having no confidence at all, only 5.2 percent indicated a great deal of confidence and 10.1 percent answered "I don't know." The increasing share of "don't know" responses may signify that many citizens simply could not keep up with details of accession negotiations. In addition, some important political actors were Euro-skeptics and commented on EU–Czech relations accordingly.

The level of confidence in the United Nations is still higher than the level of confidence in the EU. In 1998, 56.5 percent of respondents had confidence in the UN and 34 percent did not. A relatively high proportion of respondents expressed a great deal of confidence (9.2 percent) and roughly the same percentage (8.9 percent) indicated that they had no confidence at all. The proportion of those who said they "don't know" (9.6 percent) seems to indicate a lack of information.

To sum up, in 1998 the two most important government institutions – political parties and the parliament – enjoyed the lowest levels of public confidence. The nature of day-to-day political conflict as well as the temptation to sell favors may explain this situation. Less well-known political actors such as the ecology movement or the women's movement, on the other hand, are not much affected. The same is true for the EU and the UN as supra-national institutions. However, as exemplified by the EU, it is important to note that this situation may change if such an institution becomes important for decisions that affect citizens' lives directly.

Confidence in the legal system, the administration and the army

By definition, the legal system, the various branches of the administration and the army should not be partial, nor part of political competition. Thus, it is generally expected that confidence levels in these institutions should be relatively high.

Thus, it is a matter of concern that the level of confidence in the legal system decreased from 1990 to 1998. In 1990, 42.9 percent of the respondents expressed a high level of confidence in the legal system, while 57 percent did not. In 1998, the share of respondents who were confident that the legal system acted as it should decreased by 14.5 percentage points to 28.4 percent. There are a range of possible reasons why this loss of confidence in the legal system occurred. First of all, the new legal system could not be established without employing personnel who had already served the "old" system and who were not properly retrained. Second, the Czech legal system had to be adapted to the standards of the European Union. This demanding process continues to cause problems. In addition, restitution, privatization and related cases did not go undisputed. Illegal economic practices in particular, unknown under the communist regime, evolved. No legal rules existed for offences of this type at the time. They had to be enacted by the legislature and, in the meantime, the authorities could not deal adequately with this new type of crime.

In contrast, the administration as well as the army gained more confidence in the eyes of Czech citizens. Levels of confidence in the civil service increased between 1990 and 1998, from 32.4 percent to 38.3 percent. Low levels of trust were expressed by 67.4 percent of respondents in 1990. In 1998, their share decreased to 59.5 percent. There is reason to believe that this positive development reflects the improvement of the quality of public services in general, and on the communal level in particular.

Confidence in the police increased most, gaining 11.4 percent points in the period between 1990 (32.0 percent) and 1998 (43.4 percent). Levels of confidence are well above average, despite the police's negative image in the media. After 1990, the Czech police was less associated with the old regime. And, apparently, Czech citizens seem to honor the effort of the police to fight crime, and the high price they pay for it.

The army, too, has a negative image in the media. Despite that, levels of confidence increased between 1990 and 1998. In 1990, 38.9 percent of the respondents expressed rather high levels of confidence, and in 1998 this share increased to 42.2 percent. In 1990, 61 percent of the respondents expressed no or low levels of trust, while this proportion decreased to 54 percent in 1998. As in the case of the police, the "communist factor" and the "human factor" may have played a role. First, leadership structures were changed as a consequence of the democratic revolution. This was welcomed by most Czechs. Second, it was recognized that soldiers tried to perform even if they had to cope with outdated military technology. Many incidents caused by this state of affairs were met with public sympathy.

Thus, with the exception of the legal system, Czech institutions regulating everyday life or offering the same conditions for all young Czechs such as the army have slowly but steadily made inroads into public opinion. This gives reason to be optimistic about Czechs' support of representative democracy.

Confidence in security organizations

Confidence evaluations are available for three societal organizations: the churches, labor unions and major companies.

The churches enjoyed a high level of confidence in 1990 (43.1 percent). However, this level of confidence decreased to 31.7 percent in 1998. The size of the group having no confidence in churches, on the other hand, increased from 56.7 percent in 1990 to 63.4 percent in 1998. In the Czech Republic, the term "church" is primarily understood as "Catholic Church" since the size of other denominations has declined drastically. The Protestants are likely to disappear in a secularized society and so are their churches. After the fall of communism, the Catholic Church had won public support because it had openly expressed dissent with the communist regime. These sympathies vanished quickly when the restitution of former church property became a main issue on the church's agenda. Czech Catholicism turned back to its traditional pattern, i.e. liturgy rather than ecumenism. Obviously, this development has not contributed to increasing levels of public confidence.

Between 1990 and 1998, the level of confidence in labor unions increased from 26.7 percent to 37.4 percent. The size of the group with no confidence in labor unions decreased from 72.8 percent in 1990 to 51.6 percent in 1998. Although roughly half of the respondents still mistrust labor unions, the 10 percent-point increase from 1990 to 1998 must be regarded as a success. Labor unions were not popular after 1990 because of their close ties to the old regime. Their task had been to organize labor to conform to the rules of the communist regime. Labor unions had a role in organizing vacations and leisure time; however, they were usually instruments of control and suppression. They definitely did not do what unions are supposed to do, namely, represent the interest of workers against the interest of capital. The increasing level of confidence in labor unions indicates that this picture is changing. However, under the condition of privatization and a difficult economic situation in general, there is not too much space for the labor unions to maneuver and strike deals which bring advantages to their members. And it does not help either when some employers try to intimidate union representatives within their companies.

In 1998, confidence in major companies shows roughly the same level as confidence in churches or labor unions. Thus, about a third of Czech citizens have confidence in these organizations, while more than half of the populace does not. Several privatization scandals and the fear of takeovers by multinational companies have influenced the negative public image of major companies. Examples of successful multinational investments with positive side effects for local communities have not yet served to change this image. Thus, 55.5 percent of the respondents have no confidence in major companies and only 34.1 percent have such confidence.

2.3 percent reported a great deal of confidence, while 13.6 percent had no confidence at all. Respondents who did not know how to answer the question numbered 10 percent.

Confidence in the mass media

Mass media have become more and more important in the process of political communication. They are by far the main source of information about the world of politics. Investigative journalism helps to keep politicians honest by pointing to misbehavior and corruption. Do Czech citizens consider information transmitted by the mass media reliable? The answer to this question is not easy. On the one hand, confidence levels for both the press and television (TV) are above average. On the other hand, there is still a majority of Czechs who are more cautious.

In 1998, 55.5 percent of the respondents have no confidence in the press. Conflicts between top politicians and journalists lead to this negative public image of the press. It could be shown that journalists had distorted what politicians wanted to communicate. The overall pictures is that 42.6 percent of citizens do have confidence in the press. Of these, 41.1 percent report having quite a lot of confidence, while 10.6 percent have no confidence at all. This is mainly due to the many true stories about fraud in the privatization processes, machinations on the political stage and other "watchdog" reports. The share of respondents who report being confident in television is slightly higher. In addition to the general TV stations, there are several TV programs that specialize in political information and current political events. The higher confidence levels in TV media as compared to print media confirms the expectation that people tend to believe what they can see. There are still 46.9 percent of respondents who report having no confidence in TV. Of these, however, only 7.6 percent say that they have no confidence at all.

Considering all 15 institutions for which information was available in 1998, the average confidence level is 37.6 percent. Above-average confidence levels prevailed with respect to the supra-national organizations (UN, EU) and the mass media (press, TV), but also with regard to such institutions as the civil service, the police and the army. At the low end of the confidence spectrum were political parties, the parliament and the legal system as well as societal institutions such as churches, major companies and labor unions. For a smaller number of institutions, confidence levels can be compared across time. Here we can observe that confidence has declined since 1990 for the parliament, the legal system, the churches and the EU. Confidence levels have increased for labor unions and, most remarkably, for order institutions such as the civil service, the police and the army – institutions which are of high importance for the life of ordinary citizens.

The ethos of political, economic and civil community

Tolerance

Tolerance and respect for fellow citizens are regarded as important characteristics for democratic citizens. In the set of qualities children should be taught in their families, tolerance and respect rank fourth after good conduct, diligence and a sense of responsibility. A large proportion of respondents stress the importance of good interpersonal relations. For a majority, good interpersonal relations are a precondition for understanding the "other" (60.7 percent), not just effective self-assertion.

Czech society, rather homogenous and isolated until 1990, has become more and more differentiated, with regard to income, lifestyle and social status, as well as to the ethnic origin of its residents. Czech citizens were not familiar with migration before 1990, and are only gradually gaining experiences with migrants who entered the country for better job opportunities or safety from conflicts in their home countries. Apart from migration, many Czech citizens have also experienced a new societal openness with regard to formerly taboo topics, such as divorce, abortion or homosexuality. Furthermore, minorities have begun to articulate interests which are increasingly recognized by legislative measures. There has also been a renaissance of traditional values which can, at least in part, be attributed to a reaction to new social developments that are sometimes experienced as frightening.

Compared to 1990, fewer people would mind having a neighbor who belongs to another ethnic group, despite a general tendency toward xenophobia in the Czech society. In addition, respondents express higher levels of tolerance toward homosexuality than they did in 1990. While the elderly and religious believers are less tolerant on this matter, a majority would at least not mind having a homosexual neighbor. Maybe public debates on homosexual partnerships and their legal recognition have contributed to this comparatively liberal attitude toward homosexuality.

The low – and, compared to 1990, declining – levels of tolerance toward abortion and divorce might be a result of the above-mentioned renaissance of traditional values. Divorce was a subject in debates related to the amendment of family law and a partial easing of divorce. Abortion has never been politicized in Czech politics as has been the case, for example, in Poland (Kitschelt *et al.* 1999). Various anti-abortion movements exist, but no political party attempts to mobilize on this issue. Again, the level of tolerance toward abortion decreases with age. The younger generation (18–25 years) either indicate complete refusal or a high level of tolerance.

Table 4.6 Tolerance, 1998, %, Czech Republic

	Homosexuality		Abortion		Divorce	
	1990	*1998*	*1990*	*1998*	*1990*	*1998*
Never justifiable	32.6	9.2	7.7	8.3	6.8	3.7
2	4.3	3.7	2.9	4.9	2.2	1.7
3	5.9	3.1	7.1	4.9	6.0	5.2
4	3.8	2.5	3.9	5.1	5.1	4.2
5	4.4	10.8	6.4	16.7	6.1	18.3
6	12.2	7.1	21.2	8.9	29.9	10.9
7	5.4	6.8	6.9	8.5	7.7	9.1
8	6.9	6.9	14.2	15.8	14.5	16.0
9	8.9	8.9	13.5	7.9	9.4	8.9
Always justifiable	15.5	15.5	15.8	15.1	12.1	18.5
D.K., N.A.	0.1	0.1	0.3	4.0	0.1	3.5
Total	100.0	100.0	100.0	100.0	100.0	100.0

Ethics of individual achievement

In 1990, 51.7 percent of the respondents agreed that people should take more responsibility for themselves, while 47.6 percent wanted to delegate this task to the state. Probably those who supported self-responsibility in 1990 expected increasing levels of individual welfare under the condition of a free-market economy. They anticipated better rewards for their work, reflecting their performance on the job and fewer taxes meant for redistribution. In 1998, however, only 29.7 percent of Czech citizens preferred self-responsibility to a paternalistic welfare state, while 57 percent called for a stronger involvement of the state.

Before we draw any conclusion from these findings, we have to take into account the political context at the time of the fieldwork. The World Values Survey 1998 was conducted in the Czech Republic in autumn 1998. At the end of 1997, the neo-liberal Klaus government was overthrown and early elections were held in the middle of 1998. However, even after the new elections, the waves of criticism did not die down. They were directed against a type of politics that regarded any kind of regulation of economic and social policy as a "communist" enterprise. Thus, results do not necessarily reflect a desire to return to a command economy. Rather, they indicate a rejection of ultra-liberal laissez-faire politics. This interpretation is also supported by the electoral results, which gave the liberal ODS another chance. Apparently, Czech citizens do not disapprove of liberalism in general, but of the rigid forms implemented by the Klaus government.

Private ownership, state ownership and management of industry

In 1990, 72 percent of the respondents supported private ownership of companies, while 27.4 percent preferred state-run companies. Eight years later, support of private ownership declined by 19 percent points (to 53 percent). Now, 41.5 percent of citizens preferred state ownership. These figures express the disillusion prevalent in 1998 regarding the success of economic restructuring measures and its opportunity costs for the individual employee.

Again, these findings must be interpreted in the light of a type of "Manchester capitalism" that prevailed in many post-communist countries after 1990. A small group of businessmen made their fortunes under the conditions of a weak state and a judiciary not yet fully in place. They were less successful in accumulating capital, and they often operated at high risk, sometimes illegally. Their gains were often achieved at the expense of the Czech population. In 1998, several spectacular cases of illegal (or quasi-legal) business practices became public and highlighted the inability (or unwillingness) of the Klaus government to regulate the Czech economy in a decent manner. Therefore our findings can be interpreted first and foremost as a call for a government that implements a legislative framework and strict rules for business activities, rather than as a desire to go back to a socialist economy.

Who should be in charge of management decisions in a company? A total of 42.7 percent of the respondents preferred a cooperation of owners and employees in 1990, while 34 percent deemed the single responsibility of the owners adequate. In 1998, this gap narrowed. A decisive role for the owners is supported by 39 percent of the respondents, while cooperation with employees is the first choice of 35.5 percent. Employees' ownership of enterprises and the election of managers by the employees were favored by 15.6 percent in 1990, while this share decreased to 6 percent in 1998. State interventions were favored by 7 percent of the respondents in 1990; their share increased slightly to 11.7 percent in 1998. The proportion of respondents unable to express a preference also increased, from 0.6 percent in 1990 to almost 8 percent in 1998.

Again, these findings do not necessarily reflect communist nostalgia. They may instead signify a reaction to problematic side effects of less successful cases of privatization, e.g. in public transport and healthcare. The declining popularity of employees' ownership from 1990 to 1998 indicates a rejection of the alternative of a "third way," after eight years of experience with a free-market economy.

Solidarity with the poor

Social and political changes during the last ten years led to increasing inequality among Czech citizens, i.e. to unemployment, an increasing number of homeless people and poverty. Additionally, poverty as a global phenomenon with local consequences came into focus when migration rates increased. Solidarity was a popular element of the agenda of the communist regime and a central ingredient of the "new socialist personality." Respondents' attitudes reflect both this heritage as well as experience with new types of poverty. Causes of poverty in the Czech Republic are mostly ascribed to socio-economic injustice (51.4 percent), rather than to individual failure. Citizens judge the chance to escape from poverty as rather small and express a conviction that governments should take more responsibility: 62.9 percent of the respondents think that the government provides too little help for the poor. Respondents express a similar opinion with regard to helping economically less-developed countries and their governments (57.5 percent). This attitude changes when it comes to immigration. In a situation of increasing unemployment[6] many Czechs feel threatened by immigrants. Immigration is mainly related to the labor market and perceived as making it harder to find a job. This is reflected in the attitude of 91.1 percent of the respondents that employers should hire fellow citizens rather than immigrants if unemployment is high.

Conclusion

The preceding analysis has produced mixed results. On the one hand, it has shown that an overwhelming majority of Czechs prefer democracy as the ideal form of government. It can also be demonstrated that confidence in a number of important order institutions has grown since 1990. In addition, attitudes which at first glance might signal a return to communist interventionism could also be interpreted as a reaction to extreme neo-liberal policies. Thus, in these respects the democratic skeleton seems to have gained more and more support from the Czech populace. Citizens were also able to distinguish between democracy as a form of government and the way the democratic process unfolded in their country. While supportive of the former, they were rather critical of the latter. Thus, those classified as "weak democrats" often turn out to be "critical democrats" who are aware of the deficits of contemporary Czech democracy. On the other hand, there are reasons to doubt whether representative democracy can persist in the long run with such extremely low levels of confidence in political parties, the parliament and the legal system. Additional analyses of the reasons for this situation are badly needed.

Our expectations regarding the maintenance of a belief in democracy as an ideal even under the conditions of the communist regime, as well as our expectation concerning the socialization hypothesis, are not contradicted. Additional evidence on this is presented in a 1968 study of attitudes of Czech citizens (Brokl *et al.* 1999). We do not find significant differences in the level of support for democracy as an ideal between the young generation on the one hand and the old generation on the other.

During ten years of transformation, citizens may have lost their illusions and, by now, are ready for a realistic assessment of political, social and economic developments. However, even if the pace of societal and political change enforces adaptations that are sometimes difficult to bear, an increasing proportion of Czech citizens consider themselves to be very happy or generally happy (82.7 percent in 1998 compared to 65.7 percent in 1990). In the last decade we also observed an increasing number of Czechs who are satisfied with their own life. The group of people who are convinced that they have influence over their lives and feel free to make their own decisions has also increased. This evaluation of the current life situation may turn out to be a good precondition for the development of civil society and democracy.

Notes

1 I would like to thank my colleague Lubomír Brokl, who was involved in the first version of this chapter, for his further help and valuable comments.
2 Until the end of 1996, strikes occurred very sporadically – indeed, their number was almost negligible. During the first half of 1997, strike activities increased (a general strike at the Railway Company, the strike of the employees of nurseries, basic and secondary schools). However, the amount of time spent on strike activities remains insignificant.
3 According to official statistics the largest increase in the number of civic associations and organizations occurred between 1991–3 (Kroupa and Mansfeldová 1997).
4 According to the Czech surveys, 24.6 percent of citizens in 1993, 37.3 percent in 1995 and 42.9 percent in 1996 reported to be members in voluntary organizations (Kroupa and Mansfeldová 1997).
5 In 1998, labor unions had about 1.4 million members.
6 In the Czech Republic, unemployment rates were 3.5 percent in 1996, 7.5 percent in 1998 and reached over 10 percent in the end of 2002.

References

Brokl, L. (1997) "Pluralitní demokracie nebo neokorporativismus," in Brokl, L. (ed.) *Reprezentace zájmů v politickém systému České republiky*, Prague: SLON.
Brokl, L., Seidlová, A., Bečvář, J. and Rakušanová, P. (1999) *Postoje Československých občanů k demokracii v roce 1968*, Working Papers 99: 8, Prague: Institute of Sociology, CAS.
Havel, V. (1989) *Dálkový výslech*, Prague: Melantrich.
Kitschelt, H., Mansfeldová, Z., Markowski, R. and Tóka, G. (1999) *Post-Communist Party Systems: Competition, Representation, and Inter-Party Cooperation*, Cambridge: Cambridge University Press.
Kroupa, A. and Mansfeldová, Z. (1997) "Občanská sdružení a profesní komory," in Brokl, L. (ed.) *Reprezentace zájmů v politickém systému České republiky*, Prague: SLON.
Lauth, H.J. and Merkel, W. (1997) "Zivilgesellschaft und Transformation," in Lauth, H.J. and Merkel, W. (eds) *Zivilgesellschaft im Transformationsprozess*, Universität Mainz, Politikwissenschaftliche Standpunkte, Band 3.

Merkel, W. (1996a) "Theorien der Transformation: Die demokratische Konsolidierung postautoritärer Gesellschaften," in von Beyme, K. and Offe, C. (eds) *Politische Theorien in der Ära der Transformation,* PVS-Sonderheft, No. 25, Opladen.

Merkel, W. (1996b) "Institutionalisierung und Konsolidierung der Demokratie in Ostmitteleuropa," in Merkel, W., Sandschneider, E. and Segert, D. (eds) *Systemwechsel 2. Die Institutionalisierung der Demokratie,* Leske + Budrich, Opladen.

5 Slovenia in central Europe
Merely meteorological or a value kinship?

Vlado Miheljak

Introduction

A few years ago, central Europe was rediscovering itself: the collapsing communist states were taking the *Mitteleuropa* concept as a kind of short cut out of autocracy into the realm of democratic states, while central European sentiment was resurging in the consolidated democracies of the region. Then the provocative Austrian writer Peter Handke, whom the Slovenes count as one of "their own" because of his Slovene mother, baldly and cynically joked that, for him, central Europe was merely a meteorological term. This provoked a wave of ire, particularly among intellectuals in the new democracies of the region, Slovenia included. Is central Europe really only connected by geography and meteorology? Or is it also bound together by culture and values? And what is Slovenia's place in it?

Slovenia encompasses several identities and traditions. On the one hand, its political and cultural history roots it in the heartland of central Europe; on the other, it was removed from this orientation during the 70 years it spent in the political space of the former Yugoslavia. When the Yugoslav state union slid into severe political and economic crisis, as well as a crisis of identity, following the death of Tito,[1] the Slovenes once again began to discover their dormant central European identity in the 1980s.

Slovenia was then doubly different in communist times.[2] First, it was different to the other Yugoslav republics in that it was the most developed, the most pro-Western and the most liberal republic. Second, it was quite different from the other eastern and central European countries. Sociological surveys of the value orientations of the general population and generational studies of youth (see Ule 1986; Hafner-Fink 1995) in the 1980s showed that, notwithstanding the wide economic and cultural differences between the former Yugoslav republics individually, the differences between Slovenia and all the other republics were greater than those among the latter. These differences were manifested as a split between traditional and secular–rational orientations regarding, for example, authority, political authorities, religion, gender roles, national identification. Actually, the first explicit conflicts between Slovenia and the federal establishment, which was taking ever-more regressive and authoritarian stances after Slobodan Milosevic took power in Serbia, did not concern political but value issues such as views on the death penalty, homosexuality and conscientious objection (the right to civil instead of military service).

What made Slovenia so distinctive? The answer may be found, above all, in the atypical homogeneous ethnic composition and religious denomination of its population. Practically all ethnic Slovenes declaring a religious affiliation identify themselves as Catholics.[3] Its ethnic composition was also atypical for the former Yugoslavia. It alone fitted Brunner's definition (1993) of a homogeneous nation-state, in which the titular nation makes up 90 percent or more of the population. Other post-transition states that fall into this category are Poland, Hungary, Albania and Armenia. Most of the former Yugoslav republics were "multi-ethnic" in the sense that, besides a titular nation with an unquestionable majority, there were one or more culturally, economically or numerically strong ethnic groups. Bosnia and Herzegovina came in the category of a "multi-nation-state" because there was not a single titular nation, which marked it as a country with a split ethnic awareness. Ethnic composition was a very important factor in shaping the transition to democracy. In principle, the transition was far more complicated, even bloody, in ethnically heterogeneous countries (in particular the ex-Yugoslavia and the ex-Soviet Union) because there was often an "ethnification of politics" (Offe 1994: 236) which subordinated the democratization process to "sovereignization," or the process of formal democratization merely as a precondition for creating a sovereign nation-state.

Another important feature of Slovenia was its relatively high economic development, amenable industrial composition and close ties to the western European market when compared with the rest of former Yugoslav and eastern Europe in general. While the former Yugoslavia was still functioning, Slovenia – by far its most developed part – was in a good position, with a large and relatively undiscriminating market for any excess output that it could not sell on the more demanding western European market. This advantage waxed from one year to the next and consequently stoked the differences between Slovenia and the other parts of the country, not only economically but also in terms of the political atmosphere.

As a typical central European country, Slovenia withstood systematic and sometimes forcible "socialist modernization" much more easily than the other, more rural and traditionalist parts of former Yugoslavia. Its industrial composition was suited to resist this process. It was a typical central European country of small towns and it developed small-scale, market-oriented industries producing general goods, whereas the other more rural parts of the Yugoslav federation were invested by the state with heavy industry which was always unprofitable and also forcibly changed the social structure (rapid and mass transformation of farm into industrial workers) and ecologically damaging.

Consequently, Slovenia embarked on the transition adventure far better prepared than the other post-Yugoslav states. Although the actual act of independence was accompanied by a military intervention which caused Slovenia to lose the greatest part of its markets, and in spite of recessions in 1992 and 1993, by 1997 Slovenia's GDP had surpassed its level in the year the former Yugoslavia had begun to come apart, 1990. Besides Poland, it was the only transitional country to achieve this by 1997.[4] Moreover, Slovenia started from a substantially higher base level than Poland. For that year, its per capita GDP_{ppp} (Purchasing Power Parity)[5] was $14,000, by far the highest of all the transition countries.

Slovenia also stood well on certain other indicators of the potentials of and the barriers facing the transitional countries. With regard to crime rate (total registered crimes), on which Romania is the infamous leader with a staggering index of 684 in 1996 (relative to 1989), the Czech Republic recorded an index of 328, and Hungary 213, Slovenia was one of the few with an index below 100 (92).[6] Its positions on various other indicators of "sore points" for transitional countries are similarly positive and, indeed, usually the most favorable. As a consequence, it also ranks considerably below the other countries in the region on the corruption index.

Income inequality has grown far less rapidly and scandalously than in countries in which equality was an imperative prior to transition. From 1987 to 1993, the Gini index rose 65 percent in Bulgaria, while Slovenia, at 17 percent, came in lowest. The situation is similar with registered poverty[7] where, in 1995, 13.5 percent of the population were below the poverty line which, together with Estonia's 8.9 percent, is far below the average for eastern Europe, where the proportion ranges between a quarter to a fifth of the population, and is even considerably higher in the CIS (Commonwealth of Independent States).[8] Expenditures for food in 1997, at 23 percent of total consumption expenditures, were similarly among the lowest of the 4 transition countries. Finally, Slovenia's comparative advantage is reconfirmed each year by its quality-of-life scale ranking on the Human Development Index (HDI). In 1997, it ranked twenty-eighth on an absolute world ranking, surpassing some of the tail-end EU countries.[9] Only the Czech Republic (thirty-fifth), Slovakia (forty-second), and Hungary (forty-seventh) made it into the first fifty that year.

The third exceptionally important advantage over the other former Yugoslav republics, and even more so the other central and east European countries, was that Slovenia lived next door to two western countries (Italy in the West and Austria to the north), with completely open borders.[10] This enabled relatively high mobility[11] and hence information and techno-logical up-to-dateness. As a result, the collapse of the communist system did not bring the cultural shock most of the other transitional countries experienced when the borders were opened to consumer goods and new social styles, and curbs on the media were removed.[12]

Even more than a decade after democratic transition and the consequent border openings, the share of the population of the entire region that travels abroad is still by far the highest in Slovenia, as shown by Eurobarometer surveys of the EU candidate countries.[13] Whereas 77 percent of the population in Slovenia traveled abroad in the previous two years, the average for the 13 other candidates is 23 percent. Moreover, as many as 74 percent of Slovenians had visited one of the EU countries, while the candidate average is 16 percent. Knowledge of foreign languages is also comparably favorable. Slovenia has the highest percentage of the population speaking a foreign language, 91 percent, compared with the candidate average of 48 percent. A total of 71 percent speak one of the major west European languages, 46 percent English (candidate average 16 percent) and 38 percent German (candidate average 10 percent). The age distribution of knowledge of a foreign language is also substantially more than in other central and east European countries, because even in communist times the most common language taught in schools was English, followed somewhat less frequently by German.

Such was Slovenia's dowry when it embarked on transition and established itself as a consolidated democracy. Did these undeniable advantages at the very start also constitute a real advantage in consolidating democracy? Did the initial advantages hold in the post-transition stage as well?

Attitudes toward the national community

Slovenia may be described as a country without state continuity and yet with relatively high ethnic awareness. Slovenes tie their identity above all to the ethnic and not the national or political context.[14] While it was part of Yugoslavia for a long time, there was a dual identity, Slovene and Yugoslav: the Slovene was primarily an ethnic and the Yugoslav a political identity. With the process of the break-up and final collapse of the former Yugoslavia in 1990, and the foundation of the first independent state of Slovenia, a national identity gradually began to form, with a switch from the ethnic to the political context. Namely, in Slovenia the transition to democracy simultaneously constituted a transition to state sovereignty. So it is possible to speak of processes of democratization and sovereignization. In some countries, the drive for democratization was above all a way to sovereignization (e.g. Tudjman's Croatia), and vice versa in others: sovereignization was a necessary condition for democratization. The latter holds to a great degree for Slovenia since the desire for sovereignization was not the key and fundamental popular demand.

What is the basic identity, the basic features of the Slovenian?[15] The World Value Study (WVS) examines types of identity, from local to global.[16] As Table 5.1 shows, most Slovenians divide their identity between

Table 5.1 Reference to geographic location (first choice)

Geographic group	Nation								
	Hungary	Poland	Czech Republic	Slovenia	Bulgaria	Romania	Croatia	Slovakia
Town	37.8	31.9	38.7	46.0	47.2	50.4	69.3	60.2
Region	3.4	15.2	16.2	9.2	5.0	16.3	8.8	9.6
Nation	49.0	44.3	37.1	38.7	39.9	27.6	16.5	22.9
Continent	5.0	6.0	3.3	1.3	3.0	3.3	1.2	3.2
World	4.8	2.6	4.7	4.8	4.9	2.4	4.2	4.1

the local and national level, with somewhat more opting for the local level. Why is this so? The WVS (1995) survey reveals certain typical differences between countries. Namely, respondents from Hungary and Poland most often identify at the national level, in the Czech Republic roughly the same number opt for the national as the local level, while in other transition countries the preference is mostly for the local. The group of countries in which the local level predominates includes those without a state tradition (the so-called historically late nations without state continuity: Slovenia, Croatia, Slovakia) on the one hand, as well as Bulgaria and Romania, which are classified among countries with state continuity and traditions, but which also belong in a different (Orthodox Christian) cultural–religious group and derive from a different (more authoritarian) pre-democratic background.

Adding the first and second choices in a "multiple response" expression partially alters the relationship between local and national identification. Thus the Czech respondents come into the group most frequently citing a national reference, while in Slovenia and Bulgaria the frequencies of the two references are more or less equalized, although each group, with either a predominantly local or national reference, is generally preserved. The influence of personal satisfaction with the current political system in general and the assessment of the efficiency of the current government on variation in identification at the national level were examined. Assessment of the work of the government in Slovenia was not found to affect differences in identification, but satisfaction with the political system did.

With respect to the level of identification, on both choices Slovenia falls around the average of comparable countries of the region. It is difficult to unequivocally determine what is a high and what a low degree of identification. Comparison of the findings with those for established democracies

Table 5.2 Attitudes toward the national community in 11 countries (reference to the nation as a whole)

Nation	
Hungary	85.4
Poland	73.2
Czech Republic	70.4
Slovenia	73.2
Bulgaria	77.5
Romania	61.7
Croatia	55.6
Slovakia	59.2
USA	60.8
Norway	57.6
West Germany	55.3
East Germany	53.1

(USA, Norway, Germany) shows that, on average, identification with the nation is, as a whole, lower in these than in the post-transition countries. The differences between these latter countries are not unequivocal, and it is hard to find a common denominator in the post-transitional context. Thus with Germany, for instance, we find that despite wide differences in perception of the political situation, the prospects for society and the country, common and personal prospects, and differences in the political socialization of the greater part of respondents from the new and the old federal states, differences in identification are negligible. It is truly difficult to explain the differences among the post-transition countries. How can the high percentage of responses in Slovenia and the low percentage in neighboring Croatia be explained? Likewise, how can we account for the differences between the Czech Republic and Slovakia, which shared a common state for centuries? It is clear; identification with the nation as a whole is not correlated with the degree of national pride. Namely, whereas there are wide differences in identification with the nation and it is substantially lower in the three established democracies than in the post-transitional ones, this is not the case with the degree of national pride. Only in Germany do respondents (from both the old and the new federal states) express a low level of national pride. The following table presents the combined percentages of "very proud" or "quite proud" responses.[17]

The level of national pride varies considerably from one established democracy to another. It is exceptionally high in the USA (98 percent) and low in the old part of Germany (57 percent). Variation is relatively high in the central European countries such that it is approximately as high in Poland as in the USA, while the lowest level, in Slovenia, is nonetheless quite high (73.2 percent). The influence of satisfaction with the work of the present government and assessment of the present political system on national pride was examined. Satisfaction with the

Table 5.3 Identification with national community – national pride

Nation	
Hungary	91.9
Poland	97.1
Czech Republic	85.8
Slovenia	73.2
Bulgaria	77.5
Romania	84.4
Croatia	81.9
Slovakia	89.7
USA	98.0
Norway	89.1
West Germany	57.1
East Germany	62.0

work of the government did not have a substantial influence on national pride, while a correlation with perception of the political system was indicated, although it was weak. There are reasons for assuming that a high level of national pride is related to traditional authority. Using WVS (1990) data, Inglehart (1997: 85) found a high correlation between the importance of religion and national pride. Slovenia deviates here in that it shows relatively high national pride, yet it is quite secularized at the same time.

The materialist–post-materialist dimension of expressions of national pride was also examined. As Table 5.4 shows, certain differences were found between materialists and post-materialist attitudes with regard to expression of national pride which, however, do not allow a firm conclusion regarding the expected post-materialist shift away from a high level of national pride. There were no significant differences for Slovenia in 1995, while Hungary and Croatia show significant differences (namely, materialists express greater national pride).

Similarly, no significant differences were found on an urban–rural division, which was indirectly analyzed through the responses regarding size of settlement. However since the central European geographical area, and Slovenia especially, has a distinctive settlement pattern – a large number of small towns with 2,000 to 10,000 inhabitants[18] – it is very difficult to determine the type of residential milieu (urban–rural), which is an important factor in shaping the micro-socialization climate, from this size criterion. As a consequence, in the Slovenian survey we employed an additional question about the type of settlement the respondent lives in (town, suburban, village), which gives a much more meaningful response. Cross tabulation of these three settlement categories shows significant differences (at the 0.001 level) with rural respondents expressing greater national pride.

Expression of national pride does not coincide with readiness to fight for one's country.[19] Whereas in Slovenia the percentage of respondents

Table 5.4 National pride and index of materialism–post-materialism

	Materialists	Mixed type	Post-materialists
Hungary*	91.1	94.3	66.7
Poland	96.8	97.2	98.2
Czech Republic	86.7	84.9	87.9
Slovenia	90.4	92.4	88.8
Bulgaria	83.2	86.4	90.5
Romania*	89.4	81.0	71.2
Croatia*	90.1	81.6	66.5
Slovakia*	93.1	86.9	87.5

Notes
* Significant at the 0.05 level or below.

expressing national pride was the lowest in the central European region, the percentage affirming they are ready to fight for the homeland was the highest (81.9 percent). There are considerable between-country differences. Thus, in the Czech Republic, the group ready to fight for the country and the group that is not so inclined are practically even. Germany and Croatia are also interesting. The former has the unpleasant experience of fighting for the homeland deeply impressed in collective historical memory and there is a low level of readiness. In Croatia, impressions from the war that had just ended in the mid-1990s were still fresh when the survey was conducted. This probably explains the considerable difference from neighboring Slovenia, even though the two countries rank close together on the chart of basic values (position on the traditional versus secular–rational authority and the survival versus self-expression axes),[20] although they are rather wide apart with respect to readiness to fight for the homeland.

In Slovenia, readiness to fight for the homeland is not influenced by the attitude toward the present government, unlike most other countries in the region (greater satisfaction with the government indicates greater readiness to fight). There are significant differences with regard to satisfaction with the political system. When the ten-point satisfaction scale is re-coded into a three-point scale, with 1–4 categorized as satisfaction, 4–5 as a mean estimate and 6–10 as dissatisfaction, in Slovenia 79.1 percent of those who are dissatisfied would fight for the homeland, and 88.1 percent of those who are satisfied with the political system would fight (the difference is significant at the 0.016 level). The differences are univocal and significant for all countries in the region with the exception of Hungary. The rural–urban division does not distinguish respondents according to readiness to fight for the homeland. Similarly, this readiness does not vary with respect to the materialism–post-materialism axis.

Table 5.5 Would you be willing to fight for your country? (% yes)

Nation	
Hungary	61.8
Poland	72.2
Czech Republic	43.9
Slovenia	81.9
Bulgaria	55.0
Romania	70.5
Croatia	66.6
Slovakia	52.4
USA	68.5
Norway	86.6
West Germany	41.9
East Germany	44.0

Political involvement

Competent political judgment and activity, according to Hopf and Hopf (1997) do not spring from a developmental, age-defined legal status (e.g. the acquisition of active and passive voting rights), but rather by induction into the political culture through political socialization (in Almond's sense). Depending on their particular life circumstances and situation, the members of a political community achieve different levels of political maturity and competence, which vary not only between individuals but also between groups, and thus impart the predominant characteristics of a society's political culture. The determinants of political culture are sets of attitudes, values and perceptions, as well as knowledge and expectations regarding the political system. In their renowned study, *The Civic Culture*, Almond and Verba (1963; 1989) examined the status of the political culture and "awareness" of the participants in political affairs in five countries (USA, Britain, France Germany, Italy and Mexico) and constructed a typology from the empirical data with three characteristic social roles or behaviors that determine the particular type of society. The three roles are adopted in every political system: participants, subjects and parochials. The equivalent and consequence are three dominant types of political cultures: a participatory, passive submissive and a parochial culture. Participants are politically informed and interested and take a rational approach to politics; they want to take part in decisions. Passive subjects have certain formed views, attitudes toward the political system and its effectiveness but at the same time they are passive consumers of politics – usually they also respect the authorities and government without great reflection and presumptions. The parochials hardly take politics seriously, do not consider it the center of social regulation and do not have any opinions on political roles. "Civic culture" does not, however, take any pure form, rather it is always a "mixed political culture" (Almond and Verba 1989: 29). This is to say that, in any society, a certain number of people will take an active role in politics, many will be passive subjects and some will be parochials who do not even notice politics. The ratios among these three groups (particularly the first and second) determine the character of a particular society. Almond and Verba went on to draw up a schema of ideal types of developed industrial societies on the basis of this empirical research, namely, a democratic and an authoritarian. This distinction has once again become relevant after the collapse of the communist empire.

Today, a citizen's attitude toward politics is determined by cognitive political mobilization, which is dependent on the level of political interest and subjective political competence (self-rated understanding of politics),[21] as well as on the degree of involvement in politics, as evidenced by political affiliation on the one hand and a more abstract confidence in politics on the other. According to Fend (1991) one has to fulfill two "developmental roles" on entry into the world of politics. The first concerns the relationship between the capacity to show loyalty in principle to the democratic order and, at the same time, a capacity for political critique and distance, merging both dimensions into a productive stance toward politics. "Hitches" in attempts to productively synthesize these two dimensions are seen, according to Fend, in an unformed confidence in the system which can either generate radical right-wing potentials on the one hand or lower critical potentials or political activity in general due to political disinterestedness and inadequate information.

The specific task in the sphere of politics, according to Fend, concerns building party identification. Political parties serve the supporter as a generator of a kind of historical political conceptualization of society and the state. They act, then, as clarifiers and arbiters of social issues and problems. Parties with different orientations (social democratic, conservative, liberal, ecological, etc.) and similarly various civil society movements presume clear differences that allow the individual to take a particular position. Determining how a decision for or choice of a particular political party is made, which personal and social traits it is dependent upon and which socialization level it affects is, according to Fend, the subject of political socialization research. For him the formation of political identity involves a relationship between the level of political interest and the finality of choice of party. An individual is politically affiliated if their political interest is high and they support a particular party. When political interest is high but there is no affiliation to a party, the individual is undecided/seeking. And when political interest is low but the individual nonetheless is affiliated to a party they are classed as pre- or passively affiliated. Finally, one with low political interest and no party affiliation is diffuse or apolitical.

WVS (1995) examined political motivation directly, with a battery of three questions (political interest, importance of politics and political discussion). The broadest indicator is an estimate of political interest.[22]

Table 5.6 Political involvement: political interest (very or somewhat interested)

Nation	
Hungary	49.7
Poland	42.1
Czech Republic	55.9
Slovenia	43.8
Bulgaria	43.1
Romania	39.5
Croatia	42.1
Slovakia	58.0
USA	64.2
Norway	68.6
West Germany	77.9
East Germany	75.7

On self-rated political interest, Slovenia falls around the average for the central European region. The Czech Republic and Slovakia show above-average interest and Romania below-average. Despite considerable mutual differences, there is an appreciable common difference from the three established democracies (USA, Norway, West Germany). Respondents from the eight new democracies show a lower level of political interest than those from the three established democracies.

Identification with a party is relatively low in Slovenia. Slovenian respondents more frequently showed no party identity (did not say which party they would vote for) in response to the question dealing with party identification than respondents in other central European countries. They usually show an even lower level of explicit party identification in similar surveys. As such, in the WVS (1990) survey, as many as 53.4 percent did not have or reveal any direct party identification.

Political identity takes shape at the intersection of the level of political interest and party identification. Employing Fend's model, according to the data from WVS (1995), 36.3 percent of respondents were politically affiliated (affiliated to a party and with high political interest), slightly fewer, 32.4 percent, were passively involved (party affiliation with low political interest) and the least (7.6 percent) were politically interested but have no party identification. Finally, 23.8 percent were apolitical with no expressed political interest and with no party identification.

Slovenian respondents group together with Hungary, the Czech Republic and Slovakia, in which cognitive political involvement (affiliated to a

Table 5.7 Political involvement: absence of party identification (percentage of respondents failing to choose any party)

Nation	
Hungary	21.8
Poland	19.9
Czech Republic	22.7
Slovenia	31.4
Bulgaria	–
Romania	28.7
Croatia	8.1
Slovakia	13.4

Table 5.8 Typology of political identity – Slovenia

Level of political interest	Party affiliation	
	Affiliated (%)	Non-affiliated (%)
High	Politically affiliated (36.3)	"Seekers" (7.6)
Low	Passively tied (32.4)	Diffuse or apolitical (23.8)

Table 5.9 Typology of political identity – seven countries

Nation	Hungary	Poland	Czech Republic	Slovenia	Romania	Croatia	Slovakia
Politically affiliated	42.2	36.8	47.7	36.3	34.7	40.1	53.2
Passively tied	36.0	43.4	29.9	32.4	36.8	51.9	33.4
"Seekers"	7.5	5.3	8.2	7.6	4.8	2.1	4.9
Diffuse or apolitical	14.3	14.5	14.5	23.8	23.7	5.9	8.6

party, political interest expressed) predominates, whereas the political identity of Polish, Romanian and Croatian respondents predominantly takes the form of ritual or formal involvement (affiliation to a party without articulated political interest).

The second indicator of political involvement is the self-rating of the importance of politics in one's everyday life.[23] The level of importance of politics in the post-communist countries of central Europe is considerably lower than in the three established democracies, and lowest in Slovenia. It is difficult to explain the de-politicization of everyday life in Slovenia in terms of objective indices of the position of the country and its inhabitants, or subjective perceptions of the social climate. On the one hand, it is a country without state continuity, and on the other it does not have the pre-World War II democratic traditions of some of the other central European countries, so a participative political culture would not have been taken for granted. On the other hand, Slovenia had throughout enjoyed relatively good material conditions, free of great social upheavals and in a rather liberal atmosphere, which precisely passivized its citizens politically. By contrast, Poland, for example, was continuously rocked by social and political unrest, which mobilized a considerable part of its population. The new federal unit of Germany (former East Germany) also deviates

Table 5.10 Political involvement: importance of politics in 11 countries (very or rather important)

Nation	
Hungary	27.2
Poland	30.7
Czech Republic	25.9
Slovenia	14.0
Bulgaria	25.5
Romania	25.0
Croatia	26.3
Slovakia	28.5
USA	59.2
Norway	44.9
West Germany	54.8
East Germany	47.2

Table 5.11 Political involvement: political discussions with friends (frequently or occasionally)

Nation	
Hungary	72.9
Poland	67.9
Czech Republic	81.1
Slovenia	75.3
Bulgaria	71.2
Romania	75.7
Croatia	83.8
Slovakia	80.3
USA	73.2
Norway	85.9
West Germany	89.6
East Germany	88.5

considerably from the other new democracies. The attribution of greater importance to politics in everyday life in that country probably may be explained in part by the earlier political culture, which remained "inscribed" in the collective memory, and to a greater extent to the intensive events of the latter half of the 1980s when the wave of democratization struggles politicized the broad masses.

The third indicator of political involvement is the frequency of political discussions in the respondent's social circle.[24] The differences in frequency of discussions about politics between the new and established democracies are smaller than the considerable differences in the importance attributed to politics. Slovenia falls around the central European average in frequency of political discussions, but the differences are not great.

Confidence in institutions

In the context of his research into political culture in the mid-1960s, David Easton (1965) constructed his theory of political legitimacy in which the degree and form of support for the political order is the foundation of legitimacy. In contrast to the non-democratic, a democratic order is dependent on legitimacy and almost universal acceptance and acknowledgement of the rules for settling conflicts, among other things. In their study, *Beliefs in Government* (1995), Kaase and Newton maintain that legitimacy simply means that the populace approves of the institutions, procedures, norms and values of the system of government itself. However, the concept of legitimacy transcends the borders of democracy. Namely, even a non-democratic regime may be legitimate in the eyes of its subjects. As a consequence, researchers seek (not very successfully) more complex and discriminating instruments to determine confidence and support. In practice, basic indicators and complex indices based on data on confidence in institutions and the bearers of political order and authority (of every kind) are measured.

In his study of confidence in the democratic system in Slovenia, Toš (Toš 1999) found that, in general, confidence in every institution lagged behind that in the developed democratic countries. Table 5.12 presents data based on the WVS (1990)[25] and shows a marked lag in confidence in the parliament which is half that in the western European established democracies (Italy deviates here with a low level of confidence). Similar comparative lags may be seen in confidence in the police, the legal system, trade unions, civil service, the church and major companies. Confidence in the education system is approximately the same in Slovenia as in the established European democracies, while confidence in the media is higher.

Confidence in institutions, when not situationally determined (such as regarding a particular government, the person of the premier or state president), is predominantly dependent on the place of these institutions in the political cultural context and the country's state traditions. As a consequence, the high level of confidence in Great Britain in the armed forces, or the church in certain traditionally Catholic countries may be seen in this light. In particular the level of confidence in the legal system, the police and parliament coincides with the status of the political culture of a particular country. With respect to confidence in these institutions, Slovenia is closer to the new central European democracies than to the established ones.

As is evident from Table 5.13, which compares eight post-communist countries in the region, there are both common features and some differences among them in levels of confidence. Attitudes toward the church show that secularization processes have not had a great impact on confidence in the church. Both religion and confidence in the church have been preserved in some countries with the most hard-line socialism (such as Romania), but much less so in others with the most liberal communist regimes (such as Slovenia and Hungary). There are similarly no significant differences related to church denomination. Religious belief and confidence in the church are highest in Catholic Poland and Orthodox Christian Romania, while the most marked secularization is seen in the Catholic Czech Republic and Orthodox Christian Bulgaria. Catholic Slovenia is somewhat specific because a relatively high proportion, 71 percent, declares membership to a church yet, like the Czech Republic, it shows the lowest level of confidence in the church.

Although the central European post-communist countries do not differ from the established democracies in level of confidence in the church, they differ widely from them in confidence in the legal system, which is one of the major post-transitional phenomena and, at the same time, the most serious legitimacy problem in the new democracies of eastern and

Table 5.12 Confidence in institutions in selected western European countries (WVS 1990) and Slovenia in 1992 and 1995

	Sweden	Germany	Netherlands	United Kingdom	France	Italy	Europe	Slovenia 1992	Slovenia 1995
The Church	38	40	32	43	50	63	50	39	37
Armed forces	49	40	32	81	56	48	50	45	43
Education system	70	54	65	47	66	49	67	67	72
Legal system	56	65	63	54	58	32	64	50	34
Media	33	34	36	14	38	39	33	49	42
Trade unions	40	36	53	26	32	34	40	27	23
Police	74	70	73	77	67	67	75	51	46
Parliament	47	51	54	46	48	32	50	36	24
Civil service	44	39	46	44	49	27	45	40	27
Major companies	53	38	49	48	76	62	41	33	37

Table 5.13 Confidence in institutions (a great deal of confidence and quite a lot of confidence)

	Hungary	Poland	Czech Republic	Slovenia	Bulgaria	Romania	Croatia	Slovakia
The Church	42.7	65.9	31.7	37.7	51.8	77.9	57.4	57.4
Armed forces	56.6	75.1	42.2	44.7	75.7	79.9	78.6	65.7
Police	54.9	51.3	43.4	46.3	48.1	37.8	59.4	39.0
Legal system	50.8	48.3	28.4	35.9	35.5	42.7	51.4	40.9
TV	39.8	45.3	49.1	53.0	63.2	47.4	22.0	49.8
The press	30.6	43.1	42.6	43.0	41.0	34.1	22.4	41.4
Trade unions	23.9	26.5	37.4	25.2	26.9	27.9	23.8	31.9
Political parties	19.2	11.0	14.3	13.7	26.7	13.0	22.4	21.1
Parliament	37.6	31.1	19.8	24.7	42.2	18.2	41.8	28.9
Civil service	50.3	31.2	38.3	28.9	28.9	25.3	37.9	38.9
European union	57.7	47.4	43.8	42.2	52.4	39.1	33.0	49.9

central Europe. Namely, the populace in the mature democracies has a high level of confidence in the legal system, and hardly any in the media. It is precisely confidence in the media that reveals the significance of the confidence paradox in the post-transitional countries in comparison with the established democracies. That is, whereas the level of confidence in the media is relatively low and the level of confidence in the legal system relatively high (at least higher than in the media) in the established democracies, the situation in the post-transitional countries is the reverse (with some exceptions, such as Croatia and Hungary) and the populace trusts the media (particularly television), but not the legal system.[26] This reversed logic of confidence, a transitional legitimacy paradox of sorts, represents quite a serious problem in consolidating democracy. Why is this the case? Low efficiency is characteristic of the court system in the eastern and central European new democracies, as evidenced in particular by great backlogs due to the slow processing of court cases or even excessive, years-long waiting lists for cases to be heard.[27] As a consequence, the rule of law is not adequately guaranteed to individuals or institutions. On the other hand, the relatively low critical distance from the media is due to either a lack of experience with a free media or to the important affirmative role played by the media in the transition from the authoritarian one-party systems to democracy. The climate in the media was rather liberal in Slovenia in the last decade of the communist system and the media made a quite important contribution to the peaceful, conflict-free transition out of the one-party into the democratic system.

The low level of confidence in the institutions of the polity cannot be explained, either wholly or even mainly, in terms of the particular culture of trust or confidence and the general political socialization of the respondents or the post-communist countries as a whole. It is also dependent in good part on situational determinants that let down the great expectations that had been attached to the political changes. The following table shows the great decline in confidence in the legal system and in parliament after the initial years of transition (WVS 1990). Data from the 1999/2000 European Values Study is also presented for comparison. Despite the consolidation of democracy in most of the region's countries, confidence has continued to decline since the mid-1990s, or even deepened at the close of the post-transition decade. In 1999, there was a rise in confidence in the legal system in Slovenia, an exception in the region.

Attitudes toward other citizens

The attitudes that members of a political community have toward each other are relevant for the behavior of the members and their political cooperation. Of major importance is the trust in each other and the tolerance toward each other.

Table 5.14 Confidence in the legal system and parliament from 1990 to 1999

Confidence in	Year	Hungary	Poland	Czech Republic	Slovenia	Bulgaria	Romania	Croatia	Slovakia
The legal system[1]	1990	59.6	48.4	45.6	50.8	45.5	47.6	–	37.6
	1995	50.8	48.3	28.4	35.9	35.5	42.7	51.4	40.9
	1999	45.3	41.9	23.3	43.7	27.8	40.1	30.6	35.6
Parliament	1990	39.9	78.9	48.5	35.7	48.7	20.8	–	35.5
	1995	37.6	31.1	19.8	24.7	42.2	18.2	41.8	28.9
	1999	34.0	32.8	12.2	25.3	27.4	19.2	20.7	42.8

Trust and tolerance

The levels of trust in others and tolerance toward others are especially important factors in the formation of social cohesiveness. Classical philosopher and sociologist Georg Simmel argued that "trust is one of the most important synthetic forces within society" (1950: 326). Moreover, he maintains that personal acquaintance is not necessary for trust and, consequently, trust enables social interaction and cooperation with strangers. Furthermore, as Sztomka wrote much later, "Trust breeds trust; trust received is usually reciprocated" (Sztomka 1997: 14). Finally, trust is an important component of so-called social capital. "By social capital I mean features of social life – network, norms, trust – that enable participants to act together more effectively to pursue shared goals" (Putnam 1995: 664–5).

Trust is therefore a necessary but not sufficient condition for establishing and maintaining the democratic order. Of course confidence in institutions is as necessary for the normal functioning of an open society as trust in the participants. It is difficult to say what degree of trust is necessary for the "normal" functioning of an open, democratic society. Many researchers (e.g. Sztomka 1995) see the problem in post-communist consolidation of democracy as one of insufficient trust in participants and institutions. The post-communist countries show a strong lag behind the established democracies in confidence in institutions of the polity as well as trust in others.

Trust in others is low in all the central European countries examined, and it is lowest in Slovenia. This ranking is found repeatedly. In general, Slovenia counts in various studies as an example of a country with an exceptionally low level of trust in others (see Delhey and Newton 2002).

Table 5.15 Trust in others (most people can be trusted)

Nation	
Hungary	22.5
Poland	16.9
Czech Republic	27.2
Slovenia	15.3
Bulgaria	23.7
Romania	17.9
Croatia	22.8
Slovakia	25.8
USA	35.2
Norway	64.8
West Germany	39.9
East Germany	24.3

Tolerance toward others – rejection of minority groups

A frequently studied feature of post-transitional development is the emergence of strong nationalistic sentiments and marked ethnic, social and cultural distance from marginal groups. There are differences among the post-communist countries, but they are smaller than would be expected in view of the varying independence and democratization processes. Just how peaceful or violent transition was depended in great part on the complexity of the national composition of each particular country. This was at least the case with the former Yugoslavia. Thus, Slovenia was the only part of the Yugoslav entity to escape the general fate because its ethnic composition was so homogeneous and simply did not have sufficient grievances for ethnic-based clashes.

As evident from the table, the level of rejection of minority groups is considerably lower in the established than in the new central European democracies. Actually the table presents an absurd picture. Croatia, where an ethnically based war had been raging not long before, stands closest to the level typical of the established democracies.

An index of distance was computed from statements of rejection of other races, foreign workers or Muslims as neighbors[29] by allocating one point to each of the three groups cited (so that the possible score is 0 to 3 points). With 67.6 percent of respondents not rejecting any of the three groups, Slovenia shows a relatively low level of rejection of others. Deviating from the average is the high level of rejection of Muslims in the Czech Republic and Slovakia, though these countries actually have had little experience of living with Muslims. In countries that have had more experience (such as Croatia), the level of rejection is considerably lower. Slovenian respondents have had experience with both foreign workers and Muslims, and fall around the mean position between the most and the least tolerant.

Table 5.16 Rejection of minority groups

	Would not like to have as neighbours		
	People of different race	*Immigrants/foreign workers*	*Muslims*
Czech Republic	10.5	28.1	45.5
Slovakia	13.5	18.4	68.4
Poland	19.9	21.0	25.7
Hungary	18.6	24.9	MD
Slovenia	17.1	18.0	22.8
Croatia	8.4	6.8	14.3
Romania	29.7	32.8	30.4
Bulgaria	17.3	15.6	16.7
USA	7.1	9.5	12.3
Norway	8.2	9.8	19.3
West Germany	2.1	4.3	9.2
East Germany	3.6	10.0	15.8

Table 5.17 Rejection of minority groups index (no data on Muslims for Hungary)

No. cited	Poland	Czech Republic	Slovenia	Bulgaria	Romania	Croatia	Slovakia
0	65.2	45.5	67.6	71.2	53.3	79.0	28.8
1	13.6	31.8	16.0	14.5	17.6	14.5	49.4
2	10.5	15.8	7.2	8.0	12.1	4.4	16.7
3	10.7	6.9	9.1	6.3	17.0	2.0	5.8

Political culture and democratic potentials

WVS (1995) measured so-called "democratic potential" as an indicator of political culture by directly examining support for democratic rule and rejection of autocratic rule. These items produced greater differences than most of the other indicators dealt with in this chapter. Besides Bulgaria, Slovenia showed the lowest support for the pro-democracy statement "having a democratic system" and somewhat lower support for the statement "Democracy may have its problems but it's better than any other form of government." Variation among the post-transition central European countries is relatively low on these two items. The support of democracy is in all countries at a higher rate than 80 percent of all respondents. The question measuring attitudes toward autocratic rule evoked somewhat different results. However, in Slovenia the directly autocratic position was not supported and, in rejection of autocratic rule, the country shifted over to the group with few people preferring autocratic rule. With respect to the autocratic view, "Having a strong leader who does not have to bother with parliament and elections," Romania and even more so Bulgaria deviated with substantially higher support than in the other central European countries. Despite considerable variation among them, the central European countries nonetheless differ appreciably from the three established democracies (USA, Norway, Germany) on this statement. An exception here is the former East Germany, with a very low level of agreement with this autocratic view.

The items in Table 5.18 ("Having a democratic system"; "Democracy may have its problems but it's better than any other form of government"; "Having a strong leader who does not have to bother with parliament and elections," and "Having the army rule") were combined into a robust democracy–autocracy index with a range from −8 to +8 (−8 the most autocratic stance; +8 the most democratic). On this scale, Slovenia scored 2.7 points. This means that Slovenia, compared to the other central and eastern European nations, takes a median position. The score is lower than in Hungary, the Czech Republic and Croatia; however it is higher than in Bulgaria and Romania. Despite wide differences among the countries of this region, they all lag significantly behind the established democracies (less so behind the USA, more so behind Norway and Germany).

Table 5.18 Attitudes toward democracy and autocracy

	Czech Republic	Slovakia	Poland	Hungary	Slovenia	Croatia	Romania	Bulgaria	USA	Norway	West Germany	East Germany
Attitudes toward democratic rule												
Having a democratic system (very or fairly good way of governing)	90.8	92.4	MD	90.9	86.4	98.4	91.4	85.8	90.9	96.3	96.3	95.3
Democracy may have its problems but it's better than any other form of government (agree or agree strongly)	91.0	88.9	88.4	84.9	88.2	94.3	86.9	80.6	92.0	95.0	93.9	92.3
Attitudes toward autocratic rule												
Having a strong leader who does not have to bother with parliament and elections (very or fairly good)	15.9	19.0	MD	18.7	24.9	30.3	47.3	62.7	6.6	4.6	0.8	2.1

Table 5.19 Democracy–autocracy index (−8 to +8)

Hungary	3.1
Poland	–
Czech Republic	3.2
Slovenia	2.7
Bulgaria	1.2
Romania	2.2
Croatia	3.5
Slovakia	3.1
USA	3.4
Norway	4.3
West Germany	4.2
East Germany	3.4

The scale of the index was broken up into four major groups, namely:

1 "Strong democrats" (5–8 points): assess democracy very positively and autocracy negatively.
2 "Democrats" (1–4 points): differ in that their assessment of democracy is, on balance, merely positive.
3 "Undecided citizens" (0 points): composed of respondents who express a relatively balanced mixture of preferences for democracy and autocracy, or of those who feel unable to give any answer at all.
4 "Autocrats" (−1 to −8 points): respondents who give a favorable assessment of autocracy and simultaneously an unfavorable evaluation of democracy.

Table 5.20 shows the yield for the following distribution of categories for the countries of the region.

Slovenia falls somewhat behind the countries with the highest share of strong democrats yet, at the same time, has a below-average share of autocrats.

Compared with other post-communist countries, the central European countries come quite close to the established democracies. Bulgaria (with

Table 5.20 Democracy–autocracy index – four-level classification

	Autocrats	Undecided citizens	Democrats	Strong democrats
Hungary	4.8	6.9	28.3	60.0
Poland	n/a	n/a	n/a	n/a
Czech Republic	3.2	4.8	27.4	64.6
Slovenia	7.0	6.0	31.6	55.5
Bulgaria	16.9	15.4	46.1	21.6
Romania	10.3	10.8	39.9	39.0
Croatia	3.9	5.3	25.8	65.1
Slovakia	4.1	5.1	28.5	62.3

Table 5.21 Percentage of "strong democrats" in relation to the materialism–post-materialism dimension

	Materialists	*Mixed type*	*Post-materialists*
Hungary	54.9	66.9	76.9
Czech Republic	58.8	65.2	80.2
Slovenia	50.0	54.4	69.2
Bulgaria	18.9	23.2	38.6
Romania	32.6	42.4	67.3
Slovakia	59.2	63.6	73.5
Croatia	49.4	67.7	85.0

Table 5.22 "Strong democrats" in relation to rejection of minority groups index

	Rejection of minorities			
	0 cited	*1 cited*	*2 cited*	*3 cited*
Hungary	64.1	54.2	46.1	–
Czech Republic	69.2	63.8	60.2	48.1
Slovenia	60.6	54.7	42.5	29.3
Bulgaria	23.2	12.3	27.9	17.6
Romania	43.8	34.4	37.3	29.9
Slovakia	60.3	63.6	65.0	53.1
Croatia	67.2	60.3	49.1	50.0

21.6 percent) and Romania (with 39 percent) deviate considerably from them on the share of strong democrats, and most of the other post-communist countries even more so. Therefore, the category of "strong democrats" accounts for just 2 percent in Russia, 3 percent in the Ukraine and 6 percent in Belarus.

The share of strong democrats was analyzed on the materialism–post-materialism dimension. As is evident from Table 5.21, in all eight countries there is a substantially higher share of strong democrats among the post-materialist than among the materialists or the mixed type.

The distribution of strong democrats was also examined in relation to the Rejection of Minority Groups index. The following table shows the share of strong democrats in each of the four categories of the index. For Slovenia there is a significant correlation in general: strong democrats make up 60.6 percent of respondents who do not reject any minority group, and only 29.3 percent of respondents who reject all three minority groups (people of different race, immigrants/foreign workers and Muslims).

Conclusion

What may then be concluded? The position of Slovenia on the democracy–autocracy index fits the findings of some other surveys of democratic potentials (see Plasser *et al.* 1997; Fuch and Klingemann 2000). All of these studies confirm that, on the one hand, the clear majority of the citizens of Slovenia support democratic rule and that only a relatively small minority has a preference for autocratic rule; and on the other hand, they also show that the democratic potential is somewhat lower, as one would expect from its marked initial advantages, which were outlined at the beginning of this chapter.[31] Despite its various initial advantages in comparison with other relatively successful transitional countries, Slovenia's lack of a democratic tradition is its weakest point. In a country in which democratic experience is not inscribed in personal or collective memory, democratic potential is not axiomatically woven into the prevailing political culture.

Although the transition to democracy did not proceed equally smoothly in all the post-transition countries of central Europe,[32] they do not differ widely in democratic/autocratic potentials. They show lower democratic potential than the developed European countries with a long democratic tradition. However, they surpass the southern European countries (Spain, Portugal and Greece) that made the transition much earlier. Slovenia neither leads nor lags behind the other post-transitional countries of the region. While there are differences among them, the narrow group of central European countries (the Czech Republic, Slovakia, Hungary, Poland, Slovenia, Croatia and former East Germany) have many common features. In reply to Handke's provocative definition, it may be concluded that central Europe is more than just a meteorological concept – it represents a compact island of shared values in the world sea of cultures and political cultures.

Notes

1 Josip Broz Tito died in 1981.
2 For a detailed analysis of Slovenia's distinctive position in the former Yugoslavia and in the ex-communist camp, and the features of the transition to democracy, see Toš and Miheljak 2002a, b.
3 In the World Value Survey (1995), 71 percent of respondents declared themselves Catholic, 1.8 percent Protestant, 1.8 percent Orthodox, 1 percent Muslim; 21 percent of respondents who did not declare a religion came from a Catholic background.
4 See *Human Development Report for Central and Eastern Europe and CIS 1999*, United Nations Development Program (UNDP).
5 In 2000, GDPppp rose to $17,367, lengthening Slovenia's lead over the other central and eastern European countries.
6 *Human Development Report for Central and Eastern Europe and CIS 1999*, United Nations Development Program (UNDP).
7 Applying $4 per day as the poverty line (1990), the UNDP estimates that the percentage falling below it in eastern Europe and the CIS climbed from 4 percent in 1988 to 32 percent in 1994, or from 13.6 million to 119.2 million. See *Human Development Report for Central and Eastern Europe and CIS 1999*, United Nations Development Program (pp. 20–1).

8 The country data is not directly comparable because poverty is defined as a percentage of the minimum wage (less than 50 percent), yet the differences in base wages are wide.

9 Slovenia retains its ranking (twenty-ninth) in the Human Development Report for 2002, while Slovakia and Hungary achieved the greatest progress of all the central European countries.

10 Yugoslavia was exceptional in the whole of the socialist central and eastern European area in that it completely opened its borders to the West in the early 1960s, allowing its citizens to travel abroad as tourists, privately and as economic emigrants to the West.

11 From the late 1960s onwards, Slovenians, like other Yugoslav citizens, went to work in western Europe in large numbers. Economic emigration thus became a powerful modernizing impulse. This was particularly so for the less-developed parts of Yugoslavia.

12 Owing to its particular location and its smallness, Slovenia was covered by western television signals even before the era of satellite and cable television.

13 *Candidate Countries Eurobarometer 2001*, European Commission, Brussels: March 2002. Available from: europa.eu.int/comm/public_opinion. The survey covered the full slate of candidates for EU accession from central and eastern Europe: Lithuania, Latvia, Estonia, Czech Republic, Slovakia, Poland, Hungary, Slovenia, Bulgaria and Romania as well as Cyprus, Malta and Turkey.

14 Indeed, in the Slovene language, like most Slavic languages, the national entity is generally conceived of as an ethnic rather than a state entity.

15 *Slovenec* is translated variously here: Slovene is used to refer to the ethnic group as such, Slovenian to the political group, which may be made up of different ethnic groups.

16 The precise phasing of the question: "To which of these geographical groups would you say you belong first of all? (1) locality or town where you live, (2) state or region of the country where you live, (3) (the own nation), (4) (the own continent), (5) the world as a whole?" Two responses are allowed. Due to semantic difficulties, the English term 'nation' is translated in the Slovene questionnaire as 'country': the country as a whole (Slovenia).

17 Question V205 says: "How proud are you to be (substitute own nationality)? (4) Very proud, (3) quite proud, (2) not very proud, (1) not at all proud, (1) I am not (national)."

18 In the WVS (1995) survey, in Slovenia as much as 63 percent of respondents lived in towns with less than 5,000 inhabitants, yet this in no way means that they come from a rural area. The Slovenian WVS (1995) database therefore shows that, in the category of towns with 2,000 to 5,000 inhabitants, 37 percent of respondents came from an urban, 43 percent from a suburban and only 20 percent from a rural village environment.

19 Question V110 says: "Of course, we all hope that there will not be another war, but if it were to come to that, would you be willing to fight for your country? (3) yes, (1) no. Don't know and missing values (2)."

20 See Inglehart in Fuchs *et al.* (ed.) (2002).

21 Almond and Verba (1963) introduced the concept of subjective political competence to denote the subjective feeling that we can have an influence on political decisions.

22 Question V117r says: "How interested would you say are you in politics? (4) very, (3) somewhat, (2) not very, (1) not at all interested?"

23 Question V7r says: "Please say for each of the following, how important it is in your life. Would you say.... Politics is (4) very important, (3) rather important, (2) not very important, or (1) not at all important?"

24 Question V37r says: "When you get together with your friends, would you say you discuss political matters (3) frequently, (2) occasionally, or (1) never?"
25 WVS (1990) was carried out in Slovenia in 1992.
26 Some international surveys measuring confidence in institutions of the polity include confidence in the courts, and have shown an even wider difference between this and confidence in the media (high in the media and low in the courts). See *Neue Demokratien Barometer* (1995) in Plasser *et al.* (1997).
27 On numerous indicators and criteria, Slovenia is rated as one of the best-prepared EU accession candidates but, according to European Commission estimates, with respect to efficiency of the court system, it is the least adapted to EU norms.
28 In *EVS 1999/2000: the Justice System.*
29 The precise wording of the question is: "On this list are various groups of people. Could you please sort out any that you would not like to have as neighbors?"
30 No data on Muslims available for Hungary.
31 At the start of transition, Slovenia had the lead on most indicators, from the highest GDP to the lowest number of years of Leninist rule in Slovenia and former Yugoslavia (see Fuch and Klingemann 2000).
32 Consider the events in Croatia during Tudjman's time, or in Slovakia in the Meciar era.

References

Almond, G.A. and Verba, S. (1963) *The Civic Culture: Political Attitudes and Democracy in Five Nations*, Princeton, NJ: Princeton University Press.

Almond, G.A. and Verba, S. (1989) *The Civic Culture Revisited*, London: Sage.

Brunner, G. (1993) *Nationalitätenprobleme und Minderheitenkonflikte in Osteuropa: Strategien und Optionen für die Zukunft Europas*, Gütersloh: Bertelsmann Stiftung.

Candidate Countries Eurobarometer 2001, European Commission, Brussels, March 2002. Online, available at: europa.eu.int/comm/public_opinion.

Delhey, J. and Newton, K. (2002) *Who Trust? The Origins of Social Trust in Seven Nations*, Berlin: Wissenschaftszentrum Berlin für Sozialforschung (WZB).

Easton, D. (1965) *A System Analysis of Political Life*, Chicago: University of Chicago Press.

Fend, H. (1991) *Identitätentwicklung in der Adoleszenz: Lebensentwürfe, Selbstfindung und Weltanneignung in beruflichen, familiären und politischweltanschaulichen Bereichen*, Entwicklungspsychologie der Adoleszenz in der Moderne. Bd. 2. Bern/Stittgart/Toronto: Hans Huber.

Fuchs, D. and Klingemann, H. (2000) "Eastward Enlargement of the European Union and the Identity of Europe Discussion," Berlin: Wissenschaftszentrum Berlin für Sozialforschung (WZB).

Fuchs, D., Roller, E. and Wessels, B. (eds) (2002) *Bürger und Demokratie in Ost und West: Studien zur politischen Kultur und zum politischen Prozess*, Wiesbaden: Westdeutscher Verlag.

Haerpfer, C.W. (2003) *Democracy and Enlargement in Post-Communist Europe*, London: Routledge.

Hafner-Fink, M. (1995) *Socioloska razsezja razpada Jugoslavije (Sociological Dimensions of the Break-up of Yugoslavia)*, Ljubljana: Faculty of Social Sciences.

Hopf, C. and Hopf, W. (1997) *Familie, Persönlichkeit, Politik. Eine Einführung in die politische Sozialisation*, Munich: Juventa Verlag.

Human development Report for Central and Eastern Europe and CIS 1999, United Nations Development Program (UNDP).

Inglehart, R.F. (1997) *Modernization and Postmodernization: Cultural, Economic and Political Change in 43 Societies*, Princeton: Princeton University Press.

Inglehart, R. (2002) "Cleavages in the European Union: Modernization and Culture Persistence," in Fuchs, D., Roller, E. and Wessels, B. (eds) (2002) *Bürger und Demokratie in Ost und West: Studien zur politischen Kultur und zum politischen Prozess*, Wiesbaden: Westdeutscher Verlag.

Kaase, M. and Newton, K. (1995) *Beliefs in Government*, Oxford: Oxford University Press.

Offe, C. (1994) *Der Tunnel am Ende des Lichts: Erkundungen der politischen Transformation im Neuen Osten*. Frankfurt a.M: Campus Verlag.

Plasser, F., Ulram, P.A. and Waldrauch, H. (1997) *Politischer Kulturwandel in Ost-Mitteleuropa: Theorie und Empirie demokratischer Konsolidierung*, Leske + Budrich, Opladen.

Putnam, R.D. (1995) "Tuning In, Tuning out: the Strange Disappearance of Social Capital in America," *Political Science and Politics* 28.

Simmel, G. (1950) *The Sociology of Georg Simmel*, trans. by Wolff, K. (ed.) Glencoe: Free Press.

Sztomka, P. (1995) "Vertrauen. Die fehlende Ressource der postkommunistischen Gesellschaft," in Nedelmann, B. (ed.) *Politische Institutionen in Wandel: Kölner Zeitschrift für Soziologie und Sozialpsychologie*, Opladen: Sonderheft 15.

Sztomka, P. (1997) *Trust, Distrust and the Paradox of Democracy*, Berlin: Papers des Wissenschaftszentrum.

Toš, N. (1999) "Razumevanje politike in zaupanje v politike (Understanding of Politics and Beliefs in Politicians) *Teorija in praksa*: 36, 6, November/December.

Toš, N. and Miheljak, V. (eds) (2002a) *Slovenia Between Continuity and Change 1990–1997: Analyses, Documents and Data*, Berlin: Edition Sigma.

Toš, N. and Miheljak, V. (2002b) "Transition in Slovenia: Toward Democratization and the Attainment of Sovereignty," in Toš, N. and Miheljak, V. (eds) *Slovenia Between Continuity and Change 1990–1997: Analyses, Documents and Data*, Berlin: Edition Sigma, 13–41.

Ule, M. (1986) *Mladina in ideologija*. Ljubljana: Delavska enotnost.

6 Hungary
Structure and dynamics of democratic consolidation

Christian W. Haerpfer

Introduction

The end of communism started with an event at the Hungarian–Austrian border in May 1989. Hungarian politicians arguably dismantled the Iron Curtain – assisted by the Austrian Foreign Minister and observed by Hungarian and Austrian media – by providing their fellow citizens with international passports. In September 1989, the Hungarians finally permitted citizens of the German Democratic Republic to pass the same Hungarian–Austrian border to leave towards West Germany. According to some scholars (e.g. Swain 1993) these political events in Hungary at the dusk of communism were of significant importance for accelerating the speed of the central and eastern European revolution at the end of 1989. Hence, it is not an historical exaggeration to postulate that the first cracks in the Iron Curtain in the *annus mirabilis* of 1989 occurred in the Hungarian part of the communist bloc. Over 15 years after the events of 1989, the democratic transformation of the Hungarian political system is almost complete.

   This chapter focuses on an analysis of political attitudes of Hungarian citizens. Particular attention is given to support of democracy and related attitudes and values. The first section deals with support for democracy. In addition to the database especially generated for this volume, we also make use of data collected in 1994, 1996 and 1998 by the New Democracy Barometers and related surveys. This enables us to put support for democracy in Hungary in a cross-time and cross-country perspective. The second section analyzes the acceptance of political tolerance, of the principle of non-violence and support of solidarity with the poor in Hungary. The third section focuses on political motivation and protest behavior. The topic of section four is civil society. The impact of selected variables on attitudes toward democracy and autocracy is measured by multivariate regression analyses. A multivariate regression model that integrates the whole set of democratic attitudes is presented in the conclusions.

The dynamics of democratic consolidation in Hungary between 1989 and 1999

Political scientists generally tend to agree that Hungary, together with Poland and the Czech Republic, belongs to the leading troika of democratic consolidation in post-communist Europe (see Derleth 2000; Haerpfer 2002) There are different types of transformation processes. Hungary is the best example of a gradual and slow transformation. Its success was promoted through proto-forms of pluralism and market economy that existed in Hungary as early as in the 1980s. In addition, the Hungarian transformation was a non-violent one (in contrast to, say, Romania), and based upon elite consensus (Derleth 2000). Rudolf L. Tökes (1996) and Laslzo Bruszt (1990) termed it a "negotiated revolution."

The only country in central Europe in which an absolute majority evaluated the communist one-party system in a positive way is Hungary. This has to do with the special nature of the so-called "Goulash Communism" that was implemented under Secretary General János Kádár during the 1980s. Many Hungarians remember this decade as the "golden era" in modern Hungarian history. The share of citizens who value the *ancien régime* increased sharply from 51 percent in 1991 to 68 percent in 1992, decreased again to 58 percent in 1994 and remained at that comparatively high level until 1998.

In an earlier study I have reported changing levels of public support of democracy in Hungary. This index is conceptually similar but differently operationalized than the "democracy–autocracy index" which is used throughout this volume.[1] However, it also allows us to identify citizens who can be characterized as "democrats," i.e. respondents who support liberal democracy as an ideal without necessarily evaluating the performance of the political regime in a positive way. That is to say, the index of democracy does not measure the evaluation of the performance of the current government at a given point in time but the level of support for democracy as a form of government in contrast to any other non-democratic regime. Table 6.1 includes only those respondents who can be categorized as "democratic" (scores 8–10, see endnote 1). The "Haerpfer-index of democracy" encompasses the category of "democrats" (=values 9–10) as well as the group of "weak democrats" (=value 8). The "democracy–autocracy index" on the other hand, distinguishes "strong democrats," weak democrats, undecided citizens and autocrats. Its rationale and construction has been thoroughly described in the introductory chapter.[2] In Table 6.1, strong and weak democrats have been collapsed into the category "democrats" (WVS 1999). It should be stressed that because of the differences in index construction, a direct comparison of proportions of democrats in the period of 1994 to 1998 and 1999 is not possible.

More than 60 percent of Hungarian respondents can be characterized as democrats by the more restrictive Haerpfer index. Collapsing "strong"

Table 6.1 Proportion of democrats as measured by Haerpfer's democracy index 1994–8 and the democracy–autocracy index in post-communist societies, 1999

Country	NDB 3 1994	NDB 4 1996	NDB 5 1998	WVS 1999
Central Europe – mean	57	52	61	89
1. Poland	47	52	66	84
2. Czech Republic	77	69	65	95
3. Hungary	**50**	**38**	**62**	**82**
4. Slovenia	–	47	57	92
5. Slovakia	55	53	55	94
South-eastern Europe – mean	56	52	55	88
1. Romania	59	60	56	86
2. Croatia	65	51	55	97
3. Bulgaria	44	45	54	79
4. FRY	–	–	37	91
Northern Europe – mean	28	30	–	85
1. Estonia	43	46	–	90
2. Lithuania	18	27	–	80
3. Latvia	22	18	–	86
Eastern Europe – mean	21	14	30	70
1. Belarus	23	15	41	77
2. Ukraine	25	12	19	74
3. Russia	15	–	–	58

Source: NDB 3 (1994), NDB 4 (1996), NDB 5 (1998), New Baltic Barometer 1994, New Baltic Barometer 1996, WVS – World Values Survey.

(42 percent) and "weak" democrats (51 percent) the democracy–autocracy index brings the figure up to 82 percent in 1999. Thus we may well speak about an almost unanimous acceptance of democracy as a form of government in Hungary. In our earlier work, we have classified a country in which 40 percent of citizens were democrats (as measured by the Haerpfer index) in an "emerging democracy." Observing a rise to more than 60 percent democrats in 1998 justifies a classification of Hungary as a "consolidated democracy" on the micro-level, i.e. on the level of the Hungarian citizenry.[3] In the first years of political transformation we observed a high degree of skepticism with regard to democracy in general and the new Hungarian regime in particular. Only 38 percent of the respondents qualified as democrats in 1996. This share increased considerably until 1998. Together with Poland and the Czech Republic, Hungary clearly belongs to the group of stable and consolidated democracies in central and eastern Europe as far as the populace is concerned.

The Haerpfer index of democracy clearly shows the different degrees of democratization on the micro-level in post-communist Europe. In 1998, an average of 61 percent of the respondents can be characterized as democrats. With respect to public support, the countries of the central European region are already consolidated democracies. The country with the highest share of democrats is Poland (66 percent in 1998). In 1994, only 47 percent of Polish respondents could be characterized as democrats. Their share increased to 52 percent in 1996. Thus, Poland crossed the border from an emerging to a consolidated democracy some time between 1996 and 1998, and since then has been well prepared for European integration. The Czech Republic, with a share of 65 percent of democrats in 1998, occupies the second rank. Compared to the Polish trend, the development of public acceptance of democracy in the Czech Republic was reversed. In 1994, 77 percent of the Czech citizenry indicated democratic attitudes; there seemed to have been "democratic euphoria." The political development and its public perception in the period of the governments of Prime Ministers Vaclav Klaus and Milos Zeman acted as a cold shower for this initial enthusiasm and for the self-ascribed role of the Czech Republic as an "ideal-type of democratic transformation." Nevertheless it is justified to label the current Czech political system as a consolidated democracy.

According to the criteria mentioned above, three out of 15 post-communist countries have reached the status of consolidated democracy after ten years of political transformation: Poland, the Czech Republic and Hungary. In Slovenia, the Haerpfer democracy index identified 57 percent democrats in 1998, which puts Slovenian democracy just below the threshold of 60 percent. In Slovakia, a stable majority of well above 50 percent of the respondents score as democrats; in 1998 their share reached 55 percent. This development was validated by the general election in autumn 1998, when the government of Prime Minister Dzurinda replaced the government of Prime Minister Meciar, who was not known to be a strict defender of democratic values.

Summarizing results of the Haerpfer democracy index which allowed a comparison over time one can safely say that, in 1998, there is no new democratic regime in central and eastern Europe that can rely on less than 50 percent of their citizens to support democracy as an ideal. The general preference of democracy over autocracy finds an even greater expression in the results generated by the democracy–autocracy index. We want to reiterate, however, that the operationalization of the two indices is different and the proportions of democrats cannot be compared directly.

To conclude this section we will analyze the social structural composition of the four groups as defined by the democracy–autocracy index. As mentioned above, strong democrats were distinguished from weak democrats, and undecided citizens from autocrats. Who are the strong democrats in terms of the Hungarian social structure? They are primarily male (38 percent), they belong to the young generation (40 percent), received tertiary education (45 percent), live predominantly in big cities (41 percent) and belong to the middle class (46 percent). The weak democrats have their strongholds also among men (49 percent), live in the countryside (49 percent) and belong to the working class (51 percent). What is the social location of the undecided citizens? They are found primarily among women (11 percent), in the older generation (aged 55 years and above), among respondents who received primary education only (16 percent), in the lower class as well as the working class (13 percent each). Finally, who are the autocrats? They are found primarily among women (10 percent), in the lowest educational stratum (15 percent), in small villages (11 percent) and first of all in the lower class (16 percent).

Impact of public support of political principles on support of democracy

The analysis of the level of public support for political principles and values in Hungary indicates that the Hungarian democrats reach far beyond a Schumpeterian concept of democracy. They embrace a class of political ori-

Table 6.2 Democracy–autocracy index, 1999

	Strong democrats (%)	Weak democrats (%)	Undecided (%)	Autocrats (%)
Total	36	46	9	9
Gender				
Women	34	44	11	10
Men	38	49	7	7
Age				
18–34 years	40	44	7	8
35–54 years	36	47	8	9
55–90 years	32	48	11	9
Education				
Primary	22	47	16	15
Secondary	44	43	7	7
Tertiary	45	48	4	4
Town size				
100–9,999	30	49	10	11
10,000–99,999	36	47	8	9
100,000–2,000,000	41	44	9	7
Subjective class				
Lower class	24	47	13	16
Working class	27	51	13	9
Middle class	46	42	5	7
Upper class	34	49	9	9

entations which have an obvious and direct impact on the quality of the democratic process. With regard to democratic consolidation, the most important political principle is tolerance, followed by the acknowledgement of the illegitimacy of the use of violence in politics and solidarity with the poor. Political tolerance is operationalized as tolerance toward homosexuality (Table 6.3). A total of 37 percent of the respondents are tolerant toward homosexuality and homosexuals. The level of tolerance toward homosexuals is higher among men, the young, in bigger cities, in the middle class and in the higher educational strata. Intolerance toward homosexuality is more widespread in the working class, in rural Hungary, in the lowest educational groups, in the old generation and among women.

The second most significant influence on the level of public support for basic democratic principles is the respondents' rejection of violence as a legitimate means in politics (Table 6.6: Beta-coefficient = 0.13). An overwhelming majority (80 percent) of Hungarian citizens believe that the use of violence to pursue political goals is "never justified." The principle of non-violence appears to be deeply rooted in Hungarian political culture: "The Hungarian transformation was a peaceful, elite-controlled change," a "negotiated revolution. . . . This idea has had a powerful impact on the political culture: it has promoted the acceptance of such principles as

Table 6.3 Political tolerance – attitudes toward homosexuality, 1999

	Tolerant (%)	*Intolerant (%)*
Total	37	63
Gender		
Women	35	65
Men	38	62
Age		
18–34 years	47	53
35–54 years	39	61
55–90 years	21	79
Education		
Primary	19	81
Secondary	39	61
Tertiary	49	51
Town size		
100–9,999	24	76
10,000–99,999	39	61
100,000–2,000,000	44	56
Subjective class		
Lower class	24	76
Working class	29	71
Middle class	42	58
Upper class	47	53

non-violence, self-restraint, political pragmatism and readiness for negotiations. All the political leaders ... wanted to avoid violent solutions"
(Bozóki 1999: 108).

This principle, however, is in the first place limited to domestic Hungarian politics and does not necessarily apply to international politics,
the question of war and Hungarian participation in international conflicts.
One-fifth (20 percent) of the respondents believe that violence in
politics can be justified under certain circumstances, a result that casts a
shadow over Hungarian politics after ten years of political transformations.
Gender does not affect the respondent's attitude toward the question of
the legitimacy of violence in politics. This is also true for age, level of
formal education or the urban–rural dimension. Only the self-ascribed
belonging to a social class proved to be of importance: one-quarter of
respondents who attribute themselves to the working class (24 percent)
and 27 percent of the upper class agree with the general statement that
violence could be justified as a mean in politics. Among members of the
middle class and the lower class, political violence is not accepted by 80 to
90 percent.

The third most important effect on the level of support for democracy
was the level of solidarity with the poor (Table 6.5: Beta-coeffi-

Table 6.4 Legitimacy of violence in politics, 1999

	Never justified (%)	Justified (%)
Total	80	20
Gender		
Women	81	19
Men	78	22
Age		
18–34 years	79	21
35–54 years	78	22
55–90 years	81	19
Education		
Primary	81	19
Secondary	80	20
Tertiary	78	22
Town size		
100–9,999	80	20
10,000–99,999	78	22
100,000–2,000,000	81	19
Subjective class		
Lower class	88	12
Working class	76	24
Middle class	82	18
Upper class	73	27

cient = 0.10). The absolute majority of 75 percent of all citizens indicated a high level of solidarity with the poor (Table 6.5). This is especially true for women, the middle-aged, for respondents with an average level of formal education, in villages and small towns and in the lower class, which is most affected by poverty itself. Solidarity with the poor is somewhat less expressed by the higher classes, especially by the middle class and the upper class, in big cities and by men.

The relative effect of important political principles and values on the level of public support for democracy indicates that the concept of democracy in Hungary is not just limited to a set of abstract rules in the political arena, but is based on the acceptance of a pluralist society and its core political values.

Impact of political motivation and political participation on support of democracy

Political motivation

In this section, the concept of political motivation is operationalized by variables measuring "political discussion with peers," "political interest"

Table 6.5 Solidarity with the poor, 1999

	High (%)	*Medium (%)*	*Low (%)*
Total	75	23	2
Gender			
Women	76	22	3
Men	73	25	2
Age			
18–34 years	73	24	3
35–54 years	78	21	1
55–90 years	75	22	3
Education			
Primary	73	24	3
Secondary	79	21	1
Tertiary	73	24	3
Town size			
100–9,999	77	21	2
10,000–99,999	78	22	0
100,000–2,000,000	70	25	5
Subjective class			
Lower class	84	16	0
Working class	79	19	2
Middle class	72	25	3
Upper class	68	29	3

Table 6.6 Impact of political principles on support of democracy (model A; OLS multiple regression; dependent variable: democracy–autocracy index)

Political principles	Beta	Significance	R^2
X1 Tolerance	0.24	0.00	–
X2 Illegitimacy of violence as a political means	0.13	0.00	–
X3 Solidarity with the poor	0.10	0.00	–
Explained variance by model A	–	–	0.08

and the respondent's evaluation of the "importance of politics." The frequency of political discussions with peers serves as the main indicator of political motivation or involvement. In the survey 17 percent of the respondents discuss political matters frequently with their friends (Table 6.7). The majority of 56 percent of Hungarian citizens discuss political issues now and then, whereas 27 percent never discuss politics with their friends. We found a strong influence of gender on the frequency of political discussions with friends: men discuss politics more often than women. Every fifth man is involved in political discussions with his friends frequently (21 percent), whereas only 13 percent of all Hungarian women frequently debate politics. One-quarter of Hungarian men do not talk politics (24 percent) with their friends. When women are meeting, one-third of them never talk about politics (30 percent). There is a linear relationship between age and the frequency of political debate with friends. The older the citizen, the more he/she discusses politics with friends. Among the younger generation, only 10 percent are discussing political matters frequently. Roughly one-fifth of all citizens between 35 and 54 years of age, and of those aged more than 55 years, are involved in political debates with their friends frequently.

The higher the respondents' level of formal education, the more frequent are political debates among friends. In the category of respondents with the lowest level of formal education, only 11 percent discuss politics with their friends frequently. This share increases to 16 percent among those who received secondary education. The highest frequency of political debate with friends was found in the group of respondents who received tertiary education. Every fourth Hungarian university graduate discusses politics with friends frequently (26 percent). There is also a clear relationship between the urban–rural dimension and the frequency of political discussion. The larger the size of the local community, the more often political discussions take place with friends. In rural areas and small towns, only 14 percent of the population discuss politics regularly. The proportion of politically interested persons goes up to 17 percent in medium-sized towns. We found the highest frequency of political debate in cities with more than 100,000 inhabitants (19 percent) and among the middle and the upper classes. One-fifth of the middle class and 16 percent of the upper class are discussing politics frequently.

Table 6.7 Political discussion with friends, 1999

	Frequently (%)	Occasionally (%)	Never (%)
Total	17	56	27
Gender			
Women	13	57	30
Men	21	55	24
Age			
18–34 years	10	62	28
35–54 years	20	62	19
55–90 years	22	43	35
Education			
Primary	11	49	40
Secondary	16	59	26
Tertiary	26	60	14
Town size			
100–9,999	14	54	32
10,000–99,999	17	55	27
100,000–2,000,000	19	58	23
Subjective class			
Lower class	7	34	59
Working class	15	51	34
Middle class	20	61	19
Upper class	16	69	15

A second indicator for political involvement is the assessment of the importance of politics (Table 6.8). It had, however, no impact on the public level of support for democracy. Slightly less than one-third of the respondents (27 percent) state that politics is important in their life, while the remaining 73 percent indicate that politics is not important in their everyday life. The difference between men (25 percent) and women (29 percent) with regard to importance of politics in their life is rather small. Instead, we found a linear relationship with age. The older the respondent, the more he or she is inclined to think that politics is important. Hence, we found that 43 percent of the older generation is convinced that politics is important for their own life. The impact of the Second World War, communist rule until 1989 and the advent of democracy after 1989 might have contributed to the comparatively high esteem politics enjoys among older citizens. This pattern is unusual, since it is usually the middle generation who is found to be most interested in politics – as these are the citizens who participate most actively in all spheres of live. In Hungary, only 25 percent of the middle-aged indicate that they think politics is important in their lives and only 24 percent of those between 18 and 34 years gave a similar answer. The vast majority of 76 percent of all young Hungarians at the end of the twentieth century regarded their family, their work or their peers more important than politics.

Table 6.8 Importance of politics, 1999

	Important (%)	Not important (%)
Total	27	73
Gender		
Women	29	71
Men	25	75
Age		
18–34 years	24	76
35–54 years	25	75
55–90 years	43	66
Education		
Primary	23	77
Secondary	27	73
Tertiary	32	68
Town size		
100–9,999	24	76
10,000–99,999	25	75
100,000–2,000,000	32	68
Subjective class		
Lower class	18	82
Working class	25	75
Middle class	29	71
Upper class	32	68

We also found a positive relation between higher levels of formal education on the one hand and the respondents' evaluation of the importance of politics. The higher the respondent's level of formal education, the more important is politics for her or his life. Approximately one-third of university graduates (32 percent) are convinced that politics is important for their lives. In the category of respondents who received secondary education, we found 27 percent who deem politics as important in their life, while only 23 percent of respondents who received primary education report that politics is important for them.

There was also a linear relationship between size of local community and the importance of politics. The importance of politics in the respondent's life grows with the size of the local community. In cities with more than 100,000 inhabitants, including Budapest, the capital city with nearly two million residents, one-third of the population (32 percent) indicated that politics is important for their own lives. Another well-pronounced relationship was found with subjective class membership. The higher the self-ascribed position of a Hungarian citizen on the social ladder, the more important he or she thinks politics to be in her or his life (18 percent of lower class respondents as opposed to 32 percent upper class respondents).

"Interest in politics" was selected as an additional indicator of political motivation (Table 6.9). With regard to interest in politics, the Hungarian public is divided in two groups of equal size: those who are interested in politics (50 percent) and those who are not (50 percent). Significantly more men than women are interested in politics (55 percent versus 46 percent). With regard to age, there is no linear relation but nevertheless a pattern. The middle-aged generation and the elderly are more interested in politics than the younger generation. We found the highest levels of interest in politics in the group of respondents aged 35 to 54 years (56 percent). The elderly are representative for the overall distribution of political interest: 50 percent of older Hungarians (55 years and above) indicate an interest in politics, the other half does not.

A linear relationship is found for the respondents' level of formal education and their reported level of interest in politics. That is, the higher the level of education, the greater the interest in politics. Among those who received primary education only, 38 percent indicate that they are interested or very interested. This proportion increases to 49 percent in the group of those who received secondary education. In the group of respondents with the highest level of formal education, the level of respondents interested in politics increased to 62 percent. With regard to the urban–rural divide, we found a distinction between rural villages and very small towns on the one

Table 6.9 Interest in politics, 1999

	Interested (%)	Not interested (%)
Total	50	50
Gender		
Women	46	54
Men	55	45
Age		
18–34 years	44	56
35–54 years	56	44
55–90 years	50	50
Education		
Primary	38	62
Secondary	49	51
Tertiary	62	38
Town size		
100–9,999	45	55
10,000–99,999	52	48
100,000–2,000,000	52	48
Subjective class		
Lower class	29	71
Working class	44	56
Middle class	54	46
Upper class	63	37

hand (45 percent interested), and somewhat larger towns and cities on the other (52 percent interested). Subjective social class also had a strong impact upon interest in politics. The level of political interest increases with higher social status. Among the lower class, only 29 percent indicate interest in politics, the other 71 percent are not interested at all. The proportion of politically interested citizens goes up to 44 percent among members of the working class; in the middle class it grows to 54 percent. With 63 percent, political interest reaches its highest level in the upper class.

Non-institutionalized political participation

In this section, we first discuss the readiness to participate in a lawful demonstration because we use this single variable in our multivariate models to explain support of democracy. Second, we describe results generated by an index of non-institutionalized political participation (which includes "signing a petition," "joining in boycotts" and attending lawful demonstrations").

With respect to participation in lawful demonstrations, Hungarian citizens are divided: 50 percent would never participate in a political demonstration, whereas the other half might participate or had already

Table 6.10 Participation in lawful demonstrations, 1999

	Have done (%)	Might do (%)	Would never do (%)
Total	9	41	50
Gender			
Women	9	37	55
Men	10	46	44
Age			
18–34 years	8	46	46
35–54 years	13	43	44
55–90 years	8	35	58
Education			
Primary	4	31	66
Secondary	6	47	47
Tertiary	17	48	35
Town size			
100–9,999	7	35	58
10,000–99,999	11	43	47
100,000–2,000,000	10	45	45
Subjective class			
Lower class	2	22	76
Working class	7	39	54
Middle class	10	48	42
Upper class	18	32	50

participated in such demonstrations. Actual participation in the period of 1989 to 1999 is reported by 9 percent of citizens, and 41 percent say that they might do so if there were a political issue which they believe should be addressed. Respondents who have already demonstrated are found primarily among the middle-aged (35 to 54 years), among respondents who received a high level of formal education, in cities and among the middle class. Potential participants were identified primarily among men, the young (18 to 34 years), respondents with a higher level of formal education, in cities and among the middle class. Participation in demonstrations is not very popular among 55 percent of women, the elderly (55 years and older), among those who only received a low level of formal education, in rural villages and among members of the lower and the working class.

We also measured the respondents' readiness to participate or their actual participation in three different types of protest behavior (signing a petition, joining in boycotts and attending a lawful demonstration). The information has been combined in an index of protest behavior (Table 6.11). A total of 15 percent of respondents are represented at the highest level of protest behavior. These very active citizens are found more often among men (18 percent) than among women (13 percent). A medium level of protest behavior is reported by 39 percent of the respondents.

Table 6.11 Index of protest behavior, 1999

	High (%)	*Medium (%)*	*Low (%)*
Total	15	39	46
Gender			
Women	13	39	48
Men	18	39	43
Age			
18–34 years	17	39	44
35–54 years	22	40	39
55–90 years	8	39	53
Education			
Primary	4	35	61
Secondary	13	39	48
Tertiary	29	42	29
Town size			
100–9,999	9	39	53
10,000–99,999	19	37	44
100,000–2,000,000	18	41	41
Subjective class			
Lower class	2	33	64
Working class	8	41	51
Middle class	22	36	43
Upper class	22	50	28

Combined, these two groups of protesters constitute a politically active majority of 54 percent of the population. The remaining 46 percent are not active and it would be difficult to mobilize them for political action. These passive citizens are over-represented among women (48 percent, while men are 43 percent).

There is an expressed relation between age and the inclination to protest. The politically most active age group is the cohort aged 35 to 54 years: 22 percent indicate a high level of readiness for non-institutionalized political action, or have already participated that way. Among the young, 17 percent are ready to participate in all three types of political protest. Finally, 53 percent of the elderly indicate a very low level of readiness for political action. We also found a clear-cut correlation between the formal level of education and the readiness to participate in political action. Participation levels rise with higher levels of formal education. Whereas only 4 percent of Hungarians who received a low level of formal education indicate a high potential for participation in protest behavior, this share increases to 29 percent for respondents who received a high level of formal education.

Participation in protest behavior or the willingness to participate in it is primarily found in towns and cities, and only to a lower extent in the countryside. Approximately one-fifth of all urban dwellers indicate participation or the willingness to participate in political action. In the countryside, we found only one-tenth of citizens who can be regarded as potential participants in protest behavior. The majority of Hungarian villagers (53 percent) are not ready to participate in protests.

The readiness to express demands by means of political protest appears to be a characteristic of the middle classes. Of those respondents who subjectively classify themselves as middle class, 22 percent indicate that they are ready for this type of political action or to have used it already. Among respondents who describe themselves as members of the working class, we identified only 8 percent who are willing to participate in a similar manner.

Selected correlates of the democracy–autocracy index discussed above will now be included in a multivariate regression model as independent variables to test their joint explanatory power. The two indicators are "political discussion with friends" and the "readiness to participate in lawful demonstrations." Results are presented in Table 6.12. Together, the

Table 6.12 Impact of political motivation and political participation on support of democracy (model B; OLS multiple regression; dependent variable: democracy–autocracy index)

	Beta	Significance	R^2
X4 Political discussions with friends	0.19	0.00	–
X5 Participation in demonstrations	0.15	0.00	–
Explained variance by model B	–	–	0.08

two independent variables explain 8 percent of the variance in the democracy–autocracy scale. They both contribute almost equally to this result, with political motivation (political discussion with friends, beta-coefficient = 0.19) having a little bit the upper hand as compared to political protest (attending a lawful demonstration, beta coefficient = 0.15).

Impact of education on support of democracy

In post-communist societies, the proportion of "democrats" is highest among respondents who received a high level of formal education. This section of the analysis, again, makes use of results of the New Democracy surveys and relies on Haerpfer's index of democracy. Thus, we are in a position to show the development of support for democracy over time (1994, 1996, 1998) for the strategically important social group of citizens with higher education. This is the group from which future political and social elites are selected, and in this respect it is very important to know whether or not it is in support of democracy as a form of government.

In central Europe, in 1998, on average 79 percent of Hungarian citizens who had obtained or were in the process of earning an academic degree supported democracy as a regime type (as measured by the Haerpfer democracy index). For many reasons, the political orientations of this social group can be considered crucial for the persistence of the new democratic regimes. They should be the social backbone of the new democracies.

In the central European countries, the strength of citizens supporting democracy increased from 74 percent in 1994 to 79 percent in 1998 (Table 6.13). Hungary is the country with the largest share of democrats among the higher educated (76 percent in 1994 and 88 percent in 1998). The expansion of support for democracy was most dramatic in Poland: in 1994, only 65 percent of all Polish graduates supported the young Polish democracy, while in 1998 their share increased to 86 percent. The Czech pattern was quite different from the pattern in Hungary and Poland. Of all Czech graduates, 95 percent supported democracy in 1994; however, developments in Czech party politics and government apparently led to a decrease in 1998 (80 percent). The process of democratization in Slovak society was much slower than in Hungary, Poland and the Czech Republic. It also happened at a somewhat lower general level. In 1994, only 58 percent of Slovaks who achieved higher formal education supported democracy as a regime type. Their share increased to 72 in 1998 at the end of the era of Prime Minister Meciar. In Slovenia, we find a similar pattern as in the Czech Republic, a shift from democratic euphoria to greater "realism": in 1998, only 71 percent of the respondents who received tertiary education in Slovenia supported democracy, which puts Slovenia in the same group with Slovakia, well behind Hungary, Poland and the Czech Republic. Thus, Hungarian and Polish societies belong to

Table 6.13 Education and support of democracy: percentage of democrats among respondents with tertiary education, central and eastern Europe (Haerpfer democracy index; New Democracy Barometer surveys), 1994–8

	1994 (%)	1996 (%)	1998 (%)	Change 1994–8
Central Europe	74	76	79	5
1. Hungary	**76**	**65**	**88**	**12**
2. Poland	65	75	86	21
3. Czech Republic	95	88	80	−15
4. Slovakia	58	72	72	14
5. Slovenia	–	80	71	−9
South-eastern Europe	67	60	62	−5
1. Romania	79	69	77	−2
2. Bulgaria	61	60	74	13
3. Croatia	62	50	56	−6
4. FRY	–	–	41	–
Northern Europe	42	44	–	2
1. Estonia	60	62	–	2
2. Lithuania	38	40	–	2
3. Latvia	27	29	–	2
Eastern Europe	31	20	37	6
1. Belarus	32	21	47	15
2. Ukraine	36	19	26	−10
3. Russia	25	–	–	–

Sources: NDB 3 (1994), NDB 4 (1996), NDB 5 (1998), New Baltic Barometer 1994, New Baltic Barometer 1996.

the class of "mature democracies," supported by almost 90 percent of democrats. The Czech Republic, Slovakia and Slovenia fulfill the criteria of a consolidating democracy (60 percent to 80 percent democrats among the higher educated), while the Czech Republic seems to have crossed the threshold of a mature democracy in that social group (70–80 percent).

In south-eastern Europe, the level of support for democracy of respondents with a higher level of formal education is significantly lower than in central Europe. Only 67 percent of the south-east European graduates and students qualify as democrats in 1994 and their share decreased to 62 percent in 1998. In south-eastern Europe, we are able to identify two different patterns. The first one was characteristic for countries neighboring the Black Sea and the second for the republics of the former Yugoslavia. Romania and Bulgaria qualify for the category of consolidating democracy, with a share of democrats well above 70 percent. In Romania, the percentage of democrats among Romanian graduates decreased from 79 percent in 1994 to 77 percent in 1998. The strong relief felt by the Romanian public after the end of the old Ceauscescu regime probably caused the rather high level of support in 1994. In Bulgaria, we observe an increase of support for democracy by respondents who received a high level of formal education, from 61 percent in 1994 to 74 percent in 1998. Thus, Bulgaria and Romania can be labeled "consolidating democracies" with regard to respondents in the sector of tertiary levels of formal education. The pattern is different in Croatia and Serbia/Montenegro. In Croatia, the share of democrats in the group of graduates and university students decreased from 62 percent in 1994 to 56 percent in 1998. In the Federal Republic of Yugoslavia, only 41 percent of citizens who received tertiary education supported democracy. This low level of support for democracy in the group of respondents with a high level of formal education in Croatia and Serbia/Montenegro is probably caused by the earlier authoritarian regimes of Milosevic and Tudjman and the experience of war. These experiences apparently made it difficult even for those groups who are most likely to embrace democratic principles to develop democratic attitudes. Croatian society fulfils the criteria of an emerging democracy (40 percent up to 60 percent of democrats) with regard to citizens who received tertiary levels of formal education. Serbia, however, is just above the threshold of an emerging democracy.

In the Baltic countries, the level of democratization among respondents with a high level of formal education is much lower than in central and south-eastern Europe. Only 42 percent of Baltic citizens in this social group qualify as democrats in 1994. Their proportion increased only slightly in 1996 (44 percent). A clear majority of graduates support democracy in Estonia (62 percent). At 40 percent, the share of democrats is much lower in Lithuania, and in Latvia we find only 29 percent of respondents with a high level of formal education who qualify as democrats.

In eastern Europe, the share of respondents who received tertiary education and fit the category of democrats increased from 31 percent in 1994 to 37 percent in 1998. Surprisingly, we find an increasing level of public support for democracy in Belarus. In 1994, only 32 percent of respondents with a higher level of formal education qualified as democrats. However, their share increased to 47 percent in 1998 – despite the fact that during these years President Lukashenko's regime turned more and more into a dictatorship. Thus, Belarus seems to be the interesting case. The society is becoming more democratic at the grass-roots, while the government loses more and more of its already small stock of democratic characteristics. An opposite trend could be observed in Ukraine, where we find a share of 36 percent democrats in 1994 among the respondents with a high level of formal education. Their share decreased to 26 percent in 1998. In Russia – on the low end – only a minority of 25 percent of respondents with a tertiary level of formal education could be characterized as democrats in 1998.

Impact of civil society on support of democracy

The degree to which civil society is realized in a given country can be measured in many ways. One highly consensual method of measurement is to consider membership and activity in voluntary associations. We will also follow this measurement strategy.

One third of Hungarian respondents are active members of at least one voluntary association (Table 6.14). Volunteering for active service is more prevalent among men (35 percent) than women (29 percent). The most active age group participating in voluntary associations are middle-aged respondents (25 to 54 years of age; 35 percent). Young people (31 percent) are slightly more active than the elderly (29 percent).

The group most active in voluntary associations are respondents with a high level of formal education (44 percent). One-quarter of those who completed primary or secondary education are active members. The urban–rural divide has apparently no impact on the level of membership and activity in voluntary organizations. We did find an influence of subjective social class. The higher the (self-ascribed) social status, the more active is a respondent. Only 20 percent who reported belonging to the lower class are active members in voluntary associations. This share increases to 25 percent if a respondent says he is a member of the working

Table 6.14 Membership in voluntary organizations, 1999

	Active members (%)	*Not active (%)*
Total	32	68
Gender		
Women	29	71
Men	35	65
Age		
18–34 years	31	69
25–54 years	35	65
55–90 years	29	71
Education		
Primary	25	75
Secondary	26	74
Tertiary	44	56
Town size		
100–9,999	30	70
10,000–99,999	32	68
100,000–2,000,000	32	68
Subjective class		
Lower class	20	80
Working class	25	75
Middle class	36	64
Upper class	40	60

class. More than one-third of the middle class is active in the third sector and its organizations (36 percent). The most active social class, however, is the upper class, with a reported 40 percent of active members in voluntary associations.

Law-abidingness is one of the most important characteristics of a mature democratic citizen. This is particularly important precondition to ensure the rule of law in a new democracy. In Table 6.15, we present the level of the respondents' subjective law-abidingness as an index. This index combines the acceptance of three patterns of behavior: "not to claim government benefits without entitlement" (Item 1); to "pay a ticket using public transport" (Item 2); to "pay all your taxes" (Item 3). The overall result based on this index indicates that two-thirds of the Hungarian population accept the rule of law, while one-third does not – to a varying degree. Women are slightly more law-abiding (68 percent) than men (66 percent). More than 70 percent accept the rule of law in the middle-aged generation (73 percent) and among the elderly (72 percent). The young are less law-abiding. Only 56 percent of young Hungarians accept the rule of law in full; 36 percent report violating the rule of law now and then, and 8 percent do not accept the rule of law – as defined here – at all. Apparently there is a demand for educational activities that

Table 6.15 Law-abidingness, 1999

	High (%)	*Medium (%)*	*Low (%)*
Total	67	28	5
Gender			
Women	68	27	5
Men	66	29	5
Age			
18–34 years	56	36	8
35–54 years	73	24	3
55–90 years	72	24	4
Education			
Primary	68	26	6
Secondary	69	26	5
Tertiary	65	30	5
Town size			
100–9,999	68	28	4
10,000–99,999	70	25	5
100,000–2,000,000	64	30	7
Subjective class			
Lower class	62	27	11
Working class	69	25	5
Middle class	69	27	4
Upper class	62	34	4

target Hungarian youth. Level of formal education has no influence on the acceptance of the rule of law.

Results regarding the urban–rural divide are interesting. The rule of law is accepted most in villages (68 percent) and small towns (70 percent). In the big cities and in the capital, Budapest, a lower share of respondents reports abiding to the new laws and regulations (65 percent). More than one-third of the urban population (37 percent) are either not prepared to follow the law at all, or they try to avoid some of it sometimes. The strongest pillars of the rule of law in Hungary are the middle class (69 percent) on the one hand, and the working class (69 percent) on the other. The lower classes (62 percent), as well as the upper classes (62 percent), are less law-abiding than the middle and the working classes.

In the latter part of this chapter, civil society has been operationalized as the level of citizens' participation in voluntary organizations on the one hand, and their level of law-abidingness on the other (Table 6.16). Relating these two specific democratic attitudes to the democracy–autocracy index we learn that – in relative terms – the most important predictor of the two indicators is the degree to which citizens participate in civil society (membership in voluntary associations; beta-coefficient = 0.14), followed by law-abidingness (beta-coefficient = 0.12).

Democratic consolidation in Hungary – conclusions

The last step of this analysis is to test a multivariate regression model of the correlates of support of democracy in Hungary in the year 1999 (Table 6.17). This regression model combines elements of all the dimensions discussed in the previous sections. Hungary can be characterized as a consolidated democracy as far as public support for democracy as an ideal form of government is concerned: 82 percent of Hungarian citizens fit the categories of either strong or weak democrats. We distinguish four groups of predictors for the level of democratic support: political principles (dimension A), political motivation and participation (dimension B), the quality of civil society (dimension C) and the level of formal education (dimension D).

The variance explained by the regression amounts to 19 percent, almost one-fifth. Level of formal education is a powerful predictor of

Table 6.16 Impact of civil society support of democracy (model C; OLS multiple regression; dependent variable: democracy–autocracy index)

Civil society	Beta	Significance	R^2
X7 Member in associations	0.14	0.00	–
X8 Law-abidingness	0.12	0.00	–
Explained variance by Model D	–	–	0.03

Table 6.17 A multivariate regression model to explain support of democracy in Hungary, 1999 (OLS multiple regression; dependent variable (Y): democracy–autocracy index)

Dimensions	Beta	Significance
A *Political principles*		
X1 Tolerance	0.18	0.00
X2 Illegitimacy of political violence	0.15	0.00
X3 Solidarity with poor	0.10	0.00
B *Political motivation and participation*		
X4 Political motivation	0.13	0.00
X5 Protest behavior	0.09	0.01
C *Civil society*		
X6 Law-abidingness	0.12	0.00
X7 Membership in voluntary organizations	0.08	0.02
D *Social structure*		
X8 Level of formal education	0.15	0.00
Variance explained	R^2	0.19

support for democracy (beta-coefficient = 0.15). Other socio-economic variables such as age, urban–rural differences or gender are unimportant after controlling for the overpowering effect of education. Law-abidingness (beta-coefficient = 0.12) and civic participation (membership in voluntary organizations; beta-coefficient = 0.08) also contribute in a significant fashion. Two-thirds of the Hungarian respondents believe in the rule of law, not just in the abstract but as a guiding principle in everyday life. One-third of the populace are active in or members of voluntary organizations. This is considered to be an important prerequisite for a pluralist, representative democracy (Putnam 1993a, 1993b). Political motivation (beta coefficient = 0.13) and protest behavior (beta-coefficient = 0.09) contribute to explanations on a similar level. One-tenth of the respondents already participated in political demonstrations and another 40 percent are prepared to participate. Regarding other modes of protest behavior, we found support (54 percent) and rejection (46 percent) almost equally distributed (summary index combining signing a petition, joining in boycotts and attending a lawful demonstration). These findings indicate that democratic citizens in Hungary do not regard democracy as a spectator game in which one has to vote once every four years. Rather, democratic principles, values and activities have entered the political life of Hungarian citizens in a number of other ways. Hence, there is reason to believe the "strong democrats" particularly have embraced the concept of a participatory democracy.

The most important effects on support for democracy and rejection of autocracy, however, were related to basic democratic principles such as tolerance (beta-coefficient = 0.18), the illegitimacy of political violence (beta-coefficient = 0.15) and solidarity with the poor (beta-coefficient = 0.10). These democratic principles have also been found to enjoy an even greater support among the Hungarian political elite (Linz and Stepan 1996; Tökes 1997; Agh 1998; Derleth 2000). Apparently there is a congruence in these value orientations between the Hungarian public and the Hungarian elite. This strengthens our argument that democracy is safely rooted in Hungarian society at the end of the twentieth century.

Notes

1 My index of democracy consists of nine different items: Item 1: negative rating of communist political regime in the past; Item 2: positive rating of new democracy or current political regime; Item 3: optimism about the future of democratic parliaments; Item 4: support for democratic national parliament; Item 5: rejection of authoritarian leader as alternative to democracy; Item 6: rejection of a military regime as alternative to democracy; Item 7: rejection of monarchy as alternative to democracy; Item 8: rejection of return to communist political regime as alternative to democracy; Item 9: optimism about the future of democracy.

2 The democracy–autocracy index consists of two democracy items and two autocracy items. The two democracy items are: Item 1: positive rating of "Having a democratic system"; Item 2: positive rating of "Democracy may have problems but it is better than any other form of government." The two autocracy items are: Item 3: positive rating of "Having a strong leader who does not have to bother with parliament and elections"; Item 4: positive rating of "Having the army rule." The sum of the scores of the autocracy items (3, 4) is subtracted from the sum of the scores of the democracy items (1, 2), resulting in a scale which runs from +6 to −6. The groups used here are defined as follows: A. strong democrats (+5–+6); B. weak democrats (+1–+4); C. undecided citizens (0); D. autocrats (−1–−6). Missing values are excluded list-wise.

3 The process of consolidation of democracy at the meso-level and at the macro-level has to be measured with other methods. This is also true for the extent of democratization of elites and of institutions. However, I am focusing here at the extent of democratization on the micro-level of transforming societies.

References

Agh, A. (1998) *The Politics of Central Europe*, London: Sage Publications.

Bozóki, A. (1999) "Democracy in Hungary, 1990–1997," in Kaldor, M. and Vejvoda, I. (eds) *Democratization in Central and Eastern Europe*, London: Frances Pinter.

Bruszt, L. (1990) "1989: the Negotiated Revolution in Hungary," *Social Research* 5, 2.

Derleth, W.J. (2000) *The Transition in Central and Eastern European Politics*, Upper Saddle River, New Jersey: Prentice Hall.

Haerpfer, C.W. (2002) *Democracy and Enlargement in Post-Communist Europe: the Democratisation of the General Public in Fifteen Central and Eastern European Countries, 1991–1998*, London: Routledge.

Linz, J.J. and Stepan, A. (1996) *Problems of Democratic Transition and Consolidation: Southern Europe, South America, and Post-Communist Europe*, Baltimore: Johns Hopkins University Press.

Putnam, R.D. (1993a) *Bowling Alone: the Collapse and Revival of American Community*, New York: Simon & Schuster.

Putnam, R.D. (1993b) *Making Democracy Work: Civic Traditions in Modern Italy*, Princeton: Princeton University Press.

Swain, N. (1993) "Hungary," in White, S., Blatt, J. and Lewis, P.G. (eds) *Developments in East European Politics*, Basingstoke, Hampshire: Macmillan.

Tökes, R.L. (1996) *Hungary's Negotiated Revolution: Economic Reforms, Social Change, and Political Succession*, Cambridge: Cambridge University Press.

Tökes, R.L. (1997) "Party Politics and Political Participation in Postcommunist Hungary," in Dawisha, K. and Parrot, B. (eds) *The Consolidation of Democracy in East-Central Europe*, Cambridge: Cambridge University Press.

7 Slovakia

Pathways to a democratic community

Silvia Mihalikova

Introduction

Any analysis of the transformation process in the post-communist countries tends to reflect the subjective beliefs of the analyst more strongly than is the case with other research topics. This is in part a result of persistent flux in this region that hinders the development of a coherent theoretical framework for the exploration of the post-communist transformation. It is a matter of increasing contention within contemporary academic literature whether *any* theoretical framework could lead to a more objective evaluation. However, in the case of Slovakia, this postmodern dilemma has been not been terribly relevant because the unpredictable fluidity of political and socio-economic developments has rendered the Slovakian case a problematic one for analysis. Indeed, until 1998–9, Slovakia was regarded as the exception among the four Visegrad[1] countries, i.e. the anomaly in central Europe.

Observers of Slovakian politics and society habitually measure phenomena with western yardsticks. Everything that broadly resembles "the western way" is perceived as normal and standard, while deviating features are regarded as strange and unorthodox.

This method is not very precise, since it ignores the dynamic nature of the benchmark (i.e. the western capitalist system in general). Furthermore, it carries the ethnocentric notion that all countries which shy away from the direct path to political plurality and a free market economy are of a pathological nature. This latter tendency often results in a masochistic self-abasement on the part of Slovak commentators when they look at their country's deviation from the blueprint drawn at the dawn of the post-communist era by western neo-liberal enthusiasts and reformers in the East. This template basically consists of a complete rejection of communism and any form of political regulation of society and economy. The negative reflex with regard to anything perceived as non-western results from living on the "wrong" side of the Iron Curtain. History has proved this to be the case and thus the citizens and politicians of eastern Europe have been found lacking. Finally, this strong tendency to take the

West as the one and only source for explanations as well as possible models for the transformation process has prevented the analysis of east European developments in a dynamic *global* context.

This study addresses these shortcomings in order to balance the exclusive emphasis on the Western model. I will analyze global influences on east European transformation, some positive, and some posing serious challenges. Slovakia's political and socio-economic trends are explored on the basis of studies written by Slovak and foreign observers, academics, journalists and politicians, as well as on empirical data collected by the World Values Survey. The basic hypothesis is that there are no significant differences with regard to political culture and its manifestations between Slovakia and other central European countries.

Several years after gaining independence, Slovakia finds itself locked in a problematic situation. While the transformation to a market economy was comparatively successful, the results of political reforms remain, at the least, ambivalent. Hopes for a continuous and linear unfolding of democracy and its institutional and legislative environment were disappointed throughout the 1990s. The situation improved after political changes in 1998.

Moreover, the election results of 2002 can be seen as a major turning point for the country that could help to eliminate the remaining discrepancy between economic and political reform. Though it shared a common starting point with the Czech Republic, Hungary and Poland, why has Slovakia followed a different path?

The simplest answer is that in 1993 Slovakia had to start building state institutions from scratch. Furthermore, the new state differed from its peers to some extent – in terms of economic development, ethnic homogeneity and proximity to the West. It most definitely lacked the experience of Poland, the Czech Republic and Hungary in governance and administration.

While all these factors undoubtedly play an important role, we also have to pay attention to societal and political *culture* if we want to understand both the tensions within Slovak society and between Slovakia's representatives and the international community. We have to bear in mind that the post-communist societies (and this might be particularly true for Slovakia) embody only few traditions of pluralist democracy, if any. Consider that Slovakian citizens aged more than 80 years in 1993 had experienced seven regimes and eight different constitutions in their lifetimes, all without moving to another country. Only two of these periods could be considered democratic.

If we want to fully comprehend the contemporary Slovak pathway to democracy, we should first identify its historical roots and then describe its main features. This means in the first instance we have to examine the country's *non-democratic* traditions. Like other post-communist states, Slovakia has a mixed tradition of democracy and authoritarianism with roots going back at least to the early nineteenth century and the Slovak emancipation movement. Furthermore Slovakia belongs to the countries reflecting the cultural and religious heritage of two empires – namely that of the Habsburgs and the Soviet/Leninist regime. I will give a brief account of these features in the following section.

A brief history of Slovakia

Slovakia became a part of the Habsburg Empire after the defeat of the Turks in the battle of Mohacs in 1526. Through several politically calculated marriages, the Habsburg Empire grew to be one of the most diverse and wealthy in European history. However, the Empire's continuing inclusion of diverse groups sowed the seeds of its disintegration at the dawn of the nineteenth century, since the Habsburgs never solved or even acknowledged the problem of integrating the different nationalities and ethnicities living under their rule. Indeed, "the fundamental problem of the 19th century, the bringing together of peoples into some sort of mutual and moral relationship with their governments – the problem of which nationalism, liberalism, constitutionalism and democracy were diverse aspects – remained unconsidered by the responsive authorities of central Europe" (Palmer and Colton 1978: 471).

After the Austro-Hungarian *Ausgleich* (Compromise) in 1867, Slovakia was degraded to a Hungarian-ruled suburb. Count Kalman Tisza (1875–90) and his son Istvan (1903–6) pushed an official Magyar nationalism[2] to prevent further marginalization and to homogenize the population. Half of the inhabitants of the Slovakian territory were not ethnic Hungarians. This meant for non-Magyars, and Slovaks in particular, a disintegration of national symbols and heritage. Furthermore, the intelligentsia and its instruments – Slovak language, schools, newspapers and cultural and academic institutes – were closed or severely restrained (Lipták 1998).

The Slovak national movement was in a state of crisis after the closing of Matica slovenská[3] and three Slovak-speaking gymnasiums in 1875. The Hungarian government sought to weaken the national consciousness of all minorities and severely limited their right of political participation. A National Congress of Romanians, Serbs and Slovaks met in Budapest on 10 August 1895 and issued a 22-point decree on cooperation in pursuing national and political rights of all suppressed nationalities. The Hungarian answer was persecution of some participants, as well as censorship and increased monitoring of the political activity of non-Magyars.[4] Only 20 percent of citizens were entitled to vote. District functionaries, who sometimes decided according to their individual preferences whom they would allow to vote, controlled elections. Slovakian representatives in the Hungarian Parliament in Budapest were rare. There were just four in 1901, two in 1905, seven in 1906 and three in 1910. Slovaks held only 2 percent of civil service positions in the year 1910 (Lipták 1998: 21–2).

This experience of coercive Hungarian assimilation challenged Slovak political identity. At the beginning of the twentieth century, Slovakia was an underdeveloped country, largely agrarian in nature, with hardly any cultural or academic institutions. It was at this time that the Slovak diaspora in the United States became an important voice in the call for autonomy. The more than 700,000 emigrants helped to create a national identity outside Slovakia (Gawdiak 1989: 90). One expression of this development was the Cleveland Agreement, signed in October 1915, that pledged to "connect the Czech and Slovak nations into a federal union of states with complete national autonomy" (Chovanec 1994: 94). The Pittsburgh Pact, concluded in May 1918, further strengthened the movement for an independent nation-state.

The Allied victory at the end of World War I witnessed the collapse of central and eastern Europe's great multinational empires and the beginnings of the Russian revolution. The aspirations of the Slovak diaspora in America were implemented when the Czechoslovakian state emerged from the Paris Peace Negotiations in 1918. President Woodrow Wilson's 14 Points, specifically Points V and X, guaranteed that the principle of national self-determination would be granted to the nations that were newly created from the remains of the Austro-Hungarian Empire. Central Europe was meant to acquire a Wilsonian, not a Bolshevik flavor.

The merging of Czechs and Slovaks was a political calculation on both sides, because it allowed them to form a voting majority within the constitutional framework of the First Republic.[5] The Czechs regarded the Slovaks as a counterweight against the Sudeten Germans living in Bohemia, while the Slovaks regarded the Czechs as Slavic brothers and protectors against Hungarian assimilation. Both sides benefited from the creation of Czechoslovakia. The Czechs were much better prepared than Slovaks to undertake the enormous administrative and governing functions required. They benefited from their experience under Habsburg Austria, which allowed them to draw personnel from a trained cadre of bureaucrats and intelligentsia to staff positions in administration, diplomacy and the military. Slovakia on the other hand basically had to invent brand new institutions after shaking of the yoke of Hungarian rule. The "re-Slovakization of Slovakia" got under way. An entire school system was founded, publication of Slovak newspapers and journals increased, a radio broadcast industry was started and cultural institutions began to flourish. However, the Czechs' advantageous position, apparent from the very beginning of the Czechoslovakian state, allowed for a more pronounced role and visibility for the Czechs in governance. This led to the impression on the part of the Slovak population that the country was becoming a centralized state controlled from Prague rather than the initially planned federal republic.

Slovaks were nonetheless granted better conditions for fostering their own identity during the First Republic than under Hungarian rule. Great effort was focused on rebuilding and reforming Slovak society and national institutions. Another important factor was the concept of "Czechoslovakism." This ideology proclaimed that Czechs, Moravians and Slovaks formed one "Czechoslovak" nation, a brotherhood led by a strong central government in Prague. Over time, the treatment of Slovakia from Prague became paternalistic, as the Czechs tended to think *they* were able to determine what was the best for the whole country.[6]

The signatories of the Munich Agreement of 29–30 September 1938 sealed the fate of the First Republic. A new government was formed in Czechoslovakia after Beneš resigned on 4 October 1938. Dr. Emil Hácha, the chairman of the Supreme Court, became the new president and nominated Dr. Jozef Tiso as administrator of the autonomous Slovak government (Lettrich 1993: 102).

After Munich, confusion reigned on the question how an autonomous Slovakia would fit into the structure of the Federal Republic. It soon became clear that the Germans intended to form a Protectorate in the Czech part, thus accommodating the Sudeten Germans living there, and to allow Slovakia to exist as a separate state, albeit controlled by Berlin. On 21 December 1938, the Chief of the German General Staff signed an amendment to an earlier order declared by Hitler on 17 December calling for the liquidation of Czechoslovakia (Lipták 1998: 174). Slovakia became an "independent" state with the Catholic priest Jozef Tiso as President. Germany began directing Slovak foreign and military policy shortly after the March declaration of Slovak independence and Tiso's government introduced legislation on the deportation of thousands of Jews from Slovakia.

The Slovak National Uprising (1944) was the defining moment for the Slovaks during World War II. It is one of the most important events in Slovak history and is an impressive example of individual patriotism and sacrifice on the part of both soldiers and civilians who participated in the struggle to defeat Nazi Germany.

The Czechoslovak Republic was re-created on 4 April 1945 in Košice under the leadership of the formerly exiled President Eduard Beneš. After the elections one year later, the Czechoslovak Communist Party started to infiltrate key ministries of the government and began laying the groundwork for an eventual take-over (Ďurica 1996: 213).[7] Communists gained control of the ministries of information, internal trade, finance and the interior and began activities to suppress political opposition (Ďurica 1996: 214).The communist coup d'état on 25 February 1948 effectively ended any kind of independent Slovak politics. The speed of the collapse of the Democratic Party surprised every observer. The communists immediately took control of the state security apparatus and started Stalinist purges and show-trials. The Czechoslovak political system was forced completely into the Stalinist mould and was subordinated to the pursuit of Soviet interests in Europe. A reform movement led and represented by Alexander Dubček that culminated in the so-called "Prague Spring" failed and was ended by the invasion of Czechoslovakia by Warsaw Pact forces on 21 August 1968. Gustáv Husák became Chairman of the Communist Party in early 1969 and immediately re-established rigid party control over the whole society. He remained in a leading position until the end of communism in Czechoslovakia.

Post-communist Slovakia in retrospect

I will analyze the developments in Slovakia since 1989 in two sections. The first deals with the period from the collapse of communism in November 1989 until the June 1992 elections and the consequent dissolution of the Czech and Slovak Republic (formerly Czechoslovakia) on 1 January 1993 (the two events are fundamentally interconnected). The second covers the consolidating rule of Vladimir Mečiar's Movement for Democratic Slovakia (HZDS) and its two coalition partners, the Slovak National Party (SNS) and the Association of Workers of Slovakia (ZRS). The short interregnum of 1994, marked by Mečiar's fall after a vote of no confidence and the resulting early September 1994 elections, will also be analyzed here. Special attention is given to the end of this period and the September 1998 and September 2002 elections, and their impact on the image of the Slovak state, both nationally and internationally.

Each transition toward democracy has its own unique characteristics and I will use the case of Slovakia to show that, on the one hand, it is possible to manage a complicated undertaking like dividing a country peacefully. On the other hand, I will demonstrate that the Slovak case is also as an example of a transition associated with negative factors such as nationalism, xenophobia and renewal of authoritarianism. Are these ingrained in Slovak political culture? If so, how can we understand contemporary developments in Slovakia?

The response of the Slovak population to the post-1989 changes was in many respects similar to that in other post-communist countries, but it also features some unique characteristics. The most notable was the prevailing ambiguity with regard to the direction of the transition: should it be a transition toward democracy or a "new model" of authoritarianism? The priority of nationalistic demands and an independent nation-state gave observers the impression that Slovaks might prefer to live under a non-democratic state of their own nationality rather than accept a "democratically inclusive" non-national state. They might be ready to support a non-democratic government to achieve their national goals rather than press for full democracy (Shain and Linz 1995: 96).

Slovakia between 1989 and 1993

The brief period between the collapse of communism and the creation of a Slovak independent state was marked by a highly politicized struggle between the Slovak and the Czech elites about the future shape of the federation. This struggle took place in the context of a complex transformation process. The process, directed from Prague by federal politicians, involved economic and political reforms in line with the standard neo-liberal transformation package. In economics, the reforms included rapid liberalization, restructuring and small- and large-scale privatization. In the political sphere, institutions and procedures that previously played only a cosmetic role were to be transformed into genuine organs of a democratic state that embody the principles of plurality, tolerance and compromise. Only then, it was assumed, would the east European identity and the accompanying negative externalities fade. The reintegration into western civilization would follow, and with it all the benefits of a capitalist market economy rooted in democratic governance.

This posed serious challenges to the unity of Czechoslovakia. The two parts of the federation brought with them different legacies, not only from the recent past but also from more distant history. However, separation was not inevitable. First of all, the now two republics were closer in terms of basic economic and social indicators at the time of the separation than at any other time in their shared history. Second, public polls conducted before, during and after the division indicated that the majority of both Czechs and Slovaks favored the preservation of the Czechoslovakian state. Third, those who pushed for Slovakia's independence and positioned themselves at the forefront of the independent state after its creation had no history of commitment to emancipation. They were opportunists and populists. Yet many Slovaks did believe that the existing Federation was to their disadvantage, and thus they voted for political parties that promised to represent Slovak grievances. In the first chaotic and difficult years of the new democratic regime, the Slovak question provided a popular and accessible issue with which parties could rally political support. The channeling of popular discontent into Slovak nationalism turned out to be populism's easy solution for many difficult questions. This led to a radicalization of the debate around the shape of the future state. Ultimately, however, the fact that the reform policies of the new independent Slovak state did not differ dramatically from those promoted by the former federal Prague government testifies to what were in fact many shared aspirations.

Taking a closer look at this complex picture, there is no doubt that the transition initially influenced the Slovak economy more negatively than the Czech economy. Slovakia faced higher unemployment figures and the level of foreign investment was lower. Furthermore, Slovakia's heavy industry – a legacy of communist modernization and equalization policies – proved to be difficult to restructure and/or privatize. Slovakia differed slightly from its Czech counterpart with regard to ideological profiles prevalent within society, due to a milder period of normalization after 1968. Its dissident community was less active and the Slovak population was more inclined to tolerate state intervention (social planning) and paternalism. One of the causes for different political and ideological orientations in Slovakia and the Czech Lands was the different political arrangements established in the two republics during the normalization period following the Warsaw Pact army's invasion of Czechoslovakia. The purge in the Czech Lands after 1969 led to a complete turnover of the elites within political and administrative structures. The division and alienation between the communist regime and the society was broad and clearly accentuated. On the other hand, the Slovaks did at least achieve federation and vainly hoped that this would protect them from encroachment on the part of the communist regime. The logic behind this naive belief was that Slovak communist rulers would be more understanding with regard to Slovak issues and sentiments than those ruling from Prague. On the surface, normalization in Slovakia was a less stormy experience. Even though there were widespread purges of thousands of communists in Slovakia and the existential persecution of many others, in many cases the doors were left open for those expelled from the Party and/or work to make a comeback. A far greater proportion of those Slovaks who were active in the 1960s were gradually co-opted into the political and administrative structures. In addition, the rate of economic and social growth was comparatively higher in Slovakia than in Bohemia. Increasing prosperity was understood as the regime's achievement, although it was paid for with environmental devastation and further growth of the economic gap between Slovakia and the West. Thus Slovaks were more inclined to rely on and trust in the state than their Czech counterparts. These factors would increase Mečiar's appeal. Unexpressed dissent between Czechs and Slovaks with regard to issues such as the interpretation of Czechoslovakia's birth or the conduct of the two republics during World War II added to an atmosphere where Slovak independence seemed to be the only alternative.

The differences between the Czechs and Slovaks escalated in the June 1992 elections, where they found political expression. Two parties based on national lines won the elections and proved to be unable to compromise. The leaders of the Czech-based Civic Democratic Party (ODS) and the Slovak-based HZDS, Václav Klaus and Vladimír Mečiar respectively, opted to dissolve the federation. The dissolution took place on 1 January 1993, without a referendum.

While the transition to independent statehood proved to be relatively easy for the Czech Republic – she inherited the capital city and appropriated formally federal institutions – Slovakia faced the problem of building a new state almost from scratch.

Slovakia under Mečiar's rule 1994–8

A number of Slovak political scientists and foreign observers argue that, after the separation, Slovakia left the transformation path that was clearly set out by the federal government in Prague (Carpenter 1997; Kaldor and Vejvoda 1997; Szomolányi and Gould 1997; Fish 1999). Undoubtedly, there was a tendency toward regression that was intensified after the early 1994 elections. From this election a coalition government emerged in which the Movement for Democratic Slovakia, the Association of Workers of Slovakia and the Slovak National Party participated. It was led by Prime Minister Vladimír Mečiar. This coalition government constituted a majority which meant that the opposition was plainly excluded from decision-making. Furthermore, important functions were taken over by the coalition parties' candidates. In parliamentary committees, the coalition MPs held a two-third majority, that led the input of the opposition MPs to remain largely irrelevant.

These circumstances allowed Mečiar's government to abuse its power. It was able to break constitutional laws, disregard verdicts of the Constitutional Court, and develop and foster dubious economic relations. A striking illustration of deficiencies in democratic governance is the case of František Gaulieder, an MP expelled from parliament because he quit the Movement for Democratic Slovakia parliamentary caucus. In a letter to Ivan Gašparovič, speaker of the National Council of the Slovak Republic (Slovak Parliament), Gaulieder stated his intention to remain in parliament as an independent deputy. Within days, however, Gašparovič received another letter – allegedly from Gaulieder, but later denounced by the latter as fraudulent – stating that the former HZDS member would resign his seat. The case was referred to the parliament's mandate and immunity committee, in which the government coalition held the majority. Despite the fact that the committee's chairman agreed that the second letter had not been written by Gaulieder, the committee recommended that the letter be accepted. Consequently, the ruling majority in parliament voted to accept the resignation of deputy Gaulieder and to replace him with an HZDS substitute. Despite a verdict of the Constitutional Court that declared this act unconstitutional, and public protests on Gaulieder's behalf, the parliamentary majority maintained its position. Only in 1998 and 1999 did the newly formed parliament acknowledge what had occurred and provide moral and financial compensation to Mr. Gaulieder.

Among other unsavory episodes was the strange abduction of President Michal Kováč's son to Austria and the state authorities' reluctance to investigate his disappearance. Another was the involvement of Mečiar's government in privatization schemes which discontinued coupon privatization and instead redistributed property on the basis of direct sales to predetermined buyers through a Mečiar-controlled Fund of National Property. Especially revealing were the cases of Nafta Gbely, Ironworks Košice and Devín Bank (Mikloš 1998).

As a result of this deterioration of politics in Slovakia, a clear political polarization emerged by the mid-1990s. The cleavage was not along classical partisan (i.e. ideological) lines, but along a socio-political and somehow cultural axis. Two broad political camps can be distinguished (Mesežnikov 1998). The first, represented until September 1998 through the governing coalition parties, consisted of the Movement for Democratic Slovakia, the Association of Workers of Slovakia and the Slovak National Party. The second broadly encompassed the opposition parties from both the left and the right, i.e. the Christian Democratic Party, Party of the Democratic Left, Democratic Union, Democratic Party, Social Democratic Party of Slovakia, parties of the Hungarian Coalition and the Slovak Green Party. In 1996, the Christian Democratic Party, the Democratic Union and the Democratic Party established the so-called Blue Coalition. In 1997, the Social Democratic Party of Slovakia and the Slovak Green Party joined and formed the Slovak Democratic Coalition.

The first camp could be characterized as a grouping of national–authoritarian parties that pursued politics in a confrontational manner and preferred unilateral decision-making and enforcement to compromise and agreement. In contrast, the second camp was anti-authoritarian in nature and had a strong democratic and pro-European leaning. The September 1998 elections ended the semi-authoritarian government led by Mečiar – and put a halt to Slovakia's growing "democratic deficit."

Besides this polarization, tensions among legislative, executive and judicial organs were a feature of the mid-1990s. The conflict between President Michal Kováč and Prime Minister Mečiar and his government was especially pervasive. It actually resulted in a "temporary" elimination of the Presidency after a failed and muddled referendum (Mesežnikov and Bútora 1997). Conflicts between the legislative majority and the government on the one side and the judiciary on the other were reflected in the former's refusal to submit to the latter's verdicts. It could be stated, therefore, that the division of power between the main state organs remained incomplete. Indeed, the struggle for their positioning and their role in Slovak political life continued until at least 1998.

Mečiar's rule has been described as unstable though still formally democratic, since the struggle over rules and procedures took place *within* the existing (formal) framework of democratic institutions (Szomolányi and Gould 1997). This leads to another conundrum, namely the notion that having a democratic institutional framework does not necessarily mean having a functioning democracy. For instance, while laws were passed in a semblance of a democratic procedure, they were often ineffectual, since the executive force were not able (or willing) to enforce implementation.

This rather unstable political environment was also reflected in the realm of international affairs. It accounts for the disqualification of Slovakia in the west European and transatlantic integration processes. During the 1997 summit in Madrid, Slovakia was excluded from the group of countries included in the first wave of NATO enlargement, despite its obvious military readiness. Furthermore, notwithstanding the country's impressive macro-economic performance (at least until 1996/7) – and its status as an associated member of the European Community (EU) – it was not invited to further integration talks until the end of 1999. Thus the mid-1990s were years of lost opportunities for Slovakia in the field of international relations.

Despite the overall negative political development in Slovakia after 1994, economic performance improved until 1996/7 (Mikloš 1998). Indeed, the years 1994 and 1995 were marked by a revival and macroeconomic stabilization. However, 1996 brought a growing deficit. Low inflation rates and a stable currency were maintained through a strict monetary policy, involving high interest rates, which did not encourage investment. The biggest problem was a tendency of Mečiar's government to restructure economic policy according to its own interests. Lack of transparency and circumvention of laws – e.g. in the privatization process – further discouraged foreign investment and hindered economic growth. The blocking of reforms resulted in a severely imbalanced state and a slowing down of growth rates. The end of the decade therefore was characterized by attempts to stabilize the economy, to complete general reforms and to start new, more demanding reforms. These efforts were clearly expressed in the government's programmatic declaration after 1998 elections and guided its first moves toward policy implementation.

The September 1998 elections

The September 1998 elections signified a break with the policies and conduct of the previous government. Although HZDS still received the

Table 7.1 Gross Domestic Product GDP[a] rate (at constant prices), various years, %, Slovakia

Year	GDP growth
1994	4.9
1995	6.7
1996	6.2
1997	6.2
1998	4.1
1999	1.9
2000	2.2

Sources: Statistical Office of the Slovak Republic – quoted from: *National Human Development Report. Slovak Republic 2000.* Bratislava, UNDP, 2000 p. 19 (for year 2000, from Kollár and Mesežnikov 2001: 19).
Slovakia ranked with GDP purchasing parity power in US$ in 1997 (7.860) between the Czech Republic (10.380) and Hungary (6.970) (Fuchs and Klingemann 2000: 12).

Notes
a GDP revised by ESA 95 methodology. Data for 1994 to 1996 are final; data for 1997 to 1999 are preliminary.

largest single share of votes, the former opposition gained a constitutional majority in the Parliament. The election turnout was very high. Over 80 percent of eligible Slovaks voted – thanks to the participation of many young people and first-time voters.[8] The ballot thus rejected "Mečiarism" and voted for those parties committed to the redirection of Slovakia's path toward democratic consolidation and integration within the West (the two are considered virtually identical goals).

After month-long talks, a coalition agreement was reached on 28 October 1998 between the Slovak Democratic Coalition, the Party of Democratic Left, Party of the Hungarian Coalition and the Party of Civic Understanding. Theoretically, the new government had the support of 93 MPs – a constitutional majority. It sent out strong signals to the international community immediately, since it was committed to return to the path to Europe. Indeed, European integration is one of the most important challenges the new leaders are facing.

However, factions within the two strongest parties, Slovak Democratic Coalition and the Party of Democratic Left, might turn out to be the main source of tension within the government coalition. This in turn complicates and inhibits cooperation between the coalition partners in fulfilling the government program. Since the 1998 elections, three new political parties appeared on the Slovak political landscape: the Slovak Democratic and Christian Union founded by representatives of the Slovak Democratic Coalition led by Prime Minister M. Dzurinda; the SMER (meaning "direction") founded by Robert Fico, a former Vice-Chairman of the Party of the Democratic Left; and the Alliance of New Citizens, or ANO (meaning "yes") led by Pavol Rusko, the owner of the country's most popular TV station (Markíza).

In fact, Slovakia's new government has succeeded in transforming the country's image abroad, but it still needs to convince analysts that it is able to tackle problems at home. In 1999, the Dzurinda government accepted this challenge. Since this is not the place for details, it might be sufficient to indicate that after the NATO's fiftieth anniversary summit in Washington in April 1999, the prospect for Slovakian participation in the second wave of NATO enlargement became salient. As for the EU, the year's progress in Bratislava was enough to overcome former scruples with regard to Slovakian membership. The Council of Ministers' meeting in Helsinki (December 1999) decided that Slovakia should be invited to start pre-accession talks in 2000. Up to October 2002, Slovakia had closed 27 negotiation chapters and entered a qualitatively new phase of negotiations with the EU, beyond technical issues to real substantive political themes. Furthermore, Slovakia was invited to join the OECD.

The most concrete achievement of Slovakian foreign policy in 1998/9 was an improvement of relations with neighboring Hungary. The government had pledged to push through a reform of language laws to satisfy the demands of the 500,000-strong ethnic Hungarian minority, which often complained about unfair treatment by Mečiar. On 17 January 2000, the Slovak cabinet approved the European Charter of Regional and Minority Languages. The charter rules the treatment and protection of minority languages in education, the judiciary, state and local administration, the media and culture. The law can be exercised in communities where minorities make up at least 20 percent of the population. The Slovak cabinet also approved the establishment of a faculty with Hungarian-language tuition within the existing Nitra University. The faculty plans to train Hungarian-language teachers and offer other arts-related degrees. A new conflict between Slovakia and Hungary emerged in June 2001 when the Hungarian Parliament in Budapest approved a law on Hungarians living abroad. Slovakia regards this law as an attempt to intervene with Slovak legislation and does not recognize its validity.

With regard to the economy, problems persist but ambitious plans have been formulated. The government sold a large stake of the state telecom company and wants to lower the budget deficit to 2 percent of GDP. However, the pace of reforms slowed during 1999 as a result of increasing tensions between coalition parties. Furthermore, Slovakia experienced rising unemployment rates and costs of living. During the recent election period, unemployment was the most topical economic concern, with the unemployment rate reaching 14.5 percent in 1998. This trend continued in 1999, as unemployment rates reached 20.1 percent by the end of the year, with the long-term unemployed making up 43 percent of all unemployed persons (22 percent of all unemployed were unemployed for more than two years).[9]

The initial euphoria after 1998 election derived mainly from the new government's promise to fight corruption. It was soon replaced by disappointment. Surveys indicated intensified corruption in Slovakia and public access to information was not broadened. Although there were police investigations into some cases of suspected illegal practices, there were also a growing number of cases of suspected new illegal or quasi-legal politico-economic relationships. In spite of all this, Eugen Jurzyca of the Institute for Economic and Social Reforms stated that there are no significant differences in the economic performance of Slovakia and other central European countries. The growth rate of Slovakia's economy has exceeded its pre-transformation level by 1.5 percent.[10]

Slovakia stands at the beginning of a new era of change, characterized by more sophisticated politics and a slower pace of transformation. The most important pending reforms include the restructuring of the banking sector, the reform of the business environment, changes in the education and health sectors, the public state administration, improved transparency in politics and economics, and harmonization with OECD standards.

The September elections 2002: a turning point?

The results of the September elections – a victory for a bloc of center-right-wing parties – showed that voters nowadays relish a more civilized, statesmanlike and western-style brand of politics than Slovakia has experienced in its first decade of independence. This, above all, is the "message" of these elections. More than three-quarters of voters rejected authoritarian-style leaders, choosing free market politicians who resemble European Union leaders. This choice was made in spite of the probability that these leaders' reform policies will influence living standards and unemployment negatively in the short term.

What has happened? During the election campaigns, many western diplomats had predicted a return to power for the quasi-authoritarian Mečiar and the HZDS, an eventuality which could have become a barrier to Slovakia's NATO and EU membership. Although the HZDS won the election with 19.5 percent of the vote, the result was its lowest return in over a decade on the political stage, and the party was given no chance to form a government. Dzurinda's SDKÚ (Slovak Democratic and Christian Union) took the second place with 15.09 percent, and thus surprised observers who had expected the Dzurinda government's economic belt-tightening since 1998 to alienate voters from the SDKÚ. Together with the center-right-wing Hungarian Coalition Party (SMK) with 11.16 percent, Christian Democrats (KDH) with 8.25 percent and the New Citizen's Alliance (ANO) with 8.01 percent, the bloc headed by Dzurinda's party controlled 78 seats in the 150-mandate parliament, thus securing a narrow two-seat majority.

The leftist Smer party of Robert Fico finished third in the elections, with 13.46 percent, a result that excluded him from government. This was entirely unexpected, especially after polls in early September had put him in first place with a chance of reaching 20 percent and anchoring the next cabinet. Fico's recipe for Slovakia's problems was simple – justice, order and taking from the rich to help the poor. Fico's enemies were the ostentatious and illegitimately wealthy, as well as the ostentatious and helpless non-Slovak, including the Roma. The steps proposed to defeat the enemies were just as simple – cutting the Roma's social benefits and forcing the rich to prove the origin of their property. It came as little surprise that Fico was seen in the West as, in the memorable phrase of a German paper, "Mečiar-light," or that his campaign billboards were defaced by Hitler-like mustaches.

One of the major surprises of the 2002 elections were the results of the unreformed Communist Party of Slovakia (KSS) which won 6.32 percent, i.e. an 11-seat legislative caucus in the parliament assembly. This means that communists are returning to the Slovak parliament for the first time in the decade-long history of independent Slovakia. Despite the repressive history of the communist experiment in Czechoslovakia and the dissolution of the COMECON trading bloc in 1989, the KSS leadership says that it is a modern, forward-looking leftist party working for the interests of Slovak citizens. The KSS remained untouched by refusals from other parliamentary parties to cooperate in the legislature. While rejecting Slovakia's bid for NATO entry as expensive and unnecessary, the KSS did support some measures of integration within the European Union. The surprisingly successful communist result could be seen a response to the political self-destruction of viable socialist alternatives.

The outcome of September 2002 elections reassured Western governments about the maturity of Slovakia's democracy, and about the sincerity of the country's commitment to join the European Union and NATO in the months to follow

Making democracy work in Slovakia

The responses to the challenges after the collapse of communism in Slovakia resemble roughly those of other central European countries (CECs). In part, however, they differ as a result of the country's specific history and political situation. Throughout the 1990s, the level of democratization within Slovak society remained uncertain. Some commentators, as we have seen, altogether denied that democracy had taken hold, and saw its tender shoots swamped by a revived authoritarianism. Certainly, Slovakia's image in international media and organizations deteriorated significantly after 1994. Despite some positive macro-economic achievements, the country was regarded as the most problematic of the Visegrad Four by national and international observers. Since Slovak independence in January 1993, all Slovak governments have unequivocally declared the desire to become regular members of western international structures. However, until 1998, their representatives violated the basic principles of a fair dialogue with NATO and EU.[11] The state authorities received several official and unofficial *démarches* and diplomatic recommendations from western Europe and the United States that urged respect for democratic principles and civil liberties, the freedom of speech in the media and public life and increased respect for minority protection. These had little or no effect on Prime Minister Mečiar's actions. In other words, the message was sent but the receiver remained deaf, showing no signs of any positive reaction. Most exasperating was the Janus-face of Mečiar's foreign policy: it can simply be described as "You behave differently at home and in Brussels" (Wlachovský 1997). Thus it was not surprising that Slovakia was initially excluded from the list of countries invited to talks about NATO enlargement and EU membership. Although the institutional framework defined by the Slovak constitution constitutes a parliamentary democracy with free and fair elections, observers criticized that democratic principles were not implemented in daily political life.

There is a growing body of literature on this phenomenon. While it recognizes progress in building democratic institutions, the main concern articulated is the stability of these institutions, the actual implementation of democratic principles, the lack of a "spirit of democracy" among ruling elites as well as among the Slovak population. The role of the political elites is crucial, as became evident in Slovakia between 1994 and 1998, years of continued political polarization and behavior which brought the country into international isolation. Although it might sound paradoxical, the most pressing problem in Slovak foreign policy has been (and could be again) the domestic situation; namely the political elite's competitive behavior and their disrespect for democratic rules in the power game. Furthermore, the complaint of a lack of competent personnel legitimizes a recycling model for the recruitment of political personnel (Mihálikova 1996b). The same people appear on stage repeatedly – President Schuster being only one example.[12]

Another remarkable feature of Slovakian political life is that top politicians claim a "political date of birth" after November 1989, disregarding their age and political involvement in the previous regime. Apparently important factors that determine the specific configuration of the political elites of contemporary Slovakia, their attitudes and skills as well as their shortcomings, relate closely to practices and procedures common under communist rule.

Certainly this explains why Slovakia's international isolation in the mid-1990s was often explained by reference to the state's democratic deficit. Two versions of this argument circulated. The pro-Mečiar faction treated it as semantic insidiousness of an "international conspiracy against our young state" supported by "internal enemies of Slovak independence" who might be found in all social strata, in particular among intellectuals. Consequently the therapy was seen in the establishment of a special information agency, journals and media, ideally paid for and controlled by state authorities "to improve the positive image of Slovakia abroad." Simultaneously, the ruling elite tried to limit critics' freedom of speech and access to foreign media. Those critics who promoted the second interpretation of the democratic deficit took a different view. They considered the return of old and the birth of new authoritarian tendencies to be the main reason for the negative international image of Slovakia. In their opinion, only increased respect for basic democratic principles and the rule of law inside the country, as well as a clear orientation for Slovakia's foreign policy, could improve this image.

These sharply contrasting views on national politics were prevalent in the media, in statements of political parties and in everyday conversation. Slovakia appeared on the verge of becoming a divided society. This tendency was intensified by a strategy of the governing coalition, which introduced a kind of loyal mirror-society; that is, after failing to gain control over key civil society groups, HZDS and its allies established their own competing counterpart organizations, e.g. the Association of Slovak

Journalists, the Slovak Youth Congress, the General Free Labor Union and the Association of Mayors. This technique was used to create separate interest groups as well as umbrella organizations, such as the Union of Citizen's Associations and Foundations. The approach even gave rise to the creation of parallel party structures. HZDS inspired the rise of the Association of Slovak Workers (ZRS) to undermine the Party of the Democratic Left (SDL) and actively supported the establishment of the Hungarian People's Movement for Reconciliation and Prosperity, which parallels the Hungarian Coalition, and the Civic Liberal Party of Slovakia as a rival to the Democratic Union. Slovak political scientists use the term "party–state corporatism" to describe such "efforts of the ruling party to found its own party-affiliated and party-controlled organizations or to gain control over already existing groups" (Malová 1997: 93–113).

Divided society – divided political culture?

The political culture of post-communist Slovakia represents a kind of cognitive map that can be identified as a specific psychosocial constellation typical for central European countries in transition. No matter how far political and economic change has progressed, transformation processes in Slovakia have been hindered by patterns of thinking and behavior rooted in its past. De-communization appears to be more difficult than many expected. The communist mindset has proved to be harder to change than the institutional framework. Furthermore, even if establishment and procedures of the new democratic institutions will ultimately change mentalities and cultural legacies, it will not happen soon. It may well take a generation to get rid of the vestiges of the past since change must occur at two levels. These are, first, the level of personal commitment (personal values, motivations, drives, thought patterns) and, second, a more hidden level of cultural code typical for a given society (shared and objectified patterns and blueprints for acting and thinking).

Symptomatic of a society thus adrift is a kind of value confusion that manifests itself in political polarization which is much in contrast to the "certainties" characteristic to society and politics under the communist regime.

Not only elites are deeply divided. The entire population is becoming more and more politically polarized. The dividing line goes across families, informal groups and professional associations. A growing number of divorces and mental or psychological disorders are attributable to political squabbles. Perhaps this is not completely different from the situation in Poland or Hungary, but in Slovakia the condition appears especially acute.

Some examples of how political polarization has affected all social strata, regardless of the level of formal education, occupation, age, gender, religion and rural or urban residency might sufficiently demonstrate how severely this "splitting syndrome" has affected Slovakian society.

The patterns of these examples are by no means unique. They have become sufficiently commonplace to be a subject of discussion among political commentators and social and political scientists.

Even close relatives and intellectuals are not immune. Stefan and Jozef Markuš – the former a highly educated lawyer (today the Slovak Ambassador in Hungary), the latter head of Matica Slovenská, a renowned organization established in 1863 to preserve Slovak's language and culture – are politically active and influential public figures. However, they have publicly acknowledged that they do not speak to each other anymore, since they stand on opposite sides of Slovakia's political landscape. Štefan Markuš, summarizing their relationship, says: "well, we exchange Christmas postcards, that's it. I would prefer not to speak about this. It is a rather intimate issue and it hurts … Slovakia is now sharply cut into two parts. … Perhaps it is something in the Slovak character, that we are too emotional when it comes to politics" (Dorotková 1998: 2).

Other stories confirm life-long friendships broken due to political misunderstanding and dissent. For example, women who have met regularly for years cease to spend time together due to fierce arguments over Slovakia's independence and their different interpretations of history and politics. These disputes often end in unpleasant personal vituperation, breaking up the traditional Sunday dinner or birthday parties. This sociopolitical split also appears in former dissident Catholic groups whose members hated the communist regime and often gathered illegally to pray and plot. Today, they often cannot find a common language for debate.

The prevalence of a simplistic black and white picture of the world and protracted discussions about the past and present fate of the nation have been observed in all post-communist societies and among their elites. The Slovak variant includes an excessive misuse of history for the sake of political strategies. Politicians indiscriminately invoke events or personalities belonging to past centuries or contemporary Slovakia. Thus it is very popular to cite the 1,000-year oppression of the Slovak nation by Hungarians. Usually this type of argument is used to show who are and always have been our enemies. History is somehow used in a "horizontal" way, to manipulate and mobilize the public.

It is hoped that the improved political atmosphere of recent times will reduce this destructive habit. There are signs that this might be the case. However, the question remains whether the fissures opened up in the 1990s, especially in the Mečiar years, are being permanently mended or only temporarily bridged. The 2002 election campaign proved that Mečiar and his party faced almost complete domestic and international isolation. Slovak political parties joined ranks, with all major election contestants declaring they would not cooperate with Mečiar after elections, whatever the election results. It seems that the man who pushed the country to independence in 1993 was no longer deemed fit to lead the nation a decade later. The 2002 election results confirmed that a majority of citizens were aware that history would not offer them a chance to join NATO and the EU a second time.

Past versus current political system

The changes that took place in society and politics in Slovakia after November 1989 – including developments after January 1993 – brought many contradictions. Retrospectively, the majority of Slovaks regard the early 1990s skeptically. This is evident in the succession of names given to events that surrounded the collapse of the old regime. The first poetic term, the "Velvet Revolution," soon lost its popularity. By 1989, students started to talk about the "Stolen Revolution," and since then derogatory labels spread, like the "Velvet Outbreak," the "Communist Riot," the "Palace Revolution," or the "Jewish–Bolshevik Conspiracy."

Dissatisfaction in the mid-1990s mainly concerned the character of the current regime. In one survey 74.8 percent of the respondents disagreed or strongly disagreed with the statement that "we are living in democracy," 76.3 percent believed that "real politics does not respect democratic principles at all," and 75.4 percent diagnosed the "presence of authoritarian tendencies in our politics" (Miháliková 1996a: 18). In Slovakia, like in other post-communist countries, a nostalgic tendency to idealize the communist regime thrived in the 1990s, while the suffering under socialism was increasingly negated or forgotten. This became obvious in everyday life, in the (at best) lukewarm acceptance of economic transformation, and in growing anxiety about the future. Citizens seemed to miss the guarantees that had become part of their way of life under the communists.

Opinion surveys recorded almost unanimity among Slovak respondents when they were asked to indicate if they believed the former social security system to be superior over the current regime (94.4 percent). The same results were to be observed for the question of free education (96.9 percent) and free healthcare (97.4 percent) (Miháliková 1996a: 24).

According to the World Value Survey, the general support of Slovak respondents for the past political system also exceeds the level of support for the current regime:

Table 7.2 Level of support for the past and present political regime, 1999, %, Slovakia

	Low	*Medium*	*High*
Past political system	38	29	33
Current political system	46	34	20

Source: World Values Survey.

Slovaks are more supportive toward the past communist regime than other central Europeans. Only 16 percent of Czech respondents and 19 percent of Poles indicate high levels of support for the past political system, while 30 percent of Hungarians did the same.

Economic reform affects the lives of Slovakia's citizens in direct and indirect ways. It is therefore not surprising that they hold strong opinions about the extent, pace and fairness of this process. Even before 1989, a relatively large share of Slovakians systematically underestimated the extent to which a fundamental restructuring of the economy was necessary. They were not sufficiently aware of the fact that the socialist economic system had reached its limits for growth and was functioning at the expense of future generations. Throughout the mid-1990s, a majority of the population believed that the country's economy as it was structured before November 1989 did not require profound changes. That is to say, they had not accepted the need for fundamental transformation of the pre-1989 socialist economy (Table 7.3).

Those who recognized the need for change favored liberal or conservative orientations in economy and politics, namely a pro-Western course. However, for many Slovaks breaking away from communism was also important in that it gave rise to aspirations for independence. Thus the broadly positive sentiment about the end of communism was based on two contradictory impulses. First there was a genuine liberal orientation emphasizing the values of freedom, plural democracy, individual responsibility and a pro-Western foreign policy. The second impulse followed from the strong conviction that sovereignty of Slovakia was a logical outcome of the fall of the communist regime.

Through the mid-1990s, preference for the current political system (including the Mečiar years) seems to have been strongest among men and the younger generation. It was also a function of the level of formal education and command of foreign languages. Surveys indicate that more than 70 percent of students considered the post-communist order preferable to "real socialism."[13]

At the same time the Slovak population developed a strong feeling of alienation from the "new power." Levels of confidence in political

Table 7.3 "Did the pre-1989 Slovak economy require changes?," various years, %, Slovakia

	1992	1993	1994	1995	1997
No, it did not	6	6	6	5	6
Yes, but only minor changes	32	39	46	44	44
Yes, profound changes	49	49	41	44	39
Do not know	13	6	7	7	11

Source: Bútorová, Z. (ed.) (1998) *Democracy and Discontent in Slovakia: a Public Opinion Profile of a Country in Transition*, Bratislava: IVO, Bratislava, p. 24.

institutions (President, Cabinet, Parliament, coalition's deputies and opposition's deputies) are rather low. Apparently people doubt the ability of the new elites to safeguard the interests of the common people. Furthermore, a very strong sense of impoverishment prevailed, a fear of economic failure stemming from social insecurity and a pessimistic evaluation of the effects of economic transformation. As George Schöpflin (1993) has observed, low levels of trust in institutions are a part of the communist heritage. There was, and still is, very little understanding of the role of institutions as stabilizing agents that help to manage problems and prevent power accumulation of elites. Personal relations are regarded as far more authentic than the impersonal world of institutions, which is perceived as strange. Additionally it is personal, not political, loyalty or disloyalty that dominates politics.

A similar degree of high confidence (18.4 percent) in governmental institutions is shown by people in Slovakia and Hungary, compared to 8 percent in the Czech Republic and 14 percent in Poland.[14] In contrast, the Slovak army has consistently enjoyed high levels of confidence since 1993 (roughly 70 percent in the mid-1990s). In no neighboring country did the army inspire this level of confidence; nor did any other Slovak institution.[15]

In June 1997, almost 90 percent of Slovakian respondents expressed the conviction that politicians prioritize their own interests and those of their associates. Almost 80 percent believed that nepotism, utilitarianism and careerism prevail in politics. Almost as many thought that, to achieve something, one must have connections either in the government or in the opposition. It was a widely shared opinion that "the rich buy democracy, they have always done so and they always will" (Mihálikova 1997: 36).

After a short period of euphoria during and shortly after the "Velvet Revolution," the same attitudes and views that were prevalent during the old regime returned to dominate Slovak political culture in the Mečiar years: "politics is a dirty business."

Confusion in value and belief systems

The development of the Slovak society during the last decade reflects contradicting political traditions, frequent changes in officially declared basic values (both before and after 1989) and a disruption of social structures. Following from, and probably as a result of, four decades of indoctrination, citizens have still not been able to develop and internalize a new hierarchy of values. The communist mentality was not dead in the 1990s, it was simply manifested differently. It remained part of the social consciousness, convictions and behavior of the average citizen and of a large share of politicians in Slovakia. The internalization of communist thinking explains, at least partly, the prevailing preference for strident nationalism, demagogy and authoritarian patterns of governance. No matter how enthusiastically the people welcomed the fall of communism in the streets, they were not disposed to a total rejection of the socialist ethos.

One realm of contradictory beliefs in Slovakia is the relationship between the individual and the state. Slovakia has a strong tradition of collectivism and state-paternalist orientations. The results of opinion polls in the mid-1990s confirm that the shift away from the state toward individual responsibility had not taken place by then (and perhaps still has not).

No doubt the nation's severe economic problems are part of the explanation, since they easily stimulate demand for protective state intervention. This attitude corresponds with a low level of support for self-responsibility and contradicts the rather high level of support of individual competition.

The data in Table 7.4 indicate that the main difference between Slovaks, Czechs and Hungarians regarding the ethics of daily life is to be found in the higher share of Slovak respondents who believe that the state should take more responsibility – only 31.9 percent hold the opposite view, compared to 42.9 percent of Czech and 34.0 percent of Hungarian respondents (Table 7.4). With regard to all other items in question, the Czech and the Slovak sample indicate rather similar or even identical values, such as evaluation of competition, the proper fruit of hard work and attitudes toward poverty. Much larger differences are to be found between the former "Czechoslovaks" and Hungarians. As such, this data corroborates my argument that 70 years coexistence in a common state influenced the political culture of the two nations substantially.

Attitudes concerning the role of the state remained rather stable over time. The conviction that the state must retain important functions is widely shared. According to a mid-decade poll, 50 percent of the population opposed comprehensive privatization, almost 75 percent thought economic performance could not improve without serious state intervention and more than 85 percent held that the state should organize cooperation between banks, entrepreneurs and trade unions (Miháliková 1996: 28). These interventionist expectations did not, however, prevent a substantial portion of the population from favoring a free market. Clearly, this denotes confused and openly contradictory orientations among the population. On other occasions the confusion is more subtle; for instance 67.8 percent of the respondents to another poll thought Slovakia was selling off national property while the proportion believing that the country is becoming a colony of western countries was only 52.9 percent. This impression is confirmed by the results of the World Values Survey.

The data show that support for self-responsibility and ethic tolerance in Slovakia remains rather low, especially if compared to the Czech Republic. Nevertheless, the two former constituent parts of the Czecho-Slovak federation are still much closer to each other than to Hungary.

Table 7.4 Values of the community: ethics of daily life, various years, %, East Germany, Czech Republic, Slovakia and Hungary

	East Germany	Czech Republic	Slovakia	Hungary
Ethics of individual achievement				
People should take more responsibility vs. government should take more responsibility	39.7	42.9	31.9	34.0
We need larger income differences as incentives for individual efforts vs. Incomes should be made more equal	49.2	71.0	60.1	38.9
Ethics of individual competition				
Competition is good vs. Competition is harmful	91.1	89.3	89.3	91.0
In the long run, hard work usually brings a better life vs. Hard work doesn't generally bring success – it's more a matter of luck and connections	62.7	67.2	69.1	78.8
Solidarity with the poor				
People are poor in this country because society treats them unfairly	90.2	60.9	64.5	83.9
Poor people in this country have very little chance to escape from poverty	91.9	61.5	63.4	93.7
Government is doing too little for people in poverty in this country	81.3	67.1	66.0	79.7

Source: World Values Survey.

Table 7.5 Citizen support of different types of democratic community at cultural level, various years, %, East Germany, Czech Republic, Slovakia and Hungary

Countries	SRE (%)	SOL (%)	TRU (%)	WET (%)	ETO (%)
East Germany	19	86	24	33	35
Czech Republic	23	51	27	43	30
Slovakia	14	52	26	45	17
Hungary	12	82	22	43	13

Source: World Values Survey.

Notes
SRE: Self-responsibility; SOL: Solidarity; TRU: Trust in others; WET: Work ethics; ETO: Ethic tolerance. Cell entries are percentage of positive support.

Political participation

The deterioration of the economy, the inability of the political elite to manage mutual coexistence with the Czechs (in Czechoslovakia and, later, the Czech and Slovak Republic) and the increasing number of political scandals progressively undermined the confidence of the Slovak population in state policies and in the legitimacy of state institutions. By the end of 1998 people had lost trust in all political institutions.

They had also lost their illusions about the necessity and benefits of participation in political life (Przeworski 1995).[16] In the mid-1990s, roughly 80 percent of the respondents in a survey believed that citizens should delegate the solutions of important problems to politicians and limit their own involvement to the election of capable representatives and deputies. These citizens did not completely refuse to participate in political life, but indicated that participation should not be too frequent or demanding. Only 19 percent of respondents believed that they should be involved in politics and public life as much as possible (Mihálikova 1997: 42).

However, the legalization of rights to associate and to gather together in assemblies encouraged a rapid growth in the number of civil organizations. While, before November 1989, there were only 306 officially registered associations, their number increased up to almost 4,000 voluntary associations in January 1991. In February 1998, there were more than 12,500 associations registered.[17] In Spring 2001, the Ministry of Interior listed 16,849 organizations which could be considered as NGOs in a broad sense. In December 2001, the Slovak Parliament passed the Foundation Law and the amendment of the law about non-profit organizations. These legal norms precisely define the functioning of these types of NGOs. Nevertheless the Slovak party system in the late 1990s was very unstable, and strong bonds between citizens and parties were not established. Thus, political parties did not serve as a basis for an active political life in Slovak society.

Table 7.6 Political involvement, various years, %, East Germany, Czech Republic,
       Slovakia and Hungary

	East Germany	Czech Republic	Slovakia	Hungary
Importance of politics				
Very or rather important	47.2	25.9	28.5	27.2
Political interest				
Very or somewhat interested	75.7	55.9	58.0	49.7
Political discussion				
Frequently or occasionally	88.5	81.1	80.3	72.9
Active in one or more voluntary associations	45.6	29.8	27.6	31.5
Protest behavior				
Have done:				
Signing a petition	57.4	26.0	35.3	25.2
Attending lawful demonstrations	21.9	10.8	12.0	9.2
Joining in boycotts	11.2	10.1	11.3	3.2

Source: World Values Survey.

The data indicate that a majority of citizens in the respective countries do not regard participation in politics as a priority in their lives. It is impossible to determine whether this is a result of a conscious or subconscious rejection of absurdities in current politics, or of a more general trend in post-communist societies. All post-communist countries are confronted with rapidly decreasing levels of public interest in membership of political parties. In any case membership in newly created interest groups and organizations was more popular than membership in new political parties, which were somehow connected with the compromised Communist Party in public opinion in every post-communist country. The rejection of party politics is even evident in party names themselves, such as "movement," "forum," "alliance," "union," which try to deny the "party" character of the association.

With regard to types of political participation beyond party memberships, the Slovak respondents score comparatively high, especially in the more passive modes of participation, e.g. signing a petition.

Our findings indicate that "interest in politics" and "participation" measure two different items. The level of interest in politics is obviously higher than the willingness to participate in politics or take part in protests. This is also true for the younger generation that is not at all willing to act through any kind of formal organization, not least political parties. Exceptions are only those young people who consider involvement in politics as the best starting point for their future career. This pattern of behavior is not so distant from communist practices where party membership was the entry for a career.

The state of society in public perception

How did public opinion reflect the fact that Slovakia failed to be invited to negotiations with the EU and NATO together with the first group of post-communist countries? In October 1997, almost half of the citizens (47 percent) had a critical view of Slovakia's international status. As many as 59 percent thought that the country's international status deteriorated after the 1994 elections (Bútorová 1998: 177). Some 41 percent of the respondents felt this would lead to Slovakia's political, cultural and economic isolation within Europe, with 35 percent believing that the main consequence of poor international standing would be a slowing down of economic growth. Meanwhile, 32 percent foresaw new complications with regard to Slovakia's exports, and 18 percent feared a possible intensification of cooperation with the countries of the former Soviet Union.[18]

Yet the failure of the Mečiar government's policy had not discouraged citizens with regard to European integration. In the cited surveys, 74 percent of people in Slovakia supported membership in the EU, and only 21 percent opposed it. Regarding NATO, there was less unanimity: 48 percent supported membership, while 46 percent were opposed.

There is a broad consensus across all segments of Slovak society regarding the need for European integration: a majority of men and women, respondents with a lower and higher level of formal education, inhabitants of large towns and small villages, ethnic Slovaks and ethnic Hungarians support this aim. The majority of all political parties favor Slovakia's EU accession.

When evaluating the likely impacts of increasing cooperation between Slovakia and the EU, citizens' positive expectations exceed negative ones. They generally expect that integration will bring along more benefits than costs. Respondents to polls give five reasons for EU membership: overall progress, economic improvements and open markets, higher living standards, further integration into Europe through EU structures and financial aid granted by the EU. As for NATO membership, respondents expect these five gains: security and stability in the region, reforms of armed forces and armament industries within NATO structures, military progress and cooperation, NATO support for Slovakia and protection against Russia. Despite the fact that accession requires significant investments in

Table 7.7 "Do you support the entry of Slovakia into the EU and NATO?," various years, (% answers "yes," "no," "do not know") Slovakia

	October 1997	April 1998	June 1999	October 1999	August 2000	December 2000	June 2001
EU	74:14:12	79:11:10	66:24:10	66:25:9	72:19:9	74:21:5	62:26:12
NATO	52:35:13	58:31:11	35:53:12	39:50:11	50:39:11	48:46:6	41:46:13

Sources: Institute for Public Affairs, January 1999–August 2001; MIC, December 2001

the armed forces in order to reach compatibility/interoperability, experts agree that NATO membership will be a cheaper alternative for would-be members than, for example, neutrality (Pírek 1997).

A problem peculiar to Slovakia's European integration is the Roma community. Shortly after an encouraging statement from the EU Commission in July 1999 that Slovakia was doing well in meeting political criteria, a serious problem emerged with regard to the Roma minority. A relatively large group of Slovak Roma began an exodus to Finland and other West European countries and requested political asylum. Those countries, in an attempt to stop the influx of Slovak Roma, suspended its visa-free entry agreement with Slovakia. The Romany migration was perceived as economically motivated and western governments stated that, despite shortcomings in the living conditions of the Roma, Slovakia is a democratic country. Slovak authorities demanded a European harmonization of legislation to cope with the problem of Romany emigration. The "soft" legislation in countries like Finland and Norway, where asylum applicants receive sums several times larger than average Slovak monthly salaries and where applications can take as long as a year to be processed, need to be changed.

Although the EU Commission welcomed the progress made in Slovakia in the field of human rights and minorities, it urged the Slovak government to take all necessary measures to integrate the Roma minority, and especially to overcome discrimination in society and public institutions.

Conclusion

The agenda since 2002 has been clear and stands in contradiction to the greater part of the first post-communist decade where very little progress was made toward resolution of the ambiguities, contradictions and tensions in Slovak politics and society. Instead, the reinforcement and perpetuation of ambivalence in both domestic and international affairs was the HZDS leader's style.

Mečiar's legacy was a country "isolated at the heart of Europe" (as one western commentator put it) and, at least temporarily, excluded from integration talks. The Dzurinda administration did much to end Slovakia's isolation and made up lost ground. However, EU and NATO accession criteria are still challenging, with the country still struggling with socioeconomic problems.

Nonetheless, Slovakia, like the Czech Republic, Poland and Hungary, was among the first group of countries invited for EU membership and follows its neighbors into NATO. The process of transition has not been completed, though the struggle for the rules of the game seems to be over. At least the crises and conflicts of the 1990s did not lead automatically to the end of the process of democratization. However, there are some crucial empirical results concerning the democratic attitudes of the citizens. The support for the past political system is significantly higher than the support for the current political system. The belief that the state and not the individual is responsible for his or her destiny is strongly pronounced. The emphasis on the responsibility of the state is even higher than in the other Visegrad countries, which in turn have emphasized state responsibility more strongly than have the western European countries. Apparently, Slovakia's communist legacy has not entirely dissipated.

I am, however, convinced that democratization – and this also includes the attitudes of citizens – will continue, and that the citizens will not become mourning survivors, wailing over the grave of an adolescent democracy. What remains of Slovakia's "democratic deficit" is a product of the configuration of attitudes of the national elites. Thus the future will depend upon the behavior of this elite, the degree of their consensus over the "rules of the game" regarding both domestic and foreign policy as opposed to depending upon direct political participation of citizens.

The road ahead for the country is far from smooth. But the trend is clearly toward maturity. The population's comprehension of political realities evinced by the results of the 2002 elections can be seen as a major turning point for the country – away from political experiments and saviors and toward acceptance of often painful truths about the present and the past.

Notes

1 The "Visegrad Four" is an unofficial name of a consortium of the four central European post-communist countries, i.e. the Czech Republic, the Republic of Hungary, the Republic of Poland and the Slovak Republic. Before the split of the Czech and Slovak Federal Republic in 1993, the group was called the Visegrad Troika. The name was chosen in a meeting of the President of the ČSFR, Václav Havel, the Prime Minister of Hungary, József Antall, and the President of Poland, Lech Walesa, in the north Hungarian city of Visegrad on 15 February 1991. In this meeting the participants signed a declaration to promote close cooperation on the way to European integration and democracy. The meeting recalled a 1335 royal summit at the Castle of Visegrad (then the domicile of the Kings of Hungary), which brought together the kings of Poland, Bohemia and Hungary. They agreed to cooperate closely in politics and economics, and were thus a source of inspiration for their late successors to launch a successful central European initiative (see www.visegrad.org).
2 The Nationalities Act came into force in 1868.
3 Matica slovenská, the preserver of Slovak literary artefacts and culture in Martin, was closed by the Hungarians in 1875 and many of its assets confiscated.
4 *Dejiny Slovenska III (od roku 1848 do konca 19.storocia)*, (Neografia, Martin, 1992), pp. 689–91.
5 1921 census figures report 8,819,455 (65.5 percent) of citizens of Czech or Slovak nationality out of a total population of 13,613,172 Czechoslovak inhabitants. Slovaks comprised 1,913,792 of this figure. A significant number of Germans, 3,218,005 (23.4 percent), also lived within the First Republic's borders. See *Dejiny Slovenska IV* (Neografia, Martin, 1992), p. 32.

6 Also see *Slovenska IV* (Neografia, Martin, 1992), p. 46.
7 In Slovakia, the Democratic Party gained 62 percent, the communists 30.4 percent, the Workers Party 3.1 percent and the Freedom Party 3.7 percent of the votes (Ďurica 1996: 213).
8 According to a daily *SME* some 320,000 first-time voters participated in the September elections.
9 Data quoted from *National Human Development Report. Slovak Republic 2000* (Bratislava, UNDP, 2000), pp. 20–1.
10 Jurzyca argues:

> The per capita regional gross domestic product value for Slovakia ranks fourth among central European countries, behind Slovenia, the Czech Republic, and Hungary. The highest level of per capita GDP of all central European countries was recorded for the region of Prague, which is 120 per cent of the European Union average and 311 per cent of the average for central European countries. This is followed by the region of Bratislava, representing 97 per cent of the European Union average, and 250 per cent of the average for central European countries.
>
> (UNDP 2000: 25)

11 The seven-month tenure of Jozef Moravčik's coalition government (March–September 1994) could be seen as an exception to this trend.
12 Rudolf Schuster's political career started under communism. Previously, he had a high position in the Communist Party hierarchy. After 1989, he became the Chairman of the Slovak National Council and remained in this position until the first free parliamentary elections in summer 1990. After the communal elections of 1994, he became Mayor of Košice and strengthened his position as a charismatic, active and successful local politician. Schuster decided to create his own party after his failed negotiations with SDK and SDL, and when it became clear that he had no chance to be elected President by the MPs of the former Parliament. After the 1998 elections, Schuster was nevertheless appointed by SDK as its candidate for the presidential election, which he won.
13 See various surveys by Focus, MVK and Statistical Office of the Slovak Republic.
14 *Central and Eastern Eurobarometer.* No. 8, Fessel + GfK Austria, Politische Kultur, 1998.
15 For international comparison see: *Central and Eastern Eurobarometer.* No. 8, Fessel + GfK Austria, Politische Kultur, 1998; regular opinion polls conducted by the Statistical Office of the Slovak Republic as well as different Slovak survey agencies confirm this trend over the course of the 1990s.
16 The situation in Slovakia regarding mistrust and the willingness to participate in politics is very similar to other post-communist countries. Przeworski notes:

> Survey data indicate that new democracies often show a syndrome consisting of the mistrust of politics and politicians, sentiments of personal political inefficacy, low confidence in democratic institutions. Yet curiously, the belief in democracy as the best form of government does not bear an obvious relation to these attitudes.
>
> (Przeworski 1995: 59)

17 *National Human Development Report: Slovakia 1998* (United Nations Development Programme, Bratislava, 1998), p. 38.
18 *Názory verejnosti na integráciu Slovenska do NATO a EÚ.* Ústav pre výskum verejnej mienky pri Štatistickom úrade SR, Bratislava, October 1997.

References

Bútorová, Z. (ed.) (1998) *Democracy and Discontent in Slovakia: a Public Opinion Profile of a Country in Transition,* Bratislava: IVO.

Carpenter, M. (1997) "Slovakia and the Triumph of Nationalist Populism," *Communist and Post-Communist Studies* 30, 2.

Central and Eastern Eurobarometer (1998) No. 8, Fessel + GfK Austria: Politische Kultur.

Chovanec, J. (1994) *Historické a štátoprávne korene samostatnosti Slovenskej republiky,* Bratislava: Procom.

Dorotková, J. (1998) "Slovak Brothers Torn Apart by Politics," *The Slovak Spectator* 4, 2.

Ďurica, M. (1996) *Dejiny Slovenska a Slovákov,* Bratislava: SPN.

Fish, M.S. (1999) "The End of Mečiarism: a Vladimír Mečiar Retrospective," *East European Constitutional Review* 8, 1/2.

Fuchs, D. and Klingemann, H. (2000) *Eastward Enlargement of the European Union and the Identity of Europe,* Berlin: WZB.

Gawdiak, I. (1989) *Czechoslovakia – a Country Study,* Washington, DC: United States Government Printing Office.

Global Report on Slovakia (1996–8) Bratislava: Institute for Public Affairs.

Kaldor, M. and Vejvoda, I. (1997) "Democratization in Central and East European Countries," *International Affairs* 73, 1.

Kollár, M. and Mesežnikov, G. (eds) *Slovensko 2001: Súhrnná správa o stave spoločnosti,* Bratislava: Institute for Public Affairs.

Lettrich, J. (1993) *Dejiny novodobého Slovenska,* Bratislava: Archa.

Lipták, L. (1998) *Slovensko v 20.storočí,* Bratislava: Kalligram.

Malová, D. (1997) "The Development of Interest Representation in Slovakia After 1989: From 'Transmission Belts' to 'Party–State Corporatism'?," in Szomolányi, S. and Gould, J.A. (eds) *Slovakia – Problems of Democratic Consolidation: the Struggle for the Rules of the Game,* Bratislava: SPSA.

Mesežnikov, G. (1998) "Domestic Politics," *Slovakia 1996–1997: a Global Report on the State of Society,* Bratislava: Institute for Public Affairs.

Mesežnikov, G. and Bútora, M. (eds) (1997) *Slovenské referendum '97: zrod, priebeh, dôsledky,* Bratislava: Institute for Public Affairs.

Miháliková, S. (ed.) (1996a) *Orientations Toward Politics and Economy in Post-Communist East Central Europe,* Bratislava: Comenius University.

Miháliková, S. (1996b) "Understanding Slovak Political Culture," in Plasser, F. and Priberski, A. (eds) *Political Culture in East Central Europe,* Brookfield: Averbury.

Miháliková, S. (1997) *The Role of Political Cultures in the Transformation of Post-Communist Societies,* unpublished report, Bratislava: Comenius University.

Mikloš, I. (1998) "'Privatizácia," in *Slovensko 1997. Súhrnná správa o stave spoločnosti a trendoch na rok 1998,* Bratislava: Institute for Public Affairs.

National Human Development Report (2000) *Slovak Republic 2000,* Bratislava: UNDP.

Palmer, R.P. and Colton, T.J. (1978) *A History of the Modern World,* New York: A.A. Knopf.

Pírek, I. (1997) "NATO levnější než neutralita" (NATO Cheaper than Neutrality), *Profit* 33.

Przeworski, A. (1995) *Sustainable Democracy,* Cambridge: Cambridge University Press.

Przeworski, A. (1998) *Sustainable Democracy*, Cambridge: Cambridge University Press.

Schöpflin, G. (1993) "Culture and Identity in Post-Communist Europe," in White, S., Batt, J. and Lewis, P.G. (eds) *Developments in East European Politics*, Basingstoke, Hampshire: Macmillan.

Shain, Y. and Linz, J.J. (1995) *Between States: Interim Governments and Democratic Transitions*, Cambridge: Cambridge University Press.

Szomolányi, S. and Gould, J.A. (1997) *Slovakia: Problems of Democratic Consolidation and the Struggle for the Rules of the Game*, Bratislava: Slovak Political Science Association.

Wlachovský, M. (1997) "Foreign Policy," in Bútora, M. and Hunčík, P. (eds) *Global Report on Slovakia: Comprehensive Analyses from 1995 and Trends from 1996*, Bratislava: Sandor Marai Foundation.

8 Poland
Citizens and democratic politics

Renata Siemienska

Introduction

Poland, similar to other countries in central and eastern Europe, is still facing problems related to consolidating democracy and a free market economy. For almost half a century, from World War II until after the end of the 1980s, an idealized image of democracy emerged in Polish civil society. However, the ideal and the reality did not match. Many of those who expected a democratic and economic paradise after 1990 were deeply disappointed by the day-to-day reality of the emerging democratic regime. Standards of living declined steadily, the share of citizens with incomes far below the social minimum continued to rise, unemployment rates were increasing and services offered by the Polish welfare state continued to decrease. Whereas objective economic development was on the increase, subjective perceptions did not seem to match this perception.

This chapter focuses on the question of the preferred type of social, economic and political order and the processes linked to it by different groups in Polish society since 1990. This question will be discussed in light of theories proposed and empirical findings. This chapter's analyses are mainly based on data generated in the second half of the 1990s by the World Values Survey (1997, 1999) describing political value-orientations and current political behavior. However, data from the 1980s are also included when available.

I am going to discuss results of regression analyses for dependent variables measuring selected attitudes considered as being characteristic for democratic societies (see Inglehart 1997; Fuchs and Klingemann 2000; see also the discussion below). The independent variables are chosen in accordance with earlier empirical results pointing to their significance in explaining political value orientations and attitudes prevalent in different segments of society. These include age, gender, level of formal education, economic status, religious activity, trust in others, interest in politics and social value orientations. The last section of the chapter focuses on differences in attitudes and behaviors that are related to the respondents' value hierarchy and his or her position regarding the democracy–autocracy index.

There is a continuing discussion among political scientists on the definition of democracy. A variety of political systems, whose institutions function differently and create different relations between the elites and masses (Lijphart 1984; Dahl 1989; Huntington 1991) share certain characteristics that other political systems do not possess. The most important system attribute here is the legitimization of authority by free and open elections (Sartori 1994).

Similarly it is stressed that the source of any government's legitimation – democratic or otherwise – is its effectiveness (Lipset 1960; Huntington 1991). It is argued that even a government legitimized by elections may lose support when it proves to be ineffective, particularly in its economic policies. Analyses conducted in recent years with data from various countries allow the conclusion that, while economic growth does not automatically create a pluralistic society (one of the constitutive characteristics of democracy), it does increase the living standards of citizens. This in turn has a positive effect on levels of education and, thus, creates a positive condition for the implementation and functioning of democratic structures and institutions, and their support from civil society (Lipset *et al.* 1993). However, some authors point to different strategies to advance reforms:

> Reform-oriented governments can insulate themselves from popular demands and impose economic policies from above. Or, trying to mobilize support for reform programs, they can seek to orchestrate consensus by engaging in widespread concertation with parties, unions, and other organizations. [...] A reform policy is not one that emerges from broad participation, from a consensus among all the affected interests, from compromises.
>
> (Przeworski 1991: 183)

Another source of diversity is the type of the economic system linked to a particular democratic polity. Economists have often stressed that democratic states can co-exist with various types of economic systems.

In addition, various authors have pointed out that the popular definition of democracy, as majority rule, does not do justice to the many other forms of democracy (see Sartori 1987; Lijphart 1991; O'Donnell 1994). Lijphart, for example, proposed a distinction between a "majority" and a "consensus" type of democracy. While, in the majoritarian type, political power is concentrated in the hands of the majority, in consensus democracy power is shared by the various factions of a polity (Lijphart 1991).

The preceding notes have highlighted only some variations of the concept of democracy and the controversies surrounding its defining characteristics, as well as the conditions that enable its creation and persistence. Moreover, democratic regimes may change over time, something that is also true for western, "stable" democracies (Kaase and Newton

1995). Even more important, the very concept of democracy may also undergo changing interpretations (Inglehart 1990; Siemieńska 1996; 2000a, b). These changes reflect the political culture of the respective societies and are a result of political knowledge and philosophy, as well as cognition, attitudes and values. Thus, attitudes toward the political system and the concepts involved may primarily be (1) cognitive – that is, the result of conviction, information and analysis; (2) affective – that is, being a result of acceptance, aversion or indifference; and/or (3) evaluative – that is, being a result of moral convictions (Almond 1980).

In their analytical model for analyzing democracies, Fuchs and Klingemann (2006) distinguish three hierarchically structured levels, namely political culture, political structure and political process. The top-most level is that of political culture, whose constitutive elements are the fundamental values of a democracy. The next level is that of political structure, which consists of the democratic system of government of a country. The political process is concerned with the realization of the collective goals of a community by the actors.

In addition, these authors identify four types of democratic communities that they define along two dimensions: "The one dimension addresses the fundamental question who bears the principal responsibility for shaping and determining a person's life. The other dimension is concerned with the just as fundamental question of how relations between individuals should be" (Fuchs and Klingemann 2002: 24). The types of the resulting, ideal-typical democratic communities are presented in Table 8.1.

The experiences of recent years lead us to conclude that the process of transformation from autocracy to democracy is much more complicated than previously thought. It seems to depend on many factors, both of a physical (e.g. lack of private capital that prevents rapid privatization of business), as well as of a mental nature (e.g. the individual hardships that are a correlate of transformation processes). In fact, people in places like Poland were not aware of the modal political and economic mechanisms that govern traditional democracies. This led to the formation of very unrealistic images and expectations, especially with regard to future prosperity. It quickly showed that it was not possible to keep elements of the previous system which were considered positive (e.g. relative economic

Table 8.1 Types of democratic communities

Relationship with others	Responsibility for one's own fate	
	Self	State
Competition	Libertarian	Liberal
Cooperation (solidarity)	Republican	Socialist

equality via a secure minimal income) and similarly gain income opportunities characteristic for a capitalist economy. In addition, it turned out that not all of the post-communist countries were attaining the same level of stability characteristic of western democracies.

A political system's stability depends on many factors, particularly its level of legitimization. Democratic legitimization requires acceptance of the rules of the game by both the majority of citizens and the ruling elite (Linz 1978). However, as mentioned above, citizens' evaluation of any existing system also depends on its performance. In addition, the length of time a stable democratic system exists is another important source of its legitimization.

New democracies, which emerged in the early 1990s, were therefore confronted with many problems. They are developing democratic rules of the game with different results. In most, the degree of acceptance of the new rules of the game deteriorated because of a perceived decline of the economy and its gloomy prospects. Huntington (1996) points out that the readiness to accept democratic rules of the game and free market mechanisms is, in addition, determined by the type of the cultural context to which a country belongs. As he suggests, the situation in Europe is more heterogeneous than is often believed, since the division after World War II into non-communist western Europe and the communist eastern Europe did not much coincide with older cultural divisions. According to this hypothesis, the ability to adapt to a western model of politics and economics is greater in those post-communist countries that formerly belonged to the Catholic and Protestant states than to those dominated by Orthodox or Islamic culture. These differences were already highlighted in studies conducted in the early 1990s (Inglehart 1997).

An overview of Polish political and economic transformation during the 1990s

More than a decade has passed since the elections of 1989 – the turning point in Poland's political history. The last ten years were a period of confrontation between citizens' expectations and Polish reality, both with respect to the political as well as the economic system. These years brought substantial changes in the structure of the political landscape. However, during the first years the situation seemed to be clear cut: on the one hand, there was the old establishment, composed of the Polish United Workers Party (Polska Zjednoczona Partia Robotnicza; later Social Democracy of Polish Republic – Socjaldemokracja Rzeczpospolitej Polskiej), the trade unions and various other closely tied organizations and political parties. On the other hand, there was the opposition camp, which grew strong in the 1980s, and in which the main part was played by Solidarity. Solidarity was a trade union, but in addition to employees from various sectors of the national economy, it attracted politicians and intellectuals who opposed the communist system. The division between two political camps also reflected a division between "us" (the society) and "them" (the authority of the previous system). Over the ensuing years, however, this dichotomous cleavage dissolved. The breakdown was particularly notable on the right-hand side of the political divide. Parties emerged that emphasized their ties with the Catholic Church. Other parties emphasized their allegiance to the liberal side of the spectrum and still others stressed national traditions. In 1991, one could count approximately 200 political parties of which, however, only a small number had any impact on the structure of the political arena. In the 1991 parliamentary election, representatives of 29 political parties and groups were elected to parliament. The electoral law, which did not set proper hurdles for parties and party coalitions to enter parliament, allowed for such a situation.

The composition of 1993 parliament, however, changed drastically. This was mainly the result of a changed electoral law, which stipulated a minimum support of at least 5 percent of the valid votes cast. In addition, the political spectrum of the left consolidated. The Democratic Left Alliance (Sojusz Lewicy Demokratycznej – SLD) was formed, which united various parties, trade unions and non-governmental organizations with a left-wing orientation and sometimes with a communist genealogy. In this period, right-wing groups and parties, despite serious efforts, could not agree to form an electoral coalition, therefore votes cast for them (one-third of the valid votes cast) were wasted and none of these parties entered parliament. In part the shift of votes to the left was also influenced by the citizens' disappointment with the political and economic performance of governments in the first years of the decade.

Over the next years, the Polish right learned lessons from the defeat in 1993 and consolidated. In the 1997 elections, the number of political parties had decreased significantly. In this election, basically two coalitions were competing for political power. There was the left-wing post-communist Democratic Left Alliance coalition (Sojusz Lewicy Demokratycznej – SLD) and the right-wing Election Action Solidarity coalition (Akcja Wyborcza Solidarnosc – AWS). There were also several smaller political parties, including groups representing the German community. The election campaign was held under the motto of a struggle between two historically constituted political forces, the "post-communists" on the one hand, and the "former Solidarity camp" on the other. Although both coalitions obtained an almost equal number of votes in the elections, none reached an absolute majority. A coalition government was formed by the AWS with the Union of Freedom (Unia Wolności – UW) (a party from the Solidarity camp, although some of the leading activists had been PUWP members in the past). The fact that coalitions (AWS and SLD) have been the main actors in the political arena had specific consequences later on. Their leaders were forced to reach compromises and consensus. The problems arising from this necessity were particularly evident in the AWS. They resulted in changing party affiliations of parliamentarians, the formation of new factions inside the AWS, or in turning former party members into "independents." We might add here that the strength of political parties in Poland depends not so much on the number of actual members, but on how many people will vote for a proposed item of legislation in parliament. This situation is similar to that observed in other countries with only a brief period of democratic rule (e.g. Spain).

A typical feature of these two strongest political actors (AWS and SLD) is that trade union members played an important role in both coalitions. Thus, both tried to compete with one another in advocating demands for the protection of union members' interests. These interests are frequently defined as preserving the status quo, and if changes are unavoidable they want to attain the best possible deal for those employees who are likely to lose their jobs. For example, in the case of AWS, the Association of Catholic Families (Stowarzyszenie Rodzin Katolickich), strongly supported by the Church, has played an important role in this regard.

The necessity and direction of political and economic changes is based on internal and external preconditions. Internal preconditions include the transformation from a centralized economy, based on state-ownership (where effectiveness was measured more by the realization of ideological and political goals than by economic rationality) into a free market economy with its own criteria of success and failure. External preconditions include the expectations of the European Union and the adaptation to its *aquis communitaire*.

The agricultural sector poses a specific problem for Poland. The economic situation of rural inhabitants in the years before 1989 was not unbearable as a result of a combination of subsistence economy on the one hand, and relatively favorable political conditions on the other. That said, the centralized political and economic system, and an agricultural policy which did not take a clear position on the question of whether the agricultural sector should or should not remain in private hands (an exception in central and eastern Europe), seriously limited individual initiative. The lack of opportunities preserved an agricultural structure and contributed to the apathy of the individual farmer.

In the 1990s, farmers' incomes decreased to a greater extent than those of other sectors, not the least as a result of the lack of competitiveness of Polish agriculture compared to the more profitable and greatly subsidized agriculture of the European Union countries (Hausner and Marody 1999). Politicians talk a great deal about the need to restructure Polish agriculture; about its anachronistic character preserved over the last decades; about the lack of "human capital," i.e. educated people, who would be able to take part in transforming agriculture and the countryside into a worthwhile living and working environment. Peasants' parties, however, are against such reforms; they demand a policy that protects agriculture in its present form.

Democracy and democratic performance

Support of democratic rule

The change of the political system in 1989 included a fundamental change to the conception of the state and its mechanisms. The authoritarian regime had been replaced by a system in which elections, negotiations and conflicts among interest groups, and plurality of political orientations, became a reality. Such a system was basically unknown to a society which, for half a century, had experienced nothing but the highly centralized communist state.

Despite the pauperization of a significant share of the population during the 1990s, with national unemployment rates at about 12 percent, reaching up to 20 percent in some regions in 1997, 68.1 percent strongly agree or agree that "democracy may have problems but it's better than any other form of government," 8.9 percent disagree and 23 percent of the respondents remain undecided. The acceptance of democracy mainly depends on the level of formal education and the respondents' level of interest in politics (Table 8.2). Respondents with a higher level of formal education, and people with a higher level of interest in politics, more frequently believe democracy to be superior to other systems. The individual economic situation does not play a role here. In total, the variables considered in the regression model, however, explain only a relatively small part of the variance: $R^2 = 0.05$.

A more complex democracy–autocracy index is constructed by combining an index summarizing democratic attitudes with one measuring autocratic attitudes as described in the introductory chapter. Results show that, in 1999, a majority of respondents (54.8 percent), qualified as "weak democrats," while 13.3 percent were "undecided," that is, they neither supported a democratic nor an autocratic political regime. A total

Table 8.2 Predictors for the respondents' level of acceptance of democracy. Multiple regression model (standardized regression coefficients)

Independent variables	Beta
Sex	0.05
Age	0.06
Attendance of religious services	−0.02
Mat-postmat	0.03
Education	−0.23***
Family savings	0.09
Adjusted R^2	0.07

Notes
Index based on questions cited above. Minimum 3, maximum 12. Mean = 8.47, st. deviation 1.98.
*** $p<0.000$; ** $p<0.01$.

Table 8.3 Democracy–autocracy index (%)

Strong democrats	16.9
Democrats	54.8
Undecided citizens	13.3
Autocrats	15.0
Total	100.0

Source: WVS 1999.

of 16.9 percent of citizens fit the requirements for "strong democrats," and 15 percent had to be characterized as "autocrats." Respondents with a higher level of formal education tend to be more in favor of democracy as a form of government than respondents with a lower level of formal education ($r = -0.24$, $p < 0.000$). Apparently the level of formal education is the only differentiating factor; age distinguishes respondents in this respect to a much lesser degree ($r = 0.06$, $p < 0.03$). Church attendance and gender exhibit no influence.

Believing in the superiority of democracy as an ideal does not imply being blind to its actual flaws. Only agreement with the statement "In democracy, the economic system runs badly" correlates negatively with the respondents' positive evaluation of democracy in general ($r = -0.136$, $p < 0.000$). There is no statistically significant correlation between the respondents' position toward the statements "Democracies are indecisive and have too much squabbling" and "Democracies aren't any good at maintaining order," and their general evaluation of democracy as a form of government. This might indicate that the respondents are well aware of the discrepancy between democracy as an ideal and its actual performance in Polish politics.

Effectiveness of democratic rule

Some 46.7 percent of the respondents agreed with the statement "In democracy, the economic system runs badly." An overwhelming majority agreed that "Democracies are indecisive and have too much squabbling" and that "Democracies aren't any good at maintaining order" (83.2 percent and 75.7 percent respectively). The respondents' positions toward these statements were significantly correlated (correlation values between all three opinions range from 0.480 up to 0.721 with $p < 0.000$).

The evaluation of effectiveness of democratic rule is correlated with the level of formal education: respondents with a higher level of formal education evaluate the performance of the regime more positively (Table 8.4).

The economic situation of the respondent is also statistically important. Respondents with a lower income level frequently evaluated the democratic performance more negatively. Trust in institutions is of no influence here. However, a lack of trust in international institutions (the

Table 8.4 Predictors for the respondents' perception of the effectiveness of democratic rule (index); multiple regression model (standardized regression
coefficients)

Independent variables	Beta
Sex	0.05
Age	0.06
Attendance of religious services	−0.02
Mat-postmat	0.03
Education	−0.23***
Family savings	0.09**
Adjusted R^2	0.07

Notes
Index based on questions cited above. Minimum 3, maximum 12. Mean = 8.47, st. deviation
1.98.
*** $p < 0.000$; ** $p < 0.01$.

European Union and the United Nations) was correlated with an unfavorable evaluation of the effectiveness of democratic rule ($r = 0.20$,
$p < 0.000$). Apparently the respondents perceive these institutions as *the*
external forces impacting on the new political and economic order.

Conception of the state

Priority of self-responsibility

Respondents were asked to indicate whether citizens should be responsible for their own welfare, or whether they think it is the state's responsibility to provide welfare. The level of agreement with the statements "The
government should take more responsibility to ensure that everyone is
provided for" and "People should take more responsibility to provide for
themselves" was measured on a ten-point scale, where 1–4 was treated as a
clear preference for the first statement, while 7–10 was taken as a clear
preference for the latter.

A total of 41.7 percent of Poles indicated that "The government should
take more responsibility to ensure that everyone is provided for," while
36.2 percent preferred the option "People should take more responsibility
to provide for themselves." The respondents' choices were consistent with
their attitude toward people's influence on decisions affecting their own
lives. Among those who were in favor of broad government responsibility,
48 percent saw no reason for enlarging people's influence, while 30.2
percent nevertheless wanted to influence decisions that affect their own
lives. Among those who were convinced that "people should take more
responsibility to provide for themselves," the proportions were the
reversed: 30.8 percent did not wish to enlarge citizens' influence, while 58
percent indicated the opposite conviction.

A strong correlation also exists between agreement with the statement "People should take more responsibility to provide for themselves" and the opinion that "Private ownership of business and industry should be increased" ($r=0.40$, $p<0.000$). In addition, a positive attitude toward self-responsibility also correlated with a positive evaluation of the effectiveness of democratic rule ($r=0.21$, $p<0.000$). Supporters of self-responsibility are not distinguished from supporters of state responsibility by their attitudes toward governmental and administrative institutions, but they tend to express a higher level of trust in institutions of the public sphere ($r=0.15$, $p<0.000$). They have taken part, or are considering the possibility of taking part, in various types of political action. In addition they belong to the respondents with a higher level of formal education ($r=0.28$, $p<0.000$), to the younger generation ($r=0.12$, $p<0.000$), they are interested in politics ($r=16$, $p<0.000$) and exhibit a post-materialist orientation to a greater extent than respondents who advocate state responsibility ($r=0.13$, $p<0.000$).

Private or state ownership of business?

The structure of ownership of the means of production and services in Poland underwent substantial changes in the 1990s. Bankruptcies of state-owned plants, their privatization and the foundation of new companies with foreign and partly Polish capital changed not only the economy but also seriously affected the situation of the employees. In February 1997, 58.1 percent of the labor force was employed in the private sector. At the same time the unemployment rate rose up to 12.8 percent.

Respondents were asked to indicate on a ten-point scale whether they would prefer that private ownership of business and industry was increased, or whether government ownership would be the better solution. Of those polled, 21.9 percent believed that private ownership of business and industry should increase, while 37.7 percent were convinced that the government should own business and industry.

With regard to the question of management, however, only 24.4 percent favored the position that the government should appoint the managers. A large share of the respondents (44.3 percent) believed that both owners and employees should appoint managers together. Only 14.8 percent of the respondents were willing to leave management decisions to the owners alone. Roughly the same share (16.5 percent) expressed the opinion that the employees should own the business and should appoint managers.

Changes in the structure of business ownership and management are most acceptable for respondents with a higher level of formal education, a higher level of interest in politics, and a post-materialist orientation. It is worth discussing two other variables that are also statistically significant independent variables. These are gender and the economic situation of

Table 8.5 Predictors of the respondents' choice between private and state ownership and types of management; multiple regression models (standardized regression coefficients)

Independent variables	Private vs. state ownership (beta)	Type of management (beta)
Gender	0.10**	0.07*
Age	0.06*	0.06
Attendance of religious services	−0.04	−0.06
Mat-postmat	0.05*	0.09**
Education	−0.25***	−0.18***
Family savings	0.09**	0.09
Interest in politics (index)	−0.19***	−0.11***
Trust in other people	−0.03	0.06*
Adjusted R^2	0.17	0.10

Note
*** $p < 0.000$; ** $p < 0.01$; * $p < 0.05$.

the respondent. According to earlier studies, women were found to favor
governmental ownership of business more frequently and preferred
jointly appointed managers on a slightly higher level than men did.
Respondents with a lower income level also preferred a strong role for the
state in business ownership and management. This attitude reflects their
vulnerable position in the labor market since they are most likely to lose
their jobs first after privatization. In addition, these respondents tended to
reject a need for an increase of citizens' influence on political decisions.

The share of respondents opting for privatization of ownership and
management decisions was 31 percent and, thus, the lowest among the
countries of central and eastern Europe, except Slovakia, where the proportion was as low as 23 percent.

Confidence in institutions

Citizens' confidence in institutions is one important factor that stabilizes a
democratic system; more generally, in contributes to the stability of any
political system. Absence of such confidence resulted in Poland's crisis of
the early 1980s. The start of the transformation toward democracy in the
early 1990s led to the creation of new institutions that enjoyed high levels
of trust at first. However, these levels have tended to drop over the course
of the last decade.

In the beginning of 1997, political parties enjoyed the lowest level of
confidence (only 12.8 percent trusted parties a "great deal" and "quite a
lot"). Parties were followed by trade unions, with 29.9 percent approval
rates. The share of respondents trusting government, parliament and the
civil service was in the range of 30–40 percent. The next category consisted of the legal system, the police, major companies, as well as the press

and TV with a level of confidence between 45 percent and 55 percent. The Church (67.4 percent) and the armed forces (79.5 percent), however, were trusted by a majority of respondents. The latter enjoys traditionally high levels of confidence, while the Church was less trusted, compared to the early 1980s (Jasińska and Siemieńska 1983).

Environmental organizations and the women's movement are new phenomena that emerged after 1989. A large share of respondents expressed confidence in these organizations: 78.5 percent trust the environmental protection movement and 54.2 percent trust the women's movement, but neither plays an important role in the political arena.

Confidence in international organizations is at relatively high levels: 61 percent of the respondents expressed confidence in the European Union, and 67.5 percent in the United Nations.

The respondents' attitudes toward various types of governmental and administrative institutions and international organizations are quite consistent. There are two groups of citizens, one trusting and the other not trusting. This is reflected in the pattern of correlations. Almost all items are positively correlated and the correlations are statistically significant at the 0.000 level. The exceptions are the low correlations between confidence in the Church and confidence in the parliament, the environmental movement, international organizations and in major companies (although statistically significant, $p < 0.001$). Another exception is the lack

Table 8.6 Predictors of indexes of confidence in governmental institutions, administrative institutions and public organizations; multiple regression models (standardized regression coefficients)

Independent variables	Confidence		
	Governmental institutions (beta)	Administrative institutions (beta)	Public organizations (beta)
Gender	−0.03	−0.02	0.06
Age	0.05	0.11**	0.08*
Attendance of religious services	−0.01	−0.10**	−0.27***
Mat-postmat	0.05	0.02	−0.05
Education	−0.07	−0.17***	−0.18***
Family savings	−0.03	−0.02	0.07
Interest in politics (index)	0.14***	0.05	0.08*
Trust in people	−0.06	−0.05	−0.02
Adjusted R^2	0.02	0.06	0.13

Notes
Description of indices: index of confidence in governmental institutions: minimum 3, maximum 12; mean = 6.26, st. dev. = 1.89. Index of confidence in administrative organizations: minimum 4, maximum 16; mean = 10.35, st. dev. = 2.22. Index of confidence in organizations in the public sphere: minimum 2, maximum 8; mean 5.42, st. dev. = 1.54.
*** $p < 0.000$; ** $p < 0.01$; * $p < 0.05$.

of a statistically significant correlation between confidence in labor unions and confidence in the parliament and the legal system.

The set of socio-demographic social predictors used in the analyses explains the respondents' greater level of confidence in institutions of the public sphere than in administrative and governmental institutions. The variable which distinguishes trusting respondents from those who do not trust governmental institutions is interest in politics – those more interested express higher levels of confidence. For the two remaining indices, the respondents' level of education is the decisive predictor in that the lower the level of formal education, the higher the level of confidence. Furthermore, frequency of the attendance to religious services and age are indicators of greater confidence.

Citizens and civil society

Tolerance

There is widespread agreement among researchers of democracy that tolerance is one of the pillars upon which democracy rests. Once internalized, this virtue enables citizens to cope with the diversity of lifestyles that are characteristic of modern pluralistic society.

Several studies conducted at the beginning of the 1990s indicated that the post-communist societies of central and eastern Europe were characterized by less tolerance than their west European counterparts (Broek and Moor 1993). However, a more detailed analysis revealed a far more differentiated picture. Over the past few years, the level of tolerance has increased in Poland. In 1990 and 1994, tolerance and respect for other people was valued by 75 percent of the respondents as one of the qualities that children should be taught at home. In 1997, this percentage rose to 82 percent.

Age, level of formal education and interest in politics are important predictors of tolerance and social trust. Younger respondents, with a higher level of formal education and interest in politics, attach a higher value to tolerance than the elderly, respondents with a lower level of formal education and low interest in politics. In addition, gender turned out to be of some significance: women have more esteem for tolerance than men.

Some behaviors and lifestyles lead to controversy in most societies. These include homosexuality, prostitution, abortion and divorce. As previous cross-cultural studies (see Inglehart 1997) have shown, attitudes toward these issues have changed over the years, gaining more acceptance particularly in traditional democracies. This does not mean that they are accepted everywhere to the same degree, or that the process is linear. After periods of increasing acceptance, some might meet again with a strong negative reaction on the part of the society or/and certain groups

Table 8.7 Predictors of importance of tolerance and trust in others; multiple regression models (standardized regression coefficients)

Independent variables	Perceived importance of tolerance (beta)	Trust in others (beta)
Gender	−0.11***	0.00
Age	0.11***	−0.08*
Attendance of religious services	0.01	0.03
Mat-postmat	0.04	0.02
Education	−0.14***	−0.13***
Family savings	0.02	0.04
Interest in politics (index)	−0.11***	−0.05
Trust in people	−0.01	−
Adjusted R^2	0.07	0.02

Note
*** $p<0.000$; ** $p<0.01$; * $p<0.05$.

or factions of the political elite. Post-communist societies, and particularly Poland, provide a good example. The dominance of the Catholic Church, which always played an important role not only as a religious, but also as a political institution, was further strengthened by democratization (however, with a simultaneous decrease of citizens' confidence in it). This has led to an enforcement of legal restrictions for some of the issues, such as abortion or divorce (by introducing the institution of separation).

Respondents were asked to indicate their level of acceptance for homosexuality, prostitution, abortion and divorce on a ten-point scale. Scores between 1–3 points were treated as rejection of these behaviors, while scores between 8–10 points expressed acceptance. A total of 78.8 percent of the respondents considered prostitution as not justifiable, and the same is true for 70.6 percent of the respondents when it comes to homosexuality. Of those polled, 56.8 percent rejected abortion and 38.6 percent rejected divorce. Acceptance of prostitution was indicated by 3.5 percent of respondents, 8.2 percent accepted homosexuality, 12 percent abortion and 17.6 percent divorce. The respondents' attitudes toward all four issues are strongly correlated ($p<0.000$). The correlation between the attitude toward homosexuality and prostitution is particularly high ($r=0.57$, $p<0.000$); the same is true for the correlation between attitudes toward abortion and divorce ($r=0.64$, $p<0.000$). The remaining correlations range between 0.32 and 0.39.

When we configure the respondents in four groups by level of acceptance, it turns out that 46.9 percent of the respondents consider all of the behaviors in question as not justifiable, while only 6.4 percent accept all four issues as justifiable. The degree of acceptance is related to some extent to political values and party preferences (Table 8.8). With regard to the latter, the party adherents also differed the most were, on the one

Table 8.8 Level of acceptance of homosexuality, prostitution, abortion and divorce (index) and priority of political values (%)

Priority of political values**	Level of acceptance for homosexuality, prostitution, abortion and divorce (index)*				Total
	(1) Never justifiable (4–11)	(2) Some justifiable (12–19)	(3) Some justifiable (20–7)	(4) Always justifiable (28–36)	
Values never chosen	49.8	31.3	15.9	3.0	100
One value chosen	47.6	29.8	15.3	7.3	100
Two values chosen	44.7	31.5	17.5	6.2	100
Three (all) values chosen	43.6	23.1	17.9	15.4	100
Total	46.9	30.5	16.3	6.4	100

Notes
* Index: Minimum 4, maximum 36; based on four questions on the acceptance of homosexuality, prostitution, abortion and divorce, scale: 1 (never justifiable) to 10 (always justifiable).
** Priority for "Giving people more say in important government decisions," "Seeing that people have more say about how things are done at their jobs and in their communities" and "Protecting freedom of speech." A detailed description of the index is given in the paragraph "Priority of political values" (page 00).

hand, potential AWS voters, of whom 62.8 percent consider the behaviors in questions as never justifiable and only 2.3 percent regard them as always justifiable; while this relation is 28.1 percent and 9.2 percent for potential SLD voters.

The most important predictor variables of ethical tolerance are shown in Table 8.9. Younger respondents who rarely attend religious services and are more educated are more likely to be tolerant regarding the above-mentioned types of behavior. The pattern of relationships is the same as found in other countries with the exception of materialist–post-materialist values which play a significantly less important role in Poland (Inglehart 1997).

The belief that tolerance is an important virtue that should be taught to children strongly correlates with the acceptance of homosexuality ($r = 0.11$, $p < 0.000$) and divorce ($r = 0.10$, $p < 0.000$). This correlation is less strong in the case of prostitution ($r = 0.07$, $p < 0.01$) and abortion ($r = 0.08$, $p < 0.01$).

Trust in other citizens

Only 17.9 percent of the respondents believed that most people can be trusted. Only the respondents' level of formal education is of importance here: the higher the achieved level of formal education, the more likely the respondent is to express trust in other people. Age is of less importance and no other variable seems to have an influence on interpersonal social trust in Poland (see Table 8.7).

Attitudes toward immigrants

A definite majority of Poles favors a restricted immigration policy. Only 6 percent believe that immigration should not be restricted at all ("Let

Table 8.9 Predictors of the respondents' level of acceptance of homosexuality, prostitution, abortion and divorce (index); multiple regression model (standardized regression coefficients)

Independent variables	Beta
Sex	0.08
Age	−0.20***
Attendance of religious services	0.28***
Mat-postmat	−0.02
Education	0.14***
Family savings	−0.08**
Political interest (index)	0.02
Adjusted R^2	0.18

Note
*** $p < 0.000$; ** $p < 0.01$.

anyone come who wants to"); 27.7 percent of the respondents think that immigrant should "come as long as there are jobs available," 51.4 percent are in favor of introducing strict limits on the number of immigrants and 14.9 percent want to prohibit immigration completely.

It is common sense to believe that tolerance and trust in others should be important conditions for a positive attitude toward immigrants. Instead, both variables turned out to be less important preconditions than other socio-demographic variables. It is true, however, that people who trust others and want to teach tolerance to their children have slightly more positive attitudes toward immigrants (Siemienska 2001).

A higher level of formal education, younger age and a higher level of interest in politics are important predictors for a liberal attitude toward immigration. A high frequency of attending religious services has the opposite effect – respondents attending church more frequently tend to express a more restrictive attitude.

Citizens and democratic politics

Political involvement

The existence of civil society plays a key role in promoting and shaping a democratic system. It is defined as the sum of citizens' collective self-organized activities in the space between the governmental and economic sphere (see Habermas 1984; Walzer 1995; Young 1999). These activities potentially limit both economic and administrative powers.

As Putnam points out in his survey on local government in Italy, the

Table 8.10 Predictors of attitudes toward immigrants (index); multiple regression model (standardized regression coefficients)

Independent variables	Beta
Gender	0.05
Age	0.14***
Attendance of religious services	−0.09**
Mat-postmat	0.03
Education	−0.15***
Family savings	0.01
Interest in politics (index)	−0.07*
Trust in other people	0.05
Child qual: tolerance	0.01
Adjusted R^2	0.08

Notes
Index based on the questions discussed in the preceding section. Minimum – 1, maximum – 4.
*** $p < 0.000$; ** $p < 0.01$; * $p < 0.05$.

absence or marginalization of civil structures hinders the effectiveness and persistence of democratic institutions and processes:

> The success in overcoming the dilemmas of collective action and self-destruction of opportunism, which are revealed by these dilemmas, depend upon the wide social context, within which a specific game is played. Voluntary cooperation is easier within a society which has inherited a significant social capital in the form of norms of mutuality and a network of civic involvement. [...] It pertains to such features of social organization as trust, norms and relations, which may increase the effectiveness of the society, making it easier to co-ordinate action.
>
> (Putnam 1993: 258)

Another important by-product of a civil society was emphasized by Etzioni-Halevy:

> An important indicator of the public opinion in a democratic system is the ability to force the elites to become sensitive to social interests [...] The autonomy in itself cannot provide this sensibility, but rivalry of elites will make them seek support among the public, in order to maintain their position and to achieve their objectives.
>
> (Etzioni-Halevy 1993)

Other surveys indicate that values and belief systems of elites are correlated with values and belief systems prevalent in the respective society, although they are not identical. Elites are products of societies, from which they have originated, but their systems of values are not copies of those of "average" citizens (see Inglehart 1990; Siemieńska 2000a).

We will discuss several types of civil and political activities in Poland. We will show that the high level of mobilization in the 1980s did not remain stable after 1989. Moreover, this level is lower than in other post-communist countries, as well as in traditional democracies.

Interest in politics

In accordance with the Putnam model, we assume that citizens should be interested in politics since this will enable them to understand and take part in local and national decision-making and, more generally, to act competently within the public sphere.

The hypothesis that traditional democracies host a larger share of citizens seriously interested in politics than new democracies was not confirmed in previous surveys (WVS 1990–3). Rather, it might be the case that citizens become active in particular situations, especially when they are dissatisfied with the political regime. Surveys from the early 1990s have shown that in South Korea, South Africa, Lithuania, Bulgaria and Poland more respondents reported politics to play a "very important" or "quite important" role in their life than, for example, respondents in Switzerland, Austria, France, Italy or Belgium, not to mention the relatively new democracies of Spain or Portugal. Polish society was highly politicized during the 1980s. This period started with the formation of Solidarity, and ended with the 1989 parliamentary elections. All of this led to a change of the political system. This development started a phase in which politics did not matter as much as it did before. In 1990, 42 percent of the respondents indicated that politics played a "very important" or "important" role in their lives, while in 1997 this proportion decreased to 30 percent. This trend was also reflected in the frequency of discussion of political issues among peers. Consider that, in 1990, 83 percent of the respondents said that they frequently discussed political matters with friends, while in 1997 only 18 percent did so. It also may be reflected in the level of the respondents' interest in politics. In 1990, 49 percent of respondents reported that they were "very interested" or "somewhat interested," while this percentage declined to 42.1 percent in 1997 and 42.8 percent in 1999. This development was also mirrored in other post-communist countries with considerably lower levels of interest in politics than in traditional democracies (e.g. 64.2 percent in the USA, 77.9 percent in West Germany). Apparently interest in politics springs from various sources. Sometimes it is a result of a current economic and/or political situation; sometimes it is a persisting element of a long tradition of political culture.

Interest in politics depends mainly on the respondent's level of formal education and gender. Respondents with a higher level of formal education, men, respondents with a post-materialist orientation, older people, and the less religious expressed higher levels of interest in politics. The respondents' economic situation (measured by self-declared saving capacity) did not play a part here (Table 8.11).

Table 8.11 Predictors of political interest (index) in 1997; multiple regression model (standardized regression coefficients)

Independent variables	Beta
Sex	−0.20***
Age	0.09**
Attendance of religious services	0.07**
Mat-postmat	−0.09**
Education	0.30***
Family savings	0.01
Adjusted R^2	0.13

Notes
*** $p < 0.000$; ** $p < 0.01$.
Index based on the questions discussed in the preceding section. Minimum – 3, maximum – 9; mean = 5.39, st. dev. = 1.49.

Priority of political values

Longitudinal studies on the development of value and belief systems in Western countries indicate that many of the observed changes are a result of rapid economic development and the expansion of the welfare state after World War II. Inglehart (1990; 1997) suggests that societies are moving from materialist values, typical for a phase of "modernization," to patterns that can be characterized as "post-modern." He defines materialist values as values that emphasize economic and physical security while "post-materialist" values emphasize self-expression and the quality of life.

> Post-materialist are not non-Materialists, still less are they anti-Materialists. The term "Post-materialist" denotes a set of goals that are emphasized after people have attained material security, and because they have attained materialist security.
>
> (Inglehart, 1997: 35)

Inglehart considers the rise of post-materialist values to be partially responsible for the decline of state socialist regimes. However, the relationship seems to be more complicated because the prevalence and change of values and belief systems is determined by several other factors on the societal as well as the individual level.

The value orientation of the Polish respondents was measured by Inglehart's four-item battery. The respondent was asked to select the two most important goals that should be realized during the next decade. The four-item battery included two materialist goals – "maintaining order in the nation" and "fighting rising prices" – and two post-materialist goals – "giving people more say in important government decisions" and "protecting freedom of speech" (Inglehart 1977, 1990, 1997). From 1980 to 1984 the distribution of these values remained stable in Polish. However, a shift toward material values was observed in 1990 after the breakdown of the socialist system. This pattern persisted practically unchanged during the 1990s.

The political mobilization of Polish society in the 1980s occurred in a period of deep political, moral and economic crisis. It was also connected

Table 8.12 Materialist–post-materialist orientation of Polish society (%)

Year	Orientation		
	Materialist	*Mix*	*Post-materialist*
1980	22	62	16
1984	33	52	15
1990	31	59	10
1997	40	55	5

to the general limitation of civil liberties. Solidarity's demands reflected the popular value patterns in the 1980s, since this movement encompassed ten million people. Since the early 1990s, however, Poles had the impression that freedom of speech was safely attained. In contrast, "seeing that people have more say about how things are done at their jobs and in their communities" and "giving people more say in important government decisions" (Table 8.13) remained important goals in the 1980s, even after the democratic transformation. Apparently citizens thought that co-determination was not sufficiently implemented in various societal and political spheres after 1990.

These value orientations are strongly correlated (Pearson's *r* level of correlation significance $p < 0.000$). They are used to create the "priority of citizens' values" index (the mean of the index is 1.24, st. dev. 0.803; minimum 0, maximum 3) which basically taps an emancipative values dimension. The respondents who did not mention any of these items as particularly important values numbered 19 percent, 41 percent mentioned one, 35 percent mentioned two and 4 percent referred to all three values as important goals. Multiple regression analysis demonstrates that age is the strongest predictor and the only one which is statistically significant (beta = 0.192, $p < 0.000$), followed by the index of interest in politics, education, frequency of attending religious services, gender and the family's financial situation (R^2 0.045). Younger people, men, those more interested in politics, with a higher level of formal education and a lower frequency of church attendance, mention these values more frequently as important.

Political participation

Voting

In studies on the performance of democratic regimes, the role of elections is usually emphasized as the fundamental way to influence elites and their actions (see Schmitter and Karl 1991). Furthermore, free and fair

Table 8.13 Priority of citizens' values (%)

	1980*	1984*	1990	1997
"Giving people more say in important government decisions"	22	18	27	21
"Seeing that people have more say about how things are done at their jobs and in their communities"	39	30	16	29
Protecting freedom of speech	17	13	6	4

Source: Siemienska 1988.

elections are considered to be a basic element of a democratic regime. That said, some authors point out that secret elections or referenda are a form of collective tyranny of the majority over the individual and/or minorities. The latter, assumed to act rationally, should realize that he or she votes only for the pleasure of expressing their opinion, since the ability to influence the result, which is the total of all votes, is equal to zero (see Pettit 1999). However, even these authors do not believe that voting and referenda should be eliminated but, rather, supplemented. Putting this issue aside, it is necessary to realize that the problem is especially important for new democracies, where voting norms have not yet been internalized, and faith in the effectiveness of one's vote is rather low.

The level of participation in parliamentary elections in Poland is quite small. In 1991, turnout was 43.2 percent and in 1993, 52.1 percent went to the polls. This proportion decreased even more in 1997 to 47.9 percent and reached a dismal 46.3 percent in 2001. Similarly, in the local government elections of 1990, 42.3 percent of voters went to cast a ballot. In 1994, this share decreased to 33.8 percent. Older persons with a higher level of formal education were more likely to vote. Support of the different parties or party coalitions in January 1997 – that is, more than six months before the next parliamentary elections – is shown in Table 8.14.

In the 1997 survey, 18.0 percent of respondents declared that they would not take part in the elections, and 19.9 percent were undecided. Actually the percentage of non-voters was almost twice as high, a finding that substantiates the hypothesis that the respondents' intentions are not

Table 8.14 Potential electorates for the most important political parties in February 1997 (WVS survey) and votes in the elections to the Sejm (lower chamber of Polish parliament), September 21, 1997 (%)

Parties	Potential electorates of parties in February 1997	Votes in the 1997 elections to Sejm, September 21**
Election Action–Solidarity (AWS)	24.0	33.83
Alliance of Democratic Left (SLD)	17.3	27.23
Union of Freedom (UW)	6.0	13.37
Polish Peasant Party (PSL)	12.0	7.31
Movement of Rebuilt of Poland (ROP)	5.5	5.56
Labor Union (UP)	7.1	4.74*

Notes
Names of political parties: Election Action " Solidarity" – Akcja Wyborcza "Solidarnosc" (AWS); Alliance of Democratic Left – Sojusz Lewicy Demokratycznej (SLD); Union of Freedom – Unia Wolności (UW); Polish Peasant Party – Polskie Stronnictwo Ludowe (PSL); Movement of Rebuilt of Poland – Ruch Odbudowy Polski (ROP); Labor Union – Unia Pracy (UP).
* The Labor Union did not win seats in the parliament because it missed the threshold of 5 percent of votes. The German Minority – as a minority – got two seats (receiving 0.706 percent of votes).
** Source: Monitor Polski No. 64 from 30 September, 1997.

automatically identical with their future behavior (Aronson 1992; van Deth and Scarbrough 1995). It would be too rash to regard the undecided citizens as mere non-voters. In a situation of the emergence and evolution of a party system, those who are not planning to vote may also be regarded as a particularly interesting group. It is hard to determine whether the reason for not voting is lack of interest in politics, or a negative attitude toward the current policy supply in the political arena. However, survey results indicate that at least a large part of non-voters are not very interested in politics. Among those who did not plan to vote, 31 percent indicated a complete lack of interest in politics, while only 1.2 percent stated that they were very interested. But, we repeat once more that the lack of interest in politics might also result from the respondents' poor opinion about current governmental performance. In addition, non-voters also opt more often for a protective role of the state and indicate lower levels of confidence in government.

Protest as a form of political participation

Unconventional forms of political participation have become more and more popular in western societies since the 1970s (see Barnes *et al.* 1979). Dissenting citizens frequently tried to influence political elites to act in accordance with their interests by resorting to modes of participation beyond voting. Various forms of protest, which used to be regarded as unconventional, such as signing petitions, boycotts or illegal strikes, were gradually regarded as "conventional" and integrated in the repertoire of legitimate political actions (Inglehart 1997). On the other hand, elections showed lower rates of turnout in many countries, including traditional democracies.

Surveys in traditional democracies indicate that this process is becoming consolidated, especially among the higher-educated younger generation. The situation in post-communist countries, and particularly in Poland, is slightly different. The high level of protest actions in the last decades made protesting a basic mode of participation from the very beginning. However, according to national surveys, the number of respondents who state that they have taken part in unconventional forms of political protest is relatively small. In total, 20.4 percent said that they had signed petitions, 5.5 percent had taken part in boycotts, 9.8 percent had demonstrated, 4.1 percent had participated in strikes and 2.2 percent had occupied buildings. Participation in those forms of protest is not strongly correlated.

Similarly, a majority of the respondents (57 percent) declared that they might take part in one or more forms of protest. A multiple regression analysis shows that the factors, which impact on the readiness to participate, include age, interest in politics, trust in people, level of formal education and gender (listed according to the size of the standardized

Table 8.15 Predictors of readiness to protest (index I "might," index II "never");
multiple regression models (standardized regression coefficients)

Independent variables	Index I (beta)	Index II (beta)
Sex	−0.07*	0.08**
Age	−0.20***	0.22***
Attendance of religious services	−0.01	0.01
Mat-postmat	−0.03	0.06*
Education	0.08*	−0.16***
Family savings	0.004	0.02
Interest in politics (index)	0.18***	−0.24***
Trust in people	−0.09**	0.07*
Adjusted R^2	0.11	0.20

Notes
Index I "might protest": minimum 1, maximum 6; mean 2.19, st. dev. 1.39. Index II " never
protest:" minimum 1, maximum 6; mean 4.13, st. dev. 1.72.
*** $p<0.000$; ** $p<0.01$; * $p<0.05$.

regression coefficients which are all statistically significant). Younger
people, men, those more interested in politics, those expressing a higher
level of interpersonal trust and having a higher level of formal education,
more frequently declared a possible participation in various forms of
protest activities.

A larger share of respondents express a strong disinclination to
participate in protests ("never") and a comparatively low proportion indicate that they are at least theoretically willing to participate ("might").
With regard to Index I (possible future participation), 11.8 percent considered all suggested forms of protest as possible modes of participation;
28.2 percent expressed that they might never participate in any of these
forms.

Index II is based on "never" responses, and shows a similar pattern of
relationships as Index I. Respondents not interested in politics, older, with
a lower level of formal education, women and with a lower level of interpersonal trust, are most likely to reject all forms of unconventional political action.

It turned out that the current economic situation of the respondent,
measured as the family's ability to save, did not play a statistically significant role in explaining participation. The same is true for the frequency of
attending religious services. However, a more detailed analysis shows that
the economically weakest respondents (those who had to borrow money
to make ends meet) are least inclined to take part in signing petitions,
demonstrations and strikes. However this is not true for participating in
boycotts and occupying buildings.

The readiness to protest distinguishes the supporters of different political parties. Supporters of post-communist parties (Alliance of Democratic
Left – SLD, National Party of Retirees and Pensioners/Partia Emerytów i

Rencistów – KPEiR and Polish Peasant Party/Polskie Stronnictwo Ludowe – PSL) are less ready to participate in any type of protest than supporters of the "new" parties. The disinclination to participate in unconventional political action is also connected with a disinclination to vote: 56.4 percent of potential non-voters would not take part in any form of protest (Index I), and 42.3 percent definitely reject ("never") unconventional forms of political action (Index II).

Despite the existing tradition of mass participation in political protests, which distinguished Poles during the 1980s from other citizens of central and eastern Europe, at the end of the 1990s Poles participated in protests only as often as, for example, Czechs, Slovaks, Hungarians or Bulgarians (about 10 percent in all five countries), and even two times less often than Romanians. The protest frequency of the Romanians is closer to that of the United States (15.6 percent), Norway (26.1 percent) or both parts of Germany (West: 25.7 percent; East: 21.9 percent). Respondents from these countries also participated significantly more often in boycotts (about 20 percent) than Poles (5.5 percent in 1997 and 4.3 percent in 1999).

Apparently Poland's participation boom, although it is more deeply rooted than in other central east European countries, came down to a similar low level in the 1990s, after the transformation had started and at least some achievements seemed to be safe.

Active membership in voluntary organizations

According to the *Statistical Yearbook*, membership in voluntary organizations is not very high in Poland (1997). This is definitely an inheritance from the communist regime, when compulsory membership in various organizations was common practice. Only 0.6 percent of the respondents consider themselves to be active members, and a further 0.5 percent report themselves to be passive members of political parties or associations. A considerably higher share were member of trade unions (9.6 percent), of whom 1.8 percent consider themselves to be active. The events of the last 20 years, the fact that "Solidarity," and later the National Agreement of Trade Unions/Ogólnopolskie Porozumienie Związków Zawodowych – OPZZ (communist trade unions) became important actors in the political arena and play a significant role in the economic sphere, apparently helps them to attract quite a large number of people. Membership in political parties is correlated with membership in trade unions ($r = 0.107$, $p < 0.000$).

In total, the number of active members remains stable and low – 13.9 percent in 1997 and in 1999, and this figure is lower than in other central and eastern Europe countries as well as in traditional democracies. The number of active members in the Czech Republic, Slovakia, Hungary, Romania and Bulgaria is twice as high as in Poland. The share of active members in Norway and the eastern part of Germany exceeds the Polish share by four times while the US share was five times higher.

Are values and attitudes toward democracy and the liberal economy consistent?

The overall level of political interest is an indicator that differentiates democratic communities at the level of process, while the perception of the effectiveness of a democratic regime does so on the structural level (Fuchs and Klingemann 2000). Both variables are strongly correlated with attitudes that are considered characteristic of traditional (old) democracies. However, Poles did not express high levels of confidence in Polish institutions and that clearly distinguishes the society from many western societies (Inglehart 1997). Cognitive patterns prevalent in Polish society are very similar to those found in western democracies, but citizens' lack of confidence in institutions makes governing more difficult. However, similar problems for some western countries are also reported (Putnam 1993; Dalton 2002). It is also true that, in contrast to western societies, more general value orientations hardly correlate with values and attitudes analyzed here (see also Inglehart 1997). The exception is the material-ist–post-materialist orientation (Inglehart 1990; 1997), which correlates significantly with the political priorities index. The latter is not surprising because the political priorities index is based on the same variables as are used for the construction of the materialist–post-materialist index.

Similarities and differences between democrats and autocrats

The democracy–autocracy typology implies that democrats embrace a set of political values very different from those preferred by autocrats. To what degree and where can we observe these differences (Table 8.17)?

Polish democrats and autocrats differ in many respects. First of all, more democrats favor a broader concept of self-responsibility. Democrats also more often disagree with the statements, "In democracy, the economic system runs badly," "Democracies are indecisive and do too much squabbling" and "Democracies aren't good in maintaining order." Strong democrats are more interested in politics and consider it to be more important than weak democrats, undecided citizens and autocrats. However, following the news on television (not shown in Table 8.17) is common for all respondents. This indicates that watching TV is at least partially part of the phenomena of "being a viewer," and does not necessarily indicate an interest in politics. In addition, democrats participated more often in various types of protest and also express their willingness to participate more often than autocrats and undecided citizens.

Table 8.16 Pearson's correlation coefficients between selected attitudes characteristic for democratic communities

	Political priorities (index)	Political interest (index)	Effectiveness of democratic system (index)
Political priorities (index)	–	–	–
Political interest (index) (p)	–	–	–
Effectiveness of democratic system (c)	–	−0.11*	−0.11*
Confidence in governmental institutions (index) (s)	–	0.14***	–
Confidence in administrative institutions (index) (s)	–	–	–
Confidence in public sphere institutions (index) (s)	–	–	–
Confidence in international institutions (index) (s)	0.11**	0.15***	−0.20***
Private ownership of business (s)	–	−0.25***	0.30***
Self-responsibility (c)	−0.13***	0.16***	−0.21***
Protest ("never") index	0.09*	−0.33***	0.14***
Protest ("might") index	–	0.25***	–
Ethic tolerance (c)	–	0.11**	−0.18***
Immigration policy (c)	–	−0.16***	0.13***
Materialist–post-materialist orientation (c)	−0.79***	−0.12***	–
Sex	–	−0.17***	–
Age	−0.20***	–	0.12***
Attendance of religious services	–	0.10**	–
Education	0.12***	0.29***	−0.25***

Notes
Significant correlations: *** $p<0.000$, ** $p<0.001$, * $p<0.01$.
(c) – cultural level, (p) – process level, (s) – structural level.

Table 8.17 Political interest and attitudes of democrats and autocrats (%)

	Typology democrats–autocrats			
	1 strong democrats	*2 weak democrats*	*3 undecided citizens*	*4 autocrats*
Democ:bad econ				
1 strongly agree	4.2	7.1	16.7	17.2
2 agree	14.5	38.0	55.2	59.8
3 disagree	65.7	50.1	27.1	18.0
4 strongly disagree	15.7	4.8	1.0	4.9
Democ:indecision				
1 strongly agree	17.9	22.0	22.3	388
2 agrec	46.4	58.8	68.0	47.5
3 disagree	30.7	17.8	4.9	7.9
4 strongly disagree	5.0	1.4	4.9	5.8
Democ:no order				
1 strongly agree	17.3	19.0	26.0	38.1
2 agree	27.2	48.7	63.0	50.7
3 disagree	48.0	29.6	6.0	6.7
4 strongly disagree	7.5	2.7	5.0	4.5
Politics important				
1 very	12.2	5.7	4.1	5.0
2 rather	32.6	25.9	14,5	21.3
3 not very	43.1	46.8	43.4	36.3
4 not at all	12.2	21.5	37.9	37.5
Political interest				
1 very	16.3	5.4	2.1	2.5
2 some	42.9	38.0	26.7	32.1
3 not very	22.8	35.2	32.2	27.2
4 not at all	17.9	21.4	39.0	38.3
Sign petition				
1 done	33.9	21.8	9.7	14.2
2 might	29.5	30.3	20.1	23.5
3 never	36.6	47.9	70.1	62.3
Join boycott				
1 done	6.6	4.2	4.2	2.4
2 might	29.0	24.8	15.4	15.2
3 never	64.5	71.0	80.4	82.3
Attend demonstration				
1 done	13.0	9.5	5.5	4.3
2 might	34.2	31.7	22.1	25.6
3 never	52.7	58.8	72.4	70.1
Responsibility				
1 government	22.0	34.4	47.2	46.3
2 center	41.2	41.1	29.6	31.3
3 people	36.8	24.5	23.2	22.5
People trusted				
1 trusted	26.8	17.4	12.6	17.7
2 careful	73.2	82.6	87.4	82.3
No answer	80.0	77.2	69.2	67.7

Conclusion

Authors who compare countries with different historical and cultural backgrounds usually emphasize that socialist (communist) societies tend to be more oriented toward cooperation and solidarity than western societies (Fuchs and Klingemann 2000). The latter combine various features of liberal democracies between a libertarian or republican type of regime (such as the Anglo-Saxon states) and a liberal welfare state (such as Germany or the Scandinavian countries). Libertarian and republican democracies are characterized by a high level of citizen activities and participation, in part as a result of the limited role of the state in the provision of welfare.

In Poland, we observe differences in the attitudes and behaviors of democrats and autocrats. The nature of these differences is congruent with the differences hypothesized by the typology. A majority of strong democrats disagree with negative attitudes toward democracy, while autocrats – but also weak democrats and undecided citizens – disagree with these statements to a lesser extent. The same division between strong democrats on the one hand and the other three categories on the other was observed with regard to importance and interest in politics. Attitudes toward citizens' self-responsibility and interpersonal trust do not distinguish strong democrats from the other three groups as much as political values. Level of education is the most important socio-demographic factor differentiating between the categories of the democracy–autocracy index. Strong democrats usually belong to the group of respondents with a higher level of formal education.

Results of our analysis indicate that civil participation is not very widespread in Poland. It might be the case that Polish civil society, which supported a large mass protest movement during the 1980s, was based on ethical motivations which do not square well with the pragmatic and compromise-seeking orientations needed for participation in today's political life.

Our findings regarding value-orientations are in accordance with Inglehart's hypothesis of value change in modern societies. The independent variables that predict different value orientations best are the level of formal education, age and the level of interest in politics. The economic situation of the respondent's family is related to the perception of the effectiveness of democratic rule, preferences with regard to business ownership and management and tolerance. More general attitudes toward democracy do not seem to be influenced by individual-level economic variables. The materialist–post-materialist value orientation is of modest influence, and seems to be undergoing a process of transformation and crystallization.[1] The distribution of materialist and post-materialist values has a complex background, due to Poland's history and the political rebellion of Polish society against the socialist regime in the 1980s. This led to a particular relation between ethical motives and political action which – as we have mentioned above – after 1990 might prove to be incongruent with everyday political life in a democracy, which demands pragmatic moves and compromise within a given legal framework, rather than the great vision necessary to overthrow an autocratic political regime. However, the structural changes in Polish society and in the political and institutional landscape, the increase of citizens with a higher level of formal education and the rise of a generation that was not socialized under the communist rule leads us to conclude with a rather optimistic outlook regarding the support for democratic norms and values exhibited by the Polish citizenry.

Note

1 The same is true for the economic situation of the respondents. This is even more surprising if we take into account that the level of economic polarization of Polish society increased sharply after 1990.

References

Almond, G.A. (1980) "The Intellectual History of the Civic Culture Concept," in Almond, G.A. and Verba, S. (eds) *The Civic Culture Revisited*, Boston: Little, Brown & Co.

Aronson, E. (1992) *The Social Animal*, New York: W.H. Freeman.

Barnes, S., Kaase, M., Allerbeck, K.R., Farah, B., Heunks, F., Inglehart, R., Jennings, M.K., Klingemann, H.D., Marsh, A. and Rosenmayr, L. (1979) *Political Action*, Beverly Hills, London: Sage.

Dahl, R.A. (1989) *Democracy and its Critics*, New Haven: Yale University Press.

Dalton, R. (2002) *Citizen Politics: Public Opinion and Political Parties in Advanced Industrial Democracies*, New York: Seven Bridges Press.

Etzioni-Halevy, E. (1993) *The Elite Connection: Problems and Potential of Western Democracy*, Oxford: Blackwell.

Fuchs, D. and Klingemann, H. (2000) *Eastward Enlargement of the European Union and the Identity of Europe*, Berlin: WZB.

Habermas, J. (1984) *Theory of Communicative Action*, vol. 2, Boston: Beacon Press.

Hausner, J. and Marody, M. (eds) (1999) *Three Polands: the Potential for and Barriers to Integration with the European Union. EU – Monitoring III*, Warsaw: Friedrich Ebert Stiftung.

Huntington, S.P. (1991) "Democracy's Third Wave," *Journal of Democracy* 2, 2.

Huntington, S.P. (1996) *Clash of Civilizations and the Remaking of World Order*, New York: Simon and Schuster.

Inglehart, R. (1977) *The Silent Revolution: Changing Values and Political Styles*, Princeton: Princeton University Press.

Inglehart, R. (1990) *Culture Shift in Advanced Industrial Society*, Princeton: Princeton University Press.

Inglehart, R. (1997) *Modernization and Postmodernization*, Princeton: Princeton University Press.

Inglehart, R. and Siemieńska, R. (1988) "Changing Values and Political Satisfaction in Poland and the West," *Government and Opposition* 23, 4.

Jasińska, A. and Siemieńska, R. (1983) "The Socialist Personality: a Case Study of Poland," Special Issue of *International Journal of Sociology* 8, 1.

Kaase, M. and Newton, K. (1995) *Beliefs in Government*, Oxford: Oxford University Press.

Lijphart, A. (1984) *Patterns of Democracies: Majoritarian and Consensus Government in Twenty-one Countries*, New Haven: Yale University Press.

Lijphart, A. (1991) "Majority Rule in Theory and Practise, the Tenacity of a Flawed Paradigm," *International Social Science Journal* 129.

Linz, J.J. (1978) "Crisis, Breakdown and Reequilibration," in Linz, J.J. and Stepan, A. (eds) *The Breakdown of Democratic Regimes*, Baltimore: the Johns Hopkins University Press.

Lipset, S.M. (1960) *Political Man*, New York: Doubleday.

Lipset, S.M., Seong, K. and Torres, J.C. (1993) "A Comparative Analysis of the Social Requisites of Democracy," *International Social Science Journal* 136.

O'Donnell, G. (1994) "Delegative Democracy," *Journal of Democracy* 5, 1.

Pettit, P. (1999) "Republican Freedom and Contestatory Democratization," in Shapiro, I. and Casiano, H. (eds) *Democracy's Value*, Cambridge: Cambridge University Press.

Przeworski, A. (1991) *Democracy and the Market: Political and Economic Reforms in Eastern Europe and Latin America*, Cambridge: Cambridge University Press.

Putnam, R.D. (1993) *Making Democracy Work: Civic Traditions in Modern Italy*, Princeton: Princeton University Press.

Sartori, G. (1987) *The Theory of Democracy Revisited*, Chatham: Chatham House Publishers.

Sartori, G. (1994) *Demokracja (Democracy)*, Warsaw: PWN.

Schmitter, P.C. and Karl, T.L. (1991) "What Democracy Is . . . and Is Not," *Journal of Democracy* 2, 3.

Siemieńska, R. (1996) *Kobiety: nowe wyzwania – Starcie przeszłości z teraźniejszością (Women: New Challenges – Clash of the Past and the Present)*, Warsaw: Instytut Socjologii Uniwersytetu Warszawskiego.

Siemieńska, R. (2000a) "Elites' Value Orientations," in Vianello, M. and Moore, G. (eds) *Gendering Elites: Economic and Political Leadership in 27 Industrialised Societies*, New York: Macmillan.

Siemieńska, R. (2000b) *Nie mogą, nie chcą czy nie potrafią? O postawach i uczestnictwie politycznym kobiet w Polsce (They Have No Opportunities, They Do Not Want, They Are Unable, Do They? About Attitudes and Women's Political Participation in Poland)*, Warsaw: ISS UW and Friedrich Ebert Stiftung, UNESCO Chair, "Women, Society and Development," Warsaw University.

Siemieńska, R. (2001) "Post-Communist Societies: Tolerance in Transition in the 1990s," in Farnen, R., Frizsche, F., Karl, P., Kos, I. and Meyenberg, R. (eds) *Tolerance in Transition*, Oldenburg: BIS Universitat Oldenburg.

Statistical Yearbook (1997) Warsaw: Main Statistical Office.

Young, I.M. (1999) "State, Civil Society, and Social Justice," in Shapiro, I. and Casiano, H. (eds) *Democracy's Value*, Cambridge: Cambridge University Press.

van den Broek, A. and de Moor, R. (1993) "Eastern Europe after 1989," in Ester, P., Halman, L. and de Moor, R. (eds) *The Individualizing Society: Value Change in Europe and North America*, Tilburg: Tilburg University Press.

Van Deth, J.W. and Scarbrough, E. (1995) "The Concept of Values," in Van Deth, J.W. and Scarbrough, E. (eds) *The Impact of Values*, Oxford: Oxford University Press.

Walzer, M. (1995) "The Idea of Civil Society," in Walzer, M. (ed.) *Towards a Global Civil Society*, Providence: Bergham.

World Values Survey (1990–3).

World Values Survey (1995–9).

9 Latvia

Democracy as an abstract value

Ilze Koroleva and Ritma Rungule

Introduction

Latvian society experienced multiple serious changes in the twentieth century. As a consequence, children were reared within one set of social and political norms and were forced to adapt to new values and modes of social behavior as adults. The recent transition processes once more affected the whole of society's and citizens' belief systems. Postmodern and materialist values co-exist, with the former becoming increasingly popular among the younger generation since the beginning of the 1990s. In general, the belief systems of the youngest cohorts resemble those of the elderly, i.e. these individuals are closer to their grandparents than to their parents. The latter were raised under Soviet rule, while the elderly spent their childhood and adolescence in an independent Latvia (1918–40), like their grandchildren.

During the late 1980s, political participation increased substantially. Such a participation "boom" was observed in all ex-socialist countries, since this was the first chance to freely express dissenting political opinions. Levels of participation remained high until 1991, when the reforms actually began. After 1991, political action was replaced by passivity and political apathy. What are the reasons for this development?

All previous reforms were aimed at the establishment of political institutions and the development of a legal and administrative system. Many resources were devoted to this goal, i.e. institutional interests were placed before individual needs. As a result, macroeconomic indicators showed a stable and improving economic performance, while individual living standards decreased. The share of poor households is still rising. According to the official doctrine, individual welfare is the responsibility of the individual and not an issue of social politics. However, people believe that the main reasons for decreasing living standards are of a macroeconomic nature and thus cannot be influenced by the individual.

The Latvian situation fits Offe's (1996: 45) description:

> As macro events have assumed an incredible speed, the painful task of patient waiting falls upon the individuals. They must quickly adapt themselves to the new circumstances and then be ready to wait for a

long time for the fruits of this adaptation. What is required is therefore the virtues and moral resources – flexibility, patient waiting, deliberating, probing, weighing one's short-term against long-term and individual against collective preferences, tolerance of highly unequal distribution patterns [. . .]

The main characteristics of the Latvian transition are privatization, social differentiation and polarization, and alienation. The change of the whole symbolic environment in the Latvian society has challenged people's core values. The majority adapted to a kind of Orwellian "double thinking" and maintained a kind of "socialist mentality" at the same time – a feature that we understand to be a major obstacle to successful democratization and a transition to a free market economy (Lauristin *et al.* 1997).

We rely on Latvian 1996 World Values data in order to characterize the most important aspects of the development of the Latvian democratic community. In analyzing the changes that took place in Latvia after 1990, we followed the concept of the development of a democratic community and political support put forth by Dieter Fuchs and Hans-Dieter Klingemann regarding differences of attitudes toward democracy and politics between eastern and western Europe (2000: 52):

> The West–East difference we have described is concerned with differing types of democratic community. Between the countries of Europe there is little difference in the political values and behaviors that are essential to a democracy. The potential for Europeans in Western, Central and Eastern Europe to consider each other as democrats, and to integrate this understanding in their collective identity is thus considerable.

To outline the differences in opinions within the East–West axis, we have compared the opinions of people from Baltic countries and those from Norway and West Germany.

In the following sections, we employ Inglehart's model of "culture shift" (Inglehart 1990). This model enables us to understand the mechanism of change in a value system. Focusing on cultural changes beyond modernization, Inglehart predicted a universal cultural shift from materialistic to post-materialistic values. We will try to determine if and how this development is expressed in the distribution of values among the Latvian population. We are going to describe and analyze this distribution with data from the World Values Survey 1996. In the first section, having determined the general distribution of democrats and autocrats in Latvia, we analyze the level of involvement in politics, as demonstrated by interest in politics and the level of membership in associations. The second section deals with citizens' attitudes toward democracy and the third section analyzes citizens' attitudes toward other citizens.

Citizens and the democratic state

The democracy–autocracy index

According to their attitude toward democracy and autocracy, the respondents can be grouped into the following four categories: (1) "Strong democrats" assess democracy very positively and autocracy negatively. (2) "Weak Democrats" assess democracy merely positively. The group of (3) "Undecided citizens" are respondents who express a relatively balanced mixture of preferences for democracy and autocracy, or of those who felt unable to give any answer at all. (4) "Autocrats" are respondents who give a favorable assessment of autocracy and simultaneously an unfavorable evaluation of democracy.

The distribution of respondents among the four groups confirms that a majority of Latvian citizens can be classified as democrats. However, 61 percent of respondents belonged to the group of weak democrats, while only 10 percent belonged to the category of strong democrats. In total 26 percent turned out to be undecided citizens and only 3 percent could be considered autocrats. The comparatively large share of undecided citizens (roughly one-quarter of all respondents) and the large share of weak democrats suggests that the majority of Latvians holds a rather distant position with regard to democracy and its merits.

Priority of democratic rule (instead of autocratic rule)

In this section we describe in detail the distribution of attitudes and values that were combined in the democracy–autocracy index. To determine the strength of democratic attitudes among the respondents, they were first asked to indicate if they thought democracy was a good way of governing the country.

In general, the respondents support a democratic political system in Latvia. A majority (87 percent) believed that democracy was a good way of governing Latvia (although only 23 percent regarded a democratic system

Table 9.1 The democracy–autocracy index, 1996, %, Latvia

Strong democrats	10
Weak democrats	61
Undecided citizens	26
Autocrats	3

Table 9.2 Attitudes toward democracy I, 1996, %, Latvia

	Very good	Fairly good	Fairly bad	Very bad
Having a democratic political system	23	64	11	2

as very good), and only 2 percent deemed democracy a failure. Second, the respondents were asked to weigh the merits of democracy against those of other regime types.

Again, most respondents expressed support for democratic order; 81 percent agreed that democracy was the best form of government, and only 17 percent disagreed with this statement.

The prevalence of autocratic attitudes among the respondents was surveyed with questions about the respondents' attitudes toward a strong leader who does not have to bother with parliament and elections, and toward army rule.

With respect to political leadership, we observe a phenomenon quite common in the former Soviet republics. Even though citizens' support for democracy as an idea and as a set of principles is strong, a strong, autocratic leader is still perceived as an efficient way to establish and maintain order and economic growth. People support democracy as opposed to the totalitarian state they have lived in for 50 years, but democratic attitudes are not strongly rooted in civil society. Additionally it might be the case that the interrelations of the core elements of the concept of democracy are not perceived as such and thus a strong leader and democracy are not understood as contradictory.

The elderly in particular tend to express a kind of nostalgia, in that they glorify the Soviet rule or the last "golden years" of the pre-war independent Latvia, under the autocratic regime of President Karlis Ulmanis. They were much more likely to be supportive of a strong leader than younger people were. Only 9 percent of respondents younger than 30 years of age believed a strong leader to be very good for Latvia, while 22 percent of those older than 60 years did. In total, 63 percent of those

Table 9.3 Attitudes toward democracy II, 1996, %, Latvia

	Agree strongly	Agree	Disagree	Disagree strongly
Democracy may have problems, but it's better than any other form of government	19	65	15	2

Table 9.4 Attitudes toward autocracy, 1996, %, Latvia

	Very good	Fairly good	Fairly bad	Very bad
Having a strong leader who does not have to bother with parliament and elections	14	32	37	17
Having the army rule	1	5	27	68

under the age of 30 and only 39 percent of those older than 60 years deemed a strong leader to be bad for the country.

Army rule, however, was strongly condemned; 95 percent of respondents regarded it as bad for Latvia, and less than 1 percent believed it to be "very good."

Attitudes toward the desirability of a strong leadership differ between respondents from the ex-Soviet republics and respondents from Norway and West Germany, where a strong leadership is less popular than in the Baltic countries.

Effectiveness of democratic rule

After the respondents expressed their attitude toward democracy as an ideal, they were asked to rate the efficiency of democracy by indicating their agreement or disagreement to the statements shown in Table 9.6.

Even though most respondents expressed a rather strong support for democracy in general, they also believed that democracy had serious flaws. Since the establishment of a democratic political system in Latvia coincided with the collapse of a socialist, centralized economy, an economic crisis and a serious decrease in individual living standards, a majority is convinced that democracy has affected Latvian economic performance negatively. Thus, 73 percent of respondents agreed that the economic system runs badly under democratic rule. About one half of the respondents (49 percent) agreed that democracies were not good in

Table 9.5 Attitudes toward democracy and autocracy, 1996, %

	Estonia	Latvia	Lithuania	Norway	West Germany
Having a democratic system: very or fairly good way of governing	89	89	88	96	96
Having a strong leader who does not have to bother with parliament and elections: very or fairly good	38	46	64	14	10

Table 9.6 Efficiency of democracy, 1996, %, Latvia

	Agree strongly	Agree	Disagree	Disagree strongly
In democracy, the economic system runs badly	8	65	24	4
Democracies are indecisive and have too much squabbling	3	38	46	13
Democracies aren't good at maintaining order	5	44	45	6

maintaining order, and 41 percent believed that democracies were too indecisive.

Concept of the state

To determine people's perceptions of the optimal distribution of roles between individuals and the state, we asked the respondents to indicate whether they believed that the government should take more responsibility to ensure that everyone is provided for (1) versus whether people should take more responsibility to provide for themselves (10).

The respondents' answers to this question show that the Soviet years have seriously influenced peoples' concept of the relationship between government and society. More than one half of respondents (52 percent) supported the idea that the government should take more responsibility to ensure that everyone is provided for, while only 11 percent believed that people should take more responsibility for themselves. The median score (3), as well as the mean (3.89) reconfirm that a state-centered attitude toward the question of individual welfare is rather popular. The mode (1) indicates that many people hold this view very strongly.

Under the Soviet system, private initiatives were suppressed, and the ubiquitous government control and influence taught people to accept the government's leading role in every domain. Additionally, the state provision of free education and healthcare increased public reliance on the government. In Soviet society, the government and the communist party elite made all the important decisions, and private initiative was in general condemned as "capitalistic," "bourgeois" and "anti-communist." Therefore, citizens' autonomy and private initiative were replaced by dependence on state provisions of welfare. This is also confirmed by other, more recent surveys. Excessive reliance on the government and a lack of private initiative are among the most serious obstacles to successful economic development in Latvia.

The picture is less clear when it comes to the question of government

Table 9.7 State responsibility vs. self-responsibility, 1996, Latvia

The government should take more responsibility to ensure that everyone is provided for (1–3)	52%
In-between (4–7)	37%
People should take more responsibility to provide for themselves (8–10)	11%
Mean	3.89
Median	3
Mode	1
Variance	6.36

Note
* "1" corresponded to complete agreement with the first proposition (1) and "10" to complete agreement with the second proposition (10).

involvement in business ownership and management. Again, respondents were asked to indicate their own position in relation to two opposite statements: that private ownership of business and industry should be increased (1) and that government ownership of business and industry should be increased (10).

Apparently, Latvians have no clear preference structure with regard to the issue of public versus private ownership. Both positions attracted roughly the same shares of supporters, while almost one half of the respondents (48 percent) did not strongly favor either of the two propositions. One-quarter (25 percent) believed that there should be more state-owned enterprises, and just above one-quarter (27 percent) believed that the share of private ownership should increase.

When it comes to the question of how companies and industry should be managed, the respondents are again divided. Even though many respondents did not support an expansion of private ownership, only a minority favored an economy under complete government control. The return to a state-centered economy with competencies to appoint the management was the least popular option (9 percent). Most respondents replied that the managers of businesses should either be appointed by the owners (37 percent) or be selected by owners and employees together.

Both questions proved that Latvian citizens have ambiguous attitudes toward a free market economy and its specific features. On the one hand, having experienced the absurdity of a state-centered economy, citizens are against total government control, while on the other hand, they also fear the emerging market-economy and its impact on the individual employee.

Table 9.8 Government ownership vs. private ownership, 1996, Latvia

Private ownership of business and industry should be increased (1–3)	27%
In-between (4–7)	48%
Government ownership of business and industry should be increased (8–10)	25%
Mean	5.38
Median	5
Mode	5
Variance	6.74

Note
* "1" corresponded to complete agreement with the first proposition and "10" to complete agreement with the second proposition.

Table 9.9 Business and industry management, 1996, %, Latvia

The owners should run their business or appoint the managers	37
The owners and the employees should participate in the selection of managers	36
The government should be the owner and appoint the managers	9
The employees should own the business and should elect the managers	18

Political institutions and organizations

Elements of political culture such as confidence in institutions and interpersonal confidence can indicate the maturity of a political system and a civil society. In the following sections we describe the levels of trust in different categories of institutions.

Confidence in governmental institutions

The respondents' positions again confirm a discrepancy between citizens' general support for democratic principles and their dissatisfaction with the way democracy actually works in Latvia. They report low levels of confidence in the institutions that should represent their interests.

Immediately before and after the restoration of national independence in 1991, people felt united with the government and the parliament by a common goal, namely the establishment of an independent and wealthy Republic of Latvia. After 1991, economic interests and petty quarrels increasingly dominated politics and corruption flourished. Thus, citizens felt alienated from the political elite and politics in general.

Less than 11 percent of respondents trusted political parties. 25 percent trusted the parliament and 38 percent had "quite a lot" or "a great deal of" confidence in the government.

The comparatively small share of respondents trusting political parties can be explained as a consequence of the rather weak institutionalization of the party system, especially between elections. Most parties become visible only in election campaigns, while their level of activity between elections is low. In addition, a lot of the information about political parties in the media deals with internal conflicts or splits and mergers of political factions and broken pre-election promises. Thus, the public image of political parties is rather negative.

Confidence in administrative institutions

In general, the Latvian respondents report little confidence in administrative institutions. The armed forces and the police were least trusted; 69 percent did not have much confidence in each of them, 62 percent

Table 9.10 Trust in governmental institutions, 1996, %, Latvia

	A great deal of confidence	Quite a lot of confidence	Not very much confidence	No confidence at all
The parliament	2	23	47	28
The government of Latvia	3	35	40	22
Political parties	<1	10	47	43

Table 9.11 Trust in administrative institutions, 1996, %, Latvia

	A great deal of confidence	Quite a lot of confidence	Not very much confidence	No confidence at all
The legal system	3	36	44	18
The civil service	2	42	44	11
The police	2	29	47	22
The armed forces	3	28	43	26

distrusted the legal system and 55 percent had little or no confidence in the civil service.

Levels of trust in the legal system, and especially in the police, are higher in Norway and in West Germany than in the Baltic States. A remarkable exception here is Estonia, where levels of trust in the legal system are comparable with levels in Norway and Germany, and levels of trust in the police are roughly 20 percent and 30 percent higher than in Latvia and Lithuania.

Confidence in institutions of the public sphere

Altogether, the respondents reported more confidence in public organizations than in administrative and governmental institutions. Churches were trusted by the highest share of respondents (64 percent had "quite a lot" or "a great deal" of confidence in churches), closely followed by the ecology movement (62 percent) and television (58 percent). Almost half of the respondents trusted in major companies (46 percent), the press (49 percent) and the women's movement (49 percent).

Table 9.12 Confidence in order institutions, 1996, %

	Estonia	Latvia	Lithuania	Norway	West Germany
The legal system	61.6	38.3	22.2	69.5	54.5
Police	51.0	31.1	20.8	85.6	71.0

Table 9.13 Trust in public institutions, 1996, %, Latvia

	A great deal of confidence	Quite a lot of confidence	Not very much confidence	No confidence at all
The churches	18	47	24	11
Labor unions	2	48	42	9
Greens/ecology movement	12	50	29	9
The women's movement	9	40	36	15
Media	2	47	42	9
Television	4	54	36	6
Major companies	5	41	39	15

The comparatively low share of respondents who trust in major companies can be seen as an expression of the widely shared opinion that many entrepreneurs made their fortune by unfair (and sometimes illegal) means. The high proportion of people who reported having no confidence in the women's movement may echo the anti-feminist propaganda that had prevailed under the Soviets.

Confidence in international organizations

Latvian respondents report having more confidence in international organizations than in their own government. A majority (59 percent) had confidence in the EU, and almost two thirds (65 percent) had confidence in the UN; 12 percent and 10 percent, respectively, had no confidence in these organizations.

Citizens and democratic politics

Interest in politics

To determine the respondents' level of interest in politics, they were first asked to indicate how important politics was in their lives.

After the mass mobilization in the beginning of the 1990s, the importance of politics in people's lives and their interest in politics decreased. Politics and religion were ranked lowest of the six issues in question. Politics was an important issue for only 27 percent, while more than 90 percent regarded work and family as important.

Table 9.16 further reveals respondents' general level of interest in politics.

Table 9.14 Trust in international organizations, 1996, %, Latvia

	A great deal of confidence	Quite a lot of confidence	Not very much confidence	No confidence at all
The European Union	8	51	30	12
The United Nations	12	53	26	10

Table 9.15 Importance of politics, 1996, %, Latvia

Values	Very important	Rather important	Not very important	Not at all important
Family	68	26	5	1
Friends	24	57	17	2
Leisure time	20	46	28	6
Politics	5	22	44	29
Work	56	35	6	3
Religion	13	25	34	28

Table 9.16 Interest in politics, 1996, %, Latvia

Very interested	8
Somewhat interested	44
Not very interested	36
Not at all interested	12
Total	100

While the respondents in Latvia did not attach much importance to politics compared to private issues such as family and work, more than a half (52 percent) stated that they were interested in politics. Only 12 percent reported having no interest in politics at all. It might be the case that the question about importance evokes the notion of a type of involvement rather active involvement, while the question about levels of interest relates to a more passive interest.

The level of interest in politics varies considerably with regard to standard sociological categories. Men express more interest in politics than women. Age is another important factor: older respondents turned out to be more interested in politics than their younger counterparts. Respondents with a higher level of formal education are also more interested in politics than the less educated. There was no significant difference in the levels of interest in politics between ethnic Latvians and Russians.

Finally, the respondents were asked to answer a question about the frequency of political discussions with their friends, the results of which are displayed in Table 9.17.

Politics was a popular subject in debates among friends in Latvia. Only 15 percent of respondents never discussed political issues; 18 percent talked about politics with their friends often; 67 percent did so occasionally. Men are more often involved in political debates than women, and older people debate politics more frequently than the younger generation.

Respondents from Norway and West Germany indicated higher levels of political participation than Latvians and respondents from the two other Baltic countries. This might point to the fact that the development of a stable democratic regime precedes the development of a lively political culture in which politics are embedded in the lives of ordinary citizens.

Table 9.17 Political discussions with friends, 1996, %, Latvia

Frequently	18
Occasionally	67
Never	15
Total	100

Table 9.18 Political motivation, 1996, %

	Estonia	Latvia	Lithuania	Norway	West Germany
Importance of politics: very or rather important	28	27	28	45	55
Political interest: very or somewhat interested	49	52	44	69	78
Political discussion: frequently or occasionally	80	85	79	86	90

Priority of political values

In this section we analyze the respondents' priorities with regard to aims and tasks the Latvian society should reach and fulfill in the future. The respondents were first asked to indicate what they believed to be the most important aim for Latvia in the future.

In the midst of economic crisis and the transition from a socialist to a free market economy, economic survival is a central issue for the majority of citizens. It is therefore not surprising that more than three-quarters (76 percent) of respondents gave their first priority to economic growth and a further 14 percent selected improvement of the economy as their second choice. Of the four items offered, "seeing that people have more say about how things are done at their jobs," was the second most important aim: 13 percent of respondents selected it as their top priority and 41 percent mentioned it as their second choice. Military security and a beautiful environment were seen as less important than democratic order at the workplaces and in local communities.

Again respondents were asked to rate the importance of issues such as maintaining order and fighting rising prices (Table 9.20).

For a majority, "maintaining order in the nation" was most important; 56 percent selected it as their first choice and 23 percent as their second choice. "Giving people more say in important government decisions" was

Table 9.19 Latvian future aims, 1996, %, Latvia

	First choice	Second choice
A high level of economic growth	76	14
Making sure this country has strong defense forces	7	22
Seeing that people have more say about how things are done at their jobs and in their communities	13	41
Trying to make our cities and countryside more beautiful	3	19
Total	100	100

Table 9.20 Priority of political values, 1996, %, Latvia

	First choice	*Second choice*
Maintaining order in the nation	56	23
Giving people more say in important government decisions	25	26
Fighting rising prices	16	35
Protecting freedom of speech	3	13
Total	100	100

the first priority for 25 percent and 26 percent mentioned it as their second choice. While having a say in government decisions was perceived as rather important, "protecting the freedom of speech," a precondition for participation in decision-making, was evaluated as comparatively unimportant. Only 3 percent of respondents selected it as their first choice and 13 percent ranked it second. This was probably the only achievement of the last decade the respondents did not perceive as endangered. During the last ten years, prices sky-rocketed compared to the average income of people, crime was rampant and politics was considered to be largely corrupt. People felt alienated from government decision-making, and the opinion that the government worked only for its own interest was widely shared. However, freedom of speech was in no way restricted. Thus, people longed for order in the nation, for a stable economy and for more influence on government decisions, whereas freedom of speech was taken for granted.

Political participation

High levels of political participation in Latvia have been observed since the late 1980s. This type of political participation was completely different from the forced participation under Soviet rule. After regaining independence, this was the first time when people could express their views freely, establish and re-establish political parties and organizations, and participate in meetings and demonstrations. From 1992, this period of activity was followed by a period of political apathy and depression. People were disappointed with the slow pace of reforms; they had to face economic difficulties and lost trust in their own ability to influence politics. We are going to describe this development in the following sections for different types of political action.

Voting

Participation in elections is the simplest and the most widespread form of political participation. Since 1991, the turnout at elections has been decreasing continuously. In the election of the sixth parliament (*Saeima*) in 1995, the participation rate was 71.9 percent. Nineteen political parties participated in the pre-election campaign of the sixth *Saeima*. Only nine of them won seats in the parliament, but no single party won a majority. The sixth *Saeima* election was a protest election; the results were largely influenced by public disgruntlement with the existing parliament and government. The majority of the electorate voted for a different party from the one they chose in the previous election.

The results of the election were influenced by citizens' alienation from the political elite. A banking crisis and decreasing living standards had weakened people's trust in the government. Many political leaders had lost trust in themselves. Several populist parties used this moment to gain popularity by criticizing the unpopular decisions of the government – they even opened soup kitchens and distributed food. This was an excellent way to win the support of large sections of the poor. As a result, the so-called *Sigerist* Party (a populist party established by a German entrepreneur) won 16 seats in the Parliament (out of 100). This came as a big surprise for all analysts; none of the public opinion polls had predicted anything close to this result. The electorate of this party was mainly recruited from the poor and the elderly. However, this party failed to maintain its level of popularity after the election due to its inability to participate in democratic procedures and decision-making.

Beyond voting

There are many forms of political action beyond voting that require a comparatively low level of effort, e.g. signing a petition. Others, such as joining wildcat strikes, require much higher levels of effort and courage. All of these forms of action have to be analyzed in addition to voting in order to give an adequate impression of the level of political activity. The respondents were asked to indicate whether they have actually participated or might participate in a number of actions (Table 9.21).

Nearly two-fifths (39 percent) of all respondents had participated in at least one type of the listed activities, and less then one-fifth (18 percent) would never participate in any of those. Signing petitions (31 percent) and attending lawful demonstrations (20 percent) were the most popular

Table 9.21 Participation levels for different types of political action, 1996, %, Latvia

	Have done	Might do	Would never do
Signing a petition	31	40	29
Joining in boycotts	8	42	50
Attending lawful demonstrations	20	42	38
Joining unofficial strikes	3	17	80
Occupying buildings or factories	0	7	93

forms of political action. The latter is explained by the large numbers of Latvians who attended demonstrations during the process of gaining national independence (1989–91).

Illegal actions such as occupying buildings and factories and joining wildcat strikes were rather unpopular; 93 percent and 80 percent of respondents, respectively, would not participate in such activities.

Active membership in voluntary organizations

Another, more continuous, form of participation is membership in organizations, be it of an active or inactive nature.

Before the restoration of independence of Latvia, most citizens were members of at least one organization. Almost all were members of a labor union. After a rapid increase in the number of organizations in the first years of independence, people's participation decreased considerably in the first half of the 1990s.

Despite the fact that more than 30 political parties were registered in Latvia, of which nine were represented in the parliament, very few people were actually members of a political party. In this survey, less than 1 percent of respondents claimed to be active members of a political party, and 2 percent were inactive members. Even fewer people were members of environmental organizations.

The most popular organizations were church and religious organizations (4 percent active and 10 percent inactive members) and labor unions (2 percent active, 16 percent inactive members).

In general, voluntary organizations, such as charitable, art or sports associations, were not very popular among Latvian citizens. Membership levels were around 1–5 percent for organizations of this type. However, in recent years the level of active participation in voluntary organizations increased slightly. Not only the number of NGOs but also the level of financial support, e.g. from different foundations, increased, and it became easier to attract new members.

Table 9.22 Memberships in different types of organizations, 1996, %, Latvia

	Active member	Inactive member	Don't belong
Political party	1	2	97
Labor union	2	16	83
Professional association	3	6	91
Church or religious organization	4	10	87
Environmental organization	1	1	98
Charitable organization	1	1	98
Art, music or educational organization	5	5	90
Sport or recreation organization	5	4	91
Any other voluntary organization	2	2	96

The comparatively low membership levels might be due to both the still-present memory of coerced memberships under Soviet rule and the fact that many voluntary associations are still largely unknown to a majority of citizens.

Levels of participation in voluntary associations in the Baltic States are remarkably lower than in stable democracies – only 15 percent of Estonians are active in voluntary associations, the same is true for only 17 percent of Latvians and 12 percent of Lithuanians, compared to 58 percent in Norway and 60 percent in Western Germany.

Political participation in Latvia and the two other Baltic countries is of a more passive and probably more emotional nature than in Germany and Norway. Politics is more understood as political administration that is undertaken by elected professionals and not as a matter of everyday life.

Citizens and civil society

Five years after the collapse of the USSR, it was not easy to explain the meaning of such words as "community" and "society" for its former citizens. Since communist ideology degraded the individual and social heterogeneity, and set equality as the only legitimate social norm, social differentiation under the democratic regime after 1991 came as a kind of shock for Latvian citizens. In analyzing the results of questions aiming at a diagnosis of their current ability to cope with these developments, the position of the researcher is important. If we accept western values and criteria as the only standard for our analysis, a western model of society is our yardstick. However, we can also try to analyze the attitudes and values prevalent in our society as a mere indicator of change, without normative implications. In analyzing the frequencies of values and beliefs in different social groups, we may be able to understand the character and the direction of this change.

Tolerance

The respondents were asked to indicate how important they believed teaching tolerance to children to be. Tolerance and respect for other people are among the three most important qualities that Latvian respondents wish to teach their children: hard work (86 percent), responsibility (80 percent), tolerance and respect for others (73 percent). Women

Table 9.23 Membership in voluntary associations, 1996, %

	Estonia	Latvia	Lithuania	Norway	West Germany
Active in one or more voluntary associations	15	17	12	58	60

regard tolerance as more important than men (79 percent versus 65 percent).

A higher share of Protestants and Russian Orthodox evaluate tolerance as important than Catholics and non-believers do (Protestants 76.8 percent, Orthodox 75.1 percent, Catholics 71.2 percent, non-believers 69.8 percent).

A majority of the Latvian respondents consider understanding of others' preferences most important for good relationships (77 percent). Less than one-quarter (23 percent) believes the expression of one's own views to be more important (23 percent). Men favor the latter position more frequently than women do (25 percent versus 20 percent).

When it comes to tolerance for different lifestyles, i.e. active tolerance, Latvians score considerably lower compared to a rather theoretical evaluation of the value of tolerance. The respondents were asked to indicate for each of the following statements (Table 9.25) whether they thought it could always be justified, never be justified or something in between.

In recent years, homosexuality and prostitution became publicly debated issues. The attitude toward homosexuals and prostitution is more condemning than excusing. Men have a stricter attitude toward homosexuals (the mean tolerance scores for men and women were 2.65 and 3.07, respectively), and women are more reproving of prostitution (the mean tolerance scores were 3.51 for men and 2.72 for women). The attitude toward abortions was more liberal (mean value 5.29).

Table 9.24 Good human relationships, 1996, %, Latvia

To build good human relationships, it is most important to try to understand others' preferences	74
To build good human relationships, it is most important to express one's own preferences clearly	26

Table 9.25 Active tolerance, 1996, Latvia

	Homosexuality	*Prostitution*	*Abortion*	*Divorce*
Unjustifiable (1–3)	68%	64%	27%	12%
In-between (4–7)	23%	29%	49%	51%
Justifiable (8–10)	9%	7%	24%	37%
Mean	2.93	3.12	5.29	6.30
Median	1	2	5	6
Mode	1	1	5	5
Variance	6.81	6.12	7.02	5.91

Notes
1 = never justifiable; 10 = always justifiable.

Trust in the other citizen

Trust in the fellow citizen eases transactions, fosters a free flow of information and civil participation. The absence of trust easily leads to citizens' withdrawal from the public sphere and a deterioration of collective goods.

The majority of Latvian respondents think that it is necessary to be cautious in relations with other people (76 percent). Less than one-quarter (24 percent) thought that one might trust other people. Despite the widespread notions about seclusion of ethnic Latvians versus "the broad Russian soul," ethnic Latvians more often agreed that one might trust people than Russians (28 percent versus 19 percent).

Respondents from Norway (65 percent) and West Germany (40 percent) express higher levels of trust in fellow citizens than people from Baltic countries.

Table 9.26 Trust in others, 1996, %, Latvia

	Most people can be trusted
Estonia	21
Latvia	24
Lithuania	21
Norway	65
West Germany	40
East Germany	24

Solidarity with the poor

A decade ago, for Latvians poverty was perceived as a phenomenon known only in Africa and in fairy tales. Now life has changed and poverty has become a reality in Latvia. Since there is no official poverty line in Latvia, three different levels have been used for incidence analysis. The first and lowest threshold is a relative poverty line that is set at 50 percent of the mean of total monthly per capita household expenditures and constitutes 26 Ls per month per adult.[1] The second threshold is the minimum wage, which was 38 Ls per month at the end of 1996. The third poverty threshold is the crisis subsistence minimum defined by the Ministry of Welfare, which equaled 52 Ls per month per family member at the end of 1996 (UNDP 1997: 36).

A first look at the population as a whole shows that more than 10 percent of the Latvian population is very poor, living below the lowest poverty line. According to the minimum wage poverty line, 40 percent of the population is poor. This figure increases to 67 percent when applying the highest poverty line. More than half of the population has a standard of living somewhere between the low and the high poverty lines (Gassmann 2000: 11).

Poverty is an issue in Latvia and possible actions on part of the state are frequently a subject of public and private discussions. The respondents were asked to rate the amount of governmental action in the fight against poverty as too little, appropriate or too much – their answers are shown in Table 9.27.

In Latvia, poverty is perceived as a problem that may affect every citizen. The high share of respondents who believe that the government should do more to help the poor appears to be less an amazingly equivocal expression of solidarity with the poor, but rather the awareness of the vulnerability of every single citizen.

A majority believes that poverty is a result of socio-economic developments (they are poor because society does not treat them fairly). Less than one-quarter (23 percent) regard poverty as a consequence of peoples' "own laziness and passivity." Men express this opinion more often than women and Latvians more often than Russians.

The respondents were also asked to indicate whether they believed what other countries of the world were doing to help the poor was about right, too much or too little.

The respondents were not so critical in their evaluation of anti-poverty policies in foreign countries – 42 percent believed that foreign governments did as much as necessary to fight poverty, 35 percent believed them to do too little and 3 percent thought that they did too much. However it is hard to determine if the respondents' opinions are based on any current information about foreign social policies, or if they are merely a reflection of the widespread belief that everything is better "abroad."

Additionally, the respondents were asked to express their level of support for Latvia's provision of foreign aid.

Latvian provision of foreign aid was supported (completely or partly) by only 32 percent of respondents, while 64 percent rejected the notion. Given the current economic situation in Latvia, these findings are not surprising. Apparently Latvian citizens regard their country as a legitimate recipient of foreign aid, rather than as a donor.

Table 9.27 Government action against poverty, 1996, %, Latvia

Too much	1
The right amount	9
Too little	87
DK	3

Table 9.28 Latvian foreign aid, 1996, %, Latvia

Very much for	3
For to some extent	29
Somewhat against	35
Very much against	29
DK	4

Immigrants

One last important aspect of a civil society is its openness, i.e. its ability to include foreigners and immigrants. Thus the respondents were asked to describe their attitude toward immigrants who come to Latvia to work, and their views are showcased in Table 9.29.

In 1996, immigration was not an issue in Latvia. Actually, immigration levels in 1996 were lower than emigration levels from Latvia. People lost their jobs as a consequence of the liquidation of ex-Soviet industrial enterprises after 1990, not because of high levels of immigration. Since Latvian citizens had no experience with immigrants, they regarded the problem as an abstract issue that did not have much to do with real life.

Half of the respondents believed that immigrants in search of better jobs should be allowed to come into the country, while the other 50 percent thought that they should not be allowed to enter at all or that there should be strict immigration quotas.

Table 9.29 Immigrants, 1996, %, Latvia

Let anyone come who wants to	5
Let people come as long as there are jobs available	45
Place strict limits on the number of foreigners who can come here	37
Prohibit people coming here from other countries	13

Conclusion

The bulk of the population of Latvia support democracy. However, this support is not very strong; only 10 percent can be described as strong democrats, whereas 61 percent are weak democrats. The term "democracy" apparently still remains an abstract western value, not an everyday issue. This is a common feature of post-socialist countries in transition, probably due to the lack of experience with modern democracy and due to the deficits in the solution achieving fundamental social problems. Although Latvian citizens cherish the abstract notion of democracy, they are skeptical about its ability to function efficiently in reality.

Democracy in Latvia exists merely as an institutional structure, since the democratic community that could fill it with life is still weak. Its development encounters several obstacles. First, the ethnic and linguistic division between Latvians and Russian as well as a considerable income polarization. Second the still deeply rooted state-centered expectations on the part of a majority of the population and the increasing dissatisfaction with the government's capacity to cope with social and economic problems. Finally, the growing gap between the ruling elite and the majority of the population, and the elite's tendency to use its power to achieve personal goals instead of providing public goods, definitely does not support the development of a vivid democratic community.

These problems might also be, at least in part, a by-product of the absence of civil control of governance through an active civil society. Altogether, Latvian citizens are not well informed, not deeply involved in politics and rather passive with regard to political participation. Many consider democracy as, at least in part, dysfunctional. Furthermore, many do not understand the interrelations between the core elements of the concept of modern democracy. Paying lip service to the abstract ideal, they similarly demand a strong leader, limitations of certain civil freedoms and censorship. It might be the case that the support for democracy is not motivated by a concrete image of a prospective shape of the Latvian society but by a strong rejection of the past. Since the western model of democracy seems to be without alternative after the end of the Cold War, there is no second option to express this rejection. Additionally Latvia might be a further example of a "consumer democracy" as it is to be found in several East European states. People tend to prefer democracy for a promise of prosperity and not for civil liberties.

We can conclude that the process of consolidation of liberal democracy in Latvia is ongoing. The support for democracy is relatively low and, thus far, a civil society has yet to develop. There is a considerable difference between Latvia and the western European countries. In contrast, Latvia does not notably differ from the other Baltic countries.

Note

1 Exchange rate (December 1996) 1 USD = 0.556 LVL.

References

Fuchs, D. and Klingemann, H. (2000) "Eastward Enlargement of the European Union and the Identity of Europe," *West European Politics* 25, 2.

Gassmann, F. (2000) *Who and Where are the Poor in Latvia?* Riga: Ministry of Welfare of the Republic of Latvia; UNDP.

Inglehart, R. (1990) *Culture Shift in Advanced Industrial Society*, Princeton: Princeton University Press.

Lauristin, M, Vihalemm, P., Rosengren, K.E. and Weibull, L. (eds) (1997) *Return to the Western World*, Tartu: Tartu University Press.

Offe, C. (1996) *Varieties of Transition*, Cambridge: Polity Press.

UNDP (1997) *Latvia Human Development Report 1997*, Riga: UNDP.

10 Lithuania

Civic society and democratic orientation

Rasa Alisauskiene

Introduction: major characteristics of the transformation process in Lithuania

More than a decade after the beginning of the transformation process in Lithuania, the economy and politics are restructured and private ownership and a multiparty system are successfully established. Since 1990, three parliamentary elections, three presidential elections and five municipal elections have been held. In a country with 3.5 million inhabitants and about 2.3 million registered voters, the number of political parties reached 36 in 2002. Private owners manage more than 80 percent of Lithuanian companies. Lithuania re-introduced her national currency in 1993 and restored membership in major international organizations. In 1991, Lithuania expressed the wish to join the EU and the NATO, was invited to join both organizations in 2002, and subsequently attained full membership.

How do Lithuanian citizens perceive these changes? Certainly, the transformation process is influencing and partly changing their values, beliefs, attitudes and life plans. Currently, a majority supports economic reforms and the establishment of a multi-party system, despite individual economic hardships and increasing social differentiation. In order to understand current characteristics of the belief system of Lithuanians, we should also bear in mind the social context. Increasing social differentiation in Lithuanian society influences short-term attitudes and goals as well as more stable structures, such as value orientations.[1]

The Baltic countries host a population consisting of three generations that are socialized under completely different political and social regimes: the generation raised before World War II experienced an independent democratic state and a free market economy, while the middle-aged generation was socialized under an authoritarian regime. The youngest generation again grew up in an independent nation-state. This might explain some similarities in the belief systems of the elderly on the one hand and the younger generation on the other.

In the following sections, we describe the distributions of political attitudes and values of the Lithuanian sample of the World Values Survey and we will analyze the data on the background of the transition process and the current political and social context.

Citizens and democratic politics

Interest in politics

We will analyze citizens' attitudes toward democracy by their reported levels of interest in politics and political participation, and their support of autocratic and democratic modes of government.

The second presidential elections were held in November 1997; and the survey was conducted during an election campaign. Comparatively high levels of political participation and interest in politics may therefore be understood as a side-effect of this situation.

The mean score on a four-point scale is 2.09. This means that Lithuanians considered politics to be a rather important issue in their lives. There were no significant differences in this respect with regard to socioeconomic standard variables. Age, however, was an exception: the older the respondents, the more importance they accorded to politics.

Almost half of the respondents expressed at least some interest in politics. This may also be influenced by the presidential campaign (the analysis of the ten-year trend of this variable supports this assertion). However, given these circumstances, the share of respondents "not very" and "not at all" interested is amazingly high.

Table 10.1 Importance of politics in respondents' lives, 1997, %

	Very important	Rather important	Not very important	Not at all important
Total	3.9	24.2	47.8	22.7

Table 10.2 Interest in politics, 1997, %

	Very interested	Somewhat interested	Not very interested	Not at all interested	DK/NA	Mean
Total	5.4	38.5	40.2	15.4	0.5	2.34

Table 10.3 Frequency of political debates with friends, 1997, %

	Frequently	Occasionally	Never	DK/NA	Mean
Total	14.6	63.3	21.1	1.0	1.93

One in five respondents never discussed politics with friends, while one in seven did so frequently. A majority of Lithuanians discussed politics with friends at least occasionally.

All three dimensions of political interest are closely and significantly related. Respondents, who consider politics to be important in their lives, report higher levels of interest in politics, as well as higher levels of frequency of political communication.

Priority of political values

For Lithuanian citizens it is more important to be able to influence decisions on the level of the state and the community than to protect freedom of speech. This can probably be explained by the solid legal protection of freedom of speech and the freedom of the media in Lithuania. To attain freedom of speech was one of the first priorities for Lithuanians in the early years of transformation. In 1997, Lithuanian media were internationally recognized as comparatively free of governmental influence. Apparently citizens acknowledge these achievements and turn their attention to other issues, which have not reached the desired level of citizen aspiration.

The two options that describe dimensions of civil influence on political decisions on the national and local level are closely related. Freedom of speech, however, remains a separate dimension. It seems probable that a majority of citizens believe this achievement is safe and irreversible.

Table 10.4 Correlation between the dimensions of the political interest

	Importance of politics	Political interest	Political discussion
Importance of politics	1	0.6**	0.44**
Political interest	0.61**	1	0.59**
Political discussion	0.44**	0.59**	1

Notes
Pearson correlation, *significant at >0.01 level; **significant at >0.005 level.

Table 10.5 Lithuania's goals for the next ten years, 1997, %

	First priority	Second priority	No priority
Seeing that people have more say about how things are done at their jobs and in their communities	16.7	34.7	48.7
Giving people more say in important government decisions	18.3	23.3	58.4
Protecting freedom of speech	3.3	11.5	85.2

Table 10.6 Correlation between dimensions of political values of respondents

	People more say about jobs and communities	*People more say in government decisions*	*Protecting freedom of speech*
People more say about jobs and communities	1	0.25**	−0.02
People more say in government decisions	0.25**	1	−0.12**
Protecting freedom of speech	−0.02	−0.12**	1

Notes
Pearson correlation, * significant at >0.01 level; ** significant at >0.005 level.

Political participation

We now turn to the respondents' intentions to vote in general elections to assess the level of political participation. Over the last decade, voting turnout decreased, from over 70 percent in 1992 general elections to 55 percent in 1996. The presidential elections usually attract more interest: in 1997, a few months after the survey was conducted, the participation rate in the presidential elections exceeded 75 percent. In the 2002 presidential elections, the turnout decreased to 53 percent (several factors contributed to this decline: increasing economic optimism; reforms of the election procedure; and Christmas and New Year celebrations. The elections took part on 22 December and 5 January.

Five political parties collected the highest shares of votes – they are also present in the parliaments elected after the restoration of the independence. One-fifth of the respondents had not decided which party to vote for. This figure is stable over the last ten years. Only about 10 percent of respondents report not voting at all.

During the peaceful revolution in 1989–91, citizens' political activity increased significantly. Meetings and demonstrations attracted over one million participants. Six years after, the number of such events, as well as participation rates, have decreased enormously. The emerging pattern of political activity in Lithuania can be described with the following rule of thumb: the higher the demand for active participation, the less Lithuanians are willing to participate.

The level of participation is closely related to the level of formal education – respondents with an academic degree reported being most active. City dwellers are more involved than those living in rural areas. Age and gender are of no significance to political participation.

Apparently the most active citizens are inclined to participate in the majority of types of political action. Therefore, respondents who report being willing to take part in the occupation of buildings, strikes or demonstration can also be expected to participate in boycotts or signing petitions.

Table 10.7 Respondents' party preference, 1997, %

	First choice	Second choice	Never vote
Republican party	0.1	0	0.8
Liberal union	4.0	3.1	0.6
Center union	**12.1**	**7.3**	0.8
Russian union	0.8	0.6	**4.2**
Christian democratic union	3.0	2.6	1.1
Socialist party	0.7	0.3	1.3
Freedom union	0.1	0.6	0.3
Peasants party	1.8	2.1	0.6
Polish election action	0.9	0.9	**6.3**
Social democratic party	**5.9**	**7.1**	0.6
Union of political prisoners and deported persons	0.6	0.8	1.3
Lithuanian national party "Young Lithuanians"	4.3	2.6	1.8
Freedom league	0.6	1.3	1.9
Logic of life party	0.1	0.2	0.8
Democratic labor party	**7.9**	**3.9**	**16.9**
Coalition of national union and democratic party	0.6	0.9	0.4
Lithuanian national minorities alliance	1.3	1.5	2.5
Women's party	2.6	5.1	1.9
Conservative party	**16.1**	**5.8**	**16.4**
Social justice party	0.2	1.0	0.3
Christian democratic party	**5.1**	**6.9**	1.2
People party	0.2	0.5	0.3
Industrial party	1.0	1.8	0.4
National progress party	0.1	0.5	0.5
Other	0.4	0.1	0.2
None	8.8	11.4	5.1
DK	20.5	31.1	31.5

Table 10.8 Types of political participation, 1997, %

	Have done	Might do	Never do	DK/NA
Signing a petition	27.6	30.5	30.6	11.3
Joining in boycotts	4.3	31.7	49.1	15.0
Attending lawful demonstrations	15.2	40.6	35.0	9.2
Joining unofficial strikes	2.2	23.3	57.3	17.2
Occupying buildings or factories	1.3	9.9	72.6	16.2

Active membership in voluntary organizations

Membership – both active and inactive – in voluntary organizations is not very widespread in Lithuania. This might result from experiences with obligatory membership in labor unions and political organizations under the preceding Soviet regime. Additionally, citizens might not be very familiar with many of the new organizations that were founded during the 1990s.

Table 10.9 Correlation between different dimensions of political participation

	Signing a petition	Joining in boycotts	Attending lawful demonstrations	Joining unofficial strikes	Occupying buildings or factories
Signing a petition	1.00	0.51**	0.51**	0.33**	0.22**
Joining in boycotts	0.51**	1.00	0.57**	0.59**	0.43**
Attending a lawful demonstration	0.51**	0.57**	1.00	0.54**	0.30**
Joining unofficial strikes	0.33**	0.59**	0.54**	1.00	0.50**
Occupying buildings or factories	0.22**	0.43**	0.30**	0.50**	1.00

Notes
Pearson correlation, * significant at >0.01 level; ** significant at >0.005 level.

Table 10.10 Membership in voluntary organizations, 1997, %

	Active member	Inactive member	Not a member	DK/NA
Political party	1.1	2.1	96.6	0.2
Labor union	1.1	6.8	91.9	0.2
Professional organization	1.2	2.3	96.2	0.3
Religious organization	3.5	10.3	86.2	0.0
Environmental organization	0.4	1.8	97.5	0.3
Charitable organization	0.6	1.8	97.4	0.2
Art, music or educational organization	3.0	3.9	92.9	0.3
Sport or recreation organization	2.8	4.3	92.8	0.2
Other voluntary organization	0.4	0.7	91.0	7.9

Roughly 90 percent of the respondents did not belong to any voluntary organization. Of those who did, the elderly prefer religious organizations; respondents with a higher level of formal education are more often members of professional, arts, music and educational organizations, and younger respondents are more often members in sports clubs. However, overall, Lithuanians prefer to spend their leisure time with friends and relatives, traveling, doing sports or attending culture or club events. Apparently informal non-institutionalized get-together opportunities are more popular than membership in formal organizations.

Citizens and the democratic state

Attitudes towards democracy

More than 70 percent of the respondents regard the democratic system as the best choice for the country. 10 percent believe that it is a bad form of governance, 85 percent reject rule by the army. However, preference for a strong leader not responsible to parliamentary control does not seem to contradict preference for democracy as an ideal form of government for a majority of the respondents. A total of 57 percent would support a strong

Table 10.11 Different ways of governing the country – respondents' preferences, 1997, %

	Very good	Fairly good	Fairly bad	Very bad	Mean score	DK/NA
Having a democratic system	20.2	53.3	8.9	1.5	3.10	16.1
Having a strong leader who does not have to bother with parliament and elections	21.3	35.7	24.9	7.5	2.79	10.6
Having the army rule	0.8	4.5	42.9	42.5	1.60	9.3

leader; similarly, a majority of them support democracy as an ideal. This implies that the relation between the core elements of the concept of democracy remains unclear for almost half of the respondents, who might associate charisma and efficiency rather than autocratic rule with a strong leader.

A strong leader is more popular in rural areas than in the cities. Respondents with a high level of formal education are less inclined to support a strong leader than those with a low level of formal education. Age does not influence the attitude regarding a strong leader in a significant fashion.

Roughly 70 percent of respondents prefer democracy to any other regime; only 7.8 percent do not. A comparatively high level of respondents remain indecisive (20.3 percent). This corresponds with the 16.1 percent reported in Table 10.11, who did not indicate whether they agree or disagree with the statement on whether democracy is the best way of governing Lithuania. Apparently roughly one-fifth of respondents supported a "wait and see" position at the time the survey was conducted. No significant differences with regard to standard sociological categories have been observed.

The democratic orientation of the respondents is assessed by an index described in detail in the introductory chapter. Scores for democratic attitudes and autocratic attitudes are added and the latter is subtracted from the former: (1) "Strong democrats" assess democracy very positively and autocracy negatively. (2) "Weak democrats" assess democracy, on balance, positively. The group of (3) "Undecided citizens" is composed of respondents who express a balanced mixture of preferences for democracy and autocracy, or of those who felt unable to give any answer at all. (4) "Autocrats" are respondents who give a favorable assessment of autocracy as compared to a favorable evaluation of democracy.

A majority (56.9 percent) of the respondents were to be found in the category "Weak democrats." Roughly one-quarter displays decisively autocratic attitudes and 12.7 percent remain indecisive. Only 7 percent can be regarded as strong democrats.

The level of formal education is a strong predictor for attitudes toward democracy. A tenth of respondents with a higher level of formal education belong to the category "Strong democrats," while this is true for only 6 percent of those with a low or middle level of formal education. One-third

Table 10.12 Democracy as best form of government, 1997, %

	Agree strongly	Agree	Disagree	Disagree strongly	Mean score	DK/NA
Democracy may have problems, but it's better than any other form of government	17.5	54.4	6.9	0.9	3.11	20.3

Table 10.13 The democracy–autocracy index – distribution, 1997, %

	Strong democrats	Weak democrats	Autocrats	Undecided citizens
All respondents	7.0	56.9	23.5	12.7
Male	5.9	62.6	21.2	15.1
Female	7.9	51.2	25.8	10.3
>30 y.o.	7.0	60.7	20.1	12.3
30–50 y.o.	6.7	56.6	23.1	13.6
<50 y.o.	7.2	54.8	26.1	12.0
Level of formal education				
Inc. secondary	6.0	48.8	31.4	13.8
Secondary	6.1	57.7	21.7	14.6
Higher	10.1	65.6	17.4	6.9
Type of settlement				
Rural	8.3	50.3	28.7	12.7
Towns	5.9	52.6	26.7	11.3
Cities	6.5	64.8	17.3	11.3

of respondents with a low level of formal education belong to the category of autocrats. Another important variable is the size of the local community, although the relationship is ambiguous: rural areas host an overproportional share of strong democrats as well as of autocrats, while city dwellers are most likely to be found in the category "Weak democrats." The influence of age is not very pronounced. Finally, gender has an impact on the political orientation of the respondents: women are slightly over-represented as strong democrats and autocrats, while men are most likely to be found in the grouping of weak democrats. In addition, the proportion of undecided male respondents exceeds the share of female respondents who are undecided by almost 5 percent. Compared to other countries, Lithuania belongs to a group composed of Russia, Belarus and the Ukraine; that is, the countries with the lowest share of strong democrats and the highest share of autocrats and undecided citizens.

Effectiveness of democratic rule

Lithuanian respondents evaluate the efficiency of a democratic regime rather negatively. This is true for both economic performance and for such a regime's ability to maintain law and order.

One-third of the respondents are skeptical with regard to the compatibility of a democratic regime and a strong economy. The same is true for the evaluation of a democracy's ability to maintain order. However, it is also true that roughly half of the respondents disagree with the respective statements. In contrast, the opinion that democracies are indecisive is widely shared; 50 percent agree, 33 percent disagree. Again, the proportion of indecisive respondents is comparatively high for all three statements.

Table 10.14 Efficiency of a democratic regime, 1997, %

	Agree strongly	Agree	Disagree	Disagree strongly	Mean score	DK/NA
In democracy, the economic system runs badly	5.9	27.2	40.1	4.8	2.44	22.0
Democracies are indecisive and have too much squabbling	11.2	39.3	30.1	3.2	2.70	16.2
Democracies aren't any good at maintaining the order	5.2	24.9	44.1	5.6	2.37	20.2

Table 10.15 Correlation between the dimensions of the evaluation of the effectiveness of democratic rule

	Economic system runs badly	Indecisive	Maintaining order
Economic system runs badly	1.00	0.66**	0.63**
Too much squabbling	0.66**	1.00	0.68**
Order	0.63**	0.68**	1.00

Notes Pearson correlation, * significant at >0.01 level; ** significant at >0.005 level.

All in all, respondents' statements are consistent, negative (positive) evaluations of one dimension of democracy correlate significantly with negative (positive) evaluations of the other dimensions.

The eight dimensions of political attitudes shown in Tables 10.11–10.14 are closely correlated; that is, the respondents' attitudes are consistent and homogeneous. This finding might indicate that the comparatively high share of weak democrats and autocrats among the respondents is more likely to be a result of political experiences in the transition process when a strong national leader contradicted Moscow.

Concept of the state

Ethics of self-responsibility versus state paternalism

During the transformation, citizens experienced economic crises and the initial optimism and self-confidence vanished. Additionally, a majority of Lithuanian companies were privatized in 1996. Thus the respondents expected the government to introduce a more effective social policy and to provide for their welfare.

In order to gauge individual responsibility (people should take more responsibility to provide for themselves) and government's responsibility for one's own fate, respondents were asked to indicate their respective positions on a scale from 1–10, where 1 identified the paternalistic attitude ("The government should take more responsibility to ensure that

Table 10.16 Correlation between dimensions of the evaluation of democratic rule

	Democratic system	Democracy problems	Strong leader	Army rule	Democratic orientation	Economy	Squabbling	Order
Democratic system	1.00	0.36**	−0.11*	−0.12*	0.54**	−0.33**	−0.35**	−0.37**
Democracy problems	0.34***	1.00	−0.19***	−0.16***	0.56***	−0.30***	−0.23***	−0.23***
Strong leader	−0.11*	0.19**	1.00	0.16***	−0.57***	0.30***	0.30***	0.23***
Army rule	−0.12*	−0.16***	0.16**	1.00	−0.36***	0.17***	0.18***	0.22***
Democratic orientation	0.54**	0.56**	−0.57***	−0.36**	1.00	−0.43***	−0.45**	−0.44**
Economy	−0.33**	−0.30**	0.30**	0.17**	−0.43**	1.00	0.66**	0.63**
Squabbling	−0.35**	−0.23**	0.30**	0.18**	−0.45**	0.66**	1.00	0.68**
Order	−0.37**	−0.23**	0.23**	0.22**	−0.44**	0.63**	0.68**	1.00

Notes
Pearson correlation, *significant at >0.01 level; **significant at >0.005 level.

Table 10.17 Provision for individual welfare, 1997, %

	Mean score
All respondents	4.42
Male	4.52
Female	4.32
>30 y.o.	4.96
30–50 y.o.	4.70
<50 y.o.	3.78
Education	
Inc. secondary	3.62
Secondary	4.48
Higher	5.31
Type of settlement	
Rural	3.83
Towns	4.49
Cities	4.84

everyone is provided for") and 10 identified the liberal attitude ("People should take more responsibility to provide for themselves").

In the 1997 survey, the paternalistic attitude is slightly more popular among the respondents than the liberal attitude. Gender is of no influence. Respondents 50 years and older tend to expect more welfare provision by the state. Level of formal education has the strongest impact: respondents with a higher level of formal education are by far the most liberal. The same is true for urban dwellers. Urban dwellers are more liberal than those living in rural areas.

Private or state ownership of business?

In general, Lithuanian respondents show a moderately liberal orientation toward private ownership of business and industry. Respondents were asked to indicate their position on a ten-point scale: 1 was associated with a liberal statement ("Private ownership of business and industry should be increased") while 10 indicated a paternalistic attitude ("Government ownership of business and industry should be increased").

Again, the level of formal education is of importance here. Respondents with a higher level of formal education are more inclined to support private ownership than those with a lower level of formal education. Women are more paternalistically oriented than men and a tendency toward a paternalistic attitude increases with age. Type of settlement seems to be of no influence.

The findings regarding the respondents' preferences for business management confirm the impression of a moderately liberal attitude of Lithuanians when it comes to economic issues.

Table 10.18 Private or state ownership of business, 1997, %

	Mean score
All respondents	4.94
Male	4.67
Female	5.21
>30 y.o.	4.16
30–50 y.o.	4.80
<50 y.o.	5.62
Education	
Inc. secondary	5.34
Secondary	5.09
Higher	4.11
Type of settlement	
Rural	4.91
Towns	5.05
Cities	4.88

Table 10.19 Responsibility for business management, 1997, %

	Agreement (%)
The owners should run their business or appoint the managers	34.4
The owners and the employees should jointly appoint managers	23.8
The government should be the owner and appoint managers	10.1
The employees should own the business and should elect the managers	22.4

Roughly one-third of respondents opt for business owners' autonomy, one-quarter prefer owners and employees to have joint responsibility. Almost the same proportion of respondents opt for employees' ownership and responsibility.

The different dimensions of liberal and paternalistic attitudes are consistent and closely related.

Table 10.20 Correlation between the dimensions of the support for the private ownership of business

	Priority of private responsibility	Priority of private ownership	Business management
Priority of private responsibility	1.00	0.16**	0.15**
Priority of private ownership	0.16**	1.00	0.24**
Business management	0.15**	0.24**	1.00

Notes
Pearson correlation, * significant at >0.01 level; ** significant at >0.005 level.

Political institutions and organizations

From 1990 onwards, the mass media and the Church enjoyed the highest levels of confidence in Lithuania – more than 50 percent of respondents trust these institutions regardless of their political orientation. After the second presidential elections in 1997, this changed in favor of the president. In general, surveys conducted during the last ten years indicated that Lithuanian citizens are more likely to trust institutions with a symbolic role rather than legislative and executive institutions.

Independent of age, level of formal education or any other socio-economic category, administrative institutions with low levels of trust during the last decade. In general, more respondents trust the civil service rather than the legal system and the police.

Institutions in the general public sphere enjoy by far higher levels of trust than government and administration. Apparently television and press are estimated as reliable and trustworthy providers of information. In total, 76.5 percent and 70.8 percent of respondents have confidence in them, respectively. Roughly 70 percent trust the churches. Least trusted are the labor unions – even major companies enjoy higher levels of trust.

Table 10.21 Confidence in parliament, government and political parties, 1997, %

	Great deal	*Quite a lot*	*Not very much*	*None at all*
Parliament	0.6	26.0	63.3	10.1
Government	1.1	35.2	57.7	6.0
Political parties	0.3	14.0	72.1	13.6

Table 10.22 Confidence in the legal system, civil services and the police, 1997, %

	Great deal	*Quite a lot*	*Not very much*	*None at all*
Legal system	1.6	20.6	64.6	13.3
Civil service	0.9	40.1	52.7	6.3
Police	0.6	20.2	59.1	20.1

Table 10.23 Confidence in other institutions, 1997, %

	Great deal	*Quite a lot*	*Not very much*	*None at all*
Churches	14.9	54.1	28.7	2.3
Labor unions	1.5	26.2	63.0	9.3
Ecology movements	4.1	58.6	29.2	8.1
Women's movement	2.6	38.8	52.8	5.8
Press	4.6	66.2	26.5	2.7
Television	4.7	71.8	22.3	1.2
Major companies	0.8	31.5	60.4	7.3

Table 10.24 Confidence in International organizations, 1997, %

	Great deal	*Quite a lot*	*Not very much*	*None at all*
European Union	2.8	49.6	42.7	4.9
United Nations	3.4	54.3	38.3	4.0

This might be due to the role labor unions played in the Soviet Union and the compulsory labor union membership under Soviet rule.

A majority of the respondents have confidence in both the European Union and United Nations, with the UN enjoying slightly higher levels of trust than the EU.

Citizens and civic community

Horizontal relations and mediating mechanisms, such as tolerance, interpersonal and inter-group trust and social solidarity are essential characteristics of a functioning civil society. They enable citizens to participate in the public sphere according to democratic norms. In the following sections, survey results relevant for the relations between citizens in Lithuania are discussed.

The other citizen

A majority of the respondents consider tolerance and respect for others to be an important quality, which children should be taught at home.

Tolerance and respect are perceived as important by a larger share of urban residents than rural inhabitants. Respondents with a higher level of formal education are more likely to estimate this characteristic as important than those with a lower level of formal education. Age and gender is of no influence for the respondents' opinion.

Table 10.25 Tolerance and respect as important quality, 1997, %

	Important %
Tolerance and respect for other people	54.1

Table 10.26 Conditions for good human relationships, 1997, %

	Agreement %
To build good human relationships, it is most important to try to understand others' preferences	71.2
To build human relationships, it is most important to express one's own preferences clearly	28.8

Roughly three-quarters of Lithuanians consider empathy to be an important quality for good interpersonal relations. At least at the level of attitudes, they support an open and tolerant attitude toward the other citizen. However, Lithuanians are rather intolerant when it comes to socially deviant or less accepted behavior.

Altogether, the respondents regard all four modes of social behavior identified in Table 10.27 as more or less unacceptable. Homosexuality is the least justifiable behavior for the majority of people, in that only 14 percent think it is acceptable. Prostitution does not enjoy significantly higher levels of acceptance. Nearly half of the respondents (46.7 percent) think that abortion can be justified, and divorce is accepted as a justifiable behavior by 57.2 percent. Women, the elderly, rural residents and people with a lower level of formal education tolerate these behaviors to a lesser extent than men, the younger generation, city dwellers and respondents with a higher level of formal education. The high esteem of tolerance, respect and empathy in interpersonal relations expressed by a majority of respondents appears to be unrelated when it comes to toleration of these types of social behavior.

Lithuanians score low with regard to levels of interpersonal trust – a majority of 78.7 percent believes that one cannot be too careful with others. Only one citizen out of five believes that most people can be trusted. Correlations between various dimensions of tolerance and trust confirm the impression of an inconsistent belief system.

The (negative) attitudes toward homosexuality, prostitution, abortion and divorce are closely and significantly correlated. However, they do not at all correlate with the respondents' attitudes toward tolerance, respect and empathy. In addition, tolerance, trust and empathy are not

Table 10.27 Justifiability of socially less accepted behavior, 1997, %

	Mean score
Homosexuality	1.95
Prostitution	2.25
Abortion	3.88
Divorce	4.39

Note
The respondents were asked to indicate the justifiability of the above items on a scale from 10 (it can always be justified) to 1 (it can never be justified).

Table 10.28 Trust in others, 1997

	%
Most people can be trusted	21.3
You can't be too careful	78.7

Table 10.29 Correlation between the dimensions of tolerance

	Tolerance and respect	Empathy	Homosexuality	Prostitution	Abortion	Divorce	Trust in others
Tolerance and respect	1.00	0.09	−0.01	−0.04	0.02	0.06	−0.01
Empathy	0.09	1.00	0.03	−0.03	0	0.05	0.01
Homosexuality	−0.01	0.03	1.00	0.59**	0.29**	0.33**	0.02
Prostitution	−0.04	−0.03	0.59	1.00	0.40**	0.39**	0.05
Abortion	0.02	0.00	0.29	0.40**	1.00	0.60**	0.04
Divorce	0.06	0.05	0.33	0.39**	0.60**	1.00	0.00
Trust in others	−0.01	0.01	0.02	0.05	0.04	0.00	1.00

Notes
Pearson correlation, * significant at >0.01 level; ** significant at >0.005 level.

correlated. Apparently, respondents cherish the abstract notion of these qualities in inter-personal relations, but they do not exercise them, at least not to the extent one would expect on the basis of the comparatively high proportion of citizens who agree with these values. The absence of any correlation between tolerance, respect and empathy indicates that these values are not perceived as belonging to one common pattern of civil virtues. Thus, it appears that the positive attitudes are more lip service than guiding principles for one's own behavior.

Solidarity with the poor

A majority of the respondents express a high level of solidarity with the poor. This attitude is consistent with the respondents' attitude toward the government's responsibility for individual welfare (see Table 10.17).

A total of 85.9 percent of respondents believe the government does too little for the poor. However, this might be less an expression of solidarity rather than a consequence of an overall low per capita income in Lithuania. Many households live close to the poverty line. Thus, it is possible that the respondents' frame of reference is more their own situation than the fate of their (poor) fellow citizens. A general increase of foreign aid to poor countries is believed to be necessary by 42.1 percent.

However, when asked about the level of Lithuanian foreign aid, the picture is reversed, as evident in Table 10.32.

Only 28 percent of the respondents favor that Lithuania itself should provide foreign aid, while 61 percent are opposed. They regard the country's economic resources to be necessary to solve social problems at

Table 10.30 Assessment of government's action on behalf of the poor, 1997

	%
Too much	1.5
Right	7.9
Too little	85.9
DK/NA	4.7

Table 10.31 Assessment of appropriateness of the level of other countries' foreign aid, 1997

	%
Too much	1.8
Right	29.4
Too little	42.1
DK/NA	26.7

Table 10.32 Respondents' attitude toward Lithuanian provision of foreign aid, 1997

	%
Very much for	4.1
For to some extent	23.5
Somewhat against	34.9
Very much against	26.6
DK/NA	11.0

home. It seems as if respondents are convinced that Lithuania should be the recipient rather than the provider of foreign aid.

Immigrants

Immigration is a rather new phenomenon in Lithuania. The number of immigrants, primarily from eastern European countries, did not increase before 1991, and even after 1991 it remains at low levels. The country has neither experience nor resources to deal with this problem. In general, an ordinary Lithuanian citizen has never met an immigrant, and the main source of information about this subject is the media. However, a notion of strong protectionism is prevalent in the attitudes of the respondents.

A majority demands strict controls or even prohibition of immigration; 38.8 percent express liberal attitudes toward immigration, as long as their jobs are protected; only 4.4 percent want to let anyone in who wants to come. Again, it might be the case that the rather protectionist attitude toward immigration is less an expression of xenophobia, but rather a consequence of Lithuanian poor economic performance and its impact on the respondents' lives.

The correlations of the dimensions of solidarity confirm the above assertions. When asked about national and international assistance to the poor, Lithuanian respondents seem to regard themselves as potential recipients rather than as donors. Therefore, they answer these questions

Table 10.33 Attitude toward immigration, 1997

	%
Let anyone who wants to come	4.4
Let people come as long as there are jobs available	38.8
Place strict limits on number of foreigners who can come here	32.7
Prohibit people from other countries to come here	20.6
DK/NA	3.6

Notes
Pearson correlation, * significant at >0.01 level; ** significant at >0.005 level.

Table 10.34 Correlation between dimensions of solidarity

	Government help poor	International foreign aid	Lithuanian foreign aid	Immigration
Government help poor	1.00	0.33**	−0.05	−0.08
International foreign aid	0.33**	1.00	−0.01	−0.04
Lithuanian foreign aid	−0.05	−0.01	1.00	0.22**
Immigration	−0.08	−0.04	0.22**	1.00

Notes
Pearson correlation, * significant at >0.01 level; ** significant at >0.005 level.

not from the point of view of a potential donor; rather, they anticipate solidarity and assistance *from* others. The significant correlation between Lithuanian provision of foreign aid and immigration indicates a similar result: the respondents evaluate the Lithuanian economic performance as too weak to either provide foreign aid or to deal with immigration.

Conclusion

A rather low level of interest in politics characterizes the Lithuanian population. Its cyclical pattern is contextual – the closer the elections, the more interested the respondents. To participate more in national and local decision-making is an important goal for Lithuanians. Dissatisfied with their passive role in politics (a majority of Lithuanians believe that politicians perceive them mainly as voters, whose preferences count only in the election year), they are also less inclined to vote in elections. Volunteering and active participation in formal voluntary associations is also not very widespread. Lithuanians prefer to socialize and associate in informal groups.

However, despite the impression that democratic attitudes and civil values do not seem to be deeply rooted or widely shared in the Lithuanian population, one should keep in mind some cognitive differences between western European and central European publics. A large majority of Lithuanians believe in democracy as the best form of government. However, the efficiency of democratic rule is first of all judged by the respondent's personal experience of the last ten years. With 36 political parties, there have been mostly unstable governments, both on the local and on the national level. The respondents' skepticism toward the performance of the current regime, as well as their rather positive attitude toward a strong leader, may possibly be attributed to the discrepancy between the high expectations related to democracy as an ideal and the realities of everyday life and politics in a developing democracy.

Note

1 The index of social differentiation in 1988 was 4.30, while in 1991 it was 5.80. By 1992 it reached 11.50, and 12.70 in 1995. By 1998 this index was 13.00. These data were collected by Baltic Surveys/GALLUP. Index for 1988–95 presented in Abisala *et al.* (1998).

Reference

Abisala, A., Alisauskiene, R. and Dobryninas, A. (1998) *Criminality and process of democratization in Lithuania*, Vilnius: Baltic Surveys; GALLUP.

11 Estonia

Changing value patterns in a divided society

Mikk Titma and Andu Rämmer

Introduction

Like the other two Baltic States, Estonia has chosen the part of national restoration and has re-established an independent state, a democratic political system and a free market economy. These fundamental changes affected people's lives, biographies, memories and certainly their belief systems. In this chapter we will focus on the dynamics of citizens' cognitive maps during the first half of a decade of transition.

Changing values and belief systems are widely studied (see Inglehart 1990, 1998; Bardi and Schwarz 1996; Breakwell and Lyons 1996; Klingemann 1999; Rohrschneider 1999; Fuchs and Klingemann 2000; Inglehart and Baker 2000). The social psychologists Bardi and Schwarz (1996) describe unusual value patterns among the population of eastern European countries. They explain these patterns as socialization effects after decades of communist rule. We trace the dynamics of changing values in Estonia from 1990 to 1996. After a brief overview of the development of the Estonian state and economy during the last decade, we will turn to citizens' attitudes toward the restored nation-state; their involvement in political activities; their level of confidence in the newly established institutions; and, finally, their attitudes toward different categories of fellow citizens.

Although Estonia lost its independence in Word War II and was incorporated into the Soviet Union, traces of western values persist. This might have been the result of the comparatively long period of German influence in this region (Titma 1996). Estonia was already under Russian rule at the beginning of the eighteenth century, but the impact of the German elite persisted until Word War I. This elite ruled Estonia 500 years before the Northern War (1700–21) in which the European military superpower, Sweden, ceded Estonia to the rising superpower embodied by the Russian Empire. Although the German barons did not mix with the Estonian population, they fostered the formation of an Estonian national consciousness by promoting widespread literacy in the Estonian language. The first book in Estonian was published in 1535 and virtually all Estonians were literate by the end of nineteenth century.

The German–Russian rivalry ended after World War I with the formation of a democratic independent nation-state. Moreover, Estonians experienced parliamentary democracy between the two World Wars. Together with persistent hostility toward Soviet rule and the political space opened by Gorbachev's *perestroika*, Estonia was a fertile ground for the building of democratic institutions.

Another strong incentive for the turn toward democracy was to increase the independence from the Soviet Union via democratic measures such as the gradual opening and democratization of the Supreme Soviet during the late 1980s after Gorbachev's *perestroika* (Titma and Silver 1996).

The restoration of the Estonian state was declared in August 1991 and the Estonian language replaced Russian as the official language among the political elite. The current multiparty system has its roots in the *perestroika* period when two pro-independence factions, the Popular Front and the Estonian Congress competed for supporters. The *Riigikogu* (parliament) took over from the Supreme Soviet in the first free elections in 1992. Since then Estonia has inaugurated six governments.

The economy also underwent radical and rapid changes. In June 1992, Estonia was the first ex-Soviet republic to replace the plummeting Soviet *rouble*, with its own currency. The Estonian *kroon* (crown), fixed to German *Mark*, was highly trusted among Estonians, and it was a crucial prerequisite for the following radical economical reforms, the so-called "shock therapy" that introduced western consumer goods to Estonia, but also increased income differentials. Disposable income increased from 941 euros per capita in 1993 up to 2,424 euros per capita in 1996. However, the birth rate decreased from 12.43 in 1991 down to 9.35 births per 1,000 in 1996.

Changing loyalties from 1990 to 1996

At the beginning of the 1990s, the Soviet Union was still a superpower, while the Baltic States were on their way toward independence. The Baltic population realized and openly debated independence as a real possibility rather than the empty dream of some politicians. Questions of political loyalties and identification were also raised, especially for the ethnic Russians who settled in Estonia after World War II and who still account for almost 29 percent of the Estonian population. Before 1990, the Soviet Union demanded full integration of the entire population into socialist society, regardless of ethnic or national identities (Anderson *et al.* 1996). However, since Russia was at the heart of the Soviet Union, ethnic Russians somehow seemed to be in a better position than other ethnic groups. In the post-communist Baltic nation-states, the status of the groups was reversed, and the Russians found themselves in the position of a minority without full citizenship. The majority of Estonians had longed for the "return to the West" but for many Russians the new social and political order in the early 1990s came as a shock and created a high level of uncertainty (Lauristin and Heidmets 2002).

Under these circumstances it is amazing that Estonia managed to avoid any form of violent conflict during the 1990s.

All these changes influenced loyalties and units of identification for the residents of Estonia. This chapter examines the development of national and regional identifications during the first half of the 1990s. Table 11.1 lists types of identification from "the local community" to "the whole world," and the percentage of respondents who primarily identify with the respective unit in 1990, 1992 and 1996. We computed an index that identifies the respondent's locus of identification, starting with "a clear identification with the local community where you live" and ending with "the world as a whole."

In 1990, when the independence of Estonia was still questionable, two-thirds of native Estonians identified themselves with their own country. Only one-third of the Russian-speaking community identified themselves with Estonia. The local community was the second most popular source of identification for 30 percent of Estonians and 32 percent of Russians). Even Estonians seemed to have been cautious in openly declaring their loyalty with the Estonian state in 1990.

Estonian independence in 1991 resulted in a major shift in identification loci. Compared to 1990, the share of respondents who primarily identify with the republic decreased among Estonians, but it became an important reference for both groups. In 1992, when Estonia was already independent, the respective numbers were 52 percent for Estonians and

Table 11.1 Identification with main social entities by different nationalities, 1990, 1992, 1996, %, Estonia

	Year	*Estonians*	*Russian-speakers*
Local community	1990	30	32
	1992	44	40
	1996	64	53
Country (Republic)	1990	67	36
	1992	52	47
	1996	31	7
Whole world + Europe	1990	2	9
	1992	4	6
	1996	5	40
Soviet Union (Russia)	1990	1	21
	1992	0	6
No answer	1990	1	2
	1992	0	2
	1996	0	0

47 percent for Russians. Approximately half of both groups identify with Estonia in 1992. The identification with the local community among ethnic Estonians increased to 44 percent. The same is true for ethnic Russians (40 percent in 1992).

In general, the primary sources of identification of both ethnic groups converged during the first half of the 1990s. The identification with the Soviet Union and its successor Russia decreased quickly among the Russians and was replaced by increasing levels of identification with the local community and the Estonian Republic. The transition to Estonian independence apparently did not alienate ethnic Russians.

Major differences in identification only emerged later. Only 7 percent of ethnic Russians still identified primarily with Estonia in 1996. Apparently the expectations of ethnic Russian inhabitants of an independent Estonia regarding their position within the new state and society were deeply disappointed. However, they did not turn backwards to the former Soviet Union. They realized that the time of the Soviet empire was over and that their prospects in Russia might be even worse than in Estonia. An increasing share of ethnic Russians identified with Europe and the world as a whole in 1996 (40 percent compared to 6 percent in 1992). This might indicate that they expected Europe to contribute to a solution with regard to their citizenship due to the pressure the EU exercised upon Estonia as a prospective member state. Similar patterns are described for other post-communist central and eastern Europe countries (Klicperova *et al.* 1997).

In 1991, Estonian citizenship was only granted to ethnic Russians who were residents before June 1940, and to their direct descendants, which means that there are many ethnic Russians who are not Estonian citizens. Some were offered the chance to apply for Estonian citizenship. The most important condition for a successful application was the ability to speak the Estonian language fluently. In 1997, more than 100,000 Russians in Estonia had chosen to acquire citizenship from other countries, mainly from Russia. Many still have not made their decision yet. The overall number of residents without full citizenship is still unclear; as of September 1997, more than 160,000 individuals had applied for "alien's" passports (gray passports as opposed to the blue Estonian passports). The holder of a gray passport is not allowed to vote in parliamentary elections but all other citizens' rights are granted. Some 157,000 so-called "gray passports" have been printed and non-citizen residents can use them as travel and identification documents.[1]

The share of ethnic Estonians who identify primarily with their own country also decreased, from two-thirds in 1990 to one-third in 1996. Obviously there was disillusionment among Estonian citizens too. They clearly turned toward their local community as the primary geographic reference.

In the following sections we summarize our findings and compare

Estonian data with findings from the other two Baltic States, Latvia and Lithuania. Estonians identified primarily with their own country in 1990; in 1996 almost half of them indicate their local community as primary social reference. This is a common feature among the Baltic States that might indicate a calming down of nationalist impulses after achieving independence at the beginning of the 1990s. Other entities of geographic reference, especially the local community, regained importance in everyday life. Table 11.1 shows that the share of ethnic Russians who primarily refer to their local community in Estonia increased from 32 percent in 1990 up to 53 percent in 1996. The level of identification with the local community in Latvia among Russians decreased slightly from 42 percent in 1990 down to 30 percent in 1996. The Russians' level of identification with the local community remained stable (40 percent) in Lithuania during that period.

The issue of citizenship is definitely an important predictor for ethnic Russians' attitude toward the Estonian nation-state. We observe similar patterns of identification toward the respective nation-states among the Russian communities in all three Baltic States. In 1990, when all three republics were still *de jure* members of the Soviet Union (Lithuania declared its independence in 1990), approximately one-third of Russian-speakers identified themselves with the republic in which they lived. For 1992, when all republics were *de facto* independent, the Russian communities also withdrew their attachment to the Soviet Union's successor, Russia, and approximately half of them identified with the nation-state in which they lived. But in 1996, the identification with the republic remained at the 1992 level in Latvia and Lithuania, and even decreased remarkably to 7 percent in Estonia. At the same time the share of Russian-speakers who identified with Europe and the world as a whole increased considerably in all three states. In Lithuania, where it was comparatively easy to acquire citizenship, we observe a slightly growing share of ethnic Russians who indicate Lithuania as the primary reference (from 32 percent in 1990, up to 43 percent in 1992, decreasing somewhat to 35 percent in 1996). We find roughly similar, but slightly more fluctuating, patterns among Russians in Latvia. The share of those who identified primarily with Latvia was 38 percent in 1990, went up to 63 percent in 1992 and decreased again to 35 percent in 1996. The identification patterns of ethnic Lithuanians (72 percent in 1990, 62 percent in 1992, 43 percent in 1996) and Latvians (72 percent in 1990, 63 percent in 1992, 56 percent in 1996) followed similar trends. In Lithuania, ethnic Russians and Lithuanians exhibited only tiny differences in their levels of identification with the country in 1996. The integration of Russians into the new nation-state did not seem to be an issue here. In Latvia, the level for Latvians who identify primarily with the country exceeded the ethnic Russian level by 20 percent. The rather modest identification of ethnic Russians with Latvia might be a result of the still unclear conditions for the achievement of citizenship in 1996.

In the second half of the 1990s, the geographic reference map of ethnic Russians and ethnic Estonians differed more from each other than between Russians and Latvians or Lithuanians, respectively. This is especially true for the share of ethnic Russians who identified primarily with the Estonian republic. In 1990, their share was 36 percent, that is, roughly the same share that was to be found in Latvia or Lithuania. In 1992, 47 percent of the Russian respondents indicated Estonia as primary geographic reference, their share decreased sharply down to 7 percent in 1996. Apparently many Russians chose to identify with the world and Europe (40 percent) in 1996, while only 5 percent of Estonians did the same. Although the level of identification with their nation-state also decreased among ethnic Estonians during the first half of 1990s, almost one-third still identified primarily with Estonia in 1996. This finding is not really surprising since Estonia has the most rigid and restrictive practice of granting Russians Estonian citizenship.

However, the level of identification with the local community increased among Russians, up to 53 percent in 1996, so they still might see their future in Estonia, even if they refrain from a strong identification with the Estonian nation-state.

Some trends in political participation in Estonia

Political participation was not very popular in Estonia in 1996. The main reason for this might be found in a kind of normalization after euphoric political activity in the late 1980s and early 1990s, something that was observed in many eastern European countries. Additionally, the main target of citizens' protest, the Soviet Central Government in Moscow, had ceased to exist by 1996. Thus people became increasingly concerned with the problems associated with the transition to democracy.

In 1996, the boom in political participation was over and society was experiencing a period of rapid economic reforms, a kind of radical "shock therapy" that dramatically changed the conditions for individual economic survival. People were predominantly occupied by attempts to adapt to a free market economy. Although politics remained a subject in informal debates among citizens, the conversation usually concentrated on economic matters.

Politics was not a very important topic in all three Baltic States; approximately every fourth respondent indicated that politics occupied a high rank in his or her life. In this respect, there were no significant differences between Estonians and Russians. One-third of Russian-speaking respondents versus one-quarter of ethnic Estonians rated politics very or rather important (Table 11.2). However, Estonia and the two other Baltic States were behind East Germany with regard to respondents' ranking of import-

Table 11.2 Importance of politics, 1996, %, Estonia, Latvia, Lithuania and East Germany

	%
Latvia	27
Lithuania	28
East Germany	47
Estonia (overall)	28
Ethnic Estonians	25
Russian-speakers	32

ance of politics – approximately half of the respondents in East Germany indicated that politics were very important or important in their lives. This exceeded the share in the Baltic States by 20 percent. However, this is an average value for the whole Estonian population. Ethnic Estonians are considerably more interested in politics (52 percent) than Russian-speakers (46 percent) and participate more frequently in political debates (88 percent versus 72 percent). Apparently politics occupies a more important place in the lives of ethnic Estonians than for Russian-speakers.

A civil society is also characterized by active membership in voluntary associations (see Rawls 1993). However, a large share of the Estonian population (85 percent) were not participating in any voluntary association in 1996. This might be, at least in part, a result of the Soviet heritage of coercive membership to organizations like labor unions. Other types of associations, such as charitable organizations, were only introduced after 1991 and were previously unknown. Only 15 percent of the respondents were members of at least one voluntary organization. Two-thirds of such organizations were to be found within the ethnic Estonian community, while the remaining third belonged to the Russian community. However, it is difficult to interpret these figures, since the general participation level is so low.

Citizens' level of law-abidingness is a measure for their acceptance of the legislative framework of the nation-state in which they live. The strict laws under Soviet rule were followed rather selectively and for the purpose of enhancing one's own interests. In the following section, we try to answer the questions of if and how these legacies from the Soviet period might have influenced behavior in the 1990s. As shown in Table 11.3, the pattern of law-abidingness in Estonia does not differ very greatly from the other Baltic republics. However, their level of law-abidingness was slightly higher than in Latvia and Lithuania. If we compare the two ethnic communities, we gain a more detailed picture. Estonia's slightly higher level of obedience to the rule of law derives from attitudes of ethnic Estonians. However, members of both ethnic groups in Estonia were more tolerant of tax evasion than Latvians and Lithuanians (Table 11.3). In 1996, Estonia introduced a stricter financial policy than Latvia and Lithuania.

Table 11.3 Attitudes toward law and violence, 1996, %, Estonia, Latvia, Lithuania and East Germany

	Estonia (overall)	Estonians	Russian-speakers	Latvia	Lithuania	East Germany
Law-abidingness						
It is not justified to:						
Claim government benefits to which you are not entitled	95	97	90	91	94	93
Avoiding fare on public transportation	88	94	78	76	88	90
Cheating on taxes if you have a chance	83	88	75	83	86	88
Legitimacy of violence						
Using violence to pursue political goals is never justified:						
agree and strongly agree	83	86	79	83	76	85

Prior to the introduction of this policy, it was rather common for employers to pay salaries in cash to avoid paying taxes, and tax evasion was also quite common under Soviet rule. The level of law-abidingness with regard to matters such as taxation among Russian-speakers was below that of ethnic Estonians, a finding which can be explained by a longer and more deeply rooted Soviet heritage among the ethnic Russians.

In 1996, the share of those who reported a high level of law-abidingness was roughly the same in all three Baltic States (Table 11.3). However, there was a cleavage between the two ethnic communities in Estonia: Estonians indicated a higher level of law-abidingness for every single item.

There is no democracy without the opportunity to express dissenting opinions publicly. Some important types of non-violent protest include signing petitions and participating in boycotts or demonstrations. These activities were impossible under the orthodox communist regime, since dissenting socialist citizens within a socialist society were itself an oxymoron. However, peaceful demonstrations against the Soviets paved the way to independence in Estonia, while in Latvia and Lithuania some more serious violent confrontations with the Soviets in January 1991 accompanied this process (see Linz and Stepan 1996).

As such, Estonians perceived protests to a large extent as a tool to subvert an illegitimate government. Peaceful protests, in what has been termed the "singing revolution," were a vehicle for gaining freedom but did not translate into the normal politics of a democratic, independent Estonian state. The historical experience did not allow the use of these weapons against their own government during the first years of independence. Additionally, a decline with regard to all types of political involvement after the boom in political participation in the beginning of the 1990s was to be observed in all eastern European countries.

The overall level of actual or theoretical participation in protest behavior is rather low in Estonia (Table 11.4). The share of those who would never participate in any form of protest behavior is higher in Estonia than in Latvia and Lithuania. The respective numbers in the two other Baltic States were somewhat lower, and the difference is largest for signing petitions. The share of Estonian respondents that signed one or more petitions is 14 percent, only half of the share found in the other two Baltic States (31 percent), while the share found in East Germany was four times larger (64 percent). A majority of respondents in all three Baltic States would never participate in boycotts. Again, this share was highest in Estonia (64 percent). The participation rates with regard to demonstrations did not differ between the three Baltic States. As shown in Table 11.4, the willingness to participate in protest behavior was lower in all three Baltic States than in East Germany, and this pattern was especially is true for petitions and boycotts.

Figure 11.1 shows the differences between the Russian community in Estonia and ethnic Estonians in greater detail. The structure of protest

Table 11.4 Protest behavior, 1996, %, Estonia, Latvia, Lithuania and East Germany

	Petitions			Boycotts			Demonstrations		
	Have done	Might do	Would never do	Have done	Might do	Would never do	Have done	Might do	Would never do
Estonia	14	42	44	2	34	64	21	40	39
Latvia	31	40	29	8	42	50	20	42	38
Lithuania	31	34	35	5	37	58	17	45	38
East Germany	58	36	6	11	46	43	22	55	23

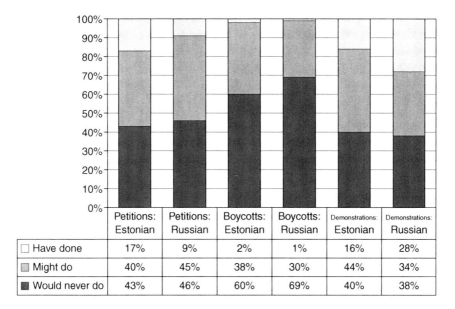

	Petitions: Estonian	Petitions: Russian	Boycotts: Estonian	Boycotts: Russian	Demonstrations: Estonian	Demonstrations: Russian
☐ Have done	17%	9%	2%	1%	16%	28%
▨ Might do	40%	45%	38%	30%	44%	34%
■ Would never do	43%	46%	60%	69%	40%	38%

Figure 11.1 Protest behavior, 1996, %, Estonia.

behavior differs between the two communities. Estonians wrote more petitions than Russians, but Russians participated in demonstrations on a significantly higher level than Estonians. There are several explanations for this pattern. The end of the 1980s saw a high level of protest due to the experience of political transformation. Protests played an important role in Estonia's transformation from a Soviet province into an independent state. While ethnic Estonians used all avenues available for protest against the Moscow government, segments of the Russian-speaking community supported Moscow-initiated actions against independence-oriented Estonian local government. We deal with that issue in more detail in the section on trust (pages 292–7).

Thus, in the first half of 1990s, a gap between the ethnic communities with regard to protest behavior emerged. Five years after declaring independence, it was psychologically difficult for ethnic Estonians to use protest behavior against their own government. At the same time, some of the Russian-speakers participated in the movement for the right to use Russian as an official language, together with Estonian, in state institutions. This reflects the transformation of the Russian-speaking community's status from that of being the dominant group in a multi-ethnic empire to being a minority group in a small national state.

Although it was not officially brokered, violence was a measure used to achieve political goals during the Soviet period. With frequent occurrence, violence as a political tool can acquire some legitimacy. Changed power relations in post-communist societies might therefore lead to violent attempts to improve the position of the dominant ethnic group which, until independence, has been a minority group in the multinational Soviet empire (Klicperova *et al.* 1997). Furthermore, though the temptation exists to use violence against former political enemies for revenge, it could equally be the case that the past experience of violence might result in an intense disgust and rejection of violence as a political instrument.

Estonia was one of the most liberal parts of the former Soviet Union, and this was also reflected in the rejection of violence – violence as a political measure was condemned by 83 percent of the Estonian and Latvian populations. This share is slightly lower than in East Germany (85 percent), but somewhat higher than in Lithuania (77 percent) and Russia (78 percent). Differences with regard to the rejection of violence were found among the different nationalities of the Estonian population: 86 percent of Estonians were against violence as a political measure, roughly the same share that is to be found in East Germany. Of Russian-speakers in Estonia, 79 percent believe that violence in politics is never justified. This is roughly the same share found in Lithuanian and Russian samples.

In comparison with the ethnic Russians in their country, Estonians tend to have a more individualistic cultural background. They also differ from Russians who moved to Estonia in the post-war period and their descendents. Historically the collectivistic Russian culture demanded unchallenged loyalty to the state. Disloyal behavior was punished by measures that would be considered violent by European standards. Estonian peasants that were ruled by German barons historically experienced more freedom than their counterparts in Russia. Additionally, Estonia had the experience of a pre-war parliamentary regime prior to being incorporated into the Soviet Union. It is possible that the parliamentary experience was stored in Estonians' collective memory. The Russian community in Estonia emerged basically as a result of post-World War II immigration from the Soviet Union; that is, from a country with a longer and more deeply rooted experience of an autocratic regime. This distinction between Estonians and Russians might support Huntington's (1996) theory of different civilizations. However, it might also be the case that these differences are less a result of the hypothetical belonging to different civilizations but due to very different experiences within the new Estonian Republic.

The historical experience of living under Soviet rule shaped patterns of understanding of political and civic culture, not only in Estonia, but also in the other Baltic States. However, all three republics were exceptions in this empire since they were incorporated into the Soviet Union two decades after its foundation, i.e. during World War II. All three republics are today economically and politically independent from the Soviet Union and Russia. The Soviet empire did not have a religious base and its legacy

– decades of autocracy and an egalitarian ideology – still has an impact on the political attitudes and behavior of its former population (Rohrschneider 1999). Indeed, we saw rather similar patterns with regard to participation in some types of protest behavior, not only between the two ethnic communities in Estonia but between the three Baltic States as well. However, we also found different attitudes between ethnic Estonians and ethnic Russians toward law and violence. Many differences between Baltic States and their Eastern neighbors might therefore derive from the fact that the Slavic countries spent more time under the Leninist regime (Reisinger 1999). The differences between ethnic Estonians and Russian-speakers with regard to law-abidingness (Table 11.3) might also be attributed to their pre-Soviet cultural experience or to the length of time spent under the Soviet regime.

All three titular Baltic nations differ according to Huntington (1996) from the other, predominantly Orthodox, neighboring Slavic successor countries of the Soviet Union. Among the three Baltic titular nations, Estonians are culturally closer to Latvians than to Lithuanians. These two nations have a Protestant background, while Lithuania belongs to the Catholic world. Baltic countries form a geographically separate group, where value and belief systems should have more in common with central European countries (with which they historically share a cultural background) than with the other former Soviet republics. However, the Estonian population is separated into two communities, the Estonian-speaking and the Russian-speaking, and they share common experiences from the Soviet period. Language also clearly distinguishes Estonia from the other two Baltic States, since Estonian is closely akin to the Finnish language and therefore totally different from the language of neighboring nations. However, among these communities, the content of historical memory differs since the Estonian community is historically strongly influenced by the Germans, while the Russians that immigrated after World War II still have strong roots in Russia where most of them still have relatives.

While attitudes toward the rule of law and violence shared by ethnic Estonians often do not differ considerably from those found in East Germany, the respective attitudes of Russian-speakers in Estonia often differ not only from those of Estonians, but also from those common in the other Baltic States. It seems, on the one hand, that ethnic Estonians are more willing to obey the law than the ethnic Russians in Estonia since they have lived in their country for many generations and Russians are mainly first- or second-generation immigrants. However, this argument is only partially admissible since Russians moved to Estonia during the Soviet period when they were the majority in the Soviet Union. The situation had changed a great deal by 1996; Estonia was an independent nation-state where Estonians formed the majority. Thus, lower ethnic Russian law-abidingness may be a function of the reaction to this changed status. On the other hand, Estonians obeyed the law more strictly than Russians even in Soviet times. However, there are still many things in common between the two ethnic communities such as a low level of interest in politics and a low level of participation in protest behavior.

Moreover, Vihalemm and Lauristin (1997) describe how collectivist values favored by the Soviet school system have been quickly replaced by more individualistic values among the young Russians. Although the Estonian and Russian communities live somewhat isolated lives (see Löfgren and Herd 2000) and share different values with regard to several issues, these differences do not exclude communication among the members of the two ethnic communities, and there are no conflicts on the level of everyday life. Thus, these differences will not stop the development of a democratic community in Estonia.

Democrats and autocrats

Some 25 percent of the Estonian population can be classified as "strong democrats" and 56 percent as "weak democrats"; only 9 percent fit the category "autocrats." When we compare the data for the two ethnic communities in Estonia, major differences emerge. While 37 percent of ethnic Estonians can be classified as strong democrats and roughly half that share as weak democrats, only 8 percent of the Russian-speaking respondents fit the category "strong democrats" and 66 percent are weak democrats. The shares of autocrats are distributed in a reverse manner: 6 percent of Estonians fit this category, while the Russian-speakers' share is twice as high (13 percent). The same is true for the share of undecided citizens, with almost twice as many ethnic Russians in this category (13 percent) than Estonians (7 percent).

In the next section we will analyze the elements of the democracy–autocracy index in more detail.

As shown in Table 11.5, the general attitude in 1996 toward the past Soviet political system was less appreciative in Estonia (47 percent) than in Lithuania (51 percent), and even in East Germany (53 percent), and comparable to the share found in Latvia (43 percent). However, although differences between the three Baltic States were small, the gap between the two ethnic communities in Estonia appeared to be a large one: 33 percent of ethnic Estonians approve the past system while this is true for over 67 percent of the ethnic Russian respondents.

The Estonian population also valued the current system higher (53 percent) than their neighbors in Latvia (42 percent) and Lithuania (49 percent). If we again compare the two language groups in Estonia, we realize that Estonians evaluate the current political system slightly more positively (62 percent) than East German respondents (60 percent), while ethnic Russians in Estonia are at the same level as respondents in Latvia (40 percent).

Support for a strong leader (38 percent) and army rule (5 percent) are

Table 11.5 Democracy index and attitudes toward political issues, 1996, %, Estonia, Latvia, Lithuania and East Germany

	Estonia (overall)	Estonians	Russian-speakers	Latvia	Lithuania	East Germany
Democracy index						
Strong democrats	25	37	8	10	7	32
Democrats	56	50	66	67	57	60
Undecided	9	7	13	10	13	4
Autocrats	9	6	13	13	23	4
Past system: fairly and very good	47	33	67	43	51	53
Current system: fairly and very good	53	62	40	42	49	60
Strong leader: fairly and very good	38	32	46	46	64	18
Army rule: fairly and very good	5	3	7	5	6	2

less prevalent in Estonia than in the other Baltic States, especially among ethnic Estonians; only 32 percent support a strong leader and 3 percent would appreciate army rule. Members of the Russian-speaking community favor a strong leader on the same level as respondents in Latvia (46 percent), and 7 percent would appreciate army rule.

Returning to the democracy index, then, we can conclude that Estonians, especially ethnic Estonians, reject autocracy on a higher level than their neighbors. The share of strong democrats (25 percent) in Estonia is closer to the share found in East Germany (32 percent) than to the share found in Latvia (10 percent) or Lithuania (7 percent). Moreover, more ethnic Estonians than East Germans fit the category of strong democrats (37 percent versus 32 percent). However, at the same time only 8 percent of the Estonian Russians can be regarded as strong democrats. This is in accordance with previous findings of Anderson *et al.* (1996) and Lauristin and Heidmets (2002) who explained this phenomenon by pointing to the lower level of modernization of the Russian community compared to the ethnic Estonians.

Confidence in institutions

The situation in the middle of the 1990s in the post-communist countries is difficult to understand without taking pre-communist history into account (see Laszlo and Farkas 1997). That said, every country deviates more or less from a generalized transition pattern. Estonia had a somewhat unique experience during the first stage of transition because it transformed the political system and the economy simultaneously. During the communist period, the Soviet party leadership had opposed Estonian independence by building up a local authoritarian, hard-line communist party called *Inter-front* that fought actively against pro-independence forces. Democratic forces that were pushing toward independence were the People's Front and the Estonian Congress. The competition of the latter two movements had a healthy impact on the vision of the new Estonian state held by the people. Thus the positions toward democracy and autocracy from Table 11.5 were developed on the basis of a bi-party system that emerged in a context of healthy competition between two distinctive understandings of democratization, understandings which were unique compared with the other Baltic States. Since Estonia was one of the first countries to start reforms, it was also able to transform the economy quickly and somewhat less painfully than other transition states, another important condition for a successful democratization process (see Linz and Stepan 1996).

Trust in the emerging nation-state is related to the level of confidence in its institutions (see Silver and Titma 1998). The quality of the civil service and the performance of institutions can increase or decrease the level of support for *the institutional system* of the state.

Steen (1996) studied confidence in institutions in the Baltic States in two steps. We proceed similarly for the year 1990, when Estonia was still formally a part of the Soviet Union, the year 1992, when Estonia was already independent but just beginning the most serious economic reforms, and finally the year 1996, when Estonia had successfully implemented economic reforms over the course of five years as an independent state (see Tables 11.6, 11.7 and 11.8). We will analyze the development of patterns of trust in institution of the two ethnic communities in Estonia.

In 1990, the Estonian population was interested and involved in politics on a high level. However, political attitudes and historical memories differed between the Estonian and non-Estonian communities (see Kaplan 1994). The same was true for attitudes toward Estonian independence and

Table 11.6 Confidence in institutions, 1990, %, Estonia

	Great deal	Quite a lot	Not very much	Not at all	Total
Republican government	20	49	23	8	100
Supreme Soviet	19	50	25	6	100
Popular Front	14	41	28	17	100
Republican media	13	51	30	6	100
Church	12	42	37	9	100
Education system	9	38	46	7	100
Social security	5	41	45	9	100
Legal system	5	28	53	14	100
Soviet army	4	18	35	43	100
State apparatus	3	36	55	6	100
Labor unions	3	24	55	18	100
Soviet government	3	14	33	50	100
Police	2	17	53	28	100

Table 11.7 Confidence in institutions, 1992, %, Estonia

	Great deal	Quite a lot	Not very much	Not at all	Total
Church	9	34	42	15	100
Estonian army	6	28	48	18	100
Education system	5	47	42	6	100
Media	5	41	45	9	100
Russian army	5	14	20	61	100
Social security	4	34	48	14	100
Local government	4	30	50	16	100
Labor unions	4	22	46	28	100
Legal system	3	25	54	18	100
Police	2	24	53	21	100
Supreme Soviet	2	24	51	23	100
Estonian Congress	2	14	40	44	100
State apparatus	1	33	53	13	100
Political system	1	17	55	27	100

Table 11.8 Confidence in institutions, 1996, % Estonia

	Great deal	Quite a lot	Not very much	Not at all	Total
Green movement	22	54	19	5	100
Women's movement	16	47	30	7	100
United Nations	14	56	24	6	100
Church	14	46	26	14	100
European Union	12	53	25	10	100
Legal system	8	54	30	8	100
State apparatus	7	54	32	7	100
Major companies	7	54	31	8	100
Labor unions	7	38	33	22	100
Press	6	49	37	8	100
Police	6	45	33	16	100
Government	6	44	36	14	100
Estonian army	6	42	37	15	100
Parliament	3	41	41	15	100
Political parties	1	22	46	31	100

the Soviet government in Moscow. This was mirrored in their specific levels of confidence in those institutions, that were polarized between the pro-independence (Estonian republican institutions) and the Soviet (Moscow-oriented) institutions. While Soviet institutions were directed from Moscow, republican institutions increased their power during *perestroika* and were dedicated to solving local problems and achieving independence.

The largest gap between levels of trust in institutions between Estonians and ethnic Russians is to be found in their evaluation of Soviet central institutions. Among the Russians, the Soviet army was seen as most prestigious (trusted by 50 percent). The Soviet central government occupied the second rank (trusted by 39 percent).

Overall, ethnic Estonians, Lithuanians and Latvians in all Baltic States evinced little trust in Soviet institutions in 1990 and evaluated their local republican political institutions as trustworthy: 88 percent of ethnic Estonians trusted the republican government in contrast to 60 percent who did not trust the Soviet government at all. Ethnic Russians in Lithuania had more faith in the Soviet institutions like the central government and the Soviet army.

The most trusted institutions for both ethnic groups were the Republican government and Supreme Soviet (local parliament) of the republic that was pushing toward independence in 1990. The republican media also enjoyed one of the highest levels of trust, since it was independent from the Soviet media that was directed from Moscow.

Russian-speakers indicated modest levels of trust in political institutions that enjoyed higher levels of trust among ethnic Estonians in general. However, there were institutions that were trusted by the members of both communities. The Republican government and Supreme Soviet were highly trusted republican institutions by both ethnic groups, which is to say the Russian population accepted the government and parliament as an institution when it addressed local political problems. The media also enjoyed a very high level of trust in the Russian community.

Let us proceed to a discussion of levels of trust in institutions in 1992. After gaining independence, the Estonian state had to win trust for the newly designed institutions on the part of all residents. In fact, the high levels of trust in institutions that were pushing toward independence vanished (see Table 11.7) and the business of daily politics that required professionals who did not exist in the immediate wake of the communist era additionally led to decreasing levels of trust. The level of support for the Supreme Soviet decreased from 69 percent in 1990 to 26 percent in 1992. Apparently the first wave of enthusiasm for Estonian institutions after the achievement of political freedom had passed and the populace was demoralized by the experience of individual economic hardship. Levels of trust in the media also decreased from 64 percent in 1990 to 46 percent in 1992; respondents also paid less attention to the news.

In 1992, Estonia's legal system enjoyed similar levels of trust among ethnic Estonians as in 1990, but the Russian community's level of support decreased considerably (from 35 percent in 1990 down to 18 percent in 1992). Unsurprisingly, trust in the police also decreased among Russians (from 27 percent in 1990 down to 17 percent in 1992): it was reorganized during that period from a (politicized) Soviet *militia* into regular police forces and, in 1992, was still in the process of establishing itself. The levels of trust in institutions that played no role in achieving independence were comparatively stable over the years. The educational system continued to enjoy higher levels of trust among ethnic Estonians (50 percent in 1990 and 57 percent in 1992) than among ethnic Russians (43 percent in 1990 and 45 percent in 1992). The social security system lost public trust as it came under pressure from the market economy. However, one-third (38 percent) of Russian-speakers as well as 39 percent of Estonians still expressed confidence in the social security system. Meanwhile, labor unions, which played a limited role under the Soviet regime, were still not evaluated as serious actors since they had not played an important part during the transformation and did not safeguard people from unemployment.

A cleavage persisted among the Estonian population with regard to trust in most of the institutions discussed: ethnic Estonians express higher levels of trust than Russian-speakers. On the other hand, the level of trust in the Russian army among ethnic Russians in Estonia remained at the same level (50 percent) in 1990 and 1992.

In 1996, Estonia was the first of the Baltic States to report substantial economic growth. The economy had started to recover from shock therapy reforms, the currency was stable, private capital dominated, wages increased and foreign capital flowed in. This allowed many governmental and non-governmental institutions to function more effectively. The overall level of politicization of the society had decreased in 1996. One reason was the routinized functioning of politics through elections and thus regular changes of governments. This would lead us to expect that the level of trust in basic institutions would also reach higher levels than in 1992.

In 1996, the respondents' positions toward the Estonian institutional landscape (see Table 11.8) became more homogenous than in 1990 and 1992. First of all, extremely positive and negative opinions became less frequent than in the early stages of transition, e.g. no institution received a very strong positive or negative evaluation. These two features describe a situation where institutions are evaluated with regard to their performance and not on the basis of ideology or political attitudes.

In addition, the Green movement, the United Nations, the women's movement, the European Union and the Church evoked the highest levels of trust. That said, none of them receive overwhelming support. These institutions were neither politicized nor were they involved in the transformation processes in Estonia. Thus they remained untouched from the ups and downs of politics and enjoy relatively high trust. Our findings indicate that the time of very polarized positions toward institutions, which might have been colored by the pros and cons toward national independence, is over.

The two most mistrusted institutions were political parties and labor unions. Indeed, one third of respondents report having no confidence in political parties and one-fifth evaluate labor unions similarly. More than half of the respondents did not trust these institutions in 1996. Apparently the people expected that labor unions would play the role they have played in the development of the advanced neighboring Nordic societies and they were disappointed when no such development occurred. There are historical features common in central and eastern Europe that might explain this phenomenon: labor unions had the status of a semi-official bureaucracy in the former Soviet Union and membership was compulsory. The structure of labor unions was not based on citizens' activity but on bureaucratic structures, and they were not flexible enough to react to citizens' needs. Low levels of trust in political parties might be a result of the lack of preparedness among respondents for party politics, i.e. political rivalry of parties with debates and fights that are common in democracies. In the former Soviet Union, the officially "correct opinion" was implemented without competition and debate. In addition, during the establishment of national independence, almost all independence-oriented political forces agreed on many issues. Compared to these features, everyday party politics might look boring, ineffective and difficult to understand.

To conclude on Estonian positions toward institutions, it seems that in 1996, five years after establishing national independence and a period of rapid economic development, the levels of trust in major institutions were stabilizing. This is not surprising as the time of rapid changes was over. Apparently, trust was no longer as politicized and institutional perform-ance rather than political attitudes determined respondents' views. This might be interpreted as a development toward a stable and democratic civil society.

Attitudes toward the other citizen

There is no civil society without the active participation of the citizens. Cit-izens' political participation in the democratic process makes it easier for democratic standards to become rooted in a society. However, the histor-ical experience of Soviet rule is not the best starting point for understand-ing and participating in democracy. Therefore, the development of democracy in the former Soviet republics can take different paths as it depends a great deal on the pre-Soviet experiences. The Czech writer and politician Havel (1989) stated that any change of the social world must start with the change in human consciousness. This is why values prevalent in a given society are of crucial importance for the transition toward democracy and a change of values accompany this development. In the following sections, we explore how people understand their relation to other citizens in society, analyzing the respective patterns of the two ethnic communities.

The semantics of "equality" and "freedom" changed during the early 1990s (Vihalemm 1997). While these concepts had previously evoked a rather strong ideological context, they now refer to individual everyday experiences. Western societies turned toward post-materialist values after they achieved considerable welfare following World War II. East Euro-peans, on the other hand, experienced economic hardship during this period, hence materialist values prevail (Saarniit 1995). This does not imply that in the aftermath of communism one can expect a linear trans-formation of the socialist value system into one reflecting the values of western democratic welfare societies. However difficult the relation between prevalent values and current behavior might be, the shared values of community at least indicate the preferred structure of the realm of the "should be" with regard to both the institutional order as well as the societal order. We employ the respondents' attitudes toward "ethics of daily life" as an operationalization of the institutional order and the respondents' attitudes toward the other citizen as an operationalization of the societal order.

Ethics of daily life

The ethics of daily life reflect, together with the respondents' attitudes toward individual competition and their level of solidarity with the poor, the expectation of who should be in charge of individual welfare and attitudes toward socio-economic differences.

Estonians occupy a rather moderate position with regard to the ethics of individual achievement (see Table 11.9): levels of support for individual responsibility were lower than in the other two Baltic States and did not differ considerably from those found in East Germany. Although Estonian culture values individualism, there is rather extensive reliance on government to secure individual welfare. Estonians compared current living standards in the Soviet Union with their Baltic neighbors before the 1990s. Following independence in 1991, they tended to compare their living standards with their Scandinavian social-democratic neighbor, Finland, that is, with a system that provides extensive social support to its citizenry. The same comparisons were made on the matter of wage differentials. A majority of Estonians think it is unfair when incomes differ by wide margins. The Russian community is more tolerant of wage differentials than ethnic Estonians (80 percent versus 56 percent in 1996). This might be explained by their reaction to economic "shock-therapy" during the first half on the 1990s. Economic reforms changed their understanding of income, from one based on the socialist guarantee to acceptance of free-market competition unconditionally. Such a conclusion does not mesh with the assumption that, although Estonians also lived for 50 years under Soviet rule, they cope better with the reforms than ethnic Russians because of their more individualistic cultural background. Differentials in perceptions in the Estonian and Russian communities on wage differentials thus call into question the notion that ethnic Russians in Estonia are less oriented toward the western values conducive to liberal democracy. It would be interesting to examine this tension with more recent data.

In 1996, respondents expressed a higher level of support for individual competition compared to the other two Baltic States. This surprisingly high esteem for individual competition might be attributed to the Lutheran background of ethnic Estonians. However, support for competition is also at a high level in the Russian community, who support competition on the same level as the Latvians. This might indicate that the market economy is working for *all* residents in Estonia. The remaining difference between Estonians and Russians might be explained by the different cultural and religious backgrounds of the two communities. As Russians belong to the Orthodox tradition, the shock caused by the radical economic reforms might have been stronger for them than for the Lutheran Estonians, since the values embedded in a free market economy might be more familiar for the latter community. However, apparently, a majority trusted their own ability to succeed under the new conditions. Amazingly the Estonians' faith in competition and hard work is, at 80 percent of respondents, even greater than in East Germany, where only 63 percent of the population believe that hard work brings a better life. This might be attributed to the outcomes of radical economic policy, which

Table 11.9 Values of the community: ethics of daily life, 1996, %, Estonia, Latvia, Lithuania and East Germany

	Estonia (overall)	Estonians	Russian-speakers	Latvia	Lithuania	East Germany
Ethics of individual achievement						
People should take more responsibility vs government should take more responsibility	36	37	35	38	49	40
We need larger income differences as incentives for individual efforts vs incomes should be made more equal	66	56	80	79	58	49
Ethics of individual competition						
Competition is good vs competition is harmful	93	95	91	92	87	91
In the long run, hard work usually brings a better life vs. hard work doesn't generally bring success – it's more a matter of luck and connections	80	84	75	69	52	63
Solidarity with the poor						
People are poor in this country because society treats them unfairly	74	66	85	77	79	90
Poor people in this country have very little chance to escape from poverty	67	54	85	74	86	92
Government is doing too little for people in poverty in this country	86	80	93	89	90	81

implemented a system where the responsibility of individuals increases, with a corresponding rise in salaries, in direct relation to employees' contribution to final production. And since purchasing power parity was, in comparison with western societies, very low, Estonians felt the buying power of every banknote directly. Interestingly, Estonians and Latvians differ considerably from Lithuania with regard to the level of support for individual competition. This discrepancy most likely reflects delayed reforms and restructuring of the Lithuanian economy.

The third aspect of the ethics of daily life is solidarity with the poor. A majority of Estonian respondents sympathized with the poor. They believed that poor people were worse off from the very beginning of the reforms. People identified as vulnerable during reforms included retired persons, inhabitants of rural areas, people with a low level of formal education or persons with educational grades that do not fit the new labor market and qualification system. Solidarity with the poor was more prominent among ethnic Russians. This might be explained by the mere fact that poverty was more likely to affect Russians than Estonians, since they were usually employed in companies and industrial plants established under Soviet rule, many of which closed down during the early stages of the transformation.

Compared to the two Baltic neighbors and to East Germany, Estonians do not differ significantly with regard to their expressed level of solidarity with the poor.

However, if we take a closer look at the poverty issue, more detailed differences between the Estonian and the Russian community are revealed. While two-thirds of Estonians believe that society treats the poor unfairly, 85 percent of Russians believe the same. This difference might express a lesser distance to socialist modes of governmental care on the part of the Russian community. Three-quarters of the Estonian population believe that the government should take care of individual welfare. Latvians (77 percent) and Lithuanians (79 percent) express similar levels of support and East Germans report even higher levels (90 percent), which might be due to the fact that the East German social system was even more paternalistic than those of the Baltic Soviet republics.

Russians and Estonians also differ in their optimism with regard to the possibility of escaping the poverty gap. While 85 percent of Russians believe that poor people have very little chance to escape from poverty, only 54 percent of Estonian respondents believe the same. Altogether, 67 percent of Estonian residents believe that poor people have very little chances of escaping the poverty trap. The Baltic neighbors (Latvia 74 percent; Lithuania 86 percent) and East Germans (92 percent) are less optimistic. Attitudes toward the governmental treatment of the poor follow a similar pattern, with 86 percent of the respondents believing that the government treated the poor unfairly (compared to 93 percent Russians and 80 percent Estonians). Estonia did not differ considerably from

East Germany or Latvia and Lithuania in this respect. Estonian society underwent a radical transformation. Apparently belief systems did the same. On one hand the respondents expressed quite a lot of optimism with regard to individuals' future prospects but, on the other hand, they were sensitive to the ramifications of the collapse of the paternalistic Soviet social system where everything was granted.

The other citizen

Attitudes toward the other citizen indicate not only what people expect from each other, but also preferences for different social settings from homogeneity to plurality. Trust among citizens is an important precondition for the free expression of dissent and political participation. Under Soviet rule, traditional loyalties and face-to-face trust on the communal level tended to become fragile under the pressure of an omnipotent state which controlled most aspects of everyday life and the family domain (Markova 1997). In Estonia, as in other central and eastern European countries, this historical legacy has not yet been overcome. Roughly, between two-thirds and four-fifth of the respondents in every central and east European country included in this survey believe that they have to be careful in dealing with other people. In Estonia, that share is 21 percent with no difference between Russians and Estonians.

Tolerance toward others can be understood as the acceptance of deviant behavior and the acceptance of minorities. In our survey, the former included attitudes toward homosexuality, prostitution, abortion and divorce. Historical experiences still shape Estonian attitudes: abortion and divorce were permitted in the Soviet Estonia, homosexuality and prostitution were not; moreover, homosexuals were treated like criminals. It still affects hostility toward homosexuality and prostitution; the difference between the two language communities can be attributed mostly to attitudes toward homosexuality. Russians are in this respect slightly more intolerant than Estonians: 61 percent of Estonians and 73 percent of Russians express extremely hostile positions toward homosexuality and 27 percent of Estonians and 16 percent of Russians tolerate homosexuality. Some 52 percent of ethnic Estonians and 58 percent of Russians also do not tolerate prostitution; 23 percent of ethnic Estonians and 21 percent of Russian-speaking respondents accept prostitution. These kinds of attitudes toward prostitution are similar in the other two Baltic States, but differ considerably from East German results (Table 11.10). Our respondents do not perceive abortion and divorce as very serious problems; this is also true for the other Baltic countries.

The share of respondents who rejected minority groups, i.e. people of different race, religion and immigrants, indicate another dimension of (in)tolerance. Since only a few residents in Estonia are of a different race, this issue is not very important for the respondents. There are some

Table 11.10 Values of the community: attitudes toward others, %, Estonia, Latvia, Lithuania and East Germany

	Estonia (overall)	Estonians	Russian-speakers	Latvia	Lithuania	East Germany
Trust in others						
Most people can be trusted	21	21	22	24	21	24
Tolerance toward others						
Acceptance of deviant behavior						
Behavior can be justified						
Divorce	80	78	81	83	57	81
Abortion	66	65	68	66	47	68
Homosexuality	22	27	16	28	14	65
Prostitution	22	23	21	32	18	54
Rejection of minority groups						
Would not like to have as neighbors						
People of different race	8	11	2	5	14	4
Immigrants/foreign workers	19	29	5	18	29	10
Muslims (or other small but salient minority group)	23	30	13	25	20	16

Muslims in Estonia but they belong to the Russian-speaking community since they originate from the former Soviet Caucasus or the Asian republics and have lived in Estonia since World War II. Estonians were treated as a minority in Estonia during the decades of Soviet rule. In reaction to this, since 1990, the Estonian media has treated Russian residents as immigrants. It is therefore not surprising that the overall level of rejection of minority groups is considerably higher among ethnic Estonians (18 percent) than among Russian-speakers (3 percent), since the latter is a (remarkably large) minority in the small republic where the overall population is only 1.4 million, 29 percent of the whole population are Russians. However, the members of these two communities do not compete on regional job markets since Russians tend to live mostly in the north Estonian industrial region where they are a majority. The Estonian hostility toward immigrants accounts for the largest share of difference between two ethnic communities – while 29 percent of ethnic Estonians reject immigrants, only 5 percent of the Russian respondents do the same. There are also considerable differences between Estonians and Russians with regard to the rejection of Muslims; 30 percent of Estonian respondents reject them, while only 13 percent of Russian-speakers do not like to live in the same neighborhood as Muslims. These findings are in accordance with the results of Anderson *et al.* (1997).

Conclusion

The transition toward democracy and its implementation in central and eastern Europe has been influenced by the legacies of communist rule and by cultural differences between these countries. Such phenomena strongly affect value patterns in all countries that lived under communist or Soviet regimes. However, while the experiences of the last 50 years have tended to resemble each other, cultural values differ and might account not only for different routes taken by different states toward democracy during the last decade, but also for these states' different standing today. If we narrow our focus down to the Baltic States, we can assume that they share similar experiences since World War I. Estonia and Latvia are culturally and religiously similar with a Lutheran background, while Lithuania belongs to the Catholic world.

Another important possible determinant of attitude formation is recent societal experience. Estonia achieved independence without violence. This was a consequence of peaceful protests during the late 1980s such as the "Singing Revolution" where people came together to sing forbidden national songs, or the "Baltic Chain" where people in all three Baltic Republics joined hands with each other to protest against the Soviet Union. However, although protests are a characteristic of civil society, after 1991 ethnic Estonians rejected all forms of protest, only five years after regaining independence, Estonians found it was psychologically difficult to use means that were employed against the Soviet Union against their own government.

Changing patterns of confidence in institutions in Estonia from 1990 to 1996 accompany the restoration of the national state and the development of civil society. One such pattern has been not only the creation and development of new institutions but also their acceptance on the part of the citizens. In 1990, when Estonia was still a *de jure* part of the Soviet Union, trust in institutions was polarized largely between the two ethnic communities with regard to the Estonian governmental and Soviet institutions. While republican institutions were clearly oriented toward independence, Soviet ones merely obeyed Moscow's orders. In 1992, when Estonia had become independent, levels of trust in institutions that played an important role in achieving Estonian independence had decreased, while trust in institutions that were not involved in politics, such as the Church, remained stable. Trust in politicized institutions like political parties and parliament was also low in 1996, five years after independence. That might indicate respondents' fatigue as a result of political and socio-economic transformations. Estonia, together with Latvia and Lithuania, differs from the other eastern European transition societies in that these countries did not have a national army or police force due to their previous incorporation in the USSR. Thus, such institutions had to be established simultaneously with the reorganization of other institutions such as the parliament. In 1996, the most serious reforms were over and patterns of trust in institutions were more homogenous than in the period of rapid change. This homogenization indicates that the two ethnic communities experienced the "shock therapy" in a broadly similar way. Differences in levels of trust between the two ethnic communities in politicized institutions like the Estonian government were striking at the beginning of 1990s, and became minor over the first half of the decade. It is significant that labor unions belonged to the most mistrusted institutions – many people were disappointed with their role in the early transformation. In addition, people's interest moved from political issues to economic ones. The perceived way to improve living conditions was not to fight for political rights but for reasonable income. There were no serious cleavages between ethnic Estonians and ethnic Russians with regard to trust in institutions in 1996. The common experience of "shock therapy" might be a solid base for the further development of a civil society in which both groups are equally represented. Moreover, although the majority of Russian residents did not have citizenship, they seemed to have accepted the rules of a market society like Estonians.

In Estonia, levels of trust in other people are much lower than in western societies, but this is known to be the case in all East European transition societies. The experience of life under Soviet rule still affects values, with rather low levels of acceptance of deviant behavior a good example of such a tendency. While members of both communities tolerated divorce and abortion, activities permitted by Soviet laws, both ethnic Estonians and Russian-speakers were intolerant toward prostitution and homosexuality which, not coincidentally, were prohibited in the Soviet Union. Russians indicated higher levels of tolerance toward minorities like immigrants, since they are themselves considered by the Estonian majority to be immigrants.

Considerable differences exist between ethnic Estonians and Russian-speakers. These differences reflect the crucial change in the two groups' status after the collapse of Soviet Union and the restoration of an independent Estonian state. Ethnic Russians were the dominating majority in the Soviet republic but suddenly they found themselves as a minority in independent Estonia. This transformation was painful and, in addition, they no longer lived in a collectivistic environment where the state took care of their life, but in a free market economy where individual performance mattered.

As a result of regained Estonian independence, a strong national movement emerged and the dominating Pro Patria party continues to rely on such sentiments. However, gradually this nationalist position has lost resonance and attitudes toward the Russian minority among ethnic Estonians have started to become more tolerant. Our data from 1990 to 1996 indicates that both sides made considerable progress toward the creation of a homogeneous civil society as indicated by our findings on the development of levels of trust in the two ethnic communities. Differences remain but they decreased considerably during the six-year period studied.

Even more important is the fact that European institutions enjoy very high levels of respect among Estonians and Russians. This might represent a good basis for the European integration of the Estonian society as a whole. In 1996, five years after declaring independence, Estonian society had managed to implement many reforms successfully over a short time. Preliminary conditions that made this success possible were as follows. First of all, Estonia was the most liberal part of Soviet Union, with the highest level of formal education of its population. Second, it was the first among the former Soviet Republics to begin reforms. Third, Estonia was the only Soviet republic, that did not experience a violent transition. Fourth, successful initial reforms enabled the implementation of the next wave. While it will take time to integrate two ethnic communities into one society, there are signs that ethnic Estonians feel less threatened by Russian-speakers every year. Our analysis shows that, although differences between the two ethnic communities existed, similarities between Estonians and Russians prevailed. The same is true if we compare value and behavior patterns between the Estonian Russians and the populations of the two other Baltic or central European states. Becoming a member of the European Union will also contribute to the further integration of two communities as it facilitates communication not only with institutions in other member states but also between Estonians and ethnic Russians.

Note

1 *Estonia Today* 25 September, 1997. For more information on the situation of Russians in Estonia and the relations between ethnic Russians and Estonian citizens, see Rose and Maley 1994; Anderson *et al.* 1996; Linz and Stepan 1996.

References

Anderson, B.A., Silver, B.D., Titma, M. and Ponarin, E.D. (1996) "Estonian and Russian Communities: Ethnic and Language Relations. Estonia's Transition from State Socialism," in Titma, M., Silver, B.D. and Anderson, B.A. (eds) *Nationalities and Society on the Eve of Independence*, Special Issue of *International Journal of Sociology* 26, 2.

Bardi, A. and Schwarz, S. (1996) "Relations Among Socio-political Values in Eastern Europe: Effects of the Communist Experience?," *Political Psychology* 17, 3.

Breakwell, G.M. and Lyons, E. (eds) (1996) *Changing European Identities: Social Psychology Analysis of Social Change*, Cornwall: Butterworth-Heinemann.

Fuchs, D. and Klingemann, H. (2000) "Eastward Enlargement of the European Union and the Identity of Europe," *West European Politics* 25, 2.

Havel, V. (1989) *In Various Directions: Essays and Articles, 1983–1989*, Scheinfeld: Schwarzenberg.

Huntington, S.P. (1996) *The Clash of Civilizations and the Remaking of World Order*, New York: Simon and Schuster.

Inglehart, R. (1990) *Culture Shift in Advanced Industrial Society*, Princeton: Princeton University Press.

Inglehart, R. (1998) "Clash of Civilizations or Global Cultural Modernization? Empirical Evidence from 61 Societies," paper presented at the 1998 meeting of the International Sociological Association, Montreal, 27–31 August.

Inglehart, R. and Baker, W. (2000) "Modernization, Cultural Change, and the Persistence of Traditional Values," *American Sociological Review* 65, 1.

Kaplan, C. (1994) "Estonia: a Plural Society on the Road to Independence," in Bremmer, I. and Taras, R. (eds) *Nation and Politics in the Soviet Successor States*, Cambridge: Cambridge University Press.

Klicperova, M., Feierbend, I.K. and Hofstetter, C.R. (1997) "In the Search for a Post-Communist Syndrome: a Theoretical Framework and Empirical Assessment," *Journal of Community and Applied Social Psychology* 7, 1.

Klingemann, H. (1999) "Mapping Political Support in the 1990s: a Global Analysis," Norris, P. (ed.) *1999 Critical Citizens: Global Support for Democratic Government*, Oxford: Oxford University Press.

Laszlo, J. and Farkas, A. (1997) "Central-Eastern European Collective Experiences," *Journal of Community and Applied Social Psychology* 7, 1.

Lauristin, M. and Heidmets, M. (2002) "Introduction: the Russian Minority in Estonia as a Theoretical and Political Issue," in Lauristin, M. and Heidmets, M. (eds) *The Challenge of the Russian Minority: Emerging Multicultural Democracy in Estonia*, Tartu: Tartu University Press.

Linz, J.J. and Stepan, A. (1996) *Problems of Democratic Transition and Consolidation: Southern Europe, South America and Post-Communist Europe*, Baltimore: The Johns Hopkins University Press.

Löfgren, J. and Herd, G.P. (2000) "Estonia and the EU: Integration and Societal Security in the Baltic Context," Research Report No. 91, Tampere: Tampere Peace Research Institute.

Markova, I. (1997) "The Individual and the Community: a Post-Communist Perspective," *Journal of Community and Applied Social Psychology* 7, 1.

Rawls, J. (1993) *Political Liberalism*, New York: Columbia University Press.

Reisinger, W.M. (1999) "Reassessing Theories of Transition Away from Authoritarian Regimes: Regional Patterns Among Postcommunist Countries," paper presented at the 1999 Annual Meeting of the Midwest Political Science Association, Chicago, 15–17 April.

Rohrschneider, R. (1999) *Learning Democracy: Democratic and Economic Values in Unified Germany*, Oxford: Oxford University Press.

Rose, R. and Maley, W. (1994) "Nationalities in the Baltic States: a Survey Study," *Studies in Public Policy 222*, Glasgow: University of Strathclyde.

Saarniit, J. (1995) "Changes in the Value Orientation of Youth and their Social Context," in Tomasi, L. (ed.) *Values and Post-Soviet Youth: The Problem of Transition*, Milan: FrancoAngeli.

Silver, B.D. and Titma, M. (1998) "Support for New Political Institutions in Estonia: the Effects of Nationality, Citizenship, and Material Well-Being," *Problems of Post-Communism* 45.

Steen, A. (1996) "Confidence in Institutions in Post-Communist Societies: the Case of the Baltic Stares," *Scandinavian Political Studies* 19, 3.

Titma, M. (1996) "Estonia: a Country in Transition," in Titma, M., Silver, B.D. and Anderson, B.A. (eds) *Nationalities and Society on the Eve of Independence*, Special Issue of *International Journal of Sociology* 26,1.

Titma, M. and Silver, B.D. (1996) "Transitions from Totalitarian Society," in Titma, M., Silver, B.D. and Anderson, B.A. (eds) *Nationalities and Society on the Eve of Independence*, Special Issue of *International Journal of Sociology* 26, 1.

Vihalemm, T. (1997) "Changing Discourses on Values in Estonia," in Lauristin, M., Vihalemm, P., Rosengren, K.E. and Weibull, L. (eds) *Return to the Western World: Cultural and Political Perspectives on the Estonian Post-Communist Transition*, Tartu: Tartu University Press.

Vihalemm, T. and Lauristin, M. (1997) "Cultural Adjustment to the Changing Societal Environment: the Case of Russians in Estonia," in Lauristin, M., Vihalemm, P., Rosengren, K.E. and Weibull, L. (eds) *Return to the Western World: Cultural and Political Perspectives on the Estonian Post-Communist Transition*, Tartu: Tartu University Press.

12 Romania

Fatalistic political cultures revisited

Alina Mungiu-Pippidi

Three meanings of political culture

Making sense of the political post-communist transition has proved to be a difficult task. In comparison, the economic transition had a clear beginning – the command economy, and a clear target – the free market. In terms of political culture, even the word "transition" has little meaning, and the early observation that East European Studies as a discipline is still far away from forging a theory of change of political culture may still be accurate (von Beyme 1996: 349). First, do we actually know where East European political culture comes from? Does it have its roots in the pre-communist past, a time that adepts of cultural legacies theories depict as doomed to "etatism" and "collectivism" even before the advent of communism (Schoepflin 1978)? Are these historical sources of eastern European political culture so corrupt as to have even perverted communism itself (Jowitt 1993)? Or does the region's political culture derive from the less remote communist times, assuming the communist regime was successful in imposing its culture upon both elites and the community? And what were the features of the community political culture during communism? As all analysts point out, comparative research in eastern Europe suffers from a "*tabula rasa* problem," as the first partially reliable comparable data were collected only as late as 1990 (Plasser and Pribersky 1996: 5). Surveys prior to this date are suspected of pro-regime bias and therefore almost useless. Second, where are these societies headed for? Perhaps the answer is toward a universal type of liberal or Western democratic political culture? But does such an entity even exist? If so how do we account for the broad range of different liberal cultures, from the individualistic Anglo-Saxons to the more collectivistic Germans, from the "feminine" Scandinavians to the "masculine" Americans (Hofstede 1998)? Differences in institutional culture among West Europeans are a common complaint within the European Union, where a "Northern" and a "Mediterranean" culture are allegedly in tense cohabitation. Even assuming we know the two ends of this continuum, what lies in between? Is "transition" a mixture of competing residual beliefs with newly acquired ones? And when does the moment arrive to decide which ones have acquired the upper hand for good?

Three distinct meanings of "political culture" have been used in connection to post-communist Europe so far. The first considers political culture to be a configuration arising out of salient patterns of public opinion with regard to politics, following the traditional approach of Almond and Verba (1963). By aggregating individual psychological data, this view creates the "national" on the basis of individual representations of politics shared by the majority of the population. Here, two distinct problems arise. First, majorities of public opinion shift constantly on a considerable number of issues. Second, many crucial political issues fall short of meeting the approval of clear majorities. There is an outstanding example of the former in eastern Europe, where the number of people saying in a survey interview that one-party systems are better than multi-party systems has decreased year after year since 1991, when a *Times Mirror* poll first asked the question. The latter often emerges in the headlines whenever polls report that public opinion is divided. On many political issues, from war to abortion, pollsters report that we face two "countries." We have two Americas, one in favor of gun control, the other in favor of unlimited freedom to buy a weapon, and two eastern Europes, one constantly voting for former communist parties, the other voting for former anti-communist parties. Majorities shift across time and across issues, making "national" political culture hard to grasp. If we believe Inglehart's (1997) ideas, then the whole post-communist world is only one "culture," where Catholics, Protestants, Orthodox and Confucians all prefer the earthly values of survival above the values of self-expression.

The second meaning of political culture refers to what the French call *mentalités. Mentalities* are more than attitudes toward politics, they are actual behaviors rooted in widespread norms about politics. Those go far beyond current issues of politics, and are only infrequently investigated. Putting one's dentist on the payroll of the European Commission as a consultant is more acceptable in some cultures than in others. Relying on majorities rather than building a broad consensus over an issue is, again, a common pattern in some countries, but not in others. *Mentalities* are better understood as "informal institutions," widespread societal norms and procedures, such as described by Douglas North. It was also North (1990) who remarked that informal institutions emerge out of habit. In times of political and economical change, they often reflect the formal institutions of the previous, rather than the current, regime. This observation may be of crucial importance in understanding post-communist societies. This approach to "political culture" is common especially in the policy literature. Studies on the legal or business culture of post-communist Europe have often taken this "institutionalist" perspective. It was even argued that any other approach than deciphering the logic of informal institutions out of their specific historical context cannot but fail to explain post-communism (Gelman 2001).

Finally, there is a more "metaphysical" vision of political culture, shared by cultural theory, area studies and comparative politics. This follows the footsteps of nineteenth-century thought (represented, for instance, by German historian Leopold Ranke) that history is an expression of national "character" or culture, and has met the endorsement in the twentieth century of a string of famous authors, ranging from George F. Kennan to Samuel Huntington or Aaron Wildavsky. Insidiously, but persistently, it is this particular vision of political culture that more often than not colors the media stories on a specific country. Similarly, Carl Schmitt's distinction between politics and the concept of the political was rediscovered in recent decades by scholars seeking a more anthropological approach to highlight the "political" texture embedded within the general cultural tissue. As Geertz once put it, "Culture [...] is not cults and customs, but the structure of meaning through which men give shape to their experience, and politics is not coups and constitutions, but one of the principal arenas in which such structures publicly unfold" (Geertz 1973: 311–12).

Needless to say, the more difficult a political transition, and the less relevant public opinion proves to be in explaining actual regime performance, the more the need increases to turn to the third variant of political culture in the effort for explanation. It works for politicians, because it lays the blame on history and the people, diminishing elite agency. It is convenient for constituencies, because it justifies poor electoral choices, assuming that the political culture of elites, regardless of their ideology, is to blame, so one needs not pay attention to politics. And finally, it is convenient for the international community, because it reinforces whatever was their initial policy approach. A country is doing poorly not because it is neglected, but is neglected because its history carries the obvious germ of its own failure, suggesting investment in that particular country cannot change its fate and is therefore a waste.

As a rule, Romania, the prime subject of this chapter, was almost always analyzed through the use of this last conceptualization of political culture. Poor performance was the consequence of a historically grounded, long-term cultural development (Shafir 1985; Wildavsky 1987; Jowitt 1993; Janos 1993). On closer inspection, however, Romania's performance is anything but "poor" considering that, in 1989, it had the worst totalitarian regime of post-communist Europe, but managed to sign the EU accession treaty in 2005, nearly 16 years after the 1989 revolution. Compared to the speedy integration of the Baltic countries, Romania has indeed performed worse – but its population is almost three times larger that of those states. Furthermore, Romania falls on the wrong side of the civilization border drawn by Samuel Huntington (1993) as it is overwhelmingly Christian Orthodox and was a tributary to the Ottoman Empire from the fifteenth to the nineteenth century. It is also allegedly haunted by Robert Kaplan's Balkan "ghosts" of nationalism and anti-Semitism. However, despite having an important and politically self-assertive Hungarian minority in Transylvania (7 percent of the total population), Romania has not become the stage for yet another "typical" Balkan ethnic conflict. Instead, it has evolved into a power-sharing polity, with Hungarian parties associated with the government since 1996. A British nineteenth-century guide also characterized Bucharest briefly as "the most dissolute" city in Europe. As for Wildavsky, who sketches four types of political culture, the "fatalistic" variant is based entirely on Romania (1987). Its inspiration lies in the Romanian folk ballad, *Mioritza*. *Mioritza* is the story of a Romanian shepherd who reacts to the news that his envious fellow shepherds plan to kill him in order to steal his herd with total passivity, taking ritual steps to meet his death and a cosmic wedding with the universe. The ballad was interpreted in various ways. Michael Shafir, a scholar of Romanian political culture, has elaborated most of the argument Wildavsky draws upon when characterizing Romania (1985). Wildavsky cross-tabulates the strength of group boundaries with the nature of norms binding groups. When norms are strong and groups are weak – so that decisions are frequently made for them by external factors – the result is what he calls a "fatalistic" political culture. In such cultures, people are unable to fully exploit both freedom – being distrustful toward the utility of the exercise of free will – and power, as low mutual trust makes collective action difficult to achieve. Wildavsky's theory is thus able to point to what is indeed the strongest determinant of Romanian history, external intervention. However, he is perhaps overly deterministic in describing a trip from gloom to doom by eternalizing bad history through the emergence of "fatalism" as a *permanent* cultural trait. There is little doubt that "external factors" have historically played a more important role than domestic agency. Romania is one of the countries that Barrington Moore Jr. considered should not be included at all in discussions on political change, as "the decisive causes of their politics lie outside their own boundaries" (1966: xii).

The Romanian national state was indeed created by a *fait accompli* in 1859, despite the preferences of the Great Powers who did not approve of the unification of Romanian principalities. In 1940, the Hitler–Stalin pact deprived Romania of important territories inhabited by Romanian citizens, striking a mortal blow to the legitimacy of constitutional monarchy. The Romanian communism that followed was entirely Soviet sponsored, and on the scrap of paper Winston Churchill handed to Stalin (according to his own narrative and Anthony Eden's *Memoirs*) Romania was marked as the country of the least interest to the West of all eastern European states. The Soviet Union was accordingly given 90 percent influence, and the West claimed a mere 10 percent sphere of influence in the country. Even the 1989 fall of Ceausescu, betrayed by the army and security apparatus, facing a yet manageable popular uprising, has also been attributed – on the basis of some evidence – to a plot led by Moscow. "Political culture" matters only when people are free to choose the form of government they prefer, and for Romanians this is a brand new experience. Only after 1989 has "political culture" started to matter more, as the whole world reached a degree of liberalization without precedent. But how much it did matter is still under dispute. On 25 December 1989, after the most violent popular uprising of all eastern European revolutions, dictator Nicolae Ceausescu and his wife were shot after a brief trial. Of the few people who assisted at the execution – quite unknown to the public at the time – some went on to play a major role in the history of post-communist Romania. Their presence at Ceaucescu's execution and the role they played in the years to come, especially in the violent repression of opposition by miners in June 1990, led several observers to conclude the popular uprising which led to the fall of Ceausescu was successful only because of a secret agreement between the army, security apparatus and some key politicians favored by Gorbachev such as Ion Iliescu. Iliescu, however, had popular appeal – he won three out of the four presidential elections in which he participated, helped by a special interpretation of the Constitution that allowed him three terms in office. It is difficult to separate decisions by formal institutions – such as this decision of the Constitutional Court – from informal institutions such as people's preference to vote for politicians who are identified with the state and related attitudes such as communism and collectivism. This suggests that any meaningful discussion of political culture must go beyond the examination of cross-sectional surveys of public opinion. In other words, if political culture is treated as an independent variable, the evidence is there to show that political culture matters little or not at all. Exogenous factors (the decision of the EU to enlarge to the Balkans) and structural constraints (the communist heritage), have such an overwhelming importance in explaining the trajectories of eastern European countries that little room is left for other explanations (Bunce 1999). If political culture is treated, however, as a dependent variable, and our concern is more to explain what triggers changes in political culture – for instance how political culture relates to political change in general – it will be worth the effort. Comparative surveys show little to no difference in legal culture, for instance. It seems that Romanians are no more willing than other eastern Europeans to cheat on taxes, travel without paying a fare on public transportation or infringe the law. Objective data, on the other hand, as monitored by the World Bank or the European Commission, point to the fact that law and order institutions in Romania show a performance that ranks lower than those of central European countries. Thus, we have to look at the relationship between formal institutions, informal institutions and public opinion to understand the complexity of political culture in times of dramatic political and social change. In other words, we have to follow the horizontal causal links roughly suggested by the theoretical model of Figure 12.1 to capture the complexity of political change, placing public opinion in a broader context. This chapter looks at Romania from such a perspective and will therefore integrate subjective data with some objective indicators as well.

The 1995 World Values Survey (WVS) data for Romania were generated in 1993 by ICCV. They provide a general comparative framework to discuss the Romanian situation. Three more-recent surveys, two from the year 2000 (2000a and 2000b), and one from 2001, jointly sponsored by the Eurobarometer and the UNDP, all executed by CURS, allow an update of the state of affairs in Romanian political culture.[1]

Figure 12.1 illustrates the complex links between formal institutions, informal institutions and political culture, in terms of the Almond and Verba definition. It helps to put my analytic tools to proper use and to understand their limitations as well. In terms of legal culture, for instance, the formal institution consists of the organization and formal procedures of the justice system, from constitutional provisions to the organization of courts. The informal institution refers to people's habits, for instance, bribing of court clerks to shorten the length of trials (usually between three and four years). "Political culture" is made up of attitudes toward formal and informal institutional arrangements. Do people like to bribe? Do they perceive this state of affairs as normal? Is it the corruption of

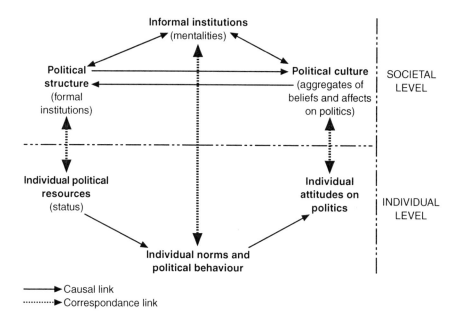

Figure 12.1 Integrating political culture into context. A theoretical model.

citizens that triggers the corruption of the judiciary, or are there institutional incentives and constraints that cause corruption with public reactions showing disapproval and discontent? Finally, we should not forget that we deal with self-reporting. Even if we find significant associations in our analysis, those will tell us something about individuals, not about countries. Figure 12.1 is a sort of mirror, separating the societal level from the individual level and tracing the correspondences between the two. Inferences from the individual level do tell us something about society as well, but the invisible border between real people and abstract aggregates should be kept in mind at all times.

The rest of this chapter will be divided in three sections and final conclusions. Each section will examine the evidence for the three major stories of Romanian political culture: the country's late and somehow incomplete separation from communism; its allegedly "peasant" character; and the country's problems of corruption and political trust. In each of these sections, I will study the attitudes of the majority of the population, trying to separate "hard to change" legacies such as development (structural constraints) from "soft" legacies (e.g. socialization, from religion to reading newspapers). Finally, I will summarize the main results of this analysis of political culture change and democratization.

Authoritarians into democrats?

Romanian exceptionalism was often invoked in connection with the way its political transition was managed by elites close to the former communist party. The transition was the outcome of a popular uprising that produced more casualties than all other eastern European regimes changes put together. More than 1,000 people died in the confusing week of the "Romanian Revolution," slaughtered first by the army in the days prior to 22 December, then by unidentified snipers. Despite this heavy toll paid primarily by denizens of the largest cities, in the first free and fair elections after the fall of communism, when central Europeans voted for anticommunist parties, Romanians voted for a party which, although not a direct communist successor, openly defended important features of the communist heritage. The National Salvation Front (NSF) started as a grassroots movement, but agencies of the former regime, such as the army and the secret services, managed to gain ever more control. The extent to which the heritage of communist times was preserved is a crucial factor in explaining transitions, but it is, in turn, dependent on how the power struggle between the communist establishment and new political elite was resolved. Romania had one of the hardest of all communist regimes in eastern Europe, and shaking it off in 1989 was possible only due to the consent of Ceausescu's own army and Securitate (the secret political police). Their agreement to a change of regime was intended as a sort of life insurance. Even before passing a new constitution in 1991, the first freely elected Romanian parliament adopted a law on national security sealing most of the communist archives indefinitely. Except for a few dignitaries who had been close to the Ceausescu family, nobody was tried for crimes during communist times. Attempts to finalize the trial of two generals who ordered the shooting of anti-Ceausescu protesters by the anti-communist government of 1996–2000 were hindered by the next government of Ion Iliescu, a former liberal apparatchik who had received power from the army in 1989. Protests against what intellectuals and the media saw as "neo-communists" at the beginning of the transition decreased considerably after the anti-communists also failed, in their turn, to deliver on their 1996 electoral promises, which caused their subsequent defeat in the 2000 elections. The warning behind these protests remains real and the absence of de-communization may render reforms ineffective. The necessity of a more than symbolic fight against communism, but the elimination of the lasting effects of residual communism, was argued for by the post-1989 civil society movement in Romania. The government of Ion Iliescu, three times victor in presidential elections, in the name of national consensus and "putting the past behind," openly fought against this vision. Yet Iliescu's electoral victories indicate that the voters' choice and values must have played some role, despite voter manipulation by the state-owned media. It is due to this silent but firm endorsement of post-communism by the public that most authors see the Romanian political transition as different from most other central European experiences. For most of the transition the society was indeed divided between urban, higher-educated people voting for the center-right and rural inhabitants and workers in state-owned bankrupt industrial mega-enterprises voting for the post-communists. The former were in favor of reform and western integration, the latter were afraid of it. In 1990, polls indicated that a majority of respondents believed that more than one political party would not be desirable, that the state should be in charge of everything and that "although he went too far, a leader of the type of Ceausescu is what we need today" (Mungiu-Pippidi 1996). This strong cleavage persisted as late as 2000, to become more and more blurred in recent years, as the distinction between anti-communists and post-communists gradually lost relevance for the policy agenda dominated by the common project of European integration. Similarly, the number of people considering the multi-party system increased, and the number of those endorsing anti-democratic alternatives decreased, as citizens were re-socialized. Not all the new democrats have become consistent democrats. Table 12.1 reflects the overlapping of those who endorse representative democracy with those who barely disguise their antipathy for politics behind a preference for technocratic, not political government, and those who openly opt for a non-democratic alternative at the same time. The number of "inconsistent" democrats has decreased since the beginning of the transition:

Table 12.1 Democratic and autocratic orientations[1]

	Democracy best	Strong leaders	Army rule	Experts
Czech Republic	91	16	5	78
Slovakia	89	19	5	78
Poland	88	–	–	–
Hungary	85	19	5	78
Slovenia	88	25	6	80
Romania 1993	87	47	25	40
Romania 2001	79	30	13	81
Bulgaria	80	62	17	46

Source: WVS 1995, except Romania 2001.

Notes
1 Surveys included the World Values Surveys 1995–2000, polled by ICCV in Romania in 1993.
Surveys quoted by year (2000a, 2000b, 2001) were all executed by the Center for Urban Sociology (CURS). Surveys 2000a and 2001 were national surveys on samples of 1,100 each. 2000b was a special survey, designed to be representative for every region, with a sample of 37,400 respondents. 2001 was a joint survey by Eurobarometer and United Nations Development Program (UNDP). 2000a and 2001 were sponsored by Freedom House and UNDP and designed by the author.
Democracy best: "Democracy may have problems but it's better than any other form of government" (agree strongly, agree); Strong leaders: "Having a strong leader who does not have to bother with parliament and elections"; Army rule: "Having the army rule"; Experts: "Having experts, not government, make decisions according to what they think is best for the country" (very good, good).

47 percent of Romanians would have preferred a strong leader to representative democracy in 1993 (WVS) compared to only 30 percent in 2001 (Eurobarometer). Non-political governments, by experts and technocrats, have remained the most popular form of government, as Romanians grew more and more dissatisfied with their politicians while becoming more committed democrats in the same time.

Nevertheless, when considering the democracy–autocracy index, we find few strong democrats in Romania (26 percent). The "strong democrats" are the consistent citizens who embrace democracy and reject autocracy. The largest group is formed by "weak democrats" (51 percent) who gave an overall positive assessment of democracy, though less strong. Finally we have 11 percent undecided (who are mostly inconsistent) and then through to "autocrats," who make up 12 percent. Overall, compared with a western democracy, such as Germany, the Romanian public is placed at the autocratic end of this index. By 1995, consistent democrats in Romania and Bulgaria were clearly lower in numbers when compared to the Czech Republic or Hungary. However, the gap has narrowed considerably over the last decade.

Several factors can explain this finding. First and foremost, we must consider the communist heritage. Romania had four million communist party members, more than double the average of the region as a whole.

Widespread institutionalization of cooperation with the communist regime combined with the strongest repression in the region (these two factors cannot be separated) are likely to be accountable for a difficult democratization. Economic development is also an important variable. Roughly 40 percent of Romania's population is still employed in agriculture – Poland has less than half this figure; Hungary and the Czech Republic less than 10 percent and even Bulgaria has only around 26 percent thus employed. These legacies and "structural constraints" compete with cultural explanations, such as blaming the Christian Orthodox denomination for its lack of appetite for democracy, compared to Catholicism and Protestantism. Another range of explanations blame the difficult economic transition that regimes have had to undertake. If a regime produces only poverty and social inequality, citizens become disenchanted regardless whether or not free and fair elections are regularly held. It becomes obvious that any explanation accounting for anti-democratic attitudes must take all these factors into account. To test various possible explanations, democratic or autocratic attitudes were used as dependent variables repeatedly in multivariate linear regression models testing these competing explanations simultaneously. The first set uses only data from Romania, thereby comparing between Romanians, democratic and less democratic. The second set uses the WVS pooled sample for the whole region. Results for two complementary Romanian models are shown in Table 12.2, one with the dependent variable "preference for strong leaders" versus "elected parliament" (I, WVS data), the other using as dependent variable the attitude toward eventual closure of parliament (II, UNDP and Eurobarometer data). The latter survey was used because it includes a question on membership in the former communist party.

Both models show that the "structural constraints" variables influence democratic attitudes importantly. Rural inhabitants are likely to be less democratic than urban ones even when controlling for income, wealth and education. Former membership in the communist party, all other things being equal, predicts a weaker commitment to democracy (Table 12.2). The young and educated are more likely to be democrats. Romanians are overwhelmingly Orthodox (already determined by birth), but no difference can be found between those who attend religious services or believe in God and those who do not when it comes to attitudes toward democracy (Table 12.2). Being an Orthodox Christian does not make one less likely to be a democrat when Romania is compared with the other countries and Christian Orthodoxy with other denominations in the pooled WVS sample (Table 12.3), which confirms previous reports by Rose *et al.* (1998), and Miller *et al.* (1998). What discriminates between democrats and non-democrats is collectivism. The more an individual believes that incomes should be close and communism was a good idea poorly put into practice, the less likely it is that one would protest if

Table 12.2 Determinants of democracy – autocracy orientations in Romania

Independent variables	Model I	Strong leader (1 for, 4 against); questions and scales	Model II	Parliament abolished (1 agree, 4 disagree); questions and scales
Wealth	Ns	Subjective satisfaction with household situation, 1 not satisfied, 4 satisfied	Ns	Individual income the previous month in five categories
Education	Ns	1 primary; 2 elementary and vocational; 3 high-school; 4 college and higher	Ns	Same
Age	0.073**	Age recoded in four groups (18–35; 36–50; 51–65; over 65)	−0.078*	Same
Rural	0.089***	1 Localities below 20,000 inhabitants; 0 all other localities	–	Same
Male	Ns	Gender, 1 Male; 0 Female	Ns	Same
Religious	Ns	Scale, 1 does not attend religious service; 1 once a month or rarely; 2 a few times a month; 3 a few times a week; 4 daily or almost daily	–	
Communist member	–		0.061*	1 member of the former communist party; 0 other
Follows politics	Ns	Discuss politics with friends, 1 frequently, 3 never	0.133***	Index constructed as the average of scores for "watch political news on TV," "read political news in the press," "discuss politics with friends"

Interested in politics	Ns	Self-reported interest in politics, 1 high, 4 low	—	
Left–right ideology scale	Ns	Scale, 1 left, 10 right	—	
Collectivism	0.054*	Scale, 1 low agreement that efforts should be made to equalize income, 10 high agreement	—	
Left–right ideology irrelevant	—		0.152***	Dichotomous variable, 1 = the right-left distinction is declared irrelevant for the respondent; 0 = the reverse
Transition frustrating	—		0.179***	Country headed in a good direction, 1 absolutely not, 4 absolutely yes
Communism good idea	—		Ns	"Communism good idea but badly put into practice," 1 fully disagree, 4 fully agree
Experts should run the country	Ns	"We should have experts running the country, instead of political governments," 1 fully agree, 4 fully disagree	—	"We should have experts running the country, instead of political governments," 1 fully agree, 4 fully disagree
Adj. R^2	0.233	0.169		

Source: I-WVS 1995; II-2001.

Notes
Figures are standardized regression coefficients (betas) ***significant at 0.000 level; **significant at 0.00 level; *significant at <0.05–0.00.; Ns = non-significant.

Table 12.3 "Hard" versus "soft" explanations of democratic orientations

Determinants	Model 1	Model 2	Scales used
Wealth	0.090*	0.089*	Subjective evaluation of financial situation of household; 1 low; 10 high
Education	0.100*	0.097*	Age finished school, in years
Age in years	−0.086*	−0.083*	Years old
Size of town	0.090*	0.083*	1 village, 8 large city
Christian Orthodox	–	0.010	Dichotomous. 1 Orthodox, 0 other
Scale denomination	0.025	–	1 Muslim, 2 Orthodox, 3 Catholic, 4 Protestant, atheist and other 0
Religious	0.005	–	Dichotomous. 1 religious, 0 other
Collectivism b	0.085*	0.086*	State vs. citizen responsibility for one's own welfare 1 State, 10 Citizen
Constant (std. error)	2.15* (0.086)	2.26* (0.076)	
N	8,559	8,559	
Adjusted R^2	0.062	0.059	

Notes
OLS regression models with dependent variable "democracy may have problems but it's better than any other form of government" (1 disagree strongly, 4 agree strongly); year of field-work: 1993 for World Values Survey. Pooled database includes Hungary, Czech Republic, Poland, Romania, Croatia, Slovenia, Slovakia and Bulgaria. Coefficients are standardized beta coefficients unless specified otherwise.
* Significant at 0.001 level.

parliament was abolished or one would prefer a strong leader to elections (Table 12.2).

Post-communist socialization seems to work. The young and those who are more exposed to information on politics are more democratic. Overall, it is the legacy of communism that burdens political transition, not other cultural factors, such as religion. And gradually, albeit slowly, this is making an impact. Learning is progressing, as Rose *et al.* (1998) have already remarked, and people grasp that elections are the most important way to assure accountability. Romanians are reluctant to give this right away – in 2002 over 90 percent defended their right to elect the president directly when a proposal was made to amend the 1991 Constitution to turn the country into a parliamentary democracy. Repeated surveys found that this issue, unlike many other political ones, was considered important by the people, that a majority of citizens was aware of the proposal and that most of them disliked it strongly.

Political scientists have long been concerned with defining core values among political values, and to establish which are most important for western civilization and liberal democracy (Conover and Feldman 1988).

Looking at models explaining support of democracy and models predicting voting behavior it becomes clear that the best discriminating question is the one asking respondents to choose between equality and freedom. These two values, the only political ones included in Milton Rokeach's values questionnaire, are indeed essential for understanding politics in post-communist countries. If one knows this choice, one can fairly predict in Romania if a person is a democrat or non-democrat, votes post-communist or anti-communist, is nationalistic or pro-European. Collectivism is associated with nationalism, ethnocentrism and voting for post-communist parties. It is eastern Europe's form of conservatism, a residual attitude grounded in communist socialization, but also in some institutional arrangements persisting from communist times. Those who are dependent on the state on practically every issue, from workers in the state industry to pensioners, and especially the poor and less educated, display considerably higher degrees of collectivism than the rest of the population. Collectivism is a "core" value because it helps to predict most political orientations, and it is the backbone of ideology, structuring internally consistent belief systems. Individuals who rate high on collectivism regret good old communist times, blame the difficult transition on the West or vote against anti-communist parties, and are socially envious. It is an ideology by default, since most of those who prefer equality to freedom do not place themselves on the left–right ideological scale, saying that ideology is irrelevant for their political choice. Materialist–post-materialist value orientations predict little to nothing in the post-communist world, mainly because most people prefer materialism and survival values. Indeed, this "survivalism," often associated with a "peasant" culture, is so dominant in Romania that it makes a story in itself.

Peasants into citizens?

Politics in poor societies and weak states may look spectacular if observed from within. It usually contains a fair amount of coups and aborted revolutions, grand reforms and brutal assassinations. If observed from afar, however, it generates an almost unbearable feeling of monotony. Coups change only the person of the dictator; assassinations prove sooner or later to have been needless. Cities always push ahead for reform, rural areas push back for stagnation. Who rules the rural, rules the country, as expressed by the famous Huntingtonian formula (1956: 292). Even the change of regimes does not modify the essential constraints under which every government – democratic or autocratic – will have to operate sooner or later. In the case of Romania, these constraints are summarized by Henry Roberts' brief formula that "problems of an agrarian society" have an adjacent ideology of their own: "survivalism." Indeed, Romanian intellectuals of the inter-war period defended this "survival society" as an *alternative* form of civilization, not the absence of it:

A minor culture, born out of improvisation and spontaneity, as well as from a total lack of will for eternity stands a better chance to last for thousands of years in its stillness.... While a major culture, emerged from the thirst to defeat both space and time is, due to its dynamism, much more exposed to catastrophes and extinction...

(Blaga 1943)

The democratic change of 1989 brought about the revival of this intellectual movement praising traditional village life and the political ideals embodied in it. Its perfect symbol is the transformation of the museum of the Communist Party into a Peasant Museum, considering that "peasant," "Romanian" and "Christian" are (or should be) synonyms. This ideology was remarkably salient in Romania throughout the twentieth century. It created a "paradox of the two villages," characterized by the contradiction between, on the one hand, an "ideal" village as imagined by intellectuals and seen as self-sufficient economically, culturally and politically. On the other hand, there was a "real" village, poor and underdeveloped. The latter has been, and still is, the main constituency of predatory elites who live on state capture, a model very similar to the one described by Huntington or Joel Migdal for Latin America. Vertical accountability stops short of the village, where regardless of electoral campaigns villagers vote invariably conservative, that is, for the communist successor parties and Ion Iliescu. As Romania has 47 percent inhabitants living in rural areas, and well over 35 percent of its economically active citizens *de facto* employed in agriculture, the "peasant" culture is an important political subculture and it needs detailed analysis.

Voting behavior in rural areas is indeed peculiar: 45 percent of the votes in rural areas were cast in the 2000 and 1996 elections for the main successor party of the communist party, the Romanian Social Democrat party (formerly the National Salvation Front, then Social Democratic Party) compared to 32 percent in urban areas. In the earlier elections of 1992 and 1990, the proportion of peasants voting for what they call "the state" was even greater, almost two times more than observed in the urban areas. This share of the vote was affected by successive splits in the dominant party, which created confusion among the electorate. In local elections, however, the post-communist party is supported almost everywhere in the rural areas. Residence in rural areas has remained the main predictor of the vote for Ion Iliescu since 1990 until 2000 even in the most complex models to explain voting behavior. Of course, not all rural areas are alike. Those rural areas that are poor and have few small city centers display the typical residual communist attitudes most prominently. In these areas, which had been fully collectivized until 1990, the vote is usually bargained between the central authority and the local leaders acting as gatekeepers between the village and the rest of the world. The local authority controls access to every resource in the area, and is instrumental in making villagers vote uniformly with the one party. In poor villages the vote is therefore practically collective, not individual, and part of the voters' indifference toward the ideology of a candidate is explained by the fact that ideology does indeed matter little under these circumstances. Equally, the organization of political life in the countryside supports this style of politics, as anti-communist parties have barely any headquarters, while the communist successor party is based in the village hall or another building of communist times. Models including all status variables also highlight the rural as a consistent predictor of obedience ("Leaders should be followed even when wrong") but not of every other authoritarian attitude. When examining political cognition, we also find the rural considerably more ignorant than the urban (Table 12.4).

Is "authoritarianism" an intrinsic feature of a rural or peasant population, or can we trace it to other determinants as well? Comparison of social indicators of urban lifestyle and similar ones of rural Romania points to several other factors explaining the difference between the urban and the rural. Rural inhabitants make only about 60 percent of the personal income of urban residents; in addition, they are older and less educated (Table 12.5). As in the case of political cognition, not only the difference between the urban and the rural, but the low income level in general is a matter for concern. Poverty and lack of political information in the rural areas are twice as bad compared to the urban areas. However, even the urban levels are far removed from the prosperity and access to information available in western Europe. As most of the "urban" is a more recent and incomplete communist creation, the "rural" element may be even more important than statistics show, going much beyond formal residence in the countryside.

What we witness in Romania's rural area is therefore a type of political culture that is typical for a modernization lag. A large amount of literature on Romania's failure to catch up in the twentieth century focuses on the lack of economic sustainability of small rural holdings, so-called subsistence farming (Mitranyi 1930; Roberts 1951). The dream of a prosperous peasantry similar to the western model was undermined by the large proportion of the population in the agricultural sector combined with a drop

Table 12.4 Urban–rural differences in political information

Questions	Urban	Rural
Follows electoral campaign daily in newspapers	23	14
One hour or more of electoral campaign watched on TV the previous day (2000)	32	16
Matters greatly if a candidate stands on the right or the left	9	5
Does not know if the left or the right stands for closer incomes	41	48
Does not know if the left or the right favors private property	39	47

Source: 2000b; see Table 12.1.

Table 12.5 Urban–rural differences of selected social indicators

Variables	Urban mean (standard error)	Rural mean (standard error)	Total population mean (standard error)
Age	44 (16)	49 (18)	46.34 (17.02)
Education	4.7 (1.4)	3.4 (1.3)	4.13 (1.50)
Personal income/month	40 Euro	21 Euro	30 Euro
Household income	65 Euro	42 Euro	54 Euro

Source: 2000b; see Table 12.1.

in productivity after the 1918–21 land reform, which destroyed all large property holdings. Nevertheless, a number of peasants managed to gain some economic autonomy, if not prosperity, by 1945 only to end up either in the Gulag or the collective farms after the Soviet army imposed communism. By 1989, except for mountainous regions, Romania was fully collectivized. A 1990 presidential decree and two land restitution acts, 1991 and 1997, have since tried to restore the 1945 property situation. This led to over 600,000 land-related law suits by 1998. While failing to reconstitute the pre-communist property, these acts managed to reconstitute the pre-communism problem of smallholdings leading to subsistence farming (Table 12.6). Furthermore, the distribution of property after 1990 empowered the local communist-era bureaucracy, who commanded both the property archives and the legal power to decide restitution matters, and turned it into a veritable predatory elite.

Other factors contributed to create a model of political dependency of the peasantry similar to that which existed before universal franchise. Among them are the persistence, even after decades of communist industrialization, of an significant population surplus in the countryside. Furthermore, the lack of productivity is evidenced by the fact that, in over 50 percent of farm holdings, most work is undertaken with horses, and the existence, for most of the transition, of a unique state agency with the legal right to buy the crops. All these variables are explanatory factors. So too are the poverty and parochialism which cuts the village from access to

Table 12.6 Size of rural property: a historical comparison

Size in hectares	% 1918	% 1949	% 1999
Under 5 (subsistence farming)	75	76.1	81.6
5–10	17.07	17.8	15.1
10–20	5.49	4.89	3.1
Over 20	2.54	1.2	0.2
Total land available	3,280,000	3,067,000	3,211,507

Sources: *Encyclopaedia of Romania*, Romanian Academy, Bucharest, 1939 and Romanian National Statistics Office (CNS).

political information. In other words, formal institutions, old and recent, contribute to the voting behavior of the peasantry as well as to their political attitudes. Attitudes of rural citizens, in turn, support these formal institutions by not rebelling against them. This vicious circle creates a black hole, so to speak, for Romanian politics, because rules applied in the more modern urban areas do not apply in the countryside. The towns vote by watching electoral campaigns, from the radical right to the radical left, but mostly for the center. The villages vote, in their own words, "for the state." The "party-state" was in opposition for four years, 1996–2000. However, this was not due to the voting behavior of the peasants, who supported Ion Iliescu in 1996 and 2000 alike, as they had already done in 1990 and 1992.

It is not surprising that Ion Iliescu was identified with the "state" in the countryside. He was the first leader to appear on television after the flight of Ceausescu and the one to hold the primetime during most of the transition. In focus groups, peasants attribute to him all the gains accomplished by the 1989 Revolution and portray him as a positive paternal figure, a strong, balanced, reliable and non-corrupt politician. Party politics is seen as the source of all evil and corruption: Electing a president directly who, in his turn, would appoint a non-political government is the ideal political system in the eyes of the peasants. When it became clear that Ion Iliescu would not enjoy a fourth term, local elites, from village hall clerks to priests, negotiated frenetically with possible successors, and polls in 2002–3 showed formidable rates of "don't knows" when trying to determine political preferences in the rural areas. What is known is that whomsoever carries the support of the village elites will get the votes of the village.

Both rural and communist states shared a certain remoteness from the legal rational type of government found even in pre-modern societies that were on their way to capitalism. Both had unpredictable patterns of distributing social and legal rights from a rational point of view, but fairly predictable for whoever is acquainted with the patterns of authority which emanate from the unwritten rules of the game. The widespread political goal in such contexts is related to "survival," understood as the quest to belong to the right status group – that is, the group well connected with the source of power and privilege. This is because benefits are still centrally distributed, be they pensions or land. This model was labeled "neo-traditionalist" by Jowitt (1993). I prefer to call it "neo-dependency," as many factors cause political dependency, making the peasants a captive constituency. The communist state replaced the old-time feudal order as the main spoiler of the peasant. This formal arrangement, rendering the peasants landless, misers and poor again, after a brief interruption between the two World Wars, recreated the political dependence from times before the vote was franchised.

This model has not endured in the post-communist urban areas and large villages to such a large extent, because of new market relationships with which it competes, even if it proved successful in slowing the market economy to become, in the words of the European Commission, "fully functional." In the simpler world of small villages, three times as many Romanians as Bulgarians or Poles live in areas where no market exists and peasants live on subsistence farming or state pensions. And this is how democratic politics still works – or, rather, does not work in Romania.

Predators into bureaucrats?

Figures on subjective perception of corruption (how widespread corruption of the public sector is) confirm the anthropological model sketched in the previous section, as most Romanians perceive that many groups are above the law. The same few people are winners regardless of the regime, and corruption is widespread. The last indicators do not single out Romania as the villain among the new members of the European Union (Table 12.7). Perceptions of corruption are widespread everywhere in the region.

Romanians do not seem to differ from other transition countries greatly on any governance-related indicators of public opinion, though objective data show Romanian governments as more corrupt and ineffectual (Mungiu-Pippidi 2002). In a general regional picture of distrust, Romanians are insignificantly below the regional average in their distrust in fellow humans and political parties, have higher rates of participation in voluntary associations (although this is based on a high membership rate in unions inherited from communist times) and attend protest rallies more often than anybody else. In no way is Romania an exceptional culture where passivity reigns and structural distrust plagues collective action, so Wildavsky's argument does not find much support. True, differences of

Table 12.7 Social trust, confidence in political parties, political participation, membership in voluntary organizations and perceptions of corruption

	Interpersonal trust	Confidence in political parties	Participation (attending lawful demonstrations)	Membership in civic organizations	Corruption perceived as widespread
Czech Republic	27	15	11	30	62
Slovakia	26	22	12	28	61
Poland	17	13	10	2	69
Hungary	22	20	9	31	42
Slovenia	15	14	9	31	68
Romania	18	14	20	31	58
Bulgaria	24	30	11	10	68

Source: WVS 1995.

participation rates, social trust or membership in civic organizations are considerable compared to western European countries. However, they are fairly typical for the post-communist world. Therefore, it is likely that the influence of communist socialization, not some specific Romanian cultural traits, is accountable for current political attitudes. Regardless of affiliation with the Catholic or Orthodox churches, eastern European countries are struggling with widespread malfunction of their administrations. This is reflected in their incapacity to provide satisfactory service without a bribe. All these countries do not pay their civil servants adequately, public resources in short supply are subject to (over)regulation, and citizens who want to escape this situation by offering and accepting bribes are encouraged by the almost total absence of formal institutions to hold them accountable. There is something remarkable about Romania, however, as the index of Transparency International (also a subjective index, but made up of the perceptions of businessmen rather than ordinary people) reveal that the country's administration and politics are more corrupt than its central European neighbors. The Freedom House Nations in Transit index of corruption also points to the predatory elite hidden in the Romanian bureaucracy. This institutional "culture" is not met passively by consumers – only 34 percent of Romanians believe changing this state of affairs is beyond their powers – but proves resilient due to the absence of a policy to dismantle the formal institutions supporting it. Citizens pay an extra tax because it is simpler to solve matters than fight the system. But there is a cost to this: trust in the new formal institutions of democracy erodes constantly.

Not only do most Romanians (62 percent) report having been mistreated by a civil servant after the fall of communism, but, of those who grant a favorable judgment to civil servants, approval ratings for judges and politicians rank below one-third of the total if we average the figures of the past decade. The majority of Romanians have come to be democrats, but blame their difficult transition on their political class (Table 12.8). The recruitment method of politicians and bureaucrats may account for their low popularity. Representatives are elected on party lists, and the government appoints judges and civil servants who are inevitably a

Table 12.8 Dissatisfied democrats

Questions	% agree
If Parliament was closed down and parties abolished, would you protest against it?	19.4
A unity government with only the best people should replace government by elected politicians	59.2
There is conflict between political class and the rest of Romanians	51.0
Failure of transition blamed on incompetent government	62.0

Source: 2001.

mixture of the communist-era bureaucracy and new recruits. As a general rule there are no public announcements of job openings in the public sector, and one can obtain a job as a civil servant by informal connections only. Politicization of the administration runs deep. Political parties have a need to support their wide range of cronies.

Even if comparable with figures for the region as a whole, public trust remains very low in Romania. People distrust their state which is still perceived, as in communist times, as a parallel entity to society. Thus, institutional social capital is low. Citizens have not yet come to claim ownership of the state, from local government to the parliament, even if they participate regularly in elections. Once elected, these bodies seem to operate alongside society rather than with it. Trust depends on performance and improves with it – trust in urban local governments doubled in Romania between 1997 and 2000, as fiscal decentralization gradually empowered mayors, who are directly elected, to start satisfying their constituencies. It remains low for central government, law and order agencies, parliament and parties, which are further removed from the voters' reach, protected by the intricacies of a proportional electoral system based on party lists.

Measures of public trust in all its variants – trust in government, in specific public agencies and in the state in general – confirms this picture (see Table 12.9). Trust is lower in urban than in rural areas, the opposite of what we would expect if trust were a basic psychological orientation arising out of an environment of scarce resources. This finding is consistent in all surveys and runs contrary to classic social capital literature, such as Almond and Verba or Putnam. It makes sense, however, in that urbanites distrust more because they bribe more frequently. Peasants rarely bribe – being cashless, they just let themselves be abused, without either bribing or protesting.

An association between social trust and political trust – be it in the public sector or the state in general – does not show in the models we discuss below. Social trust does not determine political trust. On the contrary, performance items, such as the personal experiences of a citizen in dealing with the administration, influences the degree of public trust greatly. Residual communist attitudes also hinder the accumulation of institutional social capital. The more people are frustrated with the transition to democracy and regret the loss of communism, the less trust they grant to the institutions of the new regime. The young tend to be more confident and supportive than the old, and subjective welfare rather than objective differences in income boost social capital. Members in voluntary associations are not higher on social capital than non-members. And overall, those who had negative encounters with some civil servant have developed lower attitudes of public trust.

Mistreatment by civil servants or public officials is generally interpreted as a signal to deliver payment to the civil servant or public official.

Table 12.9 Determinants of public trust

Independent variables	State	Govt	Public sector	Questions and scales
Education	Ns	Ns	Ns	1 primary; 2 elementary and vocational; 3 high school; 4 college and higher
Wealth	Ns	Ns	Ns	Factor score of average household income and total number of household utilities (low, high)
Age	Ns	−0.082*	−0.108**	Respondent's age in years
Size of town	−0.043*	−0.072*	−0.073*	1 village, 2 town under 30,000 inhabitants, 3 town 30,000–100,000 inhabitants, 4 town 100,000–200,000, 5 town 200,000 inhabitants and larger
Male	Ns	Ns	Ns	Respondent's gender (1 male, 0 female)
Subjective welfare	0.105*	0.226*	0.18*	Satisfaction with life, −1 not satisfied, not satisfied at all, 0 no answer, 1 satisfied, very satisfied
Interpersonal trust	0.129***	0.037	0.14**	"Most people can be trusted," 1 cannot be trusted, 4 can be trusted
Follows politics in the media	0.128*	0.062	0.066	Index constructed as an average of scores for "watch political news on TV"; "read political news in the press," "discuss politics with friends" (low, high)
Membership in voluntary organization	Ns	Ns	Ns	1 member, 0 non-member
Communism good idea	−0.127*	−0.242*	0.066	"Communism good idea but badly put into practice," 1 fully disagree, 4 fully agree
Mistreated by a civil servant after 1989	−0.137*	−0.215*	−0.317**	Experience with mistreatment by public servants after 1989, 1 yes, 0 no
Adjusted R^2	0.137	0.193	0.102	

Source: 2000; see Table 12.1.

Notes

Coefficients are standardized regression coefficients. *** significant at 0.000 level; ** significant at 0.00 level; * significant at <0.05–0.00; Ns non-significant. Dependent variables are trust in state (STATE), 1 little trust, 4 a lot of trust; trust in government (GOVT), factor score of evaluations of government, parliament and presidency; scale values for items range from 1, little trust, to 4, a lot of trust; trust in the public sector (PUBLIC SECTOR), factor score of evaluations for main public agencies (local governments, the courts, the prosecutors office, the post office, the police, the tax office) scale values for items range from 1, little trust, to 4, a lot of trust.

Reported bribery and reported mistreatment by the administration are correlated. As a general rule, people bribe because without this extra tax they would hardly get anything they need out of bureaucracy, and in Romania, dependency on the administration for an array of permits and licenses is far greater than in the West. Those belonging to the right network or having the right connections are excepted from this rule, a fact that can turn an impersonal relationship with the administration into a personal one. In Romania, roughly one-quarter of the respondents seem to enjoy this state of affairs. The probability that those with "connections" will get the service they require in a satisfactory manner is considerably higher than for those who do not have such contacts – even if they are in a position to pay the bribe.

The formal and informal institutions regulating administrative practice support ongoing corruption. Their origins lie in communist times. Despite its strongly modernizing rhetoric, the communist administration was just the opposite of a modern rational–legal administration. Arbitrary and discriminative, it could not have been further from the impartiality, impersonality and fairness characteristic of an ideal modern bureaucracy. The corruption of the Romanian civil service manifests itself not only in use of a public position to seek personal gain, but more broadly as the widespread infringement of the norm of impersonality and fairness that should characterize modern public service. Providing discriminatory public service as a general rule is not prompted by financial gain only, this being the norm rather than the exception in societies dominated by groups of uneven power status. These differences in power status are inherited from the recent past. According to public opinion surveys, all eastern Europeans seem discontented with the quality of their administration and political class. In practice, when we examine the situation more closely, there is a clear correlation between the degree of communization and the quality of administration, including corruption. The more intrusive the former communist regime, the greater was the arbitrary power of its agents, such as representatives of the administration. Correspondingly, their accountability to the citizenry was lower. Institutional reforms did not target this situation specifically and civil service reform acts prompted by the European Commission include practically no reward and punishment mechanism to promote a change in administrative culture. Thus such reforms are unlikely to solve the "hard" cases, such as Romania or Russia. How many years can the public function in the presence of predatory elites that no government wants or is powerful enough to shake off? The reform of public administration and of the state in general is the key to legitimating democracy and to the proper functioning of Romania in the enlarged European Union. The key group of post-communist politicians, such as Ion Iliescu, has gradually evolved from authoritarian socialists to pro-European social-democrats, but they dare not attack corruption, as the predatory elite is the most important part of their power base. This essential step, however, has to be taken to complete Romania's democratic transformation and its accession to the European Union

Conclusions

The role of "hard" constraints

"Hard" constraints to the development of democracy are legacies that cannot be modified by human agency in the period of one generation alone. Two historical "structural" legacies were found to matter in this analysis:, namely, under-development (the rural/urban ratio) and the degree of penetration by the communist regime of Romanian society (one useful proxy indicator is party membership). There is a causal link between these two factors. Communism flourished more in poorer societies, where under-development provided the necessary alibi for strong state intervention. The extreme poverty of Romanian villages inspired Ceausescu's design to "systematize" or redesign them – a reform supposed to eliminate one-half of such villages, turn a further tenth into towns and rebuild the rest. To increase the proportion of the urban population and modernize Romania by such radical policies would have been inconceivable in a country such as the Czech Republic, but such policies seemed – at least in theory – to address a real need in Romania. To impose collective farming in a situation where many farms were obviously productive such as, for example, in Poland would have also been much more difficult than under the condition of bare subsistence farming that was the rule in Romania. The debates about how to change the situation produced radical proposals even before communism. And, naturally, this deep penetration by communist rule was reinforced by the disinterest of the West. As mentioned above, Winston Churchill claimed an insignificant 10 percent of western interest in Romania when he scribbled his preferences to Stalin on what he himself called "a nasty scrap of paper." Conservative peasants in the mountains resisted the communist regime for almost ten years until they were executed, arrested or deported in the aftermath of the failed Hungarian Revolution, when it became clear the West would not stop the Sovietization of Romania (Seton-Watson 1960). Over 80,000 peasants were arrested to achieve collectivization, as well as to avert peasant resistance which was crushed in blood. Only after their leaders were completely destroyed and their lands and arms were confiscated have Romanian peasants resorted to James C. Scott's "weapons of the weak," such as cheating the collective farm. And only after the young had deserted the villages and the old barely survived "systematization" was their political dependence complete. This dependency is now felt in post-communist times. Other useful proxies of depth of penetration by the regime are the extent of collectivization and the number of dissidents by 1989. Thus, the destruction of almost every political alternative by a degree of repression which was much greater in Romania than in other central European countries with a communist legacy also accounts for a post-communist transition with a dominant party and a dominant, father-like politician.

The role of "soft" constraints

"Soft constraints" are formal institutions that can be changed (such as a poor electoral law). Similarly factors are informal institutions and opinions that hinder the emergence of democratic norms. These may also be regarded as "legacies," but they can change more easily and some have changed already. We need to examine them in connection with the tripartite model on page 313 to identify possible windows of opportunity for policy intervention. If we would only examine public opinion, rural Romania and its voting behavior, as well as administrative corruption, would remain a mystery.

Nevertheless, the importance of soft constraints is also directly determined by the nature of the former communist regime. Informal institutions multiplied and took the upper hand in guiding collective behavior due to the absurdity of formal arrangements during communism. In 1989, all Romanians were culprits, as it was illegal to store more than one kilo of sugar in one's house, have a garden without producing wheat, drive one's car every weekend and so forth. The society only survived by breaking the law, and this has become a serious obstacle to the restoration of the rule of law, especially since corruption at the top remains high. Law enforcement collapsed with Ceausescu and the new legislation is often poor, failing to set incentives and control for law-abidingness.

With regard to electoral democracy, things are much simpler to understand. Post-communist socialization works, so even individuals with an average interest in politics have learned that elections are central to the game. The less liberal a communist regime, the more autocrats are found in the beginning of the transition. High levels of inconsistency of political beliefs show the competition between the old and the new political socialization, and this can be taken as an indicator of political culture change. The number of collectivists and authoritarians decreases year after year. Similarly, the number of those who believed Romanians and Hungarians have conflicting goals and cannot cooperate politically has gradually eroded. While a majority of Romanians held this view in 1990, the proportion fell below 40 percent in the year 2000. Political socialization under the condition of support for democracy as an ideal seems to push back and alter residual communist attitudes greatly, helped by an improving economic tableau. However, political socialization works both ways. Communist ideology lingers longer in countries that have experienced harsh communist regimes, such as Romania, Bulgaria or Russia. Thus, it is not surprising to still find sizeable groups of citizens in these countries that approve of one-party systems and foster social envy. The socialization technique used by the former regimes was state terror. In contrast to this type of coercive persuasion, the new rules allow even anti-democratic parties to compete in the electoral game and in the course of time more and more Romanians turn their back on them.

Cultural legacies or institutional reproduction?

A mixture of attitudes resulting from the "old" and the "new" political regime is characteristic of a political culture in transition. The same is true for the various political institutions and their functioning. The most important evidence of "cultural legacies" is found at the level of informal institutions and can be regarded as a heritage of communism. The pre-war bureaucracies of Romania and Bulgaria were almost completely destroyed by the communist regime, yet the regime in the late 1970s already showed the same patrimonial character as the pre-war bureaucracy. This induced some observers to believe that "cultural" characteristics have survived regime change, while in fact similar contexts (big governments with little or no accountability) tend to reproduce the same features, regardless of "culture." We can clearly identify the persistence or recreation of formal institutions, which reproduce the same informal ones, creating the false feeling of "continuity," as demonstrated by the example of rural property. Those who doubt that imports of institutions are possible, from inter-war Romanian fascist thinkers to European enlargement skeptics of today, should seek the causes of new institutions failing to take root in the poor implementation of polices due to "hard" and "structural" factors, rather than "culture." Governance matters, and no nation is doomed to perpetual poor governance.

If culture is reduced to public opinion, values and beliefs, it may change faster and easier than institutions do. However, the main problems for democratization in Romania remain under-development and political dependency in the poor rural areas, as well as the difficulty to create and consolidate political organizations. A transition dominated by predatory elites due to an ongoing power struggle between an old entrenched elite and an emerging new one was more in the logic of Ceausescu's repressive Romania than in that of the week of radical Revolution, which was aided from outside and carried out by a minority of the population. The dreams of 22 December 1989, when thousands of young people invaded Ceausescu's palace, have proved to be naive: Occasional mobilization cannot easily alter a country's past. But neither can the past of a country condemn it to a different path than the one of the whole region, although it may affect the pace of a country's transformation. Difficult history matters, but it is not inescapable.

Note

Surveys included the World Values Surveys 1995–2000, polled by ICCV in Romania in 1993. Surveys quoted by year (2000a, 2000b, 2001) were all executed by the Center for Urban Sociology (CURS). Surveys 2000a and 2001 were national surveys on samples of 1,100 each. 2000b was a special survey, designed to be representative for every region, with a sample of 37,400 respondents. 2001 was a joint survey by Eurobarometer and United Nations Development Program (UNDP). 2000a and 2001 were sponsored by Freedom House and UNDP and designed by the author.

References

Almond, G. and Verba, S. (1963) *The Civic Culture*, Princeton: Princeton University Press.
von Beyme, K. (1996) *Transition to Democracy in Eastern Europe*, New York: St. Martin's Press.
Blaga, L. (1943) "The Permanence of Prehistory," *Saeculum* 9–10, quoted in Chimet, I. (1991) *Dreptul la memorie*, vol. IV, Bucuresti: Albatros, p. 143.
Bunce, V. (1999) "The Political Economy of Postsocialism," *Slavic Review* 58, 4.
Conover, P.J. and Feldman, S. (1984) "How People Organize the Political World: A Schematic Model," *American Journal of Political Science*, 28, 1.
Hofstede, G. with Arrindell, W. (1998) *Masculinity and Femininity: the Taboo Dimension of National Cultures*, Thousand Oaks, CA: Sage Publications.
Geertz, C. (1973) *The Interpretation of Cultures*, New York, Basic Books.
Gelman, V. (2001) "Post-Soviet Transitions and Democratization: Towards Theory-Building," paper presented at the 29th European Consortium of Political Research Joint Session of Workshops, Grenoble, 6–11 April.
Huntington, S.P. (1956) *Political order in changing societies*, New Haven: Yale University Press.
Huntington, S.P. (1993) "The Clash of Civilizations," *Foreign Affairs* 72, 3.
Inglehart, R. (1997) *Modernization and Post-Modernization: Cultural, Economic and Political Change in 43 Societies*, Princeton: Princeton University Press.
Janos, A. (1993) "Modernization and Decay in Historical Perspective: the Case of Romania," in Jowitt, K. (ed.) *Social Change in Romania, 1860–1940*, Berkeley: University of California Press.
Jowitt, K. (1992) *New World Disorder or the Leninist Extinction*, Berkeley: University of California Press.
Jowitt, K. (1993) *Social Change in Romania, 1860–1940*, Berkeley: University of California Press.
Kitschelt, H. (2001) "Post-Communist Economic Reform: Causal Mechanism and Concomitant Properties," paper presented at PSA Annual Meeting, San Francisco.
Miller, W.L., White, S. and Heywood, P. (1998) *Values and Political Change in Post-Communist Europe*, Basingstoke: MacMillan.
Mitranyi, D. (1930) *The Land and the Peasant in Rumania: the War and Agrarian Reform, 1917–1921*, Oxford: Oxford University Press.
Moore, Jr., B. (1966) *Social Origins of Dictatorship and Democracy*, Boston: Beacon Press.
Mungiu-Pippidi, A. (1996) *Die Rumanen nach '89*, Resita: Friederich Ebert Stiftung.

Mungiu-Pippidi, A. (2002) *Threats and Challenges: Romania after 2000*, Bucharest: UNDP and Polirom.

North, D.C. (1990), *Institutions, Institutional Change and Economic Performance*, New York: Cambridge University Press.

Plasser, F. and Pribersky, A. (1996) *Political Culture in East Central Europe*, Aldershot: Avebury.

Roberts, H. (1951) *Rumania. The Politics of an Agrarian State*, New Haven: Yale University Press.

Rose, R., Mishler, W. and Haerpfer, C. (1998) *Democracy and its Alternatives: Understanding Post-Communist Societies*, Baltimore: Johns Hopkins University Press.

Schopflin, G. (1978) *The Hungarians of Rumania*, London: MRG.

Schopflin, G. (1991) "The Political Tradition of Eastern Europe," in Graubard, S.R. (ed.) *Eastern Europe? Central Europe? Europe*, Boulder: Westview.

Scott, J.C. (1986) *Weapons of the Weak: Everyday Forms of Peasant Resistance*, New Haven: Yale University Press.

Seton-Watson, H. (1960) Th*e Pattern of Communist Revolution: a Historical Analysis*, London: Methuen.

Shafir, M. (1985) *Romania, Politics, Economics and Society: Political Stagnation and Stimulated Change*, New York: Printer Publishers Ltd.

Wildavsky, A. (1987) "Choosing Preferences by Constructing Institutions: a Cultural Theory of Preference Formation," *American Political Science Review* 81, 1.

13 Bulgaria

Democratic orientations in support of civil society

Andrey Raichev and Antony Todorov

Introduction

The objective of this chapter is to provide an inventory of the consolidation of democracy in Bulgaria. Hence, a short commentary on the historical and societal prerequisites for democracy is necessary. There are a number of specific features of the transition toward democracy in Bulgaria which, in general, relate to the specifics of "Bulgarian communism" (1944–89).

What are the specific features?

First, unlike all other ex-socialist countries, people in Bulgaria did not tend to perceive socialism as a consequence of Soviet occupation or Soviet presence. Russia played a supportive and important role in the establishment of the Bulgarian state in 1878, so the Bulgarian public never considered the Soviet Union to be a hostile power. Additionally, there was never a Soviet military presence on Bulgarian territory.

Second, urbanization, industrialization and, in more general terms, modernization took place in Bulgaria in the years of "real socialism." This development resulted in a substantial and tangible growth in the standard of living and culture. In contrast to many other post-communist countries, communist rule in Bulgaria did not cause a standstill or even a reversal of socio-economic development (see Kornai 1992; Rotschild 1993; Crampton 1995; Berend 1996; Dreyfus *et al.* 2000).

Third, the Bulgarian Communist Party never experienced a "Prague spring." Nor did the Bulgarian communists carry out Stalinist cleansings of the reformist wing as that wing matured much too late. Consequently, the changes in eastern Europe coincided with something along the lines of a much belated Prague spring in Bulgaria so that a brief Renaissance of reformist communist ideas accompanied the dissolution of the communist regime (Kalinova and Baeva 2001).

Another important feature of the Bulgarian transitional landscape is the ethnic cleansing that was carried out in the late 1980s involving

350,000 Turks, i.e. approximately 4 percent of the total Bulgarian population. At least another 350,000 were forced to assimilate, that is, to "Bulgarize" their names. However, after the changes, the Turks who remained in Bulgaria became truly integrated into the political life of this country so that Bulgaria is now "an exception to the Balkans" inasmuch as there are no intense ethnic tensions so characteristic in this region.[1]

Apart from these four factors, most of the trends that are observed in the rest of post-communist eastern Europe are also applicable to Bulgaria.

One of these trends – although it is not a characteristic feature of the transition toward a liberal democracy and market economy – is the somehow stable co-existence of anti-communists and ex-communists. In the beginning of the transition there were two main political actors in every CEE country: the anti-communist coalition, often uniting a huge number of parties, and the ex-communists, the heirs of the former communist party. Both of these actors were quite heterogeneous, which led to many splits in the course of transformation and thus provided the basis for a new, more developed palette of political parties.

For the anti-communist coalitions, this trend toward fragmentation was unsurprising. The adversaries of the communist regime had very different genealogies, some with roots in the pre-communist past, some in dissident movements and some as the product of new social movements which developed in the West decades ago. This heterogeneity is not so obvious in the heirs of the former Communist Party (CP). Usually the ruling CPs in central and eastern Europe were considered to be parties in the western sense of the term, commanding a part of the electorate and its support. In fact, the real government in the communist regimes was the Politburo and it was elected in the hierarchic and multi-level structure of the CP. Thus, the members of these "parties" were the real (and only) electoral body, although universal suffrage existed in these countries from World War II.

During the post-communist transition, the CPs transformed themselves into genuine political parties, acquiring skills and practices adapted to a pluralist political environment. These two political actors of the post-communist transition mobilized the largest share of votes during the first free elections. In Bulgaria, these were the Union of the Democratic Forces (UDF) and the Bulgarian Socialist Party (BSP), and they collected more than half of the total votes in the elections during the first part of the 1990s (see Reynier and Perrineau 2001). This is also true for most of the other former communist states.[2]

Table 13.1 Percentage of total votes for BSP and UDF in parliamentary elections, 1990–4, Bulgaria

	1990	*1991*	*1994*
% of the total number of voters	75.04	55.14	50.33

Table 13.2 Percentage of total votes for the main political parties in first parliamentary elections, central and eastern Europe, 1990

Country	Year of elections	Former CP and anti-communists	% of cast votes	Total %
Czechoslovakia	1990	Civic Forum	49.5	64.7
		CP	13.2	
Latvia	1990	Popular Front	68.2	89.7
		CP	21.5	
Lithuania	1990	Saudis	43.0	77.1
		CP	34.1	
Poland	1991	Union for Freedom	12.3	24.3
		Ex-communists	12.0	
Hungary	1990	Hungarian Democratic Forum	24.7	57.0
		FIDESZ	21.4	
		Ex-communists	10.9	
Estonia	1992	Union for Fatherland	22.0	47.8
		Coalition party	13.6	
		Centrist party	12.2	

However, it was not in every post-communist country that the ex-communists and anti-communists together were so successful. Poland is an obvious exception, since the first free elections were held before 1990. Two other exceptions were Hungary and Estonia – the ex-communists were not among the most important political parties in the first elections. Thus the bi-polar structure – ex-communists versus anti-communists – is logical but not universal. In countries where this opposition lasted only a few years or has not played the most important role in the political debate, the transition seemed to have been more successful. In the countries where this debate was much more influential and important (e.g. in Bulgaria, Romania, Ukraine), the transition proved to be more difficult and less successful.

The tension between "anti" and "ex" was especially important in Bulgaria. In the center of the debate was communism, its heritage, its consequences, its legacy. Other questions of the transition were not of similar importance, so we have to say that the transitional period in Bulgaria lasted until 2000/1. This is the main reason for the present developmental gap between Bulgaria and countries like Hungary or the Czech Republic, despite their apparently similar initial situation. Since we were not able to find substantial differences between these countries with regard to the public perception of democracy, the prevalence of democratic values or the burden of the communist past, our hypothesis is that the existing differences after a decade of transition might be explained by the different role of the opposition between anti-communists and ex-communists.

The lasting significance of this opposition in Bulgaria attaches special importance to the public perception of the communist past for the explanation of the present value structures. This analysis allows for the conclusion that this perception varies among the different generations, who keep their own individual and collective memories of communism. These memories differ and motivate the different perceptions of the transition toward democracy.

Citizens and politics

Political participation is one important element of democracies (Katz 1997: 243). Many observers expected that anti-communists would prevail over the ex-communists, that the electoral turnout rates would increase steeply and that the new political spectrum would be a result of the development of the first anti-communist coalition. None of these expectations were confirmed. The heirs of the former CP still play an essential role in the political arena, in some countries the former large anti-communist coalition disappeared and initiated several new parties located everywhere in the ideological spectrum from center-left to far-right and are not focused on anti-communism any more.[3] The turnout decreased dramatically in the whole post-communist region – on average by 20 percent.[4]

Participation rates in the first general elections in Bulgaria in 1990 and 1991 reached high levels, on average 85–90 percent. With time, however, this initial participation boom faded away – in 1996–7 only 61 to 62 percent of the electorate voted.

In the first years of the transition period, the level of interest in politics was also exceptionally high. However, this development was not stable. Roughly one-third of the respondents to the European Values Survey in 1997 stated that politics is not at all important, and for 41 percent politics is not very important. The level of reported interest in politics is a little higher: 35.2 percent are somewhat interested in politics and 36.1 percent are not very interested. High levels of interest in politics is reported by only 7.1 percent of all respondents. One-fifth is not at all interested. Interest in politics and the belief that politics is an important issue are two interrelated variables (Pearson $R = 0.327$).

In 1997, politics was perceived as a show where there is almost no role to be performed by the individual citizen-observer, since voting is almost the only mode of participation for a great majority of Bulgarian citizens. In addition, the focus of public interest shifted from political to economic problems during the transition. Once achieved, democracy was no longer a strong mobilizing factor likely to compete successfully with issues like decreasing living standards or unemployment and poverty in public opinion.

Furthermore, politics is understood as a complex yet not always honorable business. This notion of politics is at least partly caused by the

Table 13.3 Turnout in national elections, central and eastern Europe, 1990–9

	1990	1991	1992	1993	1994	1995	1996	1997	1998	1999	2000	2001	Average
Czech Republic	96.7	–	85.1	–	–	–	76.4	–	73.8	–	–	–	83.0
Slovakia	83.0	–	81.8	–	75.7	–	–	–	84.2	–	–	–	81.2
Latvia	–	–	–	89.9	–	72.6	–	–	71.9	–	–	–	78.1
Slovenia	75.7	–	85.6	–	–	–	73.7	68.6	–	–	–	–	75.9
Romania	86.2	–	76.1	–	–	–	76.0	–	–	–	56.5	–	73.7
Bulgaria	90.8	83.9	75.4	–	75.2	–	63.3	62.9	–	–	–	64.4	73.7
Russia	–	–	–	–	–	–	–	–	–	–	68.8	–	68.8
Lithuania	–	–	72.9	78.1	–	–	50.3	71.5	–	–	55.9	–	65.7
Hungary	69.5	–	–	–	68.9	–	–	–	56.3	–	–	–	64.9
Bosnia and Herzegovina	–	–	–	–	–	–	–	–	–	–	64.4	–	64.4
Estonia	–	–	66.5	–	–	68.3	–	–	–	57.4	–	–	64.1
Poland	59.7	43.3	–	52.1	–	63.5	–	47.9	–	–	61.1	46.5	53.4
Average per year	80.2	63.6	77.6	73.3	73.2	68.1	67.9	62.7	71.5	57.4	61.3	55.4	–

existing popular concept of a western type of society as a role model. The image of an American-esque society where everybody pursues their own private interests with no regard for public matters is dominant. Thus, politics is left to professional politicians and is not recognized as a matter of concern for the normal citizen.

Interest in politics, however, depends on age and the level of formal education. The elderly (aged 50+ years) tended in 1997 to report a higher level of interest than the middle generation and those under 30, who express the lowest levels of interest in politics. The level of interest in politics increases with the level of formal education (Table 13.4).

Also in 1997, generation-related differences become even more pronounced when the respondents are grouped according to the era in which they reached the age of 18:

- Democracy – respondents who have completed their eighteenth year after 1989 (9.7 percent).
- Perestroyka – respondents who have completed their eighteenth year after 1985 (13.2 percent).
- Real-socialism – respondents who have completed their eighteenth year after 1968 (29.7 percent).
- Post-Stalinist – respondents who have completed their eighteenth year after 1956 (20 percent).
- Stalinist – respondents who have completed their eighteenth year after 1944 (16.4 percent).
- Bourgeois – respondents who have completed their eighteenth year before 1944 (11.1 percent).

The "bourgeois," the "Stalinist" and the "post-Stalinist" generations express the highest level of interest in politics. However, a large share of the "bourgeois" generation also expresses no interest in politics at all (28.6 percent). The same is true for the youngest "democracy" generation, where 32.7 percent report being not interested in politics. The average figure is 19.6 percent for all respondents.

Table 13.4 Level of interest in politics, %, Bulgaria, 1997

	Very interested	Somewhat interested	Not very interested	Not at all interested	Don't know
No primary education	2.4	19.2	36.8	40.0	1.6
Primary education	6.8	32.9	33.2	24.1	3.1
Secondary, professional	4.8	39.4	37.8	17.8	0.3
Secondary, pre-university	6.1	32.0	43.5	16.3	2.0
University	15.5	45.5	31.6	4.3	3.2
Total	7.1	35.3	36.1	19.6	2.0

The same pattern emerges when the question is asked: "Do you discuss political issues with friends or within your family?" Again the "bourgeois" as well as the "Stalinist" and the "post-Stalinist" generations are the ones most likely to engage in political debates with their friends (see Table 13.5), while among the youngest generation, "democracy," 43.3 percent never discuss politics in their private lives.

Both, the "Stalinist" and the "post-Stalinist" generations consider politics as something important and debate it rather frequently with their friends. Within the communist paradigm political activities are regarded as the universal tool for social change. However, politics was prominently perceived as government policies. Apparently, those cohorts that experienced young adulthood during the establishment of communism in Bulgaria, as well as those who were politically socialized during the intensive debates accompanying de-Stalinization, are most likely to regard politics as an important issue. Conversely, the generations of "real socialism" as well as those of the "perestroyka" and "democracy" eras tend to believe that social change is mainly induced by powers outside the political realm.

The frequency of political debates among peers is also heavily influenced by the respondent's level of formal education. In particular, a higher education appears to be the decisive factor that determines the higher levels of interest in politics and an increased frequency of political debates among peers. This might imply that politics is regarded as a business that requires more sophisticated intellectual skills and is therefore left to the academics and to professional politicians.

Political values

Ten years after the beginning of the process of transition, public expectations are now focused on the standards of living. Three in four respondents insist that the most important goal for Bulgaria is to achieve economic growth, to increase prosperity and individual welfare. Other prominent goals are the maintenance of law and order in the country (50.4 percent) and curtailment of inflation (31.6 percent).

Table 13.5 Political debates, %, Bulgaria, 1997

	Frequently	*Occasionally*	*Never*	*Don't know*
Bourgeois	17.6	42.0	34.5	5.9
Stalinist	15.9	55.7	26.7	1.7
Post-Stalin	19.6	56.5	22.9	0.9
Real-socialism	9.4	71.1	17.6	1.9
Perestroyka	7.1	52.5	39.7	0.7
Democracy	4.8	43.3	51.9	0.0
Total	12.7	57.3	28.3	1.8

Some political goals linked with the transition to democracy are less frequently mentioned. Only 10.8 percent of the respondents agree with the item "more say at the workplace and in their local community as an important future goal," and only 11.9 percent of the respondents identify a greater influence on central government decisions by the ordinary citizens as being an important aim. This is a common finding in post-communist countries, where economic problems replaced political issues in the course of the transition that was almost everywhere accompanied by decreasing living standards for a majority. Of particular influence might have been the financial crisis in the winter of 1996–7 that resulted in an acute political crisis in Bulgaria. However, even if they do not express a high level of interest in politics, the highest shares of respondents who cherish greater political influence of the ordinary citizen as a future aim for Bulgaria are to be found among members of the younger generations ("perestroyka" and "democracy").

Freedom of speech is only a priority for 4.9 percent of the respondents (13.4 percent mentioned it as the second most important issue). Again, the youngest cohorts ("perestroyka" and "democracy") but also – surprisingly – the post-Stalinist generation put the greatest emphasis on freedom of speech. It might be the case that precisely those generations that were socialized into young adulthood in a phase of political liberalization appreciate freedom of speech more than generations who experienced their political socialization in times of oppression.

Protection of freedom of speech is of special importance for the educated: 11.8 percent of all respondents with an academic degree regard it as a priority issue. However, even these respondents attach greater importance to issues such as maintaining law and order and economic growth. Either freedom of speech is safely guaranteed in Bulgaria or it is still regarded as an important issue.

Political participation

Interest in politics and political participation has always been related to the process of modernization. The example of the increasing turnout in the legislative elections between 1879 and 1946 in the pre-communist period in Bulgaria confirms this hypothesis. Between 1879 and 1900, turnout rates in Bulgaria were about 30 percent; between 1900 and 1918, they reached 50 percent; in the 1920s, it increased to 80 percent, remaining on this level until 1944. After World War II, participation rates reached 90 percent (Todorov 2001). The first post-communist election in 1990 also generated a turnout of 90 percent, but during subsequent elections turnout rates gradually decreased. This fact might be an argument against the idea that the post-communist transition is the second stage of a late modernization in this region. In Bulgaria, communism did have a modernizing aspect, especially with the introduction of mass education, a system of public healthcare and the social security system, particularly in the 1970s and 1980s.

The respondents' willingness to vote in elections has been maintained at comparatively high levels: only 8.3 percent report that they will not vote, and 9.7 percent refused to answer at all. However, even the combined share of these two categories (18 percent) is far away from the level of non-participation (38 percent) that was observed over the past few years.

Interestingly the share of self-declared non-voters is to be found among respondents who came of age in the periods of "real socialism" and "perestroyka" (that is, persons aged 40–60). Here, however, two types of abstentions need to be distinguished: apolitical and political. Respondents with a lower level of formal education, who participate less in social life and have no interest in politics, are not willing to vote because of their isolation from society. Conversely, 9.6 percent of all persons with a university education (versus an average record of 8.3 percent) also admit their unwillingness to vote, but this is a political position directed against the political class. It is within this particular social stratum where a larger share of respondents would support marginal and non-traditional parties as an expression of disagreement with the mainstream.

Voting is the most conventional form of political participation in a democracy. However, other modes of participation are better indicators for the existence and the extent of an active civil society (see Table 13.6).

Between 9 percent (those who have attended lawful demonstrations) and 14.5 percent (those who might occupy buildings or factories) is the share of most active citizens that could be mobilized to participate in unconventional forms of political protest.

Unsurprisingly, the youngest cohort (aged up to 30) is most likely to participate in the more drastic modes of protest such as occupation of buildings or factories. Those who had already participated into these activities dominate in the middle cohort (40–50).

Membership in political organizations is popular for an even smaller share of the respondents: only 3.5 percent are members of a political party. Regardless of the emergence on a wide scale of associations, political parties and trade unions that followed the beginning of the transition, the organized participation in public life, only 4–5 percent of citizens were

Table 13.6 Political participation, %, Bulgaria, 1997

	Have done	Might do	Would never do
Attending lawful demonstrations	9.0	34.8	40.6
Signing a petition	5.7	31.8	38.4
Joining unofficial strikes	4.1	24.6	49.2
Joining in boycotts	2.1	17.6	58.0
Occupying buildings of factories	1.8	14.5	57.6

involved in such organizations ten years after the fall of communism. An exception is the trade unions whose active members account for about 5 percent, with another 8 percent of non-active members, adding up to a total of 12 percent. Approximately 75 percent of all Bulgarian citizens are not members of any public organization. The remaining portion is distributed over all sorts of environmental, charity, research and political organizations. This share, however, is significant. A relation exists between the type of organization and the age of its members: older respondents (aged 51+) are most likely to be members of political parties (mainly members of BSP, the successor of the old communist party). Younger respondents (aged up to 30) are predominantly members of art, music and sports associations, while the generation of the middle-aged (30–50) is composed predominantly of members of trade unions. Members of political organizations (such as political parties and trade unions) are most likely to belong to the middle generation or to the elderly, while the younger generation tends to belong to non-political organizations.

Attitudes toward democracy

Democracy, in terms of being both the substance and the aim of the transition, is loaded with predominantly positive semantics in the perception of the public. A majority of respondents prefer democracy to any other regime type in Bulgaria: 30.1 percent deem it a very good system, and 39 percent regard it as a good system. If we compare our generations, it is only the "Stalinist" generation that does not fit this general pattern of approval: the share of those who agree that democracy is a very good system for Bulgaria is comparatively small in this particular group. With decreasing age of the respondents, the share of those who agree with the statement that democracy is the best of all forms of government grows. Democracy is more appealing to younger people who are more willing to identify themselves with it as a system. Older people are more skeptical and less willing to regard democracy as an indisputable example to be followed. Here again the "Stalinist" generation expressed explicit disagreement with democracy as the best regime to a greater extent than members of the other generations (see Table 13.7).

Public approval of a political system headed by a strong leader turned out to be substantial: 21 percent of the respondents expressed their agreement with a potential strong leader. However, one should not translate this number too easily as an actual share of autocrats since, during the period when the survey was conducted, memories of the last presidential elections were still fresh and a strong leader was also understood as an efficient president. Among those 48.2 percent who deemed a head of state who is not constrained by parliament or elections as very good or good for Bulgaria, a rather large share also believed that democracy is a very good or good form of government (36.1 percent agreed with both statements).

Table 13.7 "Democracy is better than other form of government," %, Bulgaria, 1997

	Agree strongly	Agree	Disagree	Disagree strongly	Don't know	Total
Bourgeois	20.2	34.5	7.6	4.2	33.6	119
						11.1
Stalinist	22.2	32.4	15.3	4.5	25.6	176
						16.4
Post-Stalinist	28.0	32.7	15.9	5.6	17.8	214
						20.0
Real-socialism	32.7	39.0	11.3	2.8	14.2	318
						29.7
Perestroyka	37.6	36.2	10.6	3.5	12.1	141
						13.2
Democracy	39.4	36.5	7.7	1.0	15.4	104
						9.7
Column	321	381	129	40	201	1,072
Total	29.9	35.5	12.0	3.7	18.8	100.0

Thus, true autocrats who approved strong presidential powers and rejected democracy account for approximately 12 percent of all respondents. This latter figure coincides almost perfectly with the share (13.1 percent) of those respondents who regard military rule as a very good or good system for Bulgaria. This share is distributed between the "Stalinist" and the "post-Stalinist" generations, as well as, to a certain extent, the generation of "real socialism." What is apparent here is a nostalgic desire for "a better world" where stringent but clear and universal order defines the rules of the game. Conversely, the generation of "democracy," and the generations of "perestroyka" and "real socialism," oppose military rule to a considerably greater extent. In addition, disagreement with a potential military regime increases with the level of formal education (see Table 13.8).

The distribution of attitudes toward the current democratic regime is similarly structured. Calculating an index based on the respondents' attitudes toward democracy and autocracy, we analyzed the shares of strong and weak democrats and autocrats: roughly 17 percent of the respondents belong to the category of strong democrats, and 44 percent count as weak democrats.[5] A more or less clear autocratic attitude is displayed by a total of 16.1 percent (Table 13.9).

With regard to the efficiency of democracy, the respondents tend to exhibit a rather skeptical attitude. The large share that agrees with the statement that democracies are indecisive illustrate this best (51.2 percent agree or agree strongly). However, the ability of democracies to maintain order and to deal with economic problems is estimated as rather high (Table 13.10).

The highest level of skepticism toward the efficiency of democracy is expressed by respondents with a lower level of formal education and the

Table 13.8 Respondents agreeing that military rule is a very bad form of government, %, Bulgaria, 1997

Age	%
Under 18	50.0
18–30	40.5
30–41	40.2
40–51	39.6
50–61	36.4
61 and more	29.9
Level of formal education	
Under primary	21.6
Primary, under secondary	32.2
Secondary, professional	40,3
Secondary, pre-university	42.9
University	47.1

Table 13.9 Democrats and autocrats, %, Bulgaria, 1997

	Scale	*N*	%
Strong autocrats	1	80	7.5
Autocrats	2	92	8.6
Undecided	3	241	22.5
Weak democrats	4	476	44.4
Strong democrats	5	183	17.1
Total		1,072	100.0

Table 13.10 "Do you agree with the following statements?," %, Bulgaria, 1997

	Agree strongly	*Agree*	*Disagree*	*Disagree strongly*
In democracy, the economic system runs badly	12.7	24.9	35.6	10.8
Democracies aren't any good at maintaining order	12.5	25.3	34.0	11.5
Democracies are indecisive and have too much squabbling	18.4	32.8	26.8	7.7

elderly, i.e. by those respondents who experience the greatest difficulties in adjusting to the conditions of the new regime and the restructured economy.

Attitudes toward the state

The period of "real socialism" was the time of the omnipotent state. In addition to being the universal organizer of society, it was also the paternalistic provider of individual welfare on the condition of total submission to the state on the part of the citizens. Thus, the transition to democracy would necessitate the abandonment of this particular concept of the state and the establishment of individual responsibility as a common value in society.

An important peculiarity that may well influence state perception in Bulgaria relates to the fact that, from the fifteenth until the nineteenth century, Bulgaria was a part of the Ottoman Empire. This experience has given rise to a general and still persisting alienation from the state.

Attitudes toward the state predominantly mirror the respondents' evaluation of its capacity to manage the economy and ensure the success of business and companies. However, this evaluation turns out to be a negative one. Lack of trust in the state's management abilities is widespread. For example, only 10.7 percent of respondents believe that the state should own companies and appoint their managers. This share tends to become larger with increasing age, and reaches its maximum among the "Stalinist" and "post-Stalinist" generations.

Conversely, younger generations are more likely to believe that the owners of the enterprises should run them. The most popular option is that owners and their employees should manage enterprises jointly; which can be interpreted as an approval of co-determination and not as an expression of nostalgia toward "real socialism," since this view is mainly expressed by the generations of "perestroyka" and "democracy," i.e., by those aged 18–30 years (Table 13.11).

Younger respondents with a higher level of formal education as well as urban dwellers are more likely to agree with statements in favor of private economic initiatives. Conversely, the elderly as well as rural inhabitants and respondents with a lower level of formal education tend to favor a protective role for the state with regard to the economy. Apparently, there is a cleavage between those who are better adapted to the market mechanisms, and those who have become marginalized by the new economic conditions.

Interestingly no such gap can be observed when it comes to the issue of

Table 13.11 How business and industry should be managed, %, Bulgaria, 1997

	The owners run their business	Owners and employees	The government	The employees should own	Don't know
Bourgeois	13.4	16.8	12.6	15.1	42.0
Stalinist	19.9	24.4	14.2	22.7	18.8
Post-Stalinist	16.4	28.0	15.0	27.6	13.1
Real-socialism	27.4	29.9	8.8	22.6	11.3
Perestroyka	29.8	36.2	5.7	17.0	11.3
Democracy	31.7	34.6	6.7	17.3	9.6
N	248	305	115	231	173
Total	23.1	28.5	10.7	21.5	16.1

the state's responsibilities for the provision of individual welfare. Generational differences were not very pronounced when the respondents were asked to choose between individual responsibility and responsibility of the state. A substantial portion of the younger generations (inclusive of the youngest one) believed that the government has to provide for individual welfare. Apparently, Bulgarian respondents do not favor an extremely liberal position according to which everybody should provide for himself or herself without relying on the public provision of welfare.

Attitudes toward institutions

Our survey data indicates that levels of confidence in institutions are comparatively high. This survey was conducted when the new UDF government ruled for less than a year; i.e. public opinion still gave credit to the new government. At the same time, however, several other surveys observed a more skeptical, even critical, attitude toward the state administration and other institutions – an inefficiency in fighting corruption and the pursuit of private interests by representatives of the public authorities aroused particular criticism (see Table 13.9).

More than half of the respondents express a great deal or quite a lot of confidence in the Bulgarian government. However, this not true for parliament and political parties; almost two in three respondents do not express trust in political parties. This share is not significantly influenced by either age or level of formal education (however, the generation who came of age during the time of "real socialism" expressed the highest level of skepticism toward political parties). The parliament enjoys lower levels

Table 13.12 Confidence in institutions, %, Bulgaria, 1997

	A great deal	Quite a lot	Not very much	None at all	DK
Armed forces	35.3	40.5	13.0	4.4	6.8
Churches	19.0	32.6	21.6	16.7	10.0
United Nations	17.3	35.5	13.8	5.5	27.8
European Union	16.7	35.9	15.0	5.2	27.2
Television	15.2	48.1	23.1	5.9	7.7
Government	14.3	41.7	25.2	12.4	6.4
Police	11.3	36.8	30.3	15.7	5.9
Legal system	8.5	27.0	33.5	23.3	7.7
Parliament	8.3	34.0	32.6	18.3	6.7
Civil service	6.6	35.4	33.3	12.3	12.4
Labor unions	5.3	21.6	29.8	21.7	21.5
Women's movement	5.2	21.9	18.2	12.3	42.3
Press	5.1	35.9	32.9	13.9	12.1
Green movement	5.0	24.3	23.2	13.0	34.5
Political parties	4.2	22.5	40.4	24.2	8.6
Major companies	2.6	23.4	33.2	17.5	23.3

of confidence than the central government. This might indicate a skeptical attitude in general toward multi-party democracy in Bulgaria, especially with regard to its ability to protect the interests of the people. Sometimes pluralism is perceived as replacing public interests by private ones, as substituting private interests for the will of the people. In general, the state administration (except for the army) does not seem to enjoy any special public confidence.

The legal system attracts the highest level of explicit mistrust, followed by the government, which was similarly the institution that enjoyed the highest levels of trust. Obviously several cases of corruption influenced the respondents' evaluation strongly. This rather negative attitude toward the legal system is particularly pronounced among the generation of those aged 41–60 years.

The comparatively high levels of public confidence in the army are rather usual in Bulgarian society. Professional or educational status or partisan bias does not distinguish the respondents on this matter, although the youngest generation expressed a more skeptical attitude toward the army. This was especially true for those who have not yet completed their military service.

Institutions of civil society enjoy rather limited public confidence. An exception here is the Church; however, it is not actively involved in the political debate in Bulgaria. Television attracted comparatively higher levels of confidence. The women's movement and the Green movement as well as trade unions and, in principle, all civil associations, which play a role in the public arena, enjoy only low levels of confidence.

The same is also true for major companies since they are suspected to be active in illegal or quasi-legal transactions. Although the respondents valued private initiatives very highly, they do not seem to trust private entrepreneurs.

Apparently, public opinion remains cautious toward civil society institutions. They are still perceived as inefficient and suspected to pursue private interests rather than articulating and protecting the common interests of the Bulgarian society.

The European Union and the United Nations enjoyed a comparatively high level of confidence prestige in Bulgaria. It is, however, telling that more than one-quarter of the respondents refused to indicate their level of confidence in these institutions. Probably this reflects a problem of insufficient information.

Attitudes toward the other

Tolerance and respect for different lifestyles, as well as the ability to live and act in a multi-cultural, pluralist society, are important ingredients of democracy. However, while this statement is widely accepted as an indisputable truth, reality still leaves space for the improvement of levels of tolerance and respect in Bulgarian society. Tolerance in associating with others has been acknowledged as an essential element of children's education by 46.4 percent of all respondents. It is interesting to note here that this particular characteristic tends to be mentioned more frequently by the elderly (of the "bourgeois" and the "post-Stalinist" generations) rather than by their younger counterparts. This is also true with regard to views on the best way to build human relationships: should one try to understand the other person, or state one's own position? Younger people preferred the latter. It might be the case that they have internalized selfishness as one important feature of democracy "by accident," since it goes together well with the principle of free competition and the conditions of a market economy. Apparently it is difficult to draw a clear line between the sometimes opposing principles of the market on the one hand and of political democracy on the other.

Cultural liberalism has always been linked with tolerance. Attitudes toward patterns of behavior that are traditionally regarded as deviant (e.g. homosexuality, prostitution, abortion, divorce) can serve as a litmus test indicating the overall level of tolerance in a society.

In Bulgaria, mainly for historical and religious reasons, abortion and divorce have never been especially important issues. This is especially true for the period after World War II. Levels of tolerance toward these behaviors are comparatively high, with only 19 percent of all respondents believing that these behaviors are never justifiable. Homosexuality and prostitution are tolerated on much lower levels; homosexuality is regarded as never justifiable by 40.1 percent; 55.2 percent of the respondents believe this to be the case for prostitution.

Levels of tolerance increased with the respondents' level of formal education and with decreasing age. Religion may also be of importance here: Bulgarian Turks (i.e. the Muslim population) appear to be less tolerant than the Christian Bulgarians with regard to homosexuality and prostitution. However, it might be the case that the results are biased, since the two denominations make up very different shares of the sample. In any case, across the board, higher levels of tolerance toward divorce and abortion might result from the fact that these behaviors are more frequent in Bulgaria than prostitution and homosexuality. However, lower levels of tolerance toward minorities might point to a latent cruelty with regard to the weaker, more feeble members of society (Table 13.13).

In addition, Bulgarian citizens tend not to trust their fellow citizens: 59.1 percent of the respondents believe that it is not possible to trust others. Only 23.7 percent expressed the opposite viewpoint. Trust levels are highest among the younger generations (the "democracy" and the "perestroyka" cohorts), and among the elderly (the "bourgeois" cohort). Those who were socialized under socialist rule tend to express higher levels of mistrust. Apparently, trust in others is characteristic of open personalities willing to communicate with others in an open society.

Table 13.13 Attitudes toward homosexuality, prostitution, abortion and divorce, %, Bulgaria, 1997

	Never justifiable									*Always justifiable*
	1	*2*	*3*	*4*	*5*	*6*	*7*	*8*	*9*	*10*
Homosexuality	40.0	3.6	4.3	3.8	7.9	6.1	3.6	3.7	1.0	4.9
Prostitution	55.2	5.7	6.0	4.4	5.6	5.6	2.7	3.1	0.7	1.6
Abortion	19.2	2.3	4.0	4.0	12.3	8.4	5.5	10.6	4.9	18.1
Divorce	19.0	2.9	3.7	3.6	13.7	11.1	6.6	8.1	6.3	18.2

Attitudes toward the poor

A majority of the respondents (79 percent) believe that the government is doing too little for the poor. Age, the level of formal education or ethnic affiliation do not differentiate the respondents. Therefore poverty seemed to be perceived as a political problem and a task to be managed by the government.

Public opinion turns out to be much less aware of the problem of worldwide poverty: 43.2 percent of all respondents refused to answer the question of whether rich countries are making sufficient efforts to help poor ones. Critical attitudes toward rich countries are mainly expressed by the generation of the middle-aged (40–50 years). The "post-Stalinist" and the "perestroyka" generations are those most concerned about poverty in the world. It might be the case that their socialization under the conditions of an open society (compared to the past) act as a stimulus to be more aware of problems beyond the territory of their nation-state.

Opinions differ widely on Bulgarian foreign aid: 45 percent oppose it completely, while 32.7 percent agree with the potential provision of Bulgarian foreign aid. The economic hardships that have to be faced by the Bulgarians themselves seem to provoke national egoism, and similarly, Bulgaria is perceived to be a more appropriate recipient of foreign aid than a donor.

Although Bulgarian society lacks any significant experience with immigration (with the exception of Vietnamese workers in 1980s), anti-immigrant attitudes are alive and well: 44.8 percent of the respondents believe that the Bulgarian government should allow immigration only when enough jobs are available for native Bulgarians; 47.7 percent agreed to either partial or full restrictions on immigration.

Summarizing the two preceding sections, we conclude that Bulgarian society does not exhibit severely repressive characteristics, although the observed levels of tolerance are not remarkably high. Relations and political cooperation between the various ethnic communities does exist. However, Roma and Turks in Bulgaria are, on average, poorer and achieve lower levels of formal education, and thus are less capable of adapting to the conditions of the free market economy.

Conclusion

The main purpose of our analysis was to asses the progress of consolidation of democracy in Bulgaria. By the end of the 1990s, one can say that democracy in Bulgaria is established not only as a set of institutions and rules, but also in the perceptions, attitudes and values of the public. Democracy is supported by the majority of Bulgarians who, simultaneously, reject autocracy. The quota of strong democrats is decisively lower than in western European democracies, but still higher than in many other central and eastern European countries. What seems to be new in the Bulgarian political debate is the disappearance of communism as a theme of the political debate. No one fears the return of the communist regime. Thus we may conclude that, with regard to the integration of old regime conflicts, the Bulgarian transition has come to an end. Even the quite surprising outcome of the parliamentary elections in 2001, where the newly established political movement led by the former king Simeon II won a majority, cannot change this conclusion. The fact that both protagonists of the post-communist transition – UDF and BSP – have been in the opposition after 2001 will give them a chance to clarify and reshape their political profile. Meanwhile, the most important outcome of this election was that it institutionalized the end of the anti-communist and ex-communist tension. The transition in political terms is finished.

Notes

1 Many studies on this topic have been conducted after 1989 in Bulgaria. They showed that the so-called "Bulgarian ethnic model" is characterized by the political integration of the Turkish minority through the Movement for Rights and Freedom (MRF) that participate actively in the political arena and was an important part of governmental coalitions several times (from 1992 until 1994 and from 2001 until today).
2 For the results, see the electoral archive of the University of Duesseldorf (www.public.rz.uni-duesseldorf.de/~nordsiew/) and Adam Carr's electoral archive (www.iosphere.net.au/~lance/indexint.shtml).
3 The disappearance of essential anti-communist actors like the Hungarian Democratic forum, the Polish Solidarnosc, the Romanian Democratic Convention, the Czech Civic forum or the Lithuanian Saudis is an example.
4 Data is taken from the quoted electoral archives of the University of Duesseldorf and the Adam Carr archive. For Bulgaria, data are taken from the electoral archive of the New Bulgarian University.
5 This variable is constructed based on the formula: $(9 - v157) * (9 - v163) - (9 - v154) * (9 - v156)$. The resulting scale of -64 to $+64$ comprises the following five groups: group 1 – from -64 to -33; group 2 – from -34 to -1; group 3 – equal to 0; group 4 – from $+1$ to $+33$; group 5 – from $+34$ to $+64$. These groups are defined as follows: 1 – strong autocrats; 2 – autocrats; 3 – undecided; 4 – democrats; 5 – strong democrats.

References

Berend, I. (1996) *Central and Eastern Europe 1944–1993: Detour from the Periphery to the Periphery*, Cambridge: Cambridge University Press.

Crampton, R.J. (1995) *Eastern Europe in the 20th Century*, London: Routledge.

Dreyfus, M., Groppo, B., Ingerflom, C.S., Lew, R., Wolikow, S., Pennetier, C. and Pudal, B. (2000) *Le Siècle des communismes*, Paris: Les Editions de l'atelier.

Kalinova, E. and Baeva, I. (2001) *Bulgarskite prehodi 1939–2001*, Sofia: Paradigma.

Katz, R.S. (1997) *Democracy and Elections*, Oxford: Oxford University.

Kornai, J. (1992) *The Socialist System: Political Economy of Communism*, Oxford: Oxford University Press

Reynier, D. and Perrineau, P. (2001) *"Bulgarie,"* in *Dictionnaire du vote*, Paris: Seuil.

Rotschild, J. (1993) *Return to Diversity: a Political History of East–Central Europe Since World War II*, Oxford: Oxford University Press.

Todorov, A. (2001) *Izbiratelni zakoni I izbiratelna aktivnost: bulgarskiyat sluchay 1879–1946 (Electoral Laws and Electoral Participation: the Bulgarian Case)*, Istorikut: grajdanin i uchen. Sofia: Sofia University Press.

14 Russia, Belarus and Ukraine
Construction of democratic communities

Elena Bashkirova

Introduction

Robert Dahl developed a set of widely accepted criteria that a democratic regime has to meet. The criteria include the existence of civil and political rights, and legitimate and competitive elections. Dahl calls "polyarchy" the state of a country that exhibits all of these characteristics (Dahl 1971). Another common term is "liberal democracy."

There are two other sub-types of democratic regimes that are prominent in surveys on new democracies. On one hand, there are so-called defective or "boundary" regimes which have realized only some democratic features. These semi-democratic regimes stand somewhere between democracy and autocracy, and may be called "electoral democracies." This term characterizes a regime that conducts legitimate competitive elections, but is unable to guarantee civil liberties.

On the other hand, there are advanced or "progressive democracies" which display further positive features in addition to the minimum set of distinctive liberal democratic criteria and, thus, display a higher level of quality of the democratic process than many new democracies. The terms "advanced" or "progressive" and "democracy" may combine to idealize wealthy western democracies. However, based on such examples, modern political theory lists formal characteristics such as universal suffrage and freedom of speech, of association and of information, as necessary requirements for a democratic regime. These "minimum number of required features," however, are not enough for a sufficient evaluation of the state of a democratic regime. Social and economic characteristics of democratic communities should be studied in addition.

The drastic political, social and economic changes that took place in the former Soviet republics during the last decade cannot be studied as isolated phenomena. Instead, they must be understood as a specific combination of features common to post-authoritarian democratic transformations. None of the eastern European countries in transition today has ever before experienced true democracy. Thus citizens and politicians need some time to understand and accept the standards of democratic institutions and behavior. These societies are often called "young" democracies. However, some of the central European countries (e.g. Yugoslavia, the Czech Republic and Hungary) have always been more liberal as compared to others (e.g. Romania and Albania) and, therefore, might have had a better starting position.

The collapse of communism in Russia, Belarus and Ukraine did not result in a complete replacement of the ruling elite. Basically, three groups survived and constituted the base for the "new" political class. First among these groups were those members of the previous bureaucracy who coped successfully with the new political and economic situation. A second group was made up of the leaders of the new bourgeoisie (oligarchs), who merged with both the political elite and some criminal elements. The third group that survived the transition was the secret service. While the secret service stayed in the background during the 1990s, more recently the political impact of its members has increased and become visible. They act as major players who determine the rules of the game and change them if it fits their own interests.

Scholars who diagnose the weaknesses of the young Russian democracy generally refer to authoritarian modes of state control and a rather high proportion of citizens who do not accept the values of freedom and democratic choice. These authoritarian beliefs and attitudes are often attributed to a "Russian mentality." However, it would be a serious mistake to propose a social and psychological predisposition toward despotism and a strong anti-democratic character of the national political culture. Probably the specific features of Russian post-communist transformation indicate not a general rejection of democracy but a process of democratization under complicated and complex conditions.

Freedom of the individual citizen is an important feature of democracy. However, to free an individual from authoritarian repression and limitation does not automatically create a new personality able to cope with the new environment or even to contribute to its improvement. This might result in a "democracy without democrats" which could indeed be the case in Russia. Characteristic features of the Russian citizen, such as legal nihilism and a tendency to confuse freedom with anarchy and total permissiveness, have seriously disturbed the balance of interests in the Russian society and led to centrifugal or confrontational tendencies.

In addition, heavy economic and social crises in Russia, Ukraine and Belarus do more than simply hinder democratic transformations. In the former Soviet republics, people are seriously dissatisfied with the way the new democratic institutions work. They stopped believing in the capacity of the new democratic institutions to reform society and economy. Therefore the main task in analyzing the current political regime in the former Soviet republics is not simply to answer the question as to whether there is or is not a democracy. It is more important to study its specific features in a comparative and interdisciplinary framework.

In this chapter, we concentrate on the empirical analysis of the shape of civil society in Belarus, Russia and Ukraine. We utilize indicators computed in the context of the overall project by Hans-Dieter Klingemann and Dieter Fuchs using data from two waves of the Word Values Survey. We analyze the results for both the level of support for democracy as an ideal and for the current regime, and the prevalence of autocratic attitudes in comparison with West European countries. First of all, we determine the distribution of strong democrats, weak democrats, autocrats and undecided citizens in the three former Soviet republics, and analyze the socio-economic characteristics of the Russian respondents according to these categories. Then we survey the distribution of democratic and autocratic attitudes and behaviors among the citizenry of Russia, Belarus and Ukraine. The Russian sample will be studied in more detail, especially with regard to distributions of attitudes among democrats and autocrats.

The democracy–autocracy index

We measure attitudes toward democracy and autocracy with the index which has been used throughout the book. It groups respondents into four categories: "strong democrats" – the respondents who give a strong positive assessment of democracy and express a negative attitude toward autocracy; "weak democrats" who display an overall positive assessment of democracy; "undecided citizens" expressing contradictory assessments or showing difficulties in answering the respective questions; and finally "autocrats," a group that favors autocracy over democracy.

A significant difference between Germany, a country with a comparatively strong democracy, and the "young democracies" of Russia, Ukraine and Belarus is evident with respect to the proportion of "strong democrats." While in Germany a plurality of respondents belongs to this category, the respondents in the former Soviet republics are mainly concentrated in the category of "undecided citizens." Russia hosts the highest percentage of "autocrats"[1] and, in 1999, also the highest share of undecided citizens. With regard to the share of respondents found in the category "weak democrats," Ukraine and Belarus do not differ a great deal

Table 14.1 The democracy–autocracy index, 1995, 1999, %, Germany, Russia, Ukraine and Belarus

	Strong democrats		Weak democrats		Undecided citizens		Autocrats	
	1995	1999	1995	1999	1995	1999	1995	1999
Germany	54	42	39	43	6	13	0	2
Russia	2	2	32	33	50	52	16	13
Ukraine	3	5	32	42	58	46	6	7
Belarus	6	11	44	41	42	41	8	6

from Germany. In general, there is no clear trend in the three former Soviet republics, neither toward a stronger rejection of autocracy nor toward a higher level of support for democracy.

We will now present a more fine-grained analysis of the socio-economic composition of democrats and autocrats in the Russian sample, and will then turn to an analysis of attitudes and political behavior of citizens in order to determine the nature of the civil society in these countries.

Russia: socio-demographic characteristics of supporters of democracy and autocracy

"Strong democrats" are a minority in Russia (2 percent in 1995 and 1999). Urban residence and a high level of formal education are characteristics of strong democrats. In 1999, citizens of Moscow and other large cities with a population over 500,000 people were over-represented in this group (47 percent as compared to an average of 25 percent). In 1999, the percentage of respondents with a high level of formal education in the "strong democrats" category was twice that of the overall sample. Roughly one-third of the respondents qualified as "weak democrats" (32 percent in 1995 and 33 percent in 1999). Again a high level of formal education is a good predictor of membership in this group. Roughly one-third of the democrats had a high school diploma and/or an academic degree, as compared to 17 percent of the average Russian population in 1995 (21 percent in 1999). Half of the respondents belonged to the category "undecided citizens" (50 percent in 1995 and 52 percent in 1999). Socio-demographic characteristics were a low or middle level of formal education, moderate income and residence in small cities and regional capitals. Additionally, women and the elderly are slightly over-represented in this category. It summarizes not only respondents who had contradictory assessments of democracy and autocracy, but also those who found it difficult to answer the respective questions at all. Of the respondents in 1995, 16 percent (13 percent in 1999) showed the characteristics of "autocrats." Rural residents, men and highly skilled workers are over-represented here. With respect to regions, the highest proportion of autocrats lives in the Northern Caucasus (15 percent of respondents in this region, as compared to roughly 10 percent in other regions). Interestingly, age has no significant influence. Autocrats are equally represented in all age cohorts.

Support for democracy

A democratic society is characterized by citizens' support for fundamental democratic values and civil liberties. The greater the number of citizens who support these values solidly, the more deeply rooted is democracy in civil society.

Attitudes toward the national community

During the last few years, ethnic and nationalistic topics became more and more important issues in the former Soviet republics and in other eastern European countries. The connotations of "ethnos" or "nation" differ between the eastern and western hemispheres. In the Anglo-Saxon world, "nation" is defined as the aggregate of citizens of a state (this may also be true for other west European societies). In Russian and some other central and eastern European languages, "nation" is an ethnic concept. Here the question of the compatibility of democratic principles of civil society with "nationalism" becomes an important problem. Some political scientists, such as Kandel (1994) believe that democracy and this type of ethnic nationalism are incompatible, because the granting of civil rights would depend on ethnic characteristics. Others, such as Ernest Gellner (1983), on the other hand, understand "nationalism" as a viable strategy to tame ethnic rivalries and create a framework in which all ethnicities can meet as citizens, not just as members of different ethnic groups. This conceptualization would deny the possibility of the existence of "ethnic nationalism."

In order to determine how the respondents relate to their nation, they were asked to indicate their primary and secondary geographic reference, i.e. (1) locality of the town where one lives; (2) state or region of country where one lives; (3) one's nation; (4) one's continent; (5) the world as a whole.

The percentage of respondents naming Russia as first or second most important geographic reference has decreased from 67 percent in 1995 to 57 percent in 1999. In Ukraine and Belarus, this proportion remains almost stable.

Table 14.2 Proportion of respondents referring to own country in 1995 and 1999, %, Germany, Russia, Ukraine and Belarus

	1995	*1999*
Germany	55	72
Russia	67	57
Ukraine	55	58
Belarus	57	55

Table 14.3 Reference to own country, 1995, %, Russia

	Total	*Strong democrats*	*Weak democrats*	*Undecided*	*Autocrats*
Other reference	43	16	38	48	41
Own country	57	84	62	52	59

A total of 84 percent of strong democrats in Russia regard themselves as primarily belonging to their country, while this is true for only 62 percent of weak democrats and 59 percent of respondents with an autocratic orientation. Apparently, strong democrats are more inclined to identify themselves with their own country than weak democrats or autocrats. However, the significance of these findings should not be overestimated, since the absolute number of strong democrats in the Russian sample is very small.

In addition, respondents were asked to indicate how proud they are to belong to their own country, and whether they are willing to fight for their country. An index for the strength of the respondents' identification with his or her own national community was computed from the answers to these questions.

The respondents from all three former Soviet republics scored far higher with regard to the level of identification with the national community than respondents in the German sample. This is true for 1995 and 1999, although we observe a slight decrease in 1999. The smallest proportion of respondents identifying themselves with their national political community among the former Soviet republics was found in the Ukraine in 1999, when only 43 percent reached a high score of identification, while this was true for 52 percent in Russia and 61 percent in Belarus.

If we analyze the Russian sample with the categories of the democracy–autocracy index, no significant differences between strong democrats, weak democrats, undecided citizens and autocrats can be reported. However, an over-proportional percentage of autocrats (57 percent) identify strongly with their national political community.

Table 14.4 Identification with national political community, 1995 and 1999, %, Germany, Russia, Ukraine and Belarus

	Low		*Medium*		*High*	
	1995	*1999*	*1995*	*1999*	*1995*	*1999*
Germany	27	15	40	55	32	30
Russia	7	10	38	39	56	52
Ukraine	10	15	39	42	50	43
Belarus	4	9	31	31	65	61

Table 14.5 Level of identification with national political community, 1999, %, Russia

	Total	*Strong democrats*	*Weak democrats*	*Undecided*	*Autocrats*
Low	10	9	6	12	10
Medium	39	45	39	40	34
High	52	45	54	49	57

Interest in politics

People's interest in politics is one important indicator for the level of citizens' involvement in politics. The "political motivation index" was computed on the basis of the respondents' ratings of their interest in politics, the importance of politics in their lives and the frequency of political debates with their friends.

In Russia in 1995, only 14 percent, and in 1999 only 18 percent, of the respondents said that they were very interested in politics. In all three former Soviet republics, a plurality displayed a moderate level of interest. Compared to Germany, the relation between respondents with a high level of interest and respondents with a low level of interest are almost reversed: roughly one-third of all German respondents reported being very interested in politics, and 10 to 20 percent were not very interested, while a good one-third of the respondents belonged to the category "low level of interest in politics."

A more detailed analysis of the Russian sample shows that roughly one-third of the strong democrats reported being very interested in politics, while this is true for one-fifth of democrats and autocrats, and for only 15 percent of the undecided citizens. On the reverse, a proportionally high share of undecided citizens is not interested in politics (40 percent).

It should be noted that in the late 1980s and early 1990s all Russians talked politics. Almost every citizen followed the first sessions of the Congress of People's Deputies of the USSR on TV and/or participated in political actions. Political and economic strategies were debated in newspapers and magazines, at home and at work. Many people believed that

Table 14.6 Interest in politics, 1995 and 1999, %, Germany, Russia, Ukraine and Belarus

	Low		*Medium*		*High*	
	1995	*1999*	*1995*	*1999*	*1995*	*1999*
Germany	11	21	56	54	34	25
Russia	35	33	51	49	14	18
Ukraine	37	33	50	48	13	19
Belarus	25	31	54	54	21	16

Table 14.7 Interest in politics, 1999, %, Russia

	Total	*Strong democrats*	*Weak democrats*	*Undecided*	*Autocrats*
Low	33	22	24	40	31
Medium	49	48	55	46	48
High	18	29	22	15	21

these discussions would point to (and maybe even open) a pathway to fast and effective reforms – a kind of "philosopher's stone," which would help to solve all problems quickly and without pain. However, these times are long gone. The reality of the transformation process became evident for every group in Russian society. For a majority, it has resulted in an economic and social disaster. Thus, people's trust in a "miracle" has vanished and their political activity has turned into apathy and disappointment.

Current sociological studies show that Russian citizens do not consider political problems as most important. Today, politics occupies one of the least important places in their lives. Only 38 percent of Russian citizens state that politics occupies an important place in their lives. However, passive interest in politics remains on a rather high level: 67 percent get daily information about politics by the mass media; 17 percent watch TV, listen to the radio or read newspapers several times a week, while 7 percent do that once or twice a week and only 2.7 percent of Russians say that they are completely uninterested in media consumption. About 74 percent of the respondents discuss politics with their friends and 20 percent do it frequently.

These findings allow for two conclusions. First, Russian citizens are still interested in politics. A high share of the adult population watches or reads the news regularly. In addition, many respondents discuss politics at least occasionally with friends. However, a majority expresses higher levels of interest in family, friends, work and even religion. Second, under the current conditions, citizens do not believe in their ability to influence politics and they have lost their confidence in politics as an adequate measure to solve the problems of Russian society. Rather, politics is perceived as the (sometimes dirty) business of the political elite.

Civil responsibility and law abidingness

People's ideas of what is socially accepted and what is not shape their everyday behavior. Common values and norms are certainly not the only factors that influence social behavior but they are definitely very important. To determine the level of law abidingness among the respondents in the three former Soviet republics, the respondents were asked to evaluate whether a certain type of behavior can be regarded as (1) always justified, (10) never justified, or something in between for the following items: claiming government benefits to which you are not entitled; avoiding a fare on public transport; and cheating on taxes if you have chance.

A majority of the respondents in the former Soviet republics expressed a rather high level of law abidingness that does not differ too much from the levels expressed by German respondents. The Russian sample, in particular, shows a distribution that is similar to the West German sample, while only 48 percent of respondents in Belarus expressed a high level of law abidingness in 1999.

Table 14.8 Level of law-abidingness, 1995 and 1999, %, Germany, Russia, Ukraine and Belarus

	Low		Medium		High	
	1995	1999	1995	1999	1995	1999
Germany	5	6	20	21	75	74
Russia	7	4	25	22	68	73
Ukraine	10	8	27	29	63	63
Belarus	8	11	31	41	61	48

Table 14.9 Level of law-abidingness, 1999, %, Russia

	Total	Strong democrats	Weak democrats	Undecided	Autocrats
High	73	67	70	76	74
Medium	22	27	26	20	23
Low	4	5	4	4	3

If we analyze the Russian results in more detail, we find no significant differences with regard to the level of law abidingness between "strong democrats," "democrats," "undecided citizens" and "autocrats" in 1995, while in 1999 the share of "undecided citizens" exceeded the proportions of all other categories.

Active membership in voluntary associations

The survey illustrates the extremely low participation levels in the former Soviet republics. In 1995, more than 67 percent of the respondents were not a member of any voluntary organization. About 24 percent of the respondents reported being trade union members; however, only 3.6 percent of those participated actively. No more than 1.5 percent of the respondents were members of social and ecological organizations, art and cultural associations, youth or women clubs. Some 4 percent of the respondents were members of sports clubs. Moreover, only one in ten members participated actively in any voluntary organization.

Probably it is not only the stress of everyday life that prevents people from participation. It might also be the case that compulsory membership under the autocratic Soviet regime left bitter memories. In the USSR, even schoolchildren had to be members of various organizations and pay membership dues. Thus in central and eastern Europe the notion of being a member of an organization is perceived less as a matter of being part of an active civil society but rather of being forced to participate in socialist society.

Respondents were asked to indicate if they are an active member, an inactive member or not a member of the following types of organizations: political parties, labor unions, professional organizations, church or religious organizations, environmental organizations, charitable organizations, art, music or educational organizations, sport or recreational organization, or any other voluntary organization.

In the three former Soviet republics, the proportion of respondents who are members of any type of such organizations was highest in Belarus. However, it is still only a fraction of the share observed in Germany.

Rejection of violence

Citizens' attitudes toward violence as a legitimate means of political protest is important if we want to determine the character of the democracies in Russia, Ukraine and Belarus. Political protest and debate are vivid elements of a democratic regime and a civil society. However, the use of violence in political debates and struggles contradicts democratic ideals, since it denies the legitimacy of opposition and violates the physical integrity of the dissenter. The respondents were asked to indicate their readiness to reject or accept violence in rating their level of agreement with the following statement: "Using violence to pursue political goals is never justified."

After 1991, the socio-economic situation in Russia, Ukraine and Belarus deteriorated. In addition to poor economic performance and the dissolution of social networks, citizens of the ex-Soviet republics experienced a high degree of legal uncertainty. However, the overwhelming majority seems to believe that violence cannot be justified to achieve political goals

Table 14.10 Active membership in voluntary associations, 1995, %, Germany, Russia, Ukraine and Belarus

	1995
Germany	60
Russia	9
Ukraine	9
Belarus	15

Table 14.11 Legitimacy of violence, 1995, %, Germany, Russia, Ukraine and Belarus

	Disagree strongly	*Disagree*	*Agree*	*Agree strongly*
Germany	5	10	36	49
Russia	3	15	37	44
Ukraine	8	14	42	35
Belarus	5	12	33	50

and the distribution of shares between agreement and disagreement are very close to the West German sample.

Protest behavior

Participation in protest actions is an indicator for a persons' willingness to cooperate with others in expressing and achieving political goals. In this area, the respondents were asked to report actual and potential participation in different types of political protest behavior. Results were used to compute general levels of protest participation.

Altogether the general level of participation in the former Soviet republics is rather low; roughly three-quarters of the respondents reported low protest participation. Only 3 to 6 percent indicated a high level of actual or potential protest participation.

In 1995, 11 percent of the respondents in the Russian sample signed petitions, while another 30 percent indicated that they would be willing to do so. About 2.4 percent of the respondents participated in boycotts and 23 percent expressed their willingness to participate. A total of 22.5 percent participated in demonstrations and 54 percent indicated their readiness to participate; 1.5 percent participated in strikes and 17 percent were ready to join them; 0.6 percent participated in occupying buildings and enterprises and 8.4 percent were ready to follow them.

If we differentiate our findings for Russia according to the categories of the democracy–autocracy index, we find that strong democrats are more inclined to participate in political protest action than weak democrats,

Table 14.12 Protest behavior, 1995 and 1999, %, Germany, Russia, Ukraine and Belarus

	Low		*Medium*		*High*	
	1995	*1999*	*1995*	*1999*	*1995*	*1999*
Germany	15	15	33	35	52	50
Russia	73	71	24	25	3	4
Ukraine	74	70	23	24	3	6
Belarus	75	75	22	23	3	3

Table 14.13 Protest behavior, 1999, %, Russia

	Total	*Strong democrats*	*Weak democrats*	*Undecided*	*Autocrats*
Low	71	55	65	77	70
Medium	25	40	30	20	26
High	4	6	5	3	5

autocrats and undecided citizens. However, this tendency is not very pronounced, especially if we keep in mind that the absolute number of strong democrats in the Russian sample is very low.

Altogether, the hypothesis that citizens tend to delegate politics to politicians seems to be confirmed, although the level of confidence in government and governmental institutions is extremely low (see Table 14.20). A majority of citizens believe that voting is the only way to express their preferences. In addition, alienation from governmental authorities and political decision-making is a distinguishing feature of political life in Russia today. The comparatively high level of interest in politics might signify something different than in western European countries. If we bear in mind that all other characteristics of the nature of the Russian citizen seem to indicate that he or she is rather remote from politics, we might conclude that the comparatively high levels of interest they report are owed to a type of attention that is similar to an interest in a spectacle on stage. This would be a strong indicator that Russia is heading back to Tsarist times.

Support for democracy and rejection of autocracy

For a further exploration of the political culture of the three former Soviet republics, we analyze the respondents' attitudes toward democracy and autocracy. Although the two dimensions are statistically independent, it is debatable whether Russian citizens always and really make the distinction between democracy as an ideal, and democracy as it works in their own country. If they would refer to democracy as it works in their own country, this evaluation would not necessarily indicate an autocratic orientation of the individual since it remains an open question whether Russia, Ukraine and Belarus can be considered democratic regimes.

The index "attitudes towards democratic rule" was computed on the basis of the following two items: (1) the respondents' ratings of the desirability of "Having a democratic system (very good, fairly good, bad, very bad)" and (2) their evaluation of the statement "Democracy may have problems but it's better than any other form of government (strongly agree, agree, disagree, strongly disagree)."

It is noteworthy that attitudes of the Russian sample differ significantly from the other two former Soviet republics. In 1995, only half of the respondents expressed high levels of support for democracy in Russia, while this was true for three-quarters of the respondents in Ukraine and Belarus. This ratio remained unchanged as compared to 1999. The proportion of Russian respondents who supported democracy on a low level was more than twice as high as the respective share in Ukraine and Belarus. Finally, the percentage of Russian respondents expressing a moderate level of support exceeds the Ukrainian and Belarussian share by roughly 20 percent. From the former Soviet republics under consideration, the Russian population appears to be least convinced of democracy as an ideal form of government.

The index "attitudes towards autocratic rule" was computed on the basis of the respondents' ratings of the desirability of "Having a strong leader who does not have to bother with parliament and elections" or "Having the army rule" (both items: very good, fairly good, bad, very bad way of governing this country).

One should expect a reversed image when respondents were asked about their attitude toward autocratic modes of government. However, the discrepancy between Russia and the two other ex-Soviet republics disappeared when the respondents were asked to express their attitudes toward autocracy, especially in 1999. Roughly one-third of the respondents in the former Soviet republics reject autocratic modes of governance, more than half support autocracy in a moderate fashion while roughly one-fifth of the respondents are strongly in favor of an autocratic political regime. Thus, as compared to our western reference country, the share of respondents who disapprove of autocracy is disturbingly low. Something else is striking here: if we compare Table 14.14 and Table 14.15 we realize immediately that many respondents seem not to be aware of the fact that democracy and autocracy are two antagonistic concepts. In 1999, 82 percent of the Ukrainian respondents supported democracy on a rather high level. In the same year, only 27 percent clearly rejected autocracy. Apparently 55 percent of the strong supporters of democracy in Ukraine are simultaneously moder-

Table 14.14 Positive attitudes toward democratic rule, 1995 and 1999, %, Germany, Russia, Ukraine and Belarus

	Low		*Medium*		*High*	
	1995	*1999*	*1995*	*1999*	*1995*	*1999*
Germany	0	1	6	6	93	93
Russia	10	9	39	33	51	58
Ukraine	5	4	20	14	75	82
Belarus	2	2	23	13	75	85

Table 14.15 Positive attitudes toward autocratic rule, 1995 and 1999, %, Germany, Russia, Ukraine and Belarus

	Low		*Medium*		*High*	
	1995	*1999*	*1995*	*1999*	*1995*	*1999*
Germany	85	75	14	23	1	2
Russia	26	25	53	57	20	17
Ukraine	30	27	53	57	16	16
Belarus	29	35	54	46	17	19

ate or strong supporters of a strong leader and want the army to rule. This pattern repeats itself in all three countries under consideration. One possible explanation is that the relation between different elements of democracy and autocracy remain unclear for a majority of the respondents. Another piece of supportive evidence for this hypothesis can be the comparatively high proportion of respondents expressing an "undecided" or "centrist" position. It is difficult to think of a model that would fit these moderate supporters of both democracy and autocracy.

It is noteworthy that from the very beginning of the transformation, most Russians expected primarily prosperity and individual welfare from democracy, not civil liberties. An expected economic performance on the level of western democracies was a strong incentive for citizens to prefer democracy to a socialist system that had proven to be an economic failure. However, they experienced continuous recession and deterioration of individual living standards during the last decade. Since democracy did not generate the expected economic returns, citizens are disappointed and somehow disoriented. Obviously, for many citizens both regimes were unable to deliver either economic prosperity or civil liberties. This might explain why democracy and autocracy are not understood as alternatives. If the interviewers had offered a third possible regime alternative, yet unknown and not experienced by the respondents, they would have probably supported this third political model overwhelmingly. However, this experience is a distinctive feature not only in the former Soviet republics. The ideal of a "consumer democracy" can also be found in many other central and eastern European countries.

Support for the current political regime

The institutional design of a political community defines "the rules of the game" and the standards of governance. In addition to different patterns of institutional and constitutional designs, democratic communities may vary with regard to the extent they realized the democratic promise. The perceived legitimacy of a government and of the decision-making procedures allows us to asses the "quality" of a specific democratic regime. Thus citizens may support the abstract concept of democracy and at the same time criticize the specific features of the government of their country (Fuchs and Klingemann 2000). These citizens may be called "critical democrats" (Klingemann 1999). They do not oppose democracy as an ideal. On the contrary, they may be well aware of the potential of democratic government as demonstrated in other countries where democracy functions better to solve problems of everyday life. Therefore a low level of support for the current regime might indicate that the current regime is defective and not its citizens.

The level of support for the current political regime in Russia, Ukraine and Belarus was determined by a rating scale summarized below.

Table 14.16 Generalized support for the current political regime, 1995 and 1999, %, Germany, Russia, Ukraine and Belarus

	Low		Medium		High	
	1995	1999	1995	1999	1995	1999
Germany	44	43	29	28	26	28
Russia	82	84	14	14	4	3
Ukraine	71	69	22	24	7	7
Belarus	67	55	27	28	6	18

The lowest levels of support for the current political regime were found in Russia (Table 14.16), while the level of support for the past Soviet system was rather high (Table 14.17). In Belarus, the share of strong supporters of the Lukashenko regime tripled from 1995 to 1999, while in Ukraine and Russia the proportions remained roughly the same.

The level of support for the preceding Soviet regime was determined on the basis of the respondents' rating of the political system as it was ten years ago.

Half of the Russian respondents and one-third of the respondents in Ukraine and Belarus expressed a kind of "nostalgia" with the past. This may be explained by a desire of the less adaptive part of the populace to get rid of individual responsibility for one's own life. While such people tend to associate the socialist regime with a period of "stagnation," this regime, nevertheless, provided limited but guaranteed welfare. To some extent, supporters of the nationalistic parties seem to have a similar mind-set.

Analyzing levels of support by the democracy–autocracy index for the Russian sample, it becomes apparent again that even strong democrats do

Table 14.17 Generalized support for Soviet rule, 1995 and 1999, %, Russia, Ukraine and Belarus

	1995	1999
Russia	49	43
Ukraine	35	36
Belarus	38	36

Table 14.18 Support for the current regime, 1999, %, Russia

	Total	Strong democrats	Weak democrats	Undecided	Autocrats
Low	84	72	77	87	91
Medium	14	21	20	11	9
High	3	7	4	2	0

Table 14.19 Support for Soviet rule, 1999, %, Russia

	Total	Strong democrats	Weak democrats	Undecided	Autocrats
Low	28	70	43	20	18
Medium	29	14	31	29	25
High	43	16	26	51	58

not support the current regime. Russian political reality seems to generate dissatisfaction no matter whether one supports a democratic or an autocratic mode of government.

Unsurprisingly strong democrats disapprove of Soviet rule, while more than half of the respondents belonging to the category of "autocrats" and half of the "undecided citizens" rated the old system as having been good or very good. These findings corroborate the assumption that the rejection of the current regime by strong democrats does not indicate that these respondents covertly indulge in nostalgia for autocratic modes of governance. Rather, they rate both the current political regime *and* Soviet rule as non-democratic.

Confidence in governmental institutions

Levels of trust in the new institutions of democratic government might be interpreted as indicators for the extent to which citizens feel represented and served fairly by these institutions. However, low levels of trust do not necessarily indicate that these new institutions have a real problem. It might also be the case that low levels of trust are caused by the novelty of these institutions. Citizens must get acquainted with them and collect some experiences before they can develop trust and confidence. The respondents were asked to indicate their level of confidence in the parliament, the government and political parties.

Prima facie, the low level of trust in traditional state and public institutions of Russian citizens seems to resemble a trend in western post-industrial societies. However, this might be only a coincidence. Post-industrial and Russian alienation from governmental institutions are based on entirely different processes. While the former trend signifies

Table 14.20 Confidence in governmental institutions, 1995, %, Germany, Russia, Ukraine and Belarus

	Low	Medium	High
Germany	27	64	10
Russia	45	47	9
Ukraine	33	49	18
Belarus	37	50	13

increasing citizens' self-reliability and a high level of cultural individualism, the latter reflects a deep split between the political elite and ordinary citizen. This does not necessarily indicate deeply rooted non-democratic political values and orientations in Russia. Instead it may reflect the serious disappointment and indifference in Russian public opinion with regard to politics in general and the individuals' possibilities of participation in a democratic community. In addition, we observe a "re-privatization" of life after decades of collectivism and the denial of an individual life course under Soviet rule. Although this development definitely belongs to the positive features of the transition, citizens tend to perceive private interests as opposed to governmental, institutional and societal interests. As a consequence this situation results in a type of "grab and run" capitalism and does not contribute to the rule of law and the functioning of liberal democracy.

Values of the community

Ethics of individual achievement

Private property and private business ownership, individual self-expression and civil liberties are achievements of the transformation in Russia. New economic realities create new incentives and opportunity structures for citizens as employees as well as employers. However, in Russia a "new ethic of work and individual achievement" is hard to detect. High unemployment rates (13–14 percent), comparatively low wages and a decrease in real income are the more important factors that structure labor market participation.

In addition, the Russian economy today has at least three specific characteristics:

1 Long delays in wage payment (up to several months). These delays will not be compensated by public financial support because an employee who is not paid by the enterprise is not entitled to claim unemployment benefits.
2 An extremely low level of geographic mobility which is a consequence of the vast territory of Russia and the low income levels that do not allow proper transportation. Thus, people can simply not afford to move to other regions with better job opportunities.
3 Extremely weak trade unions. Thus, Russian employees lack an effective lobby that could push through their interests.

Support of an ethic of individual achievement was measured by the following question: "Now I'd like you to tell me your views on various issues. How would you place your views on this scale? '1' means you agree completely with the statement on the left; '10' means you agree completely with the statement on the right; and if your views fall somewhere in between, you can choose any number in between."

1   "The government should take more responsibility to ensure that everyone is provided for" vs. "People should take more responsibility to provide for themselves."
2   "Incomes should be made more equal" vs. "We need larger income differences as incentives for individual effort."

The index "ethics of individual achievement" was computed on the basis of the respondents' ranking of their agreement or disagreement with the two statements mentioned above.

Roughly half of the respondents express a moderate position with regard to the ethics of individual achievement. Neither a tendency toward a "Manchester capitalism" attitude nor a clear preference for a paternalistic system could be observed. However, in 1999 the proportion of respondents low on support for an ethic of individual achievement increased both in Russia and Ukraine. About 92 percent of the respondents believe that the government should guarantee the basic needs of the populace; 56 percent favor a leveling of income differences.

Ethics of individual competition

To complete the picture, the respondents were asked to indicate their agreement or disagreement with the following items. Respondents were first asked to respond to the statements: "Competition is good; it stimulates people to work hard and develop new ideas" versus "Competition is harmful; it brings out the worst in people," and "In the long run, hard work usually brings a better life" versus "Hard work doesn't generally bring success – it's more a matter of luck and connections." Responses have been summarized in an index of ethics of individual competition.

Again, a moderate position is favored by almost half of the respondents from the former Soviet republics. Another 46 percent perceived competition to be a very good thing and only 8 percent disapproved of competi-

Table 14.21 Ethics of individual achievement, 1995 and 1999, %, Germany, Russia, Ukraine and Belarus

	Low		Medium		High	
	1995	*1999*	*1995*	*1999*	*1995*	*1999*
	25	–	54	–	20	–
Russia	31	36	51	50	18	14
Ukraine	34	44	50	43	17	13
Belarus	29	19	55	55	17	26

Table 14.22 Ethics of individual competition, 1995, % Germany, Russia, Ukraine and Belarus

	Low	Medium	High
Germany	5	60	35
Russia	8	47	46
Ukraine	9	46	45
Belarus	6	41	52

tion in general. In addition, almost 81 percent of the respondents thought that the place of any person in society should be determined by his or her services to the society. Despite the high or moderate levels of support for an ethic of individual achievement and competition, the importance of work still follows the importance of the family in the hierarchy of traditional values.

However, in 1995, 83 percent of the respondents rank work as very important in their lives. Roughly half of the respondents believed that the "job should always be in the first place, even if it takes most of the free time" and only 26 percent of the respondents did not agree with this statement. Some 61 percent were of the opinion that "getting money for doing nothing is humiliation." Moreover, 82 percent believed that a "person without work becomes lazy"; another 54 percent of the respondents were convinced that "working is people's public duty."

The most important aspect of work seems to be material well-being – almost 90 percent of the respondents believe that "work should be a highly-paid one." Another 69 percent say that work "should be guaranteed." Apparently other factors are less important: "not very tense work" (17 percent); "good career opportunities" (29 percent); "long vacations and sufficient number of free days" (29 percent), or "working at a convenient time" (40 percent). However, 69 percent of the respondents would prefer an "interesting job," while 55 percent think "good colleagues" are very important. Roughly 50 percent also would like to find "a job adequate to their opportunities." With regard to the level of job satisfaction almost 60 percent of the respondents state that they were rather satisfied, while another 14 percent were very satisfied with their jobs.

Given the current situation it is hard to believe that a majority of Russian citizens are satisfied with their jobs. Probably the positive statements result from a fear of losing the job rather than from much happiness at work.

Solidarity with the poor

Finally the respondents were asked to indicate their level of solidarity with the poor people in their country. They were first asked to express which of the two following reasons for being poor comes closest to their views:

"People are poor because of laziness and lack of will power" versus "People are poor because society treats them unfairly." Second, the respondents were asked whether they believe that "most poor people in this country have a chance to escape from poverty," or if "there is very little chance of escaping poverty." Third, they were asked to rate government action with regard to the poor and to indicate if they think what "government is doing for people in poverty in this country is about the right amount or too much, or too little." The index "solidarity with the poor" was computed on the basis of the respondents' answers to these questions.

The respondents indicate a comparatively high level of solidarity with the poor. It might be the case that this is less an expression of empathy, but rather an understanding of how fast virtually anyone and everyone can become a victim of the poverty trap, including the respondents themselves.

Trust in others

Trust in the fellow citizen is one important ingredient of a functioning civil society. High levels of trust among citizens reduce transaction costs and allow for a free exchange of information and public goods, while low levels might easily foster a type of "amoral familialism," that is, a society in which the only reliable ties are of primordial nature and in which collective goods beyond the family deteriorate.

Roughly three-quarters of the respondents from the three former Soviet republics believe in 1995 that "you can't be too careful with others."

Table 14.23 Solidarity with the poor, 1995, %, Germany, Russia, Ukraine and Belarus

	Low	Medium	High
Germany	9	9	82
Russia	3	6	91
Ukraine	2	7	91
Belarus	4	9	86

Table 14.24 Trust in others, 1995 and 1999, %, Germany, Russia, Ukraine and Belarus

	Trust		No trust	
	1995	1999	1995	1999
Germany	40	36	60	64
Russia	23	23	77	77
Ukraine	29	26	71	74
Belarus	23	38	77	62

This proportion remains constant in Russia, while it increases in Ukraine by 3 percentage points and decreases in Belarus by 15 percentage points. Apparently the three countries took very different courses in the second half of the decade with regard to the inner structure of civil society.

A total of 77 percent of the Russian respondents believe that they "have to be very cautious in relations with other people," while only 23 percent state that they "are ready to trust in the majority of people." Together with low levels of trust in governmental institutions, these findings support the hypothesis of a "grab and run" mentality that nurtures anarchy and social alienation instead of civil liberties. Interestingly, strong democrats are proportionally over-represented among respondents who do not trust their fellow citizens.

Tolerance

Citizens' attitudes toward minorities and different lifestyles are of critical importance for determining the state of a democratic community. The transformation toward a liberal and democratic society demands support of a vivid socio-cultural and political pluralism. However, tolerance, like trust, cannot be implemented from above, and it is hard to determine which institutional and legislative settings within the framework of a democracy might foster these goods. Putnam (1993) suggests that in order to become tolerant, civil society also has to rely on resources other than the institutional design of a given polity. To measure social tolerance or acceptance of deviant behavior, respondents were asked to indicate, on a ten-point scale, whether they believe that homosexuality, prostitution,

Table 14.25 Trust in others, 1999, %, Russia

	Total	*Strong democrats*	*Weak democrats*	*Undecided*	*Autocrats*
No trust	77	83	74	79	74
Trust	23	17	26	21	26

Table 14.26 Level of acceptance of deviant behavior, 1995 and 1999, %, Germany, Russia, Ukraine and Belarus

	Low		*Medium*		*High*	
	1995	*1999*	*1995*	*1999*	*1995*	*1999*
Germany	19	19	36	37	46	45
Russia	65	73	32	24	4	3
Ukraine	66	77	30	19	4	4
Belarus	62	58	33	31	5	11

abortion or divorce can "always be justified" or can "never be justified" (or something in between).

The respondents in the former Soviet republics show an alarmingly low level of tolerance toward minorities and deviant behavior. This is true for 1995 and 1999, and it is also true for those identified as "strong democrats" (Table 14.27). The acceptance of a plurality of lifestyles and individual decisions does not seem to be a prominent ingredient of democratic beliefs in Russia, Ukraine and Belarus. These findings again indicate that the respondents are not fully aware of the nature of core elements of the concept of liberal democracy.

If we analyze the Russian sample in more detail, we observe an increasing level of acceptance of deviant behavior among the more democratically minded. However, it is discouraging that even a majority of strong democrats does not tolerate different lifestyles or socially deviant behavior. Barely 13 percent express a high level of tolerance.

Conclusion

Of the countries surveyed, Russia occupies the last position with regard to public support for democratic attitudes. This is not only true if we compare Russia with the other two former Soviet republics, Ukraine and Belarus, but also to all other central and east European countries studied in this book. Russia hosts the highest proportion of autocrats and the lowest proportion of strong democrats. In addition, even the strong democrats do not seem to fully understand the nature of liberal democracy. The core elements of the concept and their interrelationships tend to remain unclear. This shows in a relatively low level of constraint between these core elements characteristic of liberal democracy. Apparently Russian citizens favor some kind of "consumer democracy," a political regime that provides for individual welfare and prosperity while political virtues of democracy, such as civil liberties, are perceived as needless ornaments. Since the economic success of the Soviet regime was questionable at best, the way back is no real alternative and the current widespread dissatisfaction with democracy as it works in Russia and its economic achievements results in incoherent and contradictory attitudes.

It is striking that the other two former Soviet republics we have compared to Russia score at least partly higher as far as citizen support of

Table 14.27 Level of acceptance of deviant behavior, 1999, %, Russia

	Total	Strong democrats	Weak democrats	Undecided	Autocrats
Low	73	49	69	77	76
Medium	24	38	27	20	22
High	3	13	4	2	2

democratic attitudes is concerned. Since Russia was the heartland of Soviet socialism, the region is possibly more severely affected by the cultural heritage of Soviet ideology than any other country in this hemisphere. In addition, it might be the case that the Russian population benefited more from the old regime than any other Soviet republics and therefore was the biggest loser in terms of social welfare after 1990.

Western political scientists, who understood the radical political changes in the countries of central and east Europe and in the former USSR during the 1980s and 1990s as a triumph of democracy, soon gave up their initial optimism. They revised their positions and realized that the collapse of communism does not necessarily lead to new democracies. This "could be only one of many possible results brought to life by the fall of any authoritarian regime" (Klingemann and Hofferbert 2000). This idea also became important among eastern European researchers. Attila Agh, for example, pointed out that possible variants of the post-communist transformation include "moving back to the past regime" and maybe even an "establishment of a kind of new type of authoritarian rule" (Agh 1993). According to his analysis, the latter possibility is the most plausible. His point of view may be validated sooner than he himself initially believed, since many citizens in the former Soviet republics regard the evils of the current social and political situation in Russia as a distinctive feature of the present "democratic" regime. Guillermo O'Donnell and Philipp Schmitter describe the possible result of this public sentiment as follows: "societies move from certain authoritarian regimes to something 'uncertain' and unknown. This 'uncertain' may become a political democracy or turn into restoration of new and, most probably, more cruel form of authoritarian regime" (O'Donnell 1994).

Thus it is difficult to contradict Andrew Melville's argument that

> democracy is perceived, currently, by the Russian population not in the spirit of mass political participation and ability to influence, constantly, the process of decision-making, but like an ability to elect leaders on regular basis, while these leaders don't have any intention to accept the pressure of their voters.
>
> (Melville 1998)

In addition, Russian citizens' understanding of freedom was traditionally less connected to civil liberties than to the possibility of realizing individual preferences outside an institutional and legislative framework. This rather anarchic type of freedom has become a reality in some sectors of modern Russian society. However problematic this may be, it may also be considered as one possibility for the development of a democratic regime if these anarchic elements are channeled by legislative and executive measures. A stable and robust institutional framework may help to achieve this goal as the new Russian mentality is still in a state of flux. After the

World Values Surveys were conducted, new developments in Russia may lead to a radical change of citizens' value systems. Russian society, which had been waiting for the end of the Yeltsin era, has now elected a quite different government. Whether democracy and civil society will now find more support in Russia depends on the question of whether the current government will employ democratic or autocratic measures to solve the most pressing problems in Russia. Judging from Putin's actions, in particular with regard to his Chechen policies, let us remain pessimistic with regard to a fast transition toward democracy.

Note

1 The higher percentage of "autocrats" in Russia in comparison with the other former Soviet republics (Table 14.1) might be explained by the respondents' perception of political and social realities in Russia. Russian mass media often interpret the situation as a "power vacuum," while in Ukraine and Belarus political regimes were described as more or less authoritarian. In public opinion, most of the difficulties of the transformation period in the post-communist countries were associated with the existing political regimes. In Russia, where a strong and accountable political force was not identifiable for the ordinary citizen, this might have encouraged a higher level of support for "autocratic" values.

References

Agh, A. (1993) "The Comparative Revolution and the Transition in Central and Southern Europe," *Journal of Theoretical Politics* 5, 2.

Dahl, R. (1971) *Polyarchy: Participation and Opposition*, New Haven: Yale University Press.

Fuchs, D. and Klingemann, H. (2000) "A Comparison of Democratic Communities: American Exceptionalism and European Etatism," paper presented at *Rethinking Democracy in the New Millennium*, University of Houston, Houston, Texas, 17–20 February.

Gellner, E. (1983) *Nations and Nationalism*, Oxford: Blackwell.

Kandel, P. (1994) "Nationalism and Problems of Modernization in Post-Totalitarian World," *Polis*, 6.

Katz, R.S. (1997) *Democracy and Elections*, Oxford: Oxford University Press.

Keane, J. (1994) "Nations, Nationalism & Citizens in Europe," *International Social Science Journal* 46, 2.

Klingemann, H. (1999) "Mapping Political Support in the 1990s: a Global Analysis," Norris, Pippa (ed.) *Critical Citizens: Global Support for Democratic Government*, Oxford: Oxford University Press. Klingemann, H. and Hofferbert, R. (2000) "The Capacity of New Party Systems to Channel Discontent," Klingemann, H. and Neidhardt, F. (eds) *Zur Zukunft der Demokratie*, Berlin: edition sigma.

Melville, A. (1998) "Political Values and Orientations and Political Institutions," in Shevtsova, L. (ed.) *Political Russia*, Moscow: Carnegie Moscow Center.

O'Donnell, G. (1994) "Delegative Democracy," *Journal of Democracy* 5, 1.

Putnam, R.D. (with Robert Leonardi and Raffaella Y. Nanetti) (1993) *Making Democracy Work: Civic Traditions in Modern Italy*, Princeton: Princeton University Press.

Bibliography

Abisala, A., Alisauskiene, R. and Dobryninas, A. (1998) "Criminality and Process of democratization in Lithuania," Vilnius: Baltic Surveys; GALLUP.

Agh, A. (1993) "The Comparative Revolution and the Transition in Central and Southern Europe," *Journal of Theoretical Politics* 5, 2.

Agh, A. (1998) *The Politics of Central Europe*, London: Sage Publications.

Almond, G.A. (1980) "The Intellectual History of the Civic Culture Concept," in Almond, G.A. and Verba, S. (eds) *The Civic Culture Revisited*, Boston: Little, Brown and Company.

Almond, G.A. and Verba, S. (1963) *The Civic Culture*, Princeton: Princeton University Press.

Anderson, B.A., Silver, B.D., Titma, M. and Ponarin, E.D. (1996) "Estonian and Russian Communities: Ethnic and Language Relations. Estonia's Transition from State Socialism," in Titma, M., Silver, B.D. and Anderson, B.A. (eds) *Nationalities and Society on the Eve of Independence*. Special Issue of *International Journal of Sociology* 26, 2.

Andorka, R., Kolosi, T., Rose, R. and Vukovich, G. (eds) (1999) *A Society Transformed: Hungary in Time–Space Perspective*, Budapest: CEU Press.

Bădescu, G. (1999) "Miza politică a încrederii," *Sociologie româneasca*, New series 2.

Bădescu, G. (2003) "Încredere și democrație în țările foste comuniste," in Pop, Lucian (ed.) *Valori ale tranziției: O perspectiva empirică*, Iași: Polirom.

Barber, B.R. (1984) *Strong Democracy: Participatory Politics For a New Age*, Berkeley: University of California Press.

Bardi, A. and Schwarz, S. (1996) "Relations Among Socio-political Values in Eastern Europe: Effects of the Communist Experience?," *Political Psychology* 17, 3.

Barnes, S.H. and Simon, J. (eds) (1998) *Postcommunist Citizen*, Budapest: Erasmus Foundation and IPS of HAS.

Berend, I. (1996) *Central and Eastern Europe 1944–1993: Detour from the Periphery to the Periphery*, Cambridge: Cambridge University Press.

Berglund, S. and Aarebrot, F. (1997) *The Political History of Eastern Europe in the 20th Century: The Struggle Between Democracy and Dictatorship*, Cheltenham: Edward Elgar.

Berry, C.J. (1989) *The Idea of a Democratic Community*, New York: St. Martin's Press.

Blaga, L. (1943) "The Permanence of Prehistory," in *Saeculum* 9–10, quoted in Chimet, I. (1991) *Dreptul la memorie*, vol. IV, Bucuresti: Albatros.

Bozóki, A. (1999) "Democracy in Hungary, 1990–1997," in Kaldor, M. and Vejvoda, I. (eds) *Democratization in Central and Eastern Europe*, London: Frances Pinter.

Bozóki, A., Körösényi, A. and Schöpflin, G. (eds) (1992) *Post-Communist Transition: Emerging Pluralism in Hungary*, London: Frances Pinter.

Braudel, F. (1987) *Grammaire des Civilisations*, Paris: Arthaud – Flammarion.

Breakwell, G.M. and Lyons, E. (eds) (1996) *Changing European Identities: Social Psychology Analysis of Social Change*, Cornwall: Butterworth-Heinemann.

Brokl, L. (1997) "Pluralitní demokracie nebo neokorporativismus," in Brokl, L. (ed.) *Reprezentace zájmů v politickém systému České republiky*, Prague: SLON.

Brokl, L., Seidlová, A., Bečvář, J. and Rakušanová, P. (1999) *Postoje Československých občanůk demokracii v roce 1968*, Working Papers 99: 8, Prague: Institute of Sociology, CAS.

Bruszt, L. (1990) "1989: the negotiated revolution in Hungary," *Social Research* 5, 2.

Bunce, V. (1999) "The Political Economy of Postsocialism," *Slavic Review* 58, 4.

Bútorová, Z. (ed.) (1998) *Democracy and Discontent in Slovakia: a Public Opinion Profile of a Country in Transition*, Bratislava: IVO.

Carpenter, M. (1997) "Slovakia and the Triumph of Nationalist Populism," *Communist and Post-Communist Studies* 30, 2.

Central and Eastern Eurobarometer (1998) No. 8, Fessel + GfK Austria: Politische Kultur.

Chapman, J.W. and Shapiro, I. (eds) (1993) *Democratic Community. Nomos No. XXXV*, New York: New York University Press.

Chovanec, J. (1994) *Historické a štátoprávne korene samostatnosti Slovenskej republiky*, Bratislava: Procom.

Citizenship Statistics (1997) *Estonia Today*, Foreign Ministry's Information and fact sheet series. Online, available at: www.vm.ee/eng/estoday/1997/09cits1.html.

Conradt, D.P. (1980) "Changing German Political Culture," in Almond, G. and Verba, S. (eds) *The Civic Culture Revisited*, Newbury Park: Sage.

Crampton, R.J. (1995) *Eastern Europe in the 20th Century*, London: Routledge.

Dahl, R. (1971) *Polyarchy: Participation and Opposition*, New Haven: Yale University Press.

Dahl, R. (1989) *Democracy and its Critics*, New Haven: Yale University Press.

Dakova, V., Dreossi, B., Hyatt, J. and Socolovschi, A. (2000) *Review of the Romanian NGO Sector: Strengthening Donor Strategies*, report commissioned by Charles Stewart Mott Foundation and Charity Know How (CAF).

Dawisha, K. and Parrott, B. (eds) (1997) *The Consolidation of Democracy in East-Central Europe*, vol. 1, Cambridge: Cambridge University Press.

Derleth, W.J. (2000) *The Transition in Central and Eastern European Politics*, Upper Saddle River, New Jersey: Prentice Hall.

Diamond, L. (1999) *Developing Democracy*, Baltimore: the Johns Hopkins University Press.

Dreyfus, M., Lew, R., Interflom, C.S., Wolikow, S., Pennetier, C., Pudal, B. and Groppo, B. (2000) *Le Siècle des communismes*, Paris: Les Editions de l'Atelier.

Dorotková, J. (1998) "Slovak Brothers Torn Apart by Politics," *The Slovak Spectator* 4, 2.

Drobizheva, L. (2001) "Ethnicity in Contemporary Russia: Ethnopolicy and Praxis," Yadov, V. (ed.) *Russia: Society in Transition* Moscow: Kanon-Press-C.

Ďurica, M. (1996) *Dejiny Slovenska a Slovákov*, Bratislava, SPN.

Ekiert, G. and Hanson, S.E. (eds) (2003) *Capitalism and Democracy in Central Eastern Europe: Assessing the Legacy of Communist Rule*, Cambridge: Cambridge University Press.

Etzioni, A. (1993) *The Spirit of Community: the Reinvention of American Society*, New York: Touchstone, Simon & Schuster.

Etzioni, A. (1996) *The New Golden Rule: Community and Morality in a Democratic Society*, New York: Basic Books.

Feldman, S. (1983) "Structure and Consistency in Public Opinion: the Role of Core Beliefs and Values," *American Political Science Review* 32, 2.

Ferree, M.M., Gamson, W.A., Gerhards, G. and Rucht, D. (2000) *Collective Actors and the Public Sphere. Abortion Discourse in the U.S. and Germany*, Cambridge: Cambridge University Press.

Fischer, E.M. (ed.) (1996) *Establishing Democracies*, Boulder: Westview.

Fish, M.S. (1999) "The End of Mečiarism: a Vladimír Mečiar Retrospective," *East European Constitutional Review* 8, 1/2.

Fuchs, D. (1999) "The Democratic Culture of Unified Germany," in Norris, P. (ed.) *Critical Citizens: Global Support of Democratic Governance*, Oxford: Oxford University Press.

Fuchs, D. (1999) "Soziale Integration und politische Institutionen in modernen Gesellschaften," in Friedrichs, J. and Jagodzinski, W. (eds) *Soziale Integration: Sonderheft 39 der Kölner Zeitschrift für Soziologie und Sozialpsychologie*, Opladen: Westdeutscher Verlag.

Fuchs, D. (2000) "Die demokratische Gemeinschaft in den USA und in Deutschland," in Gerhards, J. (ed.) *Die Vermessung kultureller Unterschiede: USA und Deutschland im Vergleich*, Opladen: Westdeutscher Verlag.

Fuchs, D. and Klingemann, H. (2000) "A Comparison of Democratic Communities: American Exceptionalism and European Etatism," paper presented at *Rethinking Democracy in the New Millennium*, Texas: University of Houston, 17–20 February.

Fuchs, D. and Klingemann, H. (eds) (2000) *Citizens and the State*, Oxford: Oxford University Press.

Fuchs, D. and Klingemann, H. (2000) "Eastward Enlargement of the European Union and the Identity of Europe," *West European Politics* 25, 2.

Fuchs, D. and Roller, E. (1998) "Cultural conditions of the Transition to Liberal Democracy" in Barnes, S.H. and Simon, J. (eds) *The Postcommunist Citizen*, European Studies Series of the Hungarian Political Science Association and the Institute for Political Sciences of the Hungarian Academy of Sciences, Budapest: Erasmus Foundation and Hungarian Academy of Sciences.

Fuchs, D. and Roller, E. (1998) "Cultural Conditions of Transition to Liberal Democracies in Central and Eastern Europe," in Barnes, S.H. and Simon, J. (eds) *The Postcommunist Citizen*, Budapest: Erasmus Foundation and Hungarian Academy of Sciences.

Fuchs, D., Gerhards, J. and Roller, E. (1993) "Wir und die anderen: Ethnozentrismus in den zwölf Ländern der europäischen Gemeinschaft," *Kölner Zeitschrift für Soziologie und Sozialpsychologie* 45.

Fukuyama, F. (1999) *The Great Disruption: Human Nature and the Reconstitution of Social Order*, New York: Free Press.

Gawdiak, I. (1989) *Czechoslovakia – a Country Study*, Washington, DC: United States Government Printing Office.

Gassmann, F. (2000) *Who and Where are Poor in Latvia*, Riga: Ministry of Welfare of the Republic of Latvia; UNDP.

Geertz, C. (1973) *The Interpretation of Cultures*, New York: Basic Books.

Gellner, E. (1983) *Nations and Nationalism*, Oxford: Blackwell.

Gelman, V. (2001) "Post-Soviet Transitions and Democratization: Towards Theory-Building," paper presented at the 29th European Consortium of Political Research Joint Session of Workshops, Grenoble, 6–11 April.

Gerhards, J. (1993) "Westeuropäische Integration und die Schwierigkeiten der Entstehung einer europäischen Öffentlichkeit," *Zeitschrift für Soziologie* 22.

Ghețău, V. (1997) "Evoluția fertilității în România: De la transversal la longitudinal," *Bibliotheca Demographica No. 5/1997*, Bucharest: Romanian Academy.

Global Report on Slovakia, Bratislava: Institute for Public Affairs (1996, 1997, 1998).

Greif, A. (1994) "Cultural Beliefs and the Organization of Society: a Historical and Theoretical Reflections on Collectivist and Individualist Societies," *Journal of Political Economy* 102, 5.

Greskovits, B. (1997) *The Political Economy of Protest and Patience*, Budapest: Central European University.

Grimm, D. (1995) "Does Europe Need a Constitution?," *European Law Journal* 1.

Haerpfer, C.W. (2002) *Democracy and Enlargement in Post-Communist Europe: the Democratisation of the General Public in Fifteen Central and Eastern European countries, 1991–1998*, London: Routledge.

Hansen, M.H. (1991) *The Athenian Democracy in the Age of Demosthene:. Structure, Principles and Ideology*, Oxford: Blackwell.

Havel, V. (1989) *Dálkový výslech*, Prague: Melantrich.

Havel, V. (1989) *In Various Directions: Essays and Articles, 1983–1989*, Scheinfeld: Schwarzenberg.

Hofstede, G. with Arrindell, W. (1998) *Masculinity and Femininity: the Taboo Dimension of National Cultures*, Thousand Oaks, CA: Sage Publications.

Holmes, L. (1997) *Post Communism: an Introduction*, Oxford: Polity Press.

Huntington, S.P. (1956) *Political Order in Changing Societies*, New Haven: Yale University Press.

Huntington, S.P. (1991) *The Third Wave: Democratization in the Late Twentieth Century*, Norman: University of Oklahoma Press.

Huntington, S.P. (1993) "The Clash of Civilizations," *Foreign Affairs* 72, 3.

Huntington, S.P. (1996) *The Clash of Civilizations and the Remaking of World Order*, New York: Simon and Schuster.

Inglehart, R. (1990) *Culture Shift in Advanced Industrial Society*, Princeton: Princeton University Press.

Inglehart, R. (1997) *Modernization and Postmodernization: Cultural, Economic, and Political Change in 43 Societies*, Princeton: Princeton University Press.

Inglehart, R. (1998) "Clash of Civilizations or Global Cultural Modernization? Empirical Evidence from 61 Societies," paper presented at the 1998 meeting of the International Sociological Association, Montreal, 27–31 August.

Inglehart, R. (2000) "Globalization and Postmodern Values," *The Washington Quarterly* 23, 1, 215–28.

Inglehart, R. (2003) "How Solid is Mass Support for Democracy – and How Can We Measure It?," *Political Science and Politics* 36, 1.

Inglehart, R. and Baker, W. (2000) "Modernization, Cultural Change and the Persistence of Traditional Values," *American Sociological Review* 65, 1.

Inglehart, R. and Catterberg, G. (2003) "Trends in Political Action: the Developmental Trend and the Post-Honeymoon Decline," *International Journal of Comparative Sociology* 44, 1.

Inglehart, R. and Welzel, C. (2005) *Modernization, Cultural Change and Democracy: The Human Development Sequence*, New York: Cambridge University Press.

Janos, A. (1993) "Modernization and Decay in Historical Perspective: the Case of Romania," in Jowitt, K. (ed.) *Social Change in Romania, 1860–1940*, Berkeley: University of California.

Jowitt, K. (1992) *New World Disorder: The Leninist Extinction*, Berkeley: University of California Press.

Jowitt, K. (1993) *Social Change in Romania, 1860–1940*, Berkeley: University of California.

Jowitt, K. (1996) "The New World Disorder," in Diamond, L. and Plattner, M. (eds) *The Global Resurgence of Democracy*, Baltimore: The Johns Hopkins Press.

Kaldor, M. and Vejvoda, I. (1997) "Democratization in Central and East European Countries," *International Affairs* 73, 1.

Kalinova, E. and Baeva, I. (2001) *Bulgarskite prehodi 1939–2001*, Sofia, Ed. Paradigma.

Kandel, P. (1994) "Nationalism and Problems of Modernization in Post-Totalitarian World," *Polis* 6.

Kaplan, C. (1994) "Estonia: a Plural Society on the Road to Independence," in Bremmer, I. and Taras, R. (eds) *Nation and Politics in the Soviet Successor States*, Cambridge: Cambridge University Press.

Kaplan, R.D. (1994) *Balkan Ghosts: a Journey Through History*, New York: St. Martin's Press.

Keane, J. (1994) "Nations, Nationalism & Citizens in Europe," *International Social Science Journal* 46, 2.

Kennan, G.F. (1996) *At a Century's Ending: Reflections, 1982–1995*, London: W.W. Norton.

Kielmansegg, P.G. (1996) "Integration und Demokratie," Jachtenfuchs, M. and Kohler-Koch, B. (eds) *Europäische Integration*, Opladen: Leske + Budrich.

Király, B.K. and Bozóki, A. (eds) (1995) *Lawful Revolution in Hungary, 1989–94*, Boulder: Social Science Monographs.

Kitschelt, H. (2001) "Post-Communist Economic Reform: Causal Mechanism and Concomitant Properties," paper presented at PSA Annual Meeting, San Francisco.

Kitschelt, H., Mansfeldová, Z., Markowski, R. and Tóka, G. (1999) *Post-Communist Party Systems. Competition, Representation, and Inter-Party Cooperation*, Cambridge: Cambridge University Press.

Klicperova, M., Feierbend, I.K. and Hofstetter, C.R. (1997) "In the Search for a Post-Communist Syndrome: a Theoretical Framework and Empirical Assessment," *Journal of Community and Applied Social Psychology* 7, 1.

Klingemann, H., (1999) "Mapping Political Support in the 1990s: a Global Analysis," Norris, P. (ed.) *Critical Citizens: Global Support for Democratic Government*, Oxford: Oxford University Press.

Klingemann, H. and Fuchs, D. (2000) *Eastward Enlargement of the European Union and the Identity of Europe*, Berlin: Wissenschaftszentrum Berlin fur Sozialforschung (WZB).

Klingemann, H. and Hofferbert, R. (2000) "The Capacity of New Party Systems to Channel Discontent," Klingemann, H. and Neidhardt, F. (eds) *Zur Zukunft der Demokratie*, Berlin: edition sigma.

Kollár, M. and Mesežnikov, G. (eds) (2001) *Slovensko 2001: Súhrnná správa o stave spoločnosti*, Bratislava, Institute for Public Affairs, 2001.

Kolosi, T., Toth, I.G. and Vukovick, G. (eds) (1999) *Social Report 1998*, Budapest: TARKI.

Kornai, J. (1992) *The Socialist System: Political Economy of Communism*, Oxford: Oxford University Press.

Kroupa, A. and Mansfeldová, Z. (1997) "Občanská sdružení a profesní komory," in Brokl, L. (ed.) *Reprezentace zájmů v politickém systému České republiky*, Praha: SLON.

Kuti, É. (2001) *Nonprofit Organizations as Social Players in the Period of Transition: Roles and Challenges*, unpublished manuscript.

Laszlo, J. and Farkas, A. (1997) "Central-Eastern European Collective Experiences," *Journal of Community and Applied Social Psychology* 7, 1.

Latvia Human Development Report 1997, Riga: UNDP.

Lauristin, M. and Heidmets, M. (2002) "Intoduction: the Russian Minority in Estonia as a Theoretical and Political Issue," in Lauristin, M. and Heidmets, M. (eds) *The Challenge of the Russian Minority: Emerging Multicultural Democracy in Estonia*, Tartu: Tartu University Press.

Lauristin, M. and Vihalemm, T. (1997) "Changing Value Systems: Civilizational Shift and Local Differences," in Lauristin, M., Vihalemm, P., Rosengren, K.E. and Weibull, L. (eds) *Return to the Western World: Cultural and Political Perspectives on the Estonian Post-Communist Transition*, Tartu: Tartu University Press.

Lauristin, M, Vihalemm, P., Rosengren, K.E. and Weibull, L. (eds) (1997) *Return to the Western World*, Tartu: Tartu University Press.

Lauth, H.J. and Merkel, W. (1997) "Zivilgesellschaft und Transformation," in Lauth, H.J. and Merkel, W. (eds) *Zivilgesellschaft im Transformationsprozess*," Universität Mainz, Politikwissenschaftliche Standpunkte, Band 3.

Lepsius, M.R. (1999) "Die Europäische Union: Ökonomisch-politische Integration und kulturelle Pluralitätn," in Viehoff, R. and Segers, R.T. (eds) *Kultur, Identität, Europa: Über die Schwierigkeiten und Möglichkeiten einer Konstruktion*, Frankfurt a.M.: Suhrkamp.

Lettrich, J. (1993) *Dejiny novodobého Slovenska*, Bratislava: Archa.

Linz, J.J. and Stepan, A. (1996) *Problems of Democratic Transition and Consolidation: Southern Europe, South America and Post-Communist Europe*, Baltimore: The Johns Hopkins University Press.

Lipset, S.M. (1959) *Political Man: the Social Bases of Politics*, Garden City: Doubleday.

Lipset, S.M. (1959) "Some Social Requisites of Democracy," *American Political Science Review* 53, 1.

Lipset, S.M. (1994) "The Social Requisites of Democracy Revisited," *American Sociological Review* 59.

Lipset, S.M. (1996) *American Exceptionalism: a Double-Edged Sword*, New York: W.W. Norton.

Lipset, S.M. (2000) "Conditions for Democracy," in Klingemann, H. and Neidhardt, F. (eds) *Zur Zukunft der Demokratie*, Berlin: edition sigma.

Lipták, L. (1998) *Slovensko v 20.storočí*, Bratislava: Kalligram.

Livezeanu, I. (1995) *Cultural Politics in Greater Romania: Regionalism, Nation Building and Ethnic Struggle, 1918–1930*, Ithaca: Cornell University Press.

Löfgren, J. and Herd, G.P. (2000) "Estonia and the EU: Integration and Societal Security in the Baltic Context," *Research Report No. 91*, Tampere: Tampere Peace Research Institute.

Malová, D. (1997) "The Development of Interest Representation in Slovakia After 1989: From 'Transmission Belts' to 'Party–State Corporatism'?," in Szomolányi, S. and Gould, J.A. (eds) *Slovakia – Problems of Democratic Consolidation: the Struggle for the Rules of the Game*, Bratislava: SPSA.

Mansfeldová, Z. (1997) "Sociální partnerství v České republice," in Brokl, L. (ed.) *Reprezentace zájmů v politickém systému České republiky*, Prague: SLON.

Mansfeldová, Z. (1998) "Zivilgesellschaft in der Tschechischen und Slowakischen Republik," *Aus Politik und Zeitgeschichte* 30, 6–7.

Markova, I. (1997) "The Individual and the Community: a Post-Communist Perspective," *Journal of Community and Applied Social Psychology* 7, 1.

de Melo, M., Denizer, B., Gelb, A. and Tenev, S. (1997) "Circumstance and Choice: the Role of Initial Conditions and Policies in Transition Economies," World Bank Working Paper, Washington, DC: World Bank.

Melville, A. (1998) "Political Values and Orientations and Political Institutions," in Shevtsova, L. (ed.) *Political Russia*, Moscow: Carnegie Moscow Center.

Merkel, W. (1996) "Institutionalisierung und Konsolidierung der Demokratie in Ostmitteleuropa," in von Beyme, K. and Offe, C. (eds) *Politische Theorien in der Ära der Transformation*, PVS-Sonderheft, No. 25, Opladen.

Merkel, W. (1996) "Theorien der Transformation: Die demokratische Konsolidierung postautoritärer Gesellschaften," in von Beyme, K. and Offe, C. (eds) *Politische Theorien in der Ära der Transformation*, PVS-Sonderheft, No. 25, Opladen.

Merkel, W. (1999) *Systemtransformation: Eine Einführung in die Theorie und Empirie der Transformationsforschung*, Opladen: Leske und Budrich.

Merkel, W., Sandschneider, E. and Segert, D. (eds) (1996) *Systemwechsel 2: Die Institutionalisierung der Demokratie*, Leske + Budrich, Opladen.

Meseznikov, G. (1998) "Domestic Politics," *Slovakia 1996–1997: a Global Report on the State of Society*, Bratislava: Institute for Public Affairs.

Meseznikov, G. and Bútora, M. (eds) (1997) *Slovenské referendum '97: zrod, priebeh, dôsledky*, Bratislava: Institute for Public Affairs.

Migdal, J. (1988) *Strong Societies and Weak States*, Princeton: Princeton University Press.

Mihálikóva, S. (ed.) (1996) *Orientations Toward Politics and Economy in Post-Communist East Central Europe*, Bratislava: Comenius University.

Mihálikóva, S. (1996) "Understanding Slovak Political Culture," in Plasser, F. and Priberski, A. (eds) *Political Culture in East Central Europe*, Brookfield: Averbury.

Mihálikóva, S. (1997) *The Role of Political Cultures in the Transformation of Post-Communist Societies*, unpublished report, Bratislava: Comenius University.

Mikloš, I. (1998) "'Privatizácia" in *Slovensko 1997: Súhrnná správa o stave spoločnosti a trendoch na rok 1998*, Bratislava: Institute for Public Affairs.

Miller, W.L., White, S. and Heywood, P. (1998) *Values and Political Change in Post-Communist Europe*, Basingstoke: Macmillan.

Mishler, W. and Rose, R. (1997) "Trust, Distrust and Skepticism: Popular Evaluation of Civil and Political Institutions in Post-Communist Societies," *Journal of Politics* 59.

Mitranyi, D. (1930) *The Land and the Peasant in Rumania: the War and Agrarian Reform, 1917–1921*, Oxford: Oxford University Press.

Moore, Jr., B. (1966) *Social Origins of Dictatorship and Democracy*, Boston: Beacon Press.

Mungiu-Pippidi, A. (1996) *Die Rumanen nach '89*, Resita: Friederich Ebert Stiftung.

Mungiu-Pippidi, A. (2002) *Threats and Challenges: Romania after 2000*, Bucharest: UNDP and Polirom.

Mureşan, C. (1999) *Evoluţia demografică a României: Tendinţe vechi, schimbări recente, perspective (1870–2030)*, Cluj-Napoca: Presa Universitară Clujeană.

National Human Development Report: Slovak Republic 2000 (2000) Bratislava, UNDP.

North, D.C. (1990), *Institutions, Institutional Change and Economic Performance*, New York: Cambridge University Press.

Nozick, R. (1974) *Anarchy, State, and Utopia*, New York: Basic Books.

O'Donnell, G. (1994) "Delegative Democracy," *Journal of Democracy* 5, 1.

O'Donnell, G. (1996) "Do Economists Know Best?," in Diamond, L. and Plattner, M. (eds) *The Global Resurgance of Democracy*, Baltimore: The Johns Hopkins Press.

Offe, C. (1991) "Capitalism by Democratic Design? Democratic Theory Facing the Triple Transition in East Central Europe," *Social Research* 58.

Offe, C. (1996) *Varieties of Transition*, Cambridge: Polity Press.

Orwell, G. (1946) *Animal Farm; a Fairy Story*, New York: Harcourt, Brace and Company.

Palmer, R.P. and Colton (1978) *A History of the Modern World*, New York: A.A. Knopf.

Pírek, I. (1997) "NATO levnější než neutralita" ("NATO Cheaper than Neutrality"), *Profit* 33.

Plasser, F. and Pribersky, A. (1996) *Political Culture in East Central Europe*, Aldershot: Avebury.

Post, R.C. (1993) "Between Democracy and Community: the Legal Constitution of Social Form," in Chapman, J.W. and Shapiro, I. (eds) *Democratic Community: Nomos No. XXXV*, New York: New York University Press.

Pridham, G. and Attila Á. (eds) (2001) *Prospects for Democratic Transformation in East-Central Europe*, Manchester: Manchester University Press.

Przeworski, A. (1991) *Democracy and the Market: Political Reforms in Eastern Europe and Latin America*, Cambridge: Cambridge University Press.

Putnam, R.D. (1993) *Bowling Alone. the Collapse and Revival of American Community*, New York: Simon & Schuster.

Putnam, R.D. (1993) *Making Democracy Work: Civic Traditions in Modern Italy*, Princeton: Princeton University Press.

Rawls, J. (1993) *Political Liberalism*, New York: Columbia University Press.

Reisinger, W.M. (1999) "Reassessing Theories of Transition away from Authoritarian Regimes: Regional Patterns Among Postcommunist Countries," paper presented at the 1999 Annual Meeting of the Midwest Political Science Association, Chicago, 15–17 April.

Reynier, D. and Perrineau, P. (2001) *"Bulgarie,"* in *Dictionnaire du vote*, Paris: Seuil.

Roberts, H. (1951) *Rumania: the Politics of an Agrarian State*, New Haven: Yale University Press.

Rohrschneider, R. (1999) *Learning Democracy: Democratic and Economic Values in Unified Germany*, Oxford: Oxford University Press.

Rokeach, M. (1973) *The Nature of Human Values*, New York: Free Press.

Roller, E. (2000) "Ende des sozialstaatlichen Konsenses? Zum Aufbrechen traditioneller und zur Entstehung neuer Konfliktstrukturen in Deutschland," in Niedermayer, O. and Westle, B. (eds) *Demokratie und Partizipation*, Opladen: Westdeutscher Verlag.

Rose, R. and Maley, W. (1994) "Nationalities in the Baltic States: a Survey Study," *Studies in Public Policy* 222, Glasgow: University of Strathclyde.

Rose, R., Mishler, W. and Haerpfer, C. (1998) *Democracy and its Alternatives: Understanding Post-Communist Societies*, Baltimore: Johns Hopkins University Press.

Rotariu, T. (1993) "Aspecte demografice in Transilvania, la începutul secolului al XX-lea," *Sociologie Românesaca* 4, 2.

Rotariu, T. and Mezei, E. (1999) "Asupra unor aspecte ale migraţiei interne," *Sociologie românesaca*, Serie noua 3, 5–39.

Rotariu, T., Semeniuc, M. and Pah, I. (1996) *Studia Censualia Transilvanica: Recensământul din 1857*, Bucuresti: Editura Staff.

Rotschild, J. (1993) *Return to Diversity: a Political History of East–Central Europe Since World War II*, Oxford: Oxford University Press.

Saarniit, J. (1995) "Changes in the Value Orientation of Youth and their Social Context," in Tomasi, L. (ed.) *Values and Post-Soviet Youth: the Problem of Transition*, Milan: FrancoAngeli.

Sandu, D. (1999) *Spaţiul social al tranziţiei*. Iaşi: Polirom

Sartori, G. (1987) *The Theory of Democracy Revisited*, Chatham, NJ: Chatham House.

Scharpf, F.W. (1999) "Demokratieprobleme in der europäischen Mehrebenenpolitik," in Merkel, W. and Busch, A. (eds) *Demokratie in Ost und West: Für Klaus von Beyme*, Frankfurt a.M.: Suhrkamp.

Schöpflin, G. (1991) "The Political Tradition of Eastern Europe," in Graubard, S.R. (ed.) *Eastern Europe? Central Europe? Europe*, Boulder: Westview.

Schöpflin, G. (1993) "Culture and Identity in Post-Communist Europe," in White, S., Batt, J. and Lewis, P.G. (eds) *Developments in East European Politics*, Basingstoke: Macmillan.

Schöpflin, G. (1993) *Politics in Eastern Europe 1945–1992*, Oxford: Blackwell.

Scott, J.C. (1986) *Weapons of the Weak: Everyday Forms of Peasant Resistance*, Yale: Yale University Press.

Seton-Watson, H. (1960) Th*e Pattern of Communist Revolution: a Historical Analysis*, London: Methuen.

Shafir, M. (1985) *Romania, Politics, Economics and Society: Political Stagnation and Stimulated Change*, New York: Printer Publishers Ltd.

Shain, Y. and Linz, J.J. (1995) *Between States: Interim Governments and Democratic Transitions*, Cambridge: Cambridge University Press.

Silver, B.D. and Titma, M. (1998) "Support for New Political Institutions in Estonia: the Effects of Nationality, Citizenship, and Material Well-Being," *Problems of Post-Communism* 45.

Simon, J. (1993) "Post-paternalist Political Culture in Hungary: Relationship Between Citizens and Politics and After the Melancholic Revolution 1989–1991," *Communist and Post-Communist Studies* 26, 2.

Stan, L. and Turcescu, L. (2000) "The Romanian Orthodox Church and Post-Communist Democratization," *Europe–Asia Studies* 52, 8.

Steen, A. (1996) "Confidence in Institutions in Post-Communist Societies: the Case of the Baltic States," *Scandinavian Political Studies* 19, 3.

Stokes, G. (1997) *Three Eras of Political Change in Eastern Europe*, Oxford: Oxford University Press.

Swain, N. (1993) "Hungary," in White, S., Blatt, J. and Lewis, P.G. (eds) *Developments in East European Politics*, Basingstoke: Macmillan

Szomolányi, S. and Gould, J.A. (1997) *Slovakia: Problems of Democratic Consolidation and the Struggle for the Rules of the Game*, Bratislava: Slovak Political Science Association.

Tabuns, A. (2001) *National, State and Regime Identity in Latvia*, Riga: Baltic Study Centre.

Thomassen, J. (1995) "Support for Democratic Values," in Klingemann, H. and Fuchs, D. (eds) *Citizens and the State*, Oxford: Oxford University Press.

Titma, M. (1996) "Estonia: a Country in Transition," Titma, M., Silver, B.D. and Anderson, B.A. (eds) *Nationalities and Society on the Eve of Independence*, Special Issue of *International Journal of Sociology* 26, 1.

Titma, M. and Silver, B.D. (1996) "Transitions from Totalitarian Society," in Titma, M., Silver, B.D. and Anderson, B.A. (eds) *Nationalities and Society on the Eve of Independence*, Special Issue of *International Journal of Sociology* 26, 1.

Todorov, A. (2001) *Izbiratelni zakoni I izbiratelna aktivnost: bulgarskiyat sluchay 1879–1946 (Electoral Laws and Electoral Participation: the Bulgarian Case)*, Sofia: Sofia University Press.

Tóka, G. (1995) "Political Support in East–Central Europe," in Klingemann, H. and Fuchs, D. (eds) *Citizens and the State*, Oxford: Oxford University Press.

Tóka, G. (ed.) (1995) *The 1990 Elections to the Hungarian National Assembly*, Berlin: Sigma.

Tóka, G. and Enyedi, Z. (eds) (1999) *Elections to the Hungarian National Assembly 1994*, Berlin: Sigma.

Tökes, R.L. (1996) *Hungary's Negotiated Revolution: Economic Reforms, Social Change, and Political Succession*, Cambridge: Cambridge University Press.

Tökes, R.L. (1997) "Party Politics and Political Participation in Postcommunist Hungary," in Dawisha, K. and Parrot, B. (eds) *The Consolidation of Democracy in East–Central Europe*, Cambridge: Cambridge University Press.

Verba, S., Schlozman, K.L.M. and Brady, H.E. (1995) *Voice and Equality: Civic Volunteerism in American Politics*, Cambridge: Harvard University Press.

Vihalemm, T. (1997) "Changing Discourses on Values in Estonia," in Lauristin, M., Vihalemm, P., Rosengren, K.E. and Weibull, L. (eds) *Return to the Western World: Cultural and Political Perspectives on the Estonian Post-Communist Transition*, Tartu: Tartu University Press.

Vihalemm, T. and Lauristin, M. (1997) "Cultural Adjustment to the Changing Societal Environment: the Case of Russians in Estonia," in Lauristin, M., Vihalemm, P., Rosengren, K.E. and Weibull, L. (eds) *Return to the Western World: Cultural and Political Perspectives on the Estonian Post-Communist Transition*, Tartu: Tartu University Press.

von Beyme, K. (1996) *Transition to Democracy in Eastern Europe*, New York: St. Martin's Press.

Wagner, P. (2001) *Transformation in Eastern Europe: Beyond "East" and "West,"* unpublished manuscript.

Wildavsky, A. (1987) "Choosing Preferences by Constructing Institutions: a Cultural Theory of Preference Formation," *American Political Science Review* 81, 1.

Weber, M. (1958) *The Protestant Ethic and the Spirit of Capitalism*, New York: Charles Scribner's Sons.

Wlachovský, M. (1997) "Foreign Policy," in Bútora, M. and Hunčík, P. (eds) *Global Report on Slovakia: Comprehensive Analyses from 1995 and Trends from 1996*, Bratislava: Sandor Marai Foundation.

Zielonka, J. (ed.) (2001) *Democratic Consolidation in Eastern Europe*, volume 1: Institutional Engineering, Oxford: Oxford University Press.

Zielonka, J. (2006) *Europe as Empire: The Nature of the Enlarged European Union*, Oxford: Oxford University Press.

Index

Entries that appear in tables or figures are indicated by *t* or *f*, respectively, after the page locator.

accountability 320, 322, 330, 333
administration 107, 109; institutions 214, 269; confidence in 242; powers limited 219
age 6–7, 92–6, 113, 122, 154, 157–9, 162, 167, 245, 318*t*, 320*t*, 329, 341, 345, 348–51; elderly 238, 248, 262, 358; influence of 210, 215, 218, 221–3, 257–9, 263–4, 267–71; older generation 116, 152, 224–6; younger generation 196, 212
agricultural sector 208; employment in 317
Albania 2, 38, 42, 44–5, 57–8, 87, 120, 356
alienation 191, 236; from government authorities 366; from politics 248; social 375
American culture 38, 58; exceptionalism 32, 54
anarchy 356, 375, 377
Anglo-American countries 37–9, 42, 44–5, 55–8
anti-communist parties 16, 314, 323, 338–9, 353; coalition 337, 339; electoral promises 315
army 109, 112, 197, 312, 314, 350; national 304; public confidence in 110, 214, 350
army rule 18, 59, 104, 262*t*, 266*t*, 291, 347*t*, 367–8; opposition to 239, 346
attitudes and values 128, 237, 257, 297, 301; authoritarian 356; differences 6
Australia 35, 41, 46, 50, 55, 57–8
Austria 121, 148, 221

Austro-Hungarian Empire 104, 174–5
authoritarianism 83, 119, 165, 173, 187, 190, 209, 256, 323, 332, 356, 377; anti-authoritarian 181; revived 177, 186
autocracy 5, 41, 44, 148, 151, 205, 289, 292; attitudes towards 238*t*; elements of 368; rejection of 292, 353, 358, 366–7; support for 44, 59, 91–2*t*, 102; transition from 14
autocratic attitudes 1–2, 4, 85, 102, 104*t*, 144, 316*t*, 360; system of government 35
autocratic regimes 12, 38, 90, 93, 102–4, 237, 288, 367; nostalgia for 370; preference for 144; rejection of 26, 140, 169, 185
autocrats 13, 15–16, 18, 142, 149, 151–2, 228, 231–2, 263–5, 236–7, 290–1, 316, 345–6, 357–8, 360–1, 363, 366, 370, 375–6, 378

Baltic States 38, 42, 50, 165, 243, 245, 250, 256, 278, 282–3, 285, 289, 292–5, 298, 303
Belarus 2, 6, 16, 44–5, 57–8, 87, 143, 264, 356–62, 364, 366, 368–9, 372–6, 378; democratic beliefs 376; support for democracy 366
benchmark democracies 41–6*t*, 49–50*t*, 172
Bohemia 175, 179
bourgeois generation 341–2, 351
boycotts 92–4, 105–6, 160–1, 225–7, 248, 259, 261*t*, 285–6, 365
Bulgaria 2, 6, 9, 11, 13, 15–16, 72, 87,

121, 124–7, 133, 140–2, 164–5, 221, 227, 316, 326; citizens 339, 345; communist rule 336; confidence in the government 349; democracy 350, 353; democrats and autocrats 347*t*; ethnic communities 198, 352; financial crisis 343; Politburo 337; pre-war bureaucracies 333; Turks in 351
Bulgarian Communist Party 336
Bulgarian Socialist Party (BSP) 337, 353
business and industry 178, 267, 268, 348*t*; strict rules for 115

capitalism 206; grab-and-run 371, 375; Manchester 372
Catholic 78, 89, 96, 120, 251, 289, 303, 309
Catholic Church 12, 111, 327; dissident groups 189; states 76, 133, 206; dominance of 216; ties with the 207
Ceau_escu, Nicolae 164, 312, 325, 331–2; family 315; own army 314; regime 164
central and eastern Europe 1, 2, 4, 6, 8, 10–11, 14, 16, 34, 39, 54–5, 67, 76, 84, 150, 296, 353, 376–7; post-communist 149, 310; revolution 148; socialist 145
central European countries 38, 42, 56, 58, 88, 130–1, 144, 186, 191, 314, 332, 356; identity 119; new democracies 136; in transition 188
Christian peoples 34–5, 37, 51; Bulgarians 351
church and religious organizations 107, 112, 249–50, 293–6, 364; confidence in 111, 133, 214, 243, 269*t*, 270
citizens 9, 105, 219, 231, 250, 280–2; alienation from politics 248; influence 211; rights 280; self-reliability 371; values 223*t*
civic community 31–2, 58; associations 95, 117; culture 128, 288; engagement 49, 55, 58, 64; participation 169; revival of 106; values 94
civil rights 198, 359; distribution 325; social 31
civil service 112, 292; confidence in 110, 213, 269*t*; discriminatory 330; mistreatment by 327–30; reform acts 330 civil society 94, 101, 103, 148, 166, 168, 219–20, 270, 283, 303–4, 357, 374; associations 350;

homogeneous 305; institutions 350; movements 129; openness 254; participation 94, 231, 252; structures 13, 220, 375; support of democracy 168*t*; values 273, 275
coalition agreements 180, 183–4, 200, 207
collapse of communist system 1–2, 34–6, 72, 83, 111, 119, 121, 128, 148, 177, 190–3, 250, 305, 314, 327, 345, 353, 356, 377; economy 239; in Slovakia 186; social system 301
collectivism 25–7, 34, 56, 58, 290, 305, 312, 317–21*t*, 331–2; decades of 371; in Russian culture 288
communism 86, 200, 297, 312, 315–19*t*, 322–4, 332, 338, 342–3; de-communization 172, 179, 188; legacy of 320; never-communist zone 81; transition from 73, 85
Communist Party 106, 108, 322, 337, 339; Chairman of 177; Inter-front 292; members 316–18*t*; of Slovakia 185–6, 196, 200
communist regime 67, 71–2, 90, 102, 116, 157, 170, 176, 179, 189–90, 227, 285, 303, 314–15, 325, 330–3; dissent with 111; dissolution of 336; government 101, 122, 328, 337; institutions 93, 96, 110, 136, 250
communist rule 187, 277, 324, 339; experienced 76–7*t*, 297, 304; legacies of 192, 303; not experienced 81; socialization 231, 321, 327; successor parties 322–3
community 27; ethos 29–30; communitarian 32–3*t*, 49, 50–1; local 246, 279; values 31
Comparative Study of Electoral Systems 87
competition 187, 194*t*, 292, 296; free 351; individual 298; political 92, 108–9
Confucian 78, 309; cultural heritage 71, 74
connections 330; in the government 192; informal 328; in the opposition 192
cooperation 231; of owners and employees 115
corruption 112, 184, 314, 326, 330, 349–50; administrative 332; bribery 313, 327–8; index 121; in politics 247
crime 110, 247; abduction 180; criminal

element 356; communist times 315; rate 121

Croatia 42, 122, 124–7, 136, 139–40, 144–6, 165

cultural heritage 11–15, 36–7*t*, 56, 76, 85–8, 288–9, 333; historical 16, 35, 71, 95, 189, 231, 293, 310; soviet 377; individualistic 298, 371; map 70*f*; theory 96; traditions 34, 90, 311

cultural level 25–8, 175, 188, 351; differences 58, 206, 303; regions 75*t*, 82*t*

cultural shift 68–9, 95; Inglehart's model 236

Czech Republic 13, 45, 87–8*t*, 108, 114, 121, 124–7, 130, 133, 140, 144, 149–51, 163–4, 173, 195–6*t*, 227, 316, 326, 338, 356; Civic Democratic Party 179; Communist Party 176; crime rate 121; democracy 101–2; ecological movements 108; economy 115, 178; Havel, former President 107; institutions 110; lands 179; rejection of Muslims 139; society 113

Czechoslovakia 175–6; COMECON trading bloc 186; dissolution of the federation 177, 179; First Republic 175; unity of 178

democracy 4, 11, 13, 16–17, 44, 84, 87, 101, 105, 173, 204–5, 210, 232, 292, 332, 339, 341–3, 346*t*; acceptance of 209*t*, 216, 217–18*t*; borders of 132; deficiencies in 14, 180; elements of 368; generation 346, 348, 351; indecisive 264; modern 254; performance 210, 239, 346; preference for 7, 116, 263; pre-war 101, 131; public support for 151, 153, 155, 168; rejected 45, 346 ; socialist model of 30–1; stable 35, 83, 204, 206, 250; traditional 215, 220, 225, 228; transition to 81, 177, 120–2, 144, 282, 328, 343, 348

democracy–autocracy index 5*t*, 7*t*, 9, 18, 140, 142*t*, 143, 149, 150–2*t*, 162–3, 168, 170, 209, 210*t*, 237, 264*t*, 290–2*t*, 357*t*, 360, 365, 369

democracy and autocracy 141*t*, 366; failure to differentiate 367

democracy type 83, 85, 165; consensus of 204; consolidated 122, 136, 150–1, 164–5, 168, 170, 203; dysfunctional 254; electoral 332, 355; emerging 150, 165, 203; consumer 254, 368, 376; mature 164; modern 254; old 13; parliamentary 15, 320; pluralist 173; progressive 355

democracy, attitudes to 90, 103*t*, 150, 209, 237–8*t*, 275, 345; development constraints 331–2; level of support for 116, 164; negative 231; public 338; structural constraints 312, 314, 317

democracy, support for 3, 5–7, 9–10, 14, 26, 44–5, 59, 86, 90, 91–3 *t*, 95, 102, 110, 140, 144, 148, 154, 156–7*t*, 160–2*t*, 165, 169*t*, 254, 263, 321, 353, 358, 366; expansion of 163; in Hungary 168

democratic attitudes 1, 8, 12, 87, 91–2, 151, 165, 168, 263*t*, 275, 376–7; distribution of 87; orientations 17, 263, 316*t*, 320*t*; values 4, 13, 89, 95–6, 103, 151, 358

democratic communities 27–9, 36, 41, 45–6*t*, 56–8, 74, 85–7, 113, 138, 228, 254, 297, 368, 375; attitudes characteristic for 46, 229*t*; citizen support for 40*t*, 47–8*t*, 195*t*; consolidation 1, 3, 13, 149, 153, 183; criteria for 39, 40*t*; deficit 25, 187, 199; development of 236; institutional framework 181; operational statements 29*t*; quality of 92*t*; types of 16, 30*t*, 33*t*, 38, 94, 205*t*

democratic institutions 3, 10, 83, 187, 220; standards of 355

democratic order 138, 332; legitimacy 25; support for 238; at the workplace 246

Democratic Party 200; collapse of 176; Left Alliance coalition 207; Union 181

democratic principles 165, 169–70, 187, 190; not implemented 186; support for 242

democratic regimes 101, 204, 224, 250, 275, 377; efficiency of 104, 265*t*; political system 18, 59, 237, 277; requirements for 355; sub-types of 355; transformation 148, 223; transition 2, 14, 86, 122

democratic rule 102, 237; attitudes towards 366, 367*t*; effectiveness of 104*t*, 210–12, 228, 239, 264; evaluation of 266*t*

democratic system 140, 219, 262, 366; confidence in the 133; theory debate 26

democratization 95, 132, 163, 186, 198–9, 278, 314, 333; different degree of 86; earliest wave 68; third wave of 2; understandings of 292

democrats 15, 18, 142, 149, 228, 231, 236, 316; consistent 316; critical 28, 102, 116, 248, 368; solid 44–5, 57

demonstrations 92–3, 226, 247, 249, 259, 286–7, 365; peaceful 285; political 160

deviant behaviour 271*t*, 301, 351, 375–6; abortion 62, 77–9*t*, 113, 215–16, 251, 271, 272*t*, 301, 305, 351, 376; acceptance of 19, 375–6*t*; attitudes towards 352*t*; divorce 62, 113, 215–16, 251, 271–2*t*, 301, 305, 351, 376; homosexuality, attitudes to 62, 78, 80*t*, 81–2*t*, 113, 120, 153*t*, 215–16, 251, 271, 272*t*, 301, 305, 351, 375; intolerance 305; low levels of acceptance 304; not justifiable 216, 218; prostitution 62, 215–16, 251, 271, 272*t*, 301, 305, 351, 375

dissatisfaction 371; with the current regime 190, 220; democrats 327*t*

Dubček, Alexander 176

Dzurinda, Prime Minister M. 151, 183, 185; administration 198

East Germany 9, 71, 87–8*t*, 127, 140, 144, 195–6*t*, 282–6, 288–90, 292, 297, 298–9, 301–2; social system 300

eastern European countries 38, 44–5, 50–1, 56–8, 121, 165, 254, 274, 282, 312, 330, 355; communist 206; per capita GNP 70; post-communist 337; transformation 173, 304

ecology movement 107, 109, 129, 243

economic development 57, 70–2, 76, 83–4, 116, 120, 203, 222, 317; cultural standards 32, 119; crises 265, 356, 362; growth 70, 204, 246, 342–3; problems 193, 343, 346

economic system 204, 210; failure 368; hardships 15, 247, 256, 295, 297, 352; performance 182, 235, 364; powers, limited 219; reforms 178, 191, 278, 282, 293, 295, 298; resources 273; securities 69, 83; transformation 190, 192; transition 308, 317

economy 184; centralized 208; command 308; decline 195, 206; stable 247; subsistence 208; transformed 292

education 154–5, 167, 223, 318*t*, 320*t*, 329, 343, 350; free 190, 240; and health 184; and support of democracy 164*t*

Election Action Solidarity coalition 207

election campaign 2002 189; results 190

elections 140, 204, 209, 223–4, 247, 259, 275, 314, 320, 328, 332; of 1989 206; 1998 182–3; 1998 and 2002 177, 185; campaigns 325; contestants 189; controlled 174; first parliamentary 338; free and fair 105, 317, 338; general 89, 105, 339, 355; local government 224; municipal 256; parliamentary 207, 221, 224, 247, 256, 353; participation 105; post-communist 343; presidential 256–7, 259, 269, 312, 325; proportional system 328; protest 248; *Saeima* 248; secret 224

electoral law 207; poor 332

elite 9, 220, 223, 310, 314; communist party 240; competitive 187; consensus 149; local 325; national 90, 199; new 192, 314; personal goals 254; political 195, 216, 248, 310, 362, 371; predatory 322, 324, 327, 330, 333; ruling 277, 356; Slovak and Czech 178

equality 30, 321; of opportunity 30–1, 46

established democracies 9, 81, 124–5, 130–1, 133, 136, 139–40; confidence paradox 136 Estonia 6, 9, 11, 13, 15, 42, 87, 121, 165, 239, 243, 284, 286, 299, 300, 302–3; citizens 298, 300; communities 290, 293; economic growth 295; ethnic communities 290; ethnic Russians 15, 277–8, 281–3, 285, 288–9, 292, 295, 300–1, 303, 305–6; financial policy 283; independence 15, 280, 285, 287, 279, 305; language 277, 289; legal system 295; lost independence 277; Muslims 303; People's Front 292; political participation 282; Popular Front 278; population 288, 295; Pro Patria party 305; protest behaviour 285; state 295; two communities 297, 303, 304

Estonian state 278; citizenship 280, 282; congress 278, 292; European integration 305; local government 287; passports 280; population 288–90, 293; Republic 280

Estonians 287, 306; ethnic 282–3, 285, 289, 292, 305; governmental institutions 304

etatist 38–9, 58; anti-etatism 31, 38; policies, support for 92; tradition 46

ethics of daily life 193–4*t*, 297; motivations 231–2; tolerance 218; values 29, 31–2

ethics of individual achievement 114, 298, 371, 372–3*t*

ethnic composition 14, 88, 92, 96, 139; heterogeneity 90, 120

European civilizations 25–7, 34, 38, 56, 58, 95

European Commission 330

European Community 25, 32; countries 27, 42, 142; harmonization of legislation 198; identity 56, 58; institutions 305

European Union 25, 32, 34, 56, 211, 214, 270, 280, 294, 296, 305, 308, 326, 350; associated member 182; confidence in 108, 244; cultural zone 72; expectations of 208; integration into 151, 183, 186, 197–8, 315; interests 109; leaders 185; membership 186, 197, 256; public image 109; standards of the 110

European Union accession 109, 145, 190, 331; candidate countries 122, 146; criteria 198

European Values Study 1, 3, 11, 16, 69, 339

ex-communist 337–9, 353; countries 71–2, 78, 235; societies 16, 72, 74, 81

farming 208; collective 324, 331; subsistence 323, 326, 331

Finland 38, 44–5; social support 298

foreign aid 253, 273–4*t*; provision of 275; recipient of 352; from western Europe 94

formal institutions 262, 312, 313; of democracy 327; persistence of 333

France 32, 128, 221

free market 172, 193, 308; open borders 121; politicians 185

free market economy 14, 114–15, 203, 208, 246, 256, 277, 282, 305, 352; attitudes towards 241; transition to 236

freedom of information 355, 374

freedom of speech 81, 223, 247, 258–9*t*, 343, 355; limited 187

gender 6, 119, 152, 157, 159, 166–7, 212–3, 215, 221, 223, 225–6, 245, 251, 259, 264, 267, 271, 318*t*, 329, 358; equality 69, 108; inequalities, denial of 108

Germany 2, 6, 9, 32, 124–5, 128, 140, 148, 228, 289, 357–62, 364, 369, 373–5; community 207

Gorbachev, Mikhail 278, 312

government 30, 269; action against poverty 116, 253*t*, 273*t*; appointment of judges and civil servants 327; beliefs in 132; benefits 61; confidence in 213, 269*t*, 350, 366, 370; constraints 321; control 241; decision-making 247; effectiveness 204; legal rational 325; legitimacy of 368; non-democratic 177; non-political 325, 316; policies 342; preferences 262*t*; republican 293; responsibility 194*t*, 211, 240, 265, 273, 372; unstable 275

governmental institutions 60, 214*t*; confidence in 242*t*, 366, 370*t*; low levels of trust 375

Greece 144; Catholic Church 89, 96

Green movement 106, 294, 296, 350

Habsburg Empire 12, 34, 88–9, 95, 174

healthcare, state provision of 190, 240, 344

Hungary 6, 45, 50, 87, 88–9*t*, 120–1, 124–7, 130, 136, 140, 144, 173, 195–6*t*, 227, 316, 326, 338, 356; Coalition Party 181, 185; coercive assimilation 175; democracy in 155; failed Revolution 331; international conflicts 154; minority 183, 311; parliament 174, 184; political system 148, 150; public 159; social structure 152; transformation 153

Husák, Gustáv 177

identification 122–3*t*, 278–9*t*, 280–2; crisis 119; geographic reference 359; with the nation 124–5; with political community 360*t*

Iliescu, Ion 312, 322, 325; government of 315

illegal practices 110, 115, 184, 249, 350

immigrants 301, 303, 305, 352
immigration 113, 116, 254*t*, 275;
    attitude to 219*t*, 274*t*; strict control
    218, 274
income 203, 206, 278; inequality 121,
    194*t*, 372; low 68, 210, 213, 371;
    polarization 254; urban residents 323
independence 78, 191, 278, 281, 292,
    294, 298; without violence 303
individual 193, 209; achievement 299*t*,
    373; competition 300; freedom 31;
    performance 305; welfare 298
industrial closures 300; bankruptcies of
    state-owned plants 212; ex-Soviet 254
industrial society 67–9, 83; developed
    128; market-oriented 120; structure
    104, 120
inflation 184, 222, 247, 342
institutions 269, 292, 350; framework
    27, 254, 308, 377; change 87;
    confidence in 132–3, 134–5*t*, 138,
    213, 242, 292–4*t*, 304, 349*t*;
    democratic 178; design 90, 368;
    establishment of 304; government
    107, 112, 116; informal 309–10,
    312–13, 332–3; lack of confidence in
    228; levels of trust in 292–7, 304, 370;
    new regime 328; performance 297; in
    the public sphere 210, 212, 215, 243*t*;
    reforms 304, 330; social capital 328;
    structure 254
interest in politics 20, 63, 105, 158–9*t*,
    212, 215, 220–1, 223–8, 244–5*t*, 257,
    275, 293, 319*t*, 332, 339–41*t*, 343,
    361*t*; level of 209, 290, 361; passive
    162, 196, 362
interests of the people 101, 350;
    recognized by legislative measures
    113
intergenerational cultural shift 83–4
international community 173, 310;
    affairs 154, 181; organizations 214,
    244*t*, 270*t*
interpersonal trust 81, 218, 226, 231,
    270–3, 329
Islamic culture 206; zone 83
isolation, political 187, 189, 197
Italy 2, 89, 121, 128, 133, 221

Klaus government 103, 114–15, 151,
    179

labor unions 106, 112, 249, 270, 283,
    293–4, 296, 364; compulsory

membership 227, 260, 270;
    confidence in 111, 215, 269*t*; mistrust
    of 304; under Soviet regime 363
Latvia 12, 14, 42, 235–6, 243, 283–6,
    289–94, 299–303; citizens 249, 254;
    economic performance 239; ethnic
    citizens 252; foreign aid 253*t*; future
    aims 246*t*; independent 238; state
    responsibility 240*t*
law 222, 246–7, 264, 342; circumvention
    of 182; confidence in 243*t*;
    enforcement 332; family 113;
    ineffectual 181; Ministry of Welfare
    252; national security 315
law abidingness 41, 44–5, 57, 60, 167*t*,
    169, 284*t*, 289, 362; level of 283, 285,
    363*t*
lawful demonstration 94, 105–6, 163,
    248, 261*t*, 344; participation in 160*t*,
    161–2
legal system 107, 112, 213, 293;
    confidence in 109, 115, 116, 133,
    136–7*t*, 215, 243, 269*t*; explicit
    mistrust in 110, 350–1; framework 16,
    106, 232, 283; institutions 269, 377;
    nihilism 356; restrictions 216;
    uncertainty 364
Leninist regime 12, 35, 38, 57, 85, 146,
    289
level of formal education 6–7, 92, 152,
    156–66, 168, 204, 209–12, 215,
    218–19, 221, 224–6, 231, 245, 262–4,
    267–71, 305, 341–2, 346–9, 351–2,
    358; academic degree 259; university
    344
levels of trust 294–5; differences in 304
liberal 129, 131, 207, 267–8; attitudes
    towards immigration 274; communist
    regimes 133; community 46, 50–1,
    54, 57
liberal democracy 33*t*, 49–50, 52–3*t*, 85,
    231, 320, 337, 355, 371; core elements
    of 376; model of 30–1; transition to 95
libertarian democracy 15, 33*t*, 46,
    49–54*t*, 231; community 31, 35, 39, 57;
    model of 30
Lithuania 6, 12, 14, 42, 87–8*t*, 165, 221,
    239, 243, 250, 283–4, 286, 288–92,
    299–303; belief system 256; citizens
    269, 282; companies privatized 265;
    economic performance 275; ethnic
    Russians 281, 294; foreign aid 274*t*;
    goals 258*t*; pattern of political activity
    259

living standards 72, 204, 235, 342; decreasing 248, 339, 368; ways of improving 304

major companies 111–12 , 270, 294, 350; confidence in 214, 243–4, 269*t*
market economy 2, 73, 149, 298, 326, 337, 351; capitalist 178; mechanisms 348
materialist/post-materialist values 143, 218, 222*t*; index 228
Mečiar, Prime Minister Vladimír 14, 146, 151, 163, 177, 179–80, 185–6, 189, 192; government 182–4, 197; legacy 198
media 107, 112, 213, 294–5; consumption 362; confidence in 112, 136, 243, 269; freedom of 258; information in the 274; investigative journalism 112; Soviet 294; state-owned 315; television and press 269, 350
membership in organizations, compulsory 283
membership in voluntary associations 64, 166*t*, 167, 227, 249–50*t*, 260, 262*t*, 283, 327–8, 363, 364*t*
Milosevic, Slobodan 120, 165
minorities 113, 174, 198, 301, 305, 375–6; rejection of 139–40*t*, 143, 302–3
modernity 35, 38, 42, 57, 76; socio-economic 11–12, 35, 85, 88–9, 96
modernization 15, 70–1, 222, 292, 343; gap 15; lag 323; socialist 120; theorists 67–8, 185–8, 198; share of votes 182–3
multiparty system 256, 278, 315
Muslim 34, 37, 351; south-eastern European countries 42, 50, 56

national community 124*t*, 359–60
national independence 242, 249, 296
national pride 77–9*t*, 125–7, 145, 360
nationalism 177, 281, 311; demands 177; sentiments 139; viable strategy 359
NATO 183; chance to join 190; first wave of enlargement 182; membership 186, 197–8, 256
negotiations 209; with EU and NATO 197
neo-liberal policies 116; transformation 178

new democracies 10, 81, 130, 132, 167, 200, 220–1, 224; Barometer surveys 87, 148, 163; institutions 136, 188, 356
non-communist 74, 78, 81; western Europe 206
non-government organizations 94, 195, 249
Norway 3, 6–7, 55, 124–5, 127, 130, 140, 239, 243, 245, 250, 252; active members 227

occupation of buildings 106, 225–6, 248–9, 259, 261*t*, 344, 365
opposition 206, 338; former 183; to legitimacy of 364; to membership in the EU 197; parties 181; to reforms 208; suppressed 176
Orthodox 289; Christian 89, 96, 124, 133; culture 206; peoples 12, 34, 37, 71, 76, 78, 309; Russian 251; tradition 8, 298
Ottoman Empire 12, 34, 38, 88, 95, 348
ownership of business and industry 63, 115, 212, 213*t*, 231, 268*t*; employees 212; government 213, 241*t*, 267; private 63, 92, 256, 267–8, 371; state 115, 268*t*, 315, 348

parliament 107–9, 112, 140, 180, 288, 349; abolished 320; committees 180; confidence in 108, 116, 213, 215, 242, 269*t*, 278, 370; local 294; trust in 242, 304
participation 27, 31, 55, 128, 168, 228, 297; abolished 320; in decision-making 275; levels of 101, 235, 250; in political action 131, 248–9*t*; in voluntary associations 168, 326
parties in power 269; affiliation 129; changing 208; coalitions 224
party politics 296, 325; one-party systems 332; orientation 102; post-communist 322
party systems 57; dominant 332; emergence of 225; identification 129–30; membership 331; parallel structures 188; preference 216, 260*t*
paternalism 176, 179, 265, 267–8, 372; anti-paternalist attitude 31
perestroika 278, 294; generation 341–4, 346, 348, 351–2
pluralism 14, 26, 28, 149, 155, 204, 209, 337, 350, 376; modern 215; political 172, 375

Poland 6, 13–14, 87–9*t*, 120–1, 124–7, 133, 144, 149–51, 163, 173, 316, 326; agriculture 208; civil society 203, 221, 231; economic polarization 232; institutions, confidence in 228; political parties 206–8; politics 210, 222
police 112, 213, 293–5, 304; confidence in 243*t*, 269*t*; negative media image 110
political action 162, 212, 232, 248–9, 259, 342; legitimate 225; monitoring of 174; participation in 195–6, 248–9*t*, 270; unconventional 227
political and economic structures 179; change 188; crisis 119; strategies 361
political and social regimes 256; change 11–13; movements 107
political attitudes and behaviors 10, 35, 38, 90, 95–6, 289, 293, 296–7
political communities 34, 56, 85–6, 90, 128, 136
political culture 17, 27, 87, 128, 132–3, 140, 154, 188, 205, 242, 288, 308, 312, 313–14, 366; changes in 312; fatalistic 311; meanings of 309; in transition 333
political discussion 257–8*t*; with friends 132, 155–7*t*, 162, 221, 245*t*, 342*t*, 362
political institutions 333; confidence in 191; democratic 1; establishment of 235; imposed 86; loss of trust in 195
political interest 129–30, 155, 160, 221*t*, 228, 230*t*, 258, dimensions of 258*t*
political involvement 128, 129*t*, 130*t*, 131*t*, 132*t*, 156–7, 196*t*, 219, 285
political leadership 81, 238, 356; lost trust in themselves 248; structures 110
political motivation 9–10*t*, 19, 63, 129, 148, 155–6, 163, 168–9, 256*t*; index 361
political participation 8–9, 13, 32, 94*t*, 223, 235, 245, 250, 254, 257–61*t*, 285, 297, 301, 339, 343–4*t*; forced 247, 363; non-institutionalized 105–6, 160–2; non-participation 344; types of 260*t*; unconventional 81, 225
political parties 107, 109, 112, 196–7, 213, 247–8, 256, 259, 294–6, 337, 344–5, 349, 364; active members 227, 249; levels of confidence in 116, 242, 269*t*, 304, 370; national–authoritarian 181; nationalistic 369

political regime, current 87, 290; defective 368; non-support of 370; performance 103*t*, 225, 328; support for 60, 190*t*, 368–9*t*
political socialization 125, 128–9, 136, 332, 343
political systems 4, 124, 126, 209; maturity of 242; past, support for 190–1, 199; stability 206; transformed 292
political transformation 150, 151, 154, 287
political transition 310, 314, 320
political values 12, 26, 58, 203, 216, 228, 246, 258–9*t*, 320, 342; and behavior 85–6, 89–90, 93*t*, 96; generational differences in 16; non-democratic 371; priority of 247*t*
politicians 82*t*, 206, 275, 310, 316, 327; key 312; post-communist 330; professional 341
politics 339, 341; ability to influence 362; confrontational 181, 356; dirty 105; disappointment with 207, 248, 280, 371; importance of 131–2, 157–8*t*, 221, 244*t*, 245, 257*t*, 282–3*t*; loss of confidence in 362; in poor societies 321
poor people 61, 300; attitudes towards 352; government action for 374; homeless 116; international assistance 274
post-communist 207, 310, 315; decade 198; parties 226; societies 108, 163, 173, 189, 196, 215–16, 309
post-communist countries 87, 115, 131–3, 136, 139, 142–3, 172, 177, 190, 200, 221, 225, 280, 288, 292, 321, 336, 338, 343, 378; Baltic nation-states 278; first group 197
post-materialist 12, 69, 78, 83, 126–7; orientation 212, 221; values 222, 231, 297
post-Stalinist generation 341–3, 346, 348, 351–2
poverty 155, 192, 194*t*, 248, 323–4, 331, 339; attitudes towards 193; causes 116, 253; global 116; line 144–5, 252, 283; pauperization 209; political problem 352; and social inequality 15, 115, 317; stable 72; trap 300, 374
power 28; abuse of 180; arbitrary 330; division of 181, 311; source of 325; struggle 181, 333 pre-communist era

90, 95–6, 324; in Bulgaria 343;
experiences 297; influences from
85
privatization 111, 115, 178, 180, 182,
193, 212–13, 236; of ownership 213;
prevention of 205
protective role for the state 274, 348
protest 161, 228, 287; activities 107;
frequency 227; participation 225–7t,
289–90; political 162–3, 231, 287,
303, 364; rallies 326
Protestant 89, 111, 251, 289, 309;
Church 327; Europe 74, 78; historical
traditions 72; sects 32, 38; states 206
protest behavior 10t, 20, 148, 169, 286t,
287f, 365t; index of 161t; protest,
peaceful 148, 285; Baltic Chain 303
public opinion 310, 312, 326, 332–3;
divided 309; patterns of 309; polls
248

real socialism 347, 349; generation
341–6
reforms 184, 300, 305; blocking of 182;
effective 362; political 173; slow pace
of 247
religion 34, 38, 57, 68, 113, 119, 133,
318t, 320t, 351; decline of 67;
denominations 88, 95, 120; dominant
71, 74, 85, 96; freedom for 107;
importance of 78–9t, 126, 244;
institutions 216, 221; organizations
262; services 219, 223, 226; traditions
71, 76
representative democracy 116, 315–16;
core institution 108
republican 106; community 31–2, 50,
55t, 58; democracy 33t, 231;
government 294–5; institutions 304
revolution 105; democratic 110;
Industrial 11, 71; negotiated 149,
153; peaceful 259; radical 333;
Singing 285, 303; Velvet 192
Romania 2, 12, 72, 87–8t, 124–7, 130,
133, 140, 142, 164–5, 227, 326, 356;
anti-Semitism 311; autocratic
orientations 318–19t; civil service
330; collectivized 324; crime rate 121;
democratic transformation 331;
ethnic non-Romanians 89;
exceptionalism 314; intellectuals 321;
law and order institutions 312;
political transition 315; poor
performance of 310; population 317;

post-communist 15; pre-war
bureaucracies 333; public 316, 328;
World Value Survey 91, 94
rule of law 167, 169, 371; acceptance
168; inside the country 187;
restoration 332
rural areas 263, 318t, 322, 328, 333;
inhabitants 317, 323; population
surplus 324; property 333; residents
152, 270–1, 348, 358; Romania 323,
332; villages 159
Russia 2, 6, 12, 16, 34, 44–5, 57–8, 72,
165, 264, 280, 356–61, 364, 368–9,
372–7; democratic beliefs 366, 376;
Krasnoyarsk 87; political and social
realities 378; revolution 175
Russian 252, 254, 362, 367–8; alienation
from politics 366, 370; army, level of
trust in 295; economy 371; Empire
34, 39; new mentality 377; society 16,
362, 378

self-expression 69, 78; values 72–6,
81–4, 309
self-responsibility 15, 49–51, 54, 57, 61,
91t, 114, 154, 193, 211–12, 228, 231,
240, 265, 348–9, 369, 372
Serbia 89, 120, 165
signed petitions 80–2t, 92–4, 105–6,
160–1, 196, 225–6, 248, 259, 261t,
285–7, 365
Slovakia 14, 45, 87, 121, 124–7, 130,
144, 146, 163–4, 177, 195–6t, 227,
316, 326; army 192; Cleveland
Agreement 175; communist legacy
179, 199; constitution 186; cultural
institutes 174, 184; Democratic and
Christian Union 183, 185;
deportation of Jews 176; disrespect
for democratic rules 187; divided
society 187–8; economic
performance 178, 182t, 200;
excluded from NATO talks 180–1,
185–6; financial aid 197; national
identity 174–8; politics and society
172, 188, 192, 198; population 187;
rejection of Muslims 139; sovereignty
191; Supreme Soviet 294–5;
traditions 173
Slovenia 13–14, 42, 87, 151, 163–4, 316,
326
social class 152, 154, 158, 160, 162,
166–7; differentiation 236, 250, 256,
276

socialist 11, 13, 15, 231, 336, 351, 363, 368–9; community 31, 39, 50–1, 54–5, 57; society 133, 278, 285; system breakdown 222
socialization 6–7, 13, 314, 352; early 93, 96; effects 277; experience 85; post-communist 320, 332; under pre-communist rule 95
societal systems 26, 30, 309; community 27, 41, 45; openness 113; organizations 107, 111
solidarity 31–2, 49, 51, 54, 57, 61, 91*t*, 116, 206, 221–3, 227, 231, 274–5*t*; with the poor 92, 115, 148, 153–5*t*, 170, 252–3, 273, 297–300, 373–4*t*; social 270
south-eastern European countries 38, 88, 164–5; Orthodox 42, 51
Soviet Union 34, 39, 44, 57–8, 87, 90, 240, 260, 270, 277, 280–2, 287–9, 292, 296, 303–4, 311; army 293–4, 324, 336; former republics 13, 238, 355, 357, 362, 366–8, 372, 374, 376; heritage 283, 285; political system 369–70*t*, 290; rule 235, 247, 250, 278, 301, 371; school system 290; socialism 377; successor states 78, 81, 83
Spain 2, 38, 44–5, 50, 55, 144, 221
Stalinist 341–2; generation 345–6, 348; Hitler–Stalin pact 1940 311; purges 176, 336 state 193, 240; administration 349; attitudes to 347; centralized 175; confidence in 292, 348, 350; continuity 122, 131; dependence on 240, 321; economy 241; independent 176, 256, 289; institutions 173; intervention 178, 193, 331; loyalty to the 288; political 278; non-democratic 177; responsibility 193, 199, 212, 349; security apparatus 176; socialist regimes 222; sovereignty 15, 122; submission to the 348; terror 333; traditions 124, 133
strikes 106, 117, 226, 259, 261*t*, 365; illegal 225; wildcat 248–9
strong democrats 5–6, 13–14, 16, 18, 102, 142–3*t*, 149, 151, 228, 231, 237, 254, 263–4, 290–2, 316, 346, 357–8, 360–1, 363, 365–6, 369–70, 375–6; in Russia 360
strong leader 4, 18, 59, 103–4, 140, 238–9, 254, 262–3, 266*t*, 275, 316–17, 320, 345–6, 367–8

survival 69, 72, 78, 321, 325; by breaking the law 332; and self-expression values 76*f*; values 69, 72–3, 76, 83, 309

tolerance 8–9, 12, 14, 19, 32, 49–51, 62, 69, 78, 80–2*t*, 113–14*t*, 136–8, 169, 215, 219, 231, 250, 251*t*, 270–2*t*, 301–2, 350–2, 375; and empathy 273; importance of 216*t*; level increased 215; low level of 376; political 148, 153
trade unions 193, 206, 213, 227, 344–5, 350; communist 227; members 208, 227, 363; representatives 111; weak 371
traditional culture 67, 72, 74; orientation 69, 119, 301; values 69, 78, 322, 373
transformation 117, 213, 227, 265, 305, 368; early years 258; to a market economy 173; pace of 333; post-communist 172; process 149, 178, 205, 257, 362; in Russia 356, 371
transition 246; countries 198, 326; pattern 292; period 179, 246, 338–9, 342; post-authoritarian 355, 377; post-communist 308, 332, 337, 343, 353; post-transition countries 125, 133, 136
Transylvania 11–12, 88, 96; non-Romanian inhabitants 89
trust in others 8, 19, 32, 55, 58, 62, 80*t*, 82*t*, 91*t*, 136–8, 218–19, 252*t*, 270, 301–2, 351, 374–5*t*; lack of 210; levels of 304

Ukraine 2, 6, 9, 13, 16, 44–5, 57–8, 72, 87–8*t*, 143, 165, 264, 356–61, 364, 366–9, 372–6, 378
undecided citizens 109, 142, 149–52, 225, 228, 237, 263–4, 357, 360–3, 366, 368, 370, 375–6
unemployment 115–17, 209, 212, 254, 339, 371
United Nations 108, 211, 214, 270, 294–6, 350; confidence in 109, 244
United States 3, 5–7, 32, 35, 41, 46, 50, 54–8, 124–30, 140; President Woodrow Wilson 175
urban areas 168, 323–4*t*, 328, 336; lifestyle 323; post-communist 325; residents 162, 267, 270, 317, 331, 348, 358

values 28, 70–1, 76, 220, 339; and belief systems 235–6, 277, 289–90; under communist rule 68, 73*t*; community 299*t*, 301–2*t*; core 34, 155; materialist 12, 69, 78, 126–7, 222, 231, 321; orientations 119–20, 228, 256; patterns of 303, 305; political 1, 217*t*; socialist 297; to teach children 113, 219, 250, 270, 351

violence 279, 287–9; ethnic 2, 139, 311, 336; in politics 154*t*, 169, 284; rejection of 8, 9, 19, 29, 44, 60, 92, 153, 364

voluntary associations 101, 169, 195, 250, 275, 364; participation 92–4, 97, 106*t*, 117, 249

vote 224*t*, 344; citizens 174; collective 323; disinclination to 227; intentions to 259; shift to the left 207; urban 325

voters 90*t*, 185, 218, 256, 275; first-time 200; manipulation of 315; preferences 106, 312

voting 105–6, 223–5, 247, 321, 332, 338–9*t*, 366; apolitical abstention 344; for legislation 208; non-voters 224–5; in rural areas 322, 325

voting turnout rates 339–40*t*; decreasing 247, 259; in legislative elections 343; lower 225

weak democrats 102, 149–52, 228, 231, 237, 254, 263–5, 290, 316, 346, 357–60, 363–5, 375–6

welfare 265, 267*t*, 328–9; guaranteed 369; individual 114, 240, 273, 342, 349, 368, 376; paternalistic 347; social 377

welfare state 31, 38, 46; expansion of 222; liberal 231; paternalistic 114; values of 297

West Germany 3, 7, 41, 45–6, 57, 71, 127, 130, 148, 239, 243, 245, 250, 252, 365

western European countries 34, 37, 39, 42, 44–6, 49–51, 55–6, 58, 97, 228, 316, 320, 353

women's movements 107–9, 214, 294–6, 350; confidence in 243, 269*t*

work 62, 91–2*t*, 107, 113, 246; importance of 373; intimidation by employers 111; jobs protected 274; satisfaction 373; skilled 358

World Values Survey 1, 3, 11, 16, 29, 39, 46, 67–8, 86–7, 91–2, 104, 107, 114, 122–6, 129–30, 133, 136, 140, 144–6, 149, 173, 190, 203, 236, 257, 313, 316, 334, 357, 378

World War II 15, 88, 93, 96, 131, 157, 176, 179, 206, 222, 256, 289, 297, 351

Yugoslavia 119–22, 139, 145, 164, 356; Federal Republic 165

eBooks – at www.eBookstore.tandf.co.uk

A library at your fingertips!

eBooks are electronic versions of printed books. You can store them on your PC/laptop or browse them online.

They have advantages for anyone needing rapid access to a wide variety of published, copyright information.

eBooks can help your research by enabling you to bookmark chapters, annotate text and use instant searches to find specific words or phrases. Several eBook files would fit on even a small laptop or PDA.

NEW: Save money by eSubscribing: cheap, online access to any eBook for as long as you need it.

Annual subscription packages

We now offer special low-cost bulk subscriptions to packages of eBooks in certain subject areas. These are available to libraries or to individuals.

For more information please contact webmaster.ebooks@tandf.co.uk

We're continually developing the eBook concept, so keep up to date by visiting the website.

www.eBookstore.tandf.co.uk